MAKING HISTORY

Modern Europe in the World through Primary Sources

Janet Watson

Kendall Hunt
publishing company

Kendall Hunt
publishing company

www.kendallhunt.com
Send all inquiries to:
4050 Westmark Drive
Dubuque, IA 52004-1840

Copyright © 2010 by Kendall Hunt Publishing Company

ISBN 978-0-7575-8400-8

Printed in the United States of America
10 9 8 7 6 5 4 3 2 1

CONTENTS

Columbus's Letter to the King and Queen of Spain
Christopher Columbus 1

The Devastation of the Indies: A Brief Account
Bartolomé de Las Casas 5

Concerning Christian Liberty
Martin Luther 21

Dear Christians, One and All, Rejoice
Martin Luther 45

Of Cannibals
Michel de Montaigne 47

The Social Contract
Jean-Jacques Rousseau 55

What Is Enlightenment?
Immanuel Kant 77

The Interesting Narrative of the Life of Olaudah Equiano, or
Gustavus Vassa, the African
Olaudah Equiano 81

The Condition of the Working Class in England
Friedrich Engels 103

Hard Times
Charles Dickens 141

Recollections: The French Revolution of 1848
Alexis de Tocqueville 153

Class Struggles in France
Karl Marx 161

My Indian Mutiny Diary
William Howard Russell 177

The Mutinies and the People
A Hindu (Samhu Chandra Mookerjee) 183

Mafeking Diary: A Black Man's View of a White Man's war
> Sol T. Plaatje. 187

Two Treaties: from the Hague Convention *and the* Treaty of Vereeniging. 197

Hymn of Hate
> Ernst Lissauer 201

The Return of the Soldier
> Rebecca West 203

Civilization and Its Discontents
> Sigmund Freud 211

A Writer at War
> Vasily Grossman 219

Survival at Auschwitz
> Primo Levi 233

The People Who Walked On (This Way to the Gas, Ladies and Gentlemen)
> Tadeusz Borowski. 245

Columbus's Letter to the King and Queen of Spain

Christopher Columbus

Most High and Mighty Sovereigns,

In obedience to your Highnesses' commands, and with submission to superior judgment, I will say whatever occurs to me in reference to the colonization and commerce of the Island of Espanola, and of the other islands, both those already discovered and those that may be discovered hereafter.

In the first place, as regards the Island of Espanola: Inasmuch as the number of colonists who desire to go thither amounts to two thousand, owing to the land being safer and better for farming and trading, and because it will serve as a place to which they can return and from which they can carry on trade with the neighboring islands:

1. That in the said island there shall be founded three or four towns, situated in the most convenient places, and that the settlers who are there be assigned to the aforesaid places and towns.

2. That for the better and more speedy colonization of the said island, no one shall have liberty to collect gold in it except those who have taken out colonists' papers, and have built houses for their abode, in the town in which they are, that they may live united and in greater safety.

3. That each town shall have its alcalde [Mayor] ... and its notary public, as is the use and custom in Castile.

4. That there shall be a church, and parish priests or friars to administer the sacraments, to perform divine worship, and for the conversion of the Indians.

5. That none of the colonists shall go to seek gold without a license from the governor or alcalde of the town where he lives; and that he must first take oath to return to the place whence he sets out, for the purpose of registering faithfully all the gold he may have found, and to return once a month, or once a week, as the time may have been set for him, to render account and show the quantity of said gold; and this shall be written down by the notary before the alcalde, or, if it seems better, that a friar or priest, deputed for the purpose, shall be also present.

6. That all the gold thus brought in shall be smelted immediately, and stamped with some mark that shall distinguish each town; and that the portion which belongs to your Highnesses shall be weighed, and given and consigned to each alcalde in his own town, and registered by the above-mentioned priest or friar, so that it shall not pass through the hands of only one person, and there shall be no opportunity to conceal the truth.

7. That all gold that may be found without the mark of one of the said towns in the possession of any one who has once registered in accordance with the above order shall

From "Columbus' Letter to the King and Queen of Spain, 1494".

1

be taken as forfeited, and that the accuser shall have one portion of it and your Highnesses the other.

8. That one per centum of all the gold that may be found shall be set aside for building churches and adorning the same, and for the support of the priests or friars belonging to them; and , if it should be thought proper to pay any thing to the alcaldes or notaries for their services, or for ensuring the faithful performance of their duties, that this amount shall be sent to the governor or treasurer who may be appointed there by your Highnesses.

9. As regards the division of the gold, and the share that ought to be reserved for your Highnesses, this, in my opinion, must be left to the aforesaid governor and treasurer, because it will have to be greater or less according to the quantity of gold that may be found. Or, should it seem preferable, your Highnesses might, for the space of one year, take one half, and the collector the other, and a better arrangement for the division be made afterward.

10. That if the said alcaldes or notaries shall commit or be privy to any fraud, punishment shall be provided, and the same for the colonists who shall not have declared all the gold they have.

11. That in the said island there shall be a treasurer, with a clerk to assist him, who shall receive all the gold belonging to your Highnesses, and the alcaldes and notaries of the towns shall each keep a record of what they deliver to the said treasurer.

12. As, in the eagerness to get gold, every one will wish, naturally, to engage in its search in preference to any other employment, it seems to me that the privilege of going to look for gold ought to be withheld during some portion of each year, that there may be opportunity to have the other business necessary for the island performed.

13. In regard to the discovery of new countries, I think permission should be granted to all that wish to go, and more liberality used in the matter of the fifth, making the tax easier, in some fair way, in order that many may be disposed to go on voyages.

I will now give my opinion about ships going to the said Island of Espanola, and the order that should be maintained; and that is, that the said ships should only be allowed to discharge in one or two ports designated for the purpose, and should register there whatever cargo they bring or unload; and when the time for their departure comes, that they should sail from these same ports, and register all the cargo they take in, that nothing may be concealed.

- In reference to the transportation of gold from the island to Castile, that all of it should be taken on board the ship, both that belonging to your Highnesses and the property of every one else; that it should all be placed in one chest with two locks, with their keys, and that the master of the vessel keep one key and some person selected by the governor and treasurer the other; that there should come with the gold, for a testimony, a list of all that has been put into the said chest, properly marked, so that each owner may receive his own; and that, for the faithful performance of this duty, if any gold whatsoever is found outside of the said chest in any way, be it little or much, it shall be forfeited to your Highnesses.

- That all the ships that come from the said island shall be obliged to make their proper discharge in the port of Cadiz, and that no person shall disembark or other person be permitted to go on board until the ship has been visited by the person or persons deputed for that purpose, in the said city, by your Highnesses, to whom the master shall show all that he carries, and exhibit the manifest of all the cargo, it may be seen and examined if the said ship brings any thing hidden and not known at the time of lading.

- That the chest in which the said gold has been carried shall be opened in the presence of the magistrates of the said city of Cadiz, and of the person deputed for that purpose by your Highnesses, and his own property be given to each owner.

I beg your Highnesses to hold me in your protection; and I remain, praying our Lord God for your Highnesses' lives and the increase of much greater States.

The Devastation of the Indies: A Brief Account

Bartolomé de Las Casas

Translated from the Spanish by Herma Briffault

The Indies were discovered in the year one thousand four hundred and ninety-two. In the following year a great many Spaniards went there with the intention of settling the land. Thus, forty-nine years have passed since the first settlers penetrated the land, the first so-claimed being the large and most happy isle called Hispaniola, which is six hundred leagues in circumference. Around it in all directions are many other islands, some very big, others very small, and all of them were, as we saw with our own eyes, densely populated with native peoples called Indians. This large island was perhaps the most densely populated place in the world. There must be close to two hundred leagues of land on this island, and the seacoast has been explored for more than ten thousand leagues, and each day more of it is being explored. And all the land so far discovered is a beehive of people; it is as though God had crowded into these lands the great majority of mankind.

And of all the infinite universe of humanity, these people are the most guileless, the most devoid of wickedness and duplicity, the most obedient and faithful to their native masters and to the Spanish Christians whom they serve. They are by nature the most humble, patient, and peaceable, holding no grudges, free from embroilments, neither excitable nor quarrelsome. These people are the most devoid of rancors, hatreds, or desire for vengeance of any people in the world. And because they are so weak and complaisant, they are less able to endure heavy labor and soon die of no matter what malady. The sons of nobles among us, brought up in the enjoyments of life's refinements, are no more delicate than are these Indians, even those among them who are of the lowest rank of laborers. They are also poor people, for they not only possess little but have no desire to possess worldly goods. For this reason they are not arrogant, embittered, or greedy. Their repasts are such that the food of the holy fathers in the desert can scarcely be more parsimonious, scanty, and poor. As to their dress, they are generally naked, with only their pudenda covered somewhat. And when they cover their shoulders it is with a square cloth no more than two varas in size. They have no beds, but sleep on a kind of matting or else in a kind of suspended net called *hamacas*. They are very clean in their persons, with alert, intelligent minds, docile and open to doctrine, very apt to receive our holy Catholic faith, to be endowed with virtuous customs, and to behave in a godly fashion. And once they begin to hear the tidings of the Faith, they are so insistent on knowing more and on taking the sacraments of the Church and on observing the divine cult that, truly, the missionaries who are here need to be endowed by God with great patience in order to cope with such eagerness. Some of the secular Spaniards who have been here for many years say that the goodness of the Indians is undeniable and that if this gifted people could be brought to know the one true God they would be the most fortunate people in the world.

Yet into this sheepfold, into this land of meek outcasts there came some Spaniards who immediately behaved like ravening wild beasts, wolves, tigers, or lions that had been starved for many days. And Spaniards have behaved in no other way during the past forty years, down to the present time, for they are still acting like ravening beasts, killing, terrorizing, afflicting, torturing, and destroying the native peoples, doing all this with the strangest and most varied new methods of cruelty, never seen or heard of before, and to such a degree that this Island of Hispaniola, once so populous (having a population that I estimated to be more than three millions), has now a population of barely two hundred persons.

The island of Cuba is nearly as long as the distance between Valladolid and Rome; it is now almost completely depopulated. San Juan and Jamaica are two of the largest, most productive and attractive islands; both are now deserted and devastated. On the northern side of Cuba and Hispaniola lie the neighboring Lucayos comprising more that sixty islands including those called *Gigantes*, beside numerous other islands, some small some large. The least felicitous of them were more fertile and beautiful than the gardens of the King of Seville. They have the healthiest lands in the world, where lived more than five hundred thousand souls; they are now deserted, inhabited by not a single living creature. All the people were slain or died after being taken into captivity and brought to the Island of Hispaniola to be sold as slaves. When the Spaniards saw that some of these had escaped, they sent a ship to find them, and it voyaged for three years among the islands searching for those who had escaped being slaughtered, for a good Christian had helped them escape, taking pity on them and had won them over to Christ; of these there were eleven persons and these I saw.

More than thirty other islands in the vicinity of San Juan are for the most part and for the same reason depopulated, and the land laid waste. On these islands I estimate there are 2,100 leagues of land that have been ruined and depopulated, empty of people.

As for the vast mainland, which is ten times larger than all Spain, even including Aragon and Portugal, containing more land than the distance between Seville and Jerusalem, or more than two thousand leagues, we are sure that our Spaniards, with their cruel and abominable acts, have devastated the land and exterminated the rational people who fully inhabited it. We can estimate very surely and truthfully that in the forty years that have passed, with the infernal actions of the Christians, there have been unjustly slain more than twelve million men, women, and children. In truth, I believe without trying to deceive myself that the number of the slain is more like fifteen million.

The common ways mainly employed by the Spaniards who call themselves Christian and who have gone there to extirpate those pitiful nations and wipe them off the earth is by unjustly waging cruel and bloody wars. Then, when they have slain all those who fought for their lives or to escape the tortures they would have to endure, that is to say, when they have slain all the native rulers and young men (since the Spaniards usually spare only the women and children, who are subjected to the hardest and bitterest servitude ever suffered by man or beast), they enslave any survivors. With these infernal methods of tyranny they debase and weaken countless numbers of those pitiful Indian nations.

Their reason for killing and destroying such an infinite number of souls is that the Christians have an ultimate aim, which is to acquire gold, and to swell themselves with riches in a very brief time and thus rise to a high estate disproportionate to their merits. It should be kept in mind that their insatiable greed and ambition, the greatest ever seen in the world, is the cause of their villainies. And also, those lands are so rich and felicitous, the native peoples so meek and patient, so easy to subject, that our Spaniards have no more consideration for them than beasts. And I say this from my own knowledge of the acts I witnessed. But I should not say "than beasts" for, thanks be to God, they have treated beasts with some respect; I should say instead like excrement on the public squares. And thus they have deprived the Indians of their lives and souls, for the millions I mentioned have died without the Faith and without the benefit of the sacraments. This is a well-known and proven fact which even the tyrant Governors, themselves killers, know and admit. And never have the Indians in all the Indies committed any act against the Spanish Christians, until those Christians have first and many times committed countless cruel aggressions against them or against neighboring nations. For in the beginning the Indians regarded the Spaniards as angels from Heaven. Only after the Spaniards had used violence against them, killing, robbing, torturing, did the Indians ever rise up against them.

Hispaniola

On the Island Hispaniola was where the Spaniards first landed, as I have said. Here those Christians perpetrated their first ravages and oppressions against the native peoples. This was the first land in the New World to be destroyed and depopulated by the Christians, and here they began their subjection of the women and children, taking them away from the Indians to use them and ill use them, eating the food they provided with their sweat and toil. The Spaniards did not content themselves with what the Indians gave them of their own free will, according to their ability, which was always too little to satisfy enormous appetites, for a Christian eats and consumes in one day an amount of food that would suffice to feed three houses inhabited by ten Indians for one month. And they committed other acts of force and violence and oppression which made the Indians realize that these men had not come from Heaven. And some of the Indians concealed their foods while others concealed their wives and children and still others fled to the mountains to avoid the terrible transactions of the Christians.

And the Christians attacked them with buffets and beatings, until finally they laid hands on the nobles of the villages. Then they behaved with such temerity and shamelessness that the most powerful ruler of the islands had to see his own wife raped by a Christian officer.

From that time onward the Indians began to seek ways to throw the Christians out of their lands. They took up arms, but their weapons were very weak and of little service in offense and still less in defense. (Because of this, the wars of the Indians against each other are little more than games played by children.) And the Christians, with their horses and swords and pikes began to carry out massacres and strange cruelties against them. They attacked the towns and spared neither the children nor the aged nor pregnant women nor women in childbed, not only stabbing them and dismembering them but cutting them to pieces as if dealing with sheep in the slaughter house. They laid bets as to who, with one stroke of the sword, could split a man in two or could cut off his head or spill out his entrails with a single stroke of the pike. They took infants from their mothers' breasts, snatching them by the legs and pitching them headfirst against the crags or snatched them by the arms and threw them into the rivers, roaring with laughter and saying as the babies fell into the water, "Boil there, you offspring of the devil!" Other infants they put to the sword along with their mothers and anyone else who happened to be nearby. They made some low wide gallows on which the hanged victim's feet almost touched the ground, stringing up their victims in lots of thirteen, in memory of Our Redeemer and His twelve Apostles, then set burning wood at their feet and thus burned them alive. To others they attached straw or wrapped their whole bodies in straw and set them afire. With still others, all those they wanted to capture alive, they cut off their hands and hung them round the victim's neck, saying, "Go now, carry the message," meaning, Take the news to the Indians who have fled to the mountains. They usually dealt with the chieftains and nobles in the following way: they made a grid of rods which they placed of forked sticks, then lashed the victims to the grid and lighted a smoldering fire underneath, so that little by little, as those captives screamed in despair and torment, their souls would leave them.

I once saw this, when there were four or five nobles lashed on grids and burning; I seem even to recall that there were two or three pairs of grids where others were burning, and because they uttered such loud screams that they disturbed the captain's sleep, he ordered them to be strangled. And the constable, who was worse than an executioner, did not want to obey that order (and I know the name of that constable and know his relatives in Seville), but instead put a stick over the victims' tongues, so they could not make a sound, and he stirred up the fire, but not too much, so that they roasted slowly, as he liked. I saw all these things I have described, and countless others.

And because all the people who could do so fled to the mountains to escape these inhuman, ruthless, and ferocious acts, the Spanish captains, enemies of the human race, pursued them with the fierce dogs they kept which attacked the Indians, tearing them to pieces and devouring them. And because on few and far between occasions, the Indians justifiably killed some Christians, the Spaniards made a rule among themselves that for every Christian slain by the Indians, they would slay a hundred Indians.

The Kingdoms That Once Existed on the Island Hispaniola

On the island Hispaniola there were five very large principalities ruled by five very powerful Kings to whom almost all the other rulers paid tribute, since there were other princes in distant provinces who recognized no one as their superior. There was a kingdom called Maguá, the last syllable accented, which name means "The Realm of the Fertile Lowlands," This land is among the most notable and admirable places in the world, for it stretches across the island from the southern sea to the northern sea, a distance of eighty leagues. It averages five leagues in width but at times is eight to ten and is of very high altitude from one part to another and is drained by more that thirty thousand rivers and creeks, twelve of the rivers being as large as the Ebro and Duero and Guadalquivir combined. All the rivers flow from the western highland, And since men and women were separated, there could be no marital relations. And the men died in the mines and the women died on the ranches from the same causes, exhaustion and hunger. And thus was depopulated that island which had been densely populated.

· · · ·

I will speak only briefly of the heavy loads the Indians were made to carry, loads weighing three to four arrobas, Christian tyrants and captains had themselves carried in hammocks borne by two Indians. This shows that they treated the Indians as beasts of burden. But were I to describe all this and the buffetings and beatings and birchings endured by the Indians at their labors, no amount of time and paper could encompass this task.

And be it noted that the worst depredations on these islands in the New World began when tidings came of the death of Her most Serene Highness, Queen Isabel, which occurred in the year one thousand five hundred and four. Because, up to that time, only a few provinces on the island of Hispaniola had been destroyed in unjust wars, but not the entire island, since, for the most part, the island was under the royal protection of the Queen and she, may God rest her, took admirable and zealous care of these people, their salvation and prosperity, as we saw with our own eyes and touched with our hands.

Another rule should be noted: in all parts of the Indies, wherever they have landed or passed through, the Christians have always committed atrocities against the Indians, have perpetrated the slaughters and tyrannies and abominable oppressions against innocent people that we have described, and have added worse and more cruel acts, ever since God allowed them most suddenly to fall into dishonor and opprobrium.

The Islands of San Juan and Jamaica

The Spaniards passed over to the islands of San Juan and Jamaica (both of them veritable gardens and beehives of activity) in the year one thousand five hundred and nine, with the aim and purpose of making these islands a part of Hispaniola.

And on those islands the Spaniards perpetrated the same acts of aggression against the Indians and the wicked deeds described above, adding to them many outstanding cruelties, massacres and burnings of the people, or executing them by flinging them to the fierce dogs, torturing and oppressing the survivors, condemning them to the hard labor of the mines, thus eradicating them from the earth, despoiling the land of those unfortunate and innocent people. Before the arrival of the Spaniards there had lived on these islands more than six hundred thousand souls, it has been stated. I believe there were more than one million inhabitants, and now, in each of the two islands, there are no more than two hundred persons, all the others having perished without the Faith and without the holy sacraments.

The Island of Cuba

In the year one thousand five hundred and eleven, the Spaniards passed over to the island of Cuba, which as I have said is at the same distance from Hispaniola as the distance between Valladolid and Rome, and which was a province of Canú to the Gulf of Urabá, hugging the coast for a hundred leagues. And it includes much land in the interior, to the south. The people of this province have been afflicted and killed. The land has been laid waste over the years from one thousand four hundred and ninety-eight until today, as was Santa Marta. The Spaniards have perpetrated some outstanding cruelties on these islands. There have been many massacres. Here I will not dwell on the killings, the pillage, the many acts of wickedness, but will merely say that on Cartagena were perpetrated the same acts as in other parts.

. . . .

The Coast of Pearls, Paria and the Island of Trinidad

Along the coast of Paria as far as the Gulf of Venezuela, a distance of two hundred leagues, the destruction carried out by the Spaniards has been noteworthy. They have attacked and have taken alive as many people at they could, to sell them as slaves. The Spaniards often take captives into their houses, as domestic servants, treating them well for a time, treating them like sons and daughters, the captives regarding the Spaniards like fathers, and serving them to the best of their ability. Then the Spaniards after a while betray their trust. It is painful to tell of how many injuries are then inflicted on these people by the Spaniards, ever since they invaded the coastal region in the year one thousand five hundred and ten and down to the present time. I will recount only two or three instances of cruelty, from which can be judged the other innumerable and hideous acts deserving all the fires of hell.

On the island of Trinidad, which is much larger than Sicily and much more felicitous, close to the mainland at Paria, is where the Indians are the best to be found in the Indies, as to goodness and virtues. The Spanish tyrant, with sixty or seventy men, all rascals and experienced thieves, sent a messenger to proclaim that they had come to dwell on the island in peace with the Indians. The people welcomed them as if they were kinsmen, as if they were their sons, and treated them with cheerful kindness, serving them, bringing them gifts and giving them their surplus food, as is the custom in the Indies, everywhere. They gave generously of all the products needed by the Spaniards, and they build a big house, large enough to accommodate all of them, according to the desire expressed by the Spaniards who said they wanted to live together, but in reality it was because of a plan they had, which they soon carried out. When the double roof of straw was made, so that those within could not see outside, they had as many Indians as possible come into the house, with the pretense that they were needed to do some finishing work, then the Spaniards posted guards so that no one could leave, the guards standing with unsheathed swords. Then they forbade the Indians to make a move, and tied them up, and whenever one of the Indians tried to escape he was cut to pieces.

Some of the Indians managed to escape, either wounded or unharmed, and they, with the villagers who had not entered the house, seized another house and with bows and arrows defended themselves against the Spaniards until the Christians set fire to the house, burning to death all the Indians inside it.

Then, with their captives who numbered one hundred and eighty or two hundred, the Spaniards went down to their ships, hoisted sail and voyaged to San Juan, where half the number of Indians were sold as slaves, after which they voyaged to Hispaniola where the remainder of the captives were sold.

When I remonstrated with the captain–general for such outstanding acts of wickedness and betrayal, as I encountered him in San Juan, his response was this: "Sir, after all, I have only obeyed the orders I was given when I was sent to the Indies, for I was told 'If you cannot conquer them by war, then capture them, no matter how.'" And he told me that, in truth, he had all his life lacked a mother and father and had never been treated kindly except by the Indians on the island of Trinidad. He said this to explain his great confusion and the worsening of his sins which had been many on the mainland, and now the taking captive Indians to whom he had promised safety.

See what acts were these: capturing Indians to sell them into slavery.

On another occasion, our Dominican Order having been given permission to preach and convert the native people who were without enlightenment and hope of salvation, they sent a religious eminently learned in theology and of great virtue and holiness, along with a lay friar to survey the land and to find with the help of an Indian a site favorable to the establishment of a monastery. They were welcomed like angels from Heaven upon their arrival in a settlement and their words were listened to with attention, devotion, and good cheer. By words I mean their gestures, for they mainly used sign language, not knowing or understanding the language of the Indians.

By chance, after the ship that brought them had gone away, another vessel came and the Spaniards on it, using their customary deceitfulness, took on board the chief ruler of these lands, without the knowledge of the Dominican friars. The ruler's name was Don Alonso, which was either a name the Dominican friars had given him or had been given by some other Spaniards, since the Indians are very fond of being called by a Christian name, asking for and being given one even before they know enough of the Faith to be baptized. Thus, the Spaniards duped the aforesaid Don Alonso into boarding the ship with his wife and a certain number of his followers, and there they celebrated a fiesta. Finally the Spaniards persuaded seventeen other Indians to board the ship, which they did, confident that because the Dominican religious were in their land the Spaniards would not harm them. Once they had the Indians on board, the traitorous Spaniards hoisted sail and voyaged to Hispaniola where all the captives were sold into slavery.

All the people of the land, upon seeing their chief ruler and his wife borne away, came to the Dominican friars, intending to kill them. The friars, confronted with such an act of wickedness, were so full of anguish that they wanted to die, being ready to give their lives in reparation for such an act of wickedness, especially since this unjust act was a hindrance to their preaching the word of God to the Indians. They soothed the Indians as best they could, assuring them that by the next ship they would send a letter to Hispaniola and would have the Indian chief and his followers returned to this land. Then God brought a ship to that place, in confirmation of the damnation of those that governed, and the Dominican friars wrote many times asking for the return of the Indians who had been so unjustly taken captive. But those who read the letters were never willing to do justice, because to some among them had been allocated their share of those Indians who had so wickedly been taken captive by the tyrants.

The two friars had promised the Indians that within four months they would see their chieftain, Don Alonso, return with his wife and followers, so when they did not return either within four months or eight months, the Indians became restless and the friars prepared to give their lives, as they had offered to do before. And the Indians thus took a just vengeance on these innocents when they slew them. Because the Indians thought the Dominicans had been the cause of the betrayal, and because they had seen no truth in their promise that within four months their chief would return, and because until then (as today) the Indians could see no difference between the friars and the Spanish tyrants, thieves, and bullies wreaking havoc everywhere in this land. Without a doubt the blessed friars suffered unjustly and thus, according to our holy Faith, they are, as true martyrs, with God in Heaven, blessed martyrs who willingly came to the Indies, in obedience to their Order, to preach and expound the holy Faith and save all those souls and to endure whatever labors or sufferings were offered them for the sake of our crucified Lord, Jesus Christ.

Once again, on account of the wicked Christians and their nefarious acts, Indians had killed another two friars, this time of the Order of St. Dominic's Friars Preachers and one Franciscan, in which death I was a witness and by a divine miracle escaped death myself, the story of which would fill men with terror. But the story is too long to describe here, it must wait for the Day of Judgment when everything will be made clear and God will revenge such outrageous offenses as are committed by the Spaniards in the Indies, by Spaniards who call themselves Christians.

And again, in these provinces on that part of the Venezuelan coast called Cape Codera, there was a village ruled by a chief called Higoroto, a proper name common among these peoples. He was so good and his people so virtuous that when a great number of Spaniards came in ships they were given help in repairs, food, rest, care, and comfort. These Indians felt safe from the kind of death they heard about from those who fled into their province where many tyrannies had caused much affliction. Higoroto sent these survivors to the nearby Island of Pearls, where were many Christians, instead of killing them as he could have done. And all the Christians in the village ruled by Higoroto called it "the house and home" of everyone. And a wretch of a Spanish tyrant decided to attack this village.

They sent a ship and invited many Indians to embark on it and, trustingly, many men, women, and children went aboard. Then the Spaniards hoisted sail and voyaged to the island of San Juan, where all the captives were sold as slaves.

. . . .

I arrived in San Juan at about that same time, and saw along with the King in the Indies, the Emperor granted and conceded the government and jurisdiction of the large kingdom of Venezuela, much larger than Spain, to some German merchant adventurers in exchange for certain concessions and agreements. Those merchants, upon entering the land with three hundred or more men, encountered people as tame as sheep, as were all the native peoples in the Indies everywhere, until they suffered injury at the hands of the Spaniards. And here were committed, I believe, incomparably more cruelties than those we have described, acts more irrational and ferocious than any inflicted by the most ferocious lions and tigers and rabid wolves. Because the actions were carried out with more avidity and blind greed, with more subtle determination to rob the Indians of their gold and silver than all the tyrants who had gone before. They subordinated all shame, all fear of God and of the King, forgetting that they were mortal men, having greater freedom, since they possessed all the jurisdiction of the land.

They ravaged, destroyed, incarnadined, and depopulated these dominions extending over more than four hundred leagues that had been supremely happy and admirable provinces, densely populated, rich in gold. Here the conquerors have slain the total population of diverse nations; on many leagues they have not left a single human being alive, except for the few who took refuge in caves, in the bowels of the earth, to escape the alien and pestilential knives. Those German merchants have killed and uprooted innocent generations, employing a variety of strange iniquities and impieties (as I consider them), and they are still, today, unremittingly doing the same thing.

Of the infinite number of offenses and outrages perpetrated in this region, I will give only four or five examples. From these it will be possible to judge the methods that have been used here to effect the devastation and depopulation we have mentioned above.

They captured the supreme ruler of this province, without any cause other than to extract from him gold, through torture. He broke loose and fled to the mountains where he stirred up the people who were hiding there in the underbrush. They hunted down those in revolt and there ensued great slaughters, and all those taken captive were sold openly as slaves. In all the provinces where these conquerors came, no matter where, they were welcomed with songs and dances and gifts of gold in great quantity. And this continued until the conquerors seized the noble ruler of the province. The hospitality of the people was repaid by terror, which spread through the land as the people were put to the sword.

On one occasion, when the Indians came out to welcome the conquerors, they were all placed in a big house of straw and at a command were slaughtered. Some Indians escaped from the bloody hands of those bestial men by climbing the wooden stanchions. The commander then set fire to the house, burning to death all the ones who had escaped death by the sword.

A great many villages were depopulated, the few survivors of the massacres fleeing to the mountains for safety.

The conquerors arrived in a large province bordering the province and kingdom of Santa Marta, where the Indians were dwelling in peace, occupied at their crafts in their houses, their haciendas, doing their usual work. The conquerors remained for some time in the villages, consuming the Indians' food and provisions, while the Indians served them whole-heartedly, enduring continual oppression and importunities, the intolerably gross behavior of the conquerors, their enormous appetites — one man eating at a single meal more than would suffice for a family of ten Indians in a month.

Of their own free will, the Indians gave them at this time large quantities of gold, and performed countless services of a friendly nature. Finally, wanting to depart, the tyrants decided to repay the Indians in the following way.

The German tyrant who was the Governor (and we believe he was a heretic, for he neither attended Mass nor allowed any of his men or the Indians serving them to attend Mass, the Germans all being Lutherans or known as such), commanded that all the Indians and their wives and children be herded into a huge corral surrounded with stakes which the

Indians themselves had driven into the ground. And he commanded that no food be given them until each one had ransomed himself by promising to bring back gold from his house, so much for himself, so much for his wife, so much for his child or children. Many Indians were allowed to go to their houses from which they brought back the required gold. But then the tyrant hired some rascally Spaniards to go to the houses where the ransomed Indians had resumed their lives, and to bring them back to the corral, where they were submitted once more to torture from hunger and thirst, and told they could ransom themselves again for more gold. Some Indians ransomed themselves several times. Others, who had no more gold to give, having all they possessed, were kept in the corral until they died of hunger.

Thus the German tyrant ravaged and destroyed and depopulated a province rich in gold that had been densely inhabited. And in a large valley of this province, forty leagues in extent, he burnt a settlement comprised of one thousand houses.

This diabolical tyrant decided to push into the interior of Peru, desiring to explore the country for gold. For this unhappy journey he took with him a great number of the surviving Indians chained together, each of them carrying a cargo weighing four arrobas. And when one of the Indians would weaken or faint from hunger and weariness, they cut off his head at the chain, so as not to delay or stop the march of the others, and the head would fall to one side of the road while the body fell to the other side. And the burden the dead man had carried was distributed among the other captive Indians.

To recount the provinces razed by this tyrant, the towns and settlements he burned, the people he killed, the particular cruelties he perpetrated, and the massacres he carried out on this march into the interior is not possible, and the plain truth is unbelievable.

Other tyrants who succeeded him in Venezuela also followed the route he took into the interior, as did the tyrants in command at Santa Marta, all with the same damnable avid desire to discover a hoard of gold in Peru. And they found more than two hundred leagues of the land so burnt, so devastated, that land which had been filled with a happy people, that even they, cruel tyrants as they were, looked in horror at the traces left by that first tyrant, on his march into Peru.

The truth of all this has been proved by many witnesses called upon by the Council of the Indies, and their testimony is in the possession of that same Council. Yet never has a single one of those tyrants been burnt at the stake. And their acts of outrageous wickedness that have been proven seem to mean nothing to the ministers of justice who have had to deal with the Indies. Because of their mortal blindness they have never examined the crimes, the ravages and massacres that have been perpetrated and are still being perpetrated by all the tyrant-Governors of the Indies. But they do, now and then, examine the cruelties committed by some knave or other, thus losing to the King some thousands of castellanos, satisfied to argue these little-proven and so very general and confused cases. And they do not even know how to certify these minor cases or reveal, as they should in duty bound to God and the King, the fact that the German tyrants have robbed the King of more than three million castellanos' worth of gold. Because that province of Venezuela, where they ruined and despoiled more than four hundred leagues of land, is the land richest in gold and was the most densely populated of any land in the Indies. And they diverted from the King and wasted more crown revenues in that one kingdom, than the revenues of all the Kings of Spain, a total of millions in the sixteen years since those German tyrants and enemies of God and the King began to occupy that land. And those damages, from now until the end of the world, cannot be remedied unless God by a miracle resuscitates all those thousands of souls that have perished. These are the temporal damages they have caused the King. It would be well to consider what kind and how many damages and dishonors and blasphemies they have perpetrated against God and God's law and what recompense can be made for the countless souls burning in hell because of the greed and inhumanity of those bestial German tyrants.

And now, as to the inhumanity and ruthlessness of those tyrants, I will conclude with this statement. From the time they entered the land until today, they have sent many shiploads of captive Indians to sell them as slaves in Santa Marta, Hispaniola, Jamaica, and the island of San Juan. More than one million Indians. And they continue to do this, the transaction seen and known but dissimulated by the Royal Audiencia of Hispaniola, which hitherto has favored such crimes committed by the tyrants on the islands and on the mainland which they have penetrated for a distance of four hundred leagues, subjecting the mainland Venezuela and Santa Marta. Yet their actions on the mainland could still be checked and remedied. These Indians have given no cause to be enslaved. It is only because of blind perversity and the determination to satisfy their insatiable greed that these avaricious tyrants act as they have acted in the Indies. This alone impels them to take captive meek and innocent people from their houses, separating husbands from wives, fathers from sons, and to brand them with the royal seal and to sell them as slaves.

That Part of the Mainland Called Florida

Into these mainland provinces have gone three tyrants at different times from the year one thousand five hundred and ten or eleven, to commit the nefarious acts that have been committed by other tyrants, especially two of them, in other parts of the Indies, so as to rise in rank beyond their merits. And all three tyrants have come to a bad end, losing their lives and possessions, the houses they built in other times with the blood and sweat of the Indians, and their memory is erased from the earth as if they had never lived. They left the entire world scandalized and their names have become a byword of horror and infamy. God ended their lives before they could do more harm. And God has punished them for the evil deeds they committed, deeds I know about, having seen them with my own eyes.

The fourth and the latest tyrant-Governor was appointed with a great to-do in this year one thousand five hundred and thirty-eight. Nothing has been heard of him for three years but we are sure that if he is still alive, wherever he has gone he will have inflicted many cruelties, will have destroyed many nations, for he is of the same breed as those who have ravaged and destroyed most provinces and perpetrated most vile deeds, along with his comrades, but we believe still more strongly that God may have given him the same ending to his life that He gave the other tyrants.

Three of four years after writing the above, I learned that those tyrants who conquered Florida have departed that land, leaving behind them their dead leader. He had committed unheard-of cruelties, which his inhuman comrades repeated against those innocent and harmless peoples. Thus my surmise has been proven not to have been false. His vile deeds were too many and too terrible to recount. I will only reaffirm what I said at the beginning, to wit: The more the conquerors discover new lands, the more lands and peoples do they destroy and with ever greater iniquities against God and man. It is wearisome to dwell on their bloody deeds, the deeds not of men but of wild beasts. I will not tell of their cruelties in detail, but will only relate as an example the following.

On these lands lived a population that was wise, well disposed, politically well organized. As usual, the tyrants perpetrated massacres with the aim of instilling and spreading terror. They afflicted, they killed the people, they took captives and compelled them to carry intolerable loads, like beasts of burden. And when one of the burden-bearers sank under the load, they cut off his head at the neck-chain, so as not to interrupt the march of the others, since they were all chained together, and as I have related above, the head fell to one side of the road, while the body fell to the other.

When the conquerors entered a town, they were greeted cheerfully and were given all the food they required and were assigned six hundred Indians to carry their loads and attend to their horses for their journeys into the interior.

· · · ·

A relative of the leading tyrant returned unexpectedly he embraced them and had the trumpets sound, letting them understand that from then on he would ask for nothing. But he told them that everything they had given him, and everything he had taken or destroyed up to then was justified, now that he had taken them under his protection, and was his by right.

Later on, the native ruler of all these mainland provinces came with his numerous attendants. His name was Atubaliba, and he and his followers were all naked and carried only mock weapons, knowing nothing of swords and pikes, how they could wound, knowing nothing about horses, how they could run, or of what kind of men were these Spaniards who would attack and set upon them demons, if need be, to rob them of gold.

This native King arrived and called out: "Where are these Spaniards? Let them come out, for I will not move from here until they recompense me for the vassals they have taken from me or killed, and for the towns they have destroyed and the wealth they have taken from me!"

The Spaniards came out and assaulted his followers, killing many, after which they captured the ruler who had been borne in state on a litter. They bargained with him for his ransom. He promised to give them gold worth four million castellanos. And he gave them fifteen millions' worth. Upon which, they promised to release him, but they did not keep their promise (as they never did with the Indians in the Indies). Instead, they took him to his people so he could command them to assemble, for he had told them that no leaf on any tree anywhere stirred without his command, but if the people assembled, believing it was at his command, he feared they would slay him.

Despite all this, they condemned him to be burned alive, although some more merciful Spaniards implored the captain to strangle him before burning him. As he heard his sentence pronounced, this Indian ruler asked, "Why will you burn me? What have I done? Did you not promise to release me if I gave you gold? And did I not give you more than you asked for? But since this is what you want, then send me to your King." And he said many other things of this kind, in confusion and revolt against the great injustice of the Spaniards. And finally they burned him.

Consider here the justice and merit of this war against the Indians, the capture of this great ruler and his sentence and execution; consider the behavior or these great tyrants and the rich treasures they took from that powerful chieftain and from other great people of the realm, or the countless wicked and cruel deeds committed in exterminating these peoples, and committed by men who call themselves Christians.

I will now mention a few such actions that were witnessed by a Franciscan friar at the beginning of the invasion of Peru, and which he set down in writing, signing his name. He sent this report in translations to various parts of the Castilian Kingdoms. One of them, signed by him, is in my possession, and I will quote from it.

> I, the undersigned, Fray Marcos de Niza, of the Franciscan Order called Friars Minor, Father Superior of the said friars, in the province of Peru, who was one of the first religious to accompany the first Christian conquerors of the said province, do state and bear witness to the truth of what I saw with my own eyes in that land, mainly concerning the treatment and conquest of the native peoples.

To begin with, I am a witness with a certain knowledge and experience of the Indians, and I can assert that the Indians of Peru are the most benevolent and kindly disposed to the Christians that I have ever seen. I saw that they gave generously to the Spaniards gold and silver and precious stones and everything they possessed when asked for, all of them being ready to serve and never hostile, always peaceful so long as they were not given occasion by cruel treatment to be warlike, receiving the Spaniards into the villages with generosity and honor, giving them food and what slaves male and female they required.

Furthermore, I bear witness that without cause or occasion, the Spaniards upon entering the lands of the Indians and after their cacique, Atabaliba, had given the Christians more than two millions' worth of gold and all the land he possessed, without resistance, the said cacique was burnt alive.

Atabaliba was the ruler of the entire land, and in pursuit of him, they burned alive his captain–general, Cochilimaca, who had come in peace to the Spanish Governor, in the company of other nobles. And within a few days the Spaniards burned him and Chamba, another noble of the Quito province, who had given no cause, was guilty of no act against them.

Furthermore, they burnt alive Chapera, a lord of the Canaries, again unjustly. They even took Albia, the greatest of the nobles in Quito and, after torturing him in many ways to persuade him to tell where the gold of Atabaliba was hidden, which he could not do because it seems he did not know, they burned his feet. Likewise in Quito they burned Cozopanga, the ruler of all the dependencies of Quito. He had come in peace, at the command of Sebastién de Benalcázar, a captain of the Spanish Governor, and because he did not give the great quantity of gold asked for, they burned him and a number of other nobles and caciques. And as far as I was able to ascertain, the Spaniards did this with the intention of leaving no prince or chieftain alive in the entire country.

Furthermore, when the Spaniards had collected a great deal of gold from the Indians, they shut them up in three big houses, crowding in as many as they could, then set fire to the houses, burning alive all that were in them, yet those Indians had given no cause nor made any resistance. And it happened there that a clergyman, Ocaña by name, snatched a boy from the fire, but another Spaniard took him and flung him back into the flames where he was reduced to ashes. And that Spaniard who had flung the boy into the flames dropped dead on the way back to the captain—general's tent. And I was the one who saw to it that he was not given burial.

Furthermore, I affirm that with my own eyes I saw Spaniards cut off the nose, hands, and ears of Indians, male and female, without provocation, merely because it pleased them to do it, and this they did in so many places that it would take a long time to recount. And I have seen Spaniards urge their dogs to tear the Indians to pieces, this I have seen many times. Likewise I have seen the Spaniards burn so many houses and villages that I would be unable to give the number. I have also seen the Spaniards take suckling infants by the arms and fling them as far away as they could, and have seen other outrages and cruelties perpetrated without reason, which filled me with horror, so many that it would take too long to recount.

Likewise, I saw how they summoned the caciques and the chief rulers to come, assuring them safety, and when they peacefully came, they were taken captive and burned.

And in my presence they burned two Indians, and although I preached against it I was unable to prevent it. And God knows, and as far as I can comprehend, the uprising of the Indians in Peru occurred for no other reason than because of such outrages and the many other causes the Spaniards gave them. Nor did the Spaniards ever keep their word, but instead, without any reason and unjustly and tyrannically, they destroyed the Indians, their lands, their properties, committing such acts that the Indians preferred to die rather than endure them.

Moreover, I can say from having heard the Indians relate it, there is much more gold hidden than displayed, but which, because of their maltreatment, they will not reveal while they are so maltreated. They prefer to die, as others have died before them. And in the said maltreatments, Our Lord has been offended and our king betrayed and defrauded, for this land could easily provide food for all Castile, but it would be very difficult to recuperate the land now, it seems to me.

All the above words are those of the Franciscan Father Superior, and they came to me from the Bishop of Mexico, signed by him, testifying to the fact that they were affirmed by the said Franciscan, Fray Marcos de Niza.

Now, consider what this holy Father says he witnessed, because he traveled through fifty or a hundred leagues of this land and was there from the beginning, for nine or ten years, when very few religious accompanied the four or five thousand Spaniards who invaded Peru, attracted by the smell of gold, and they swept through many great kingdoms and provinces, which they have now destroyed and laid waste in perpetrating the acts which I have related, and many others even more savage and cruel. Truly, they have until now destroyed a thousand times more souls than I have recounted, and with ever less fear of God and of the King and piety, for they have wiped out a great portion of the human family. They have killed in these realms within ten years more than four million souls, and are still killing.

A few days ago they tortured with sharpened reeds and then killed a great queen, the wife of the Inca, King of all these realms which the Christians seized and laid waste. And they took the queen, his wife, and against all justice and reason killed her, even though it is said that she was with child, for the sole reason to cause suffering to her husband.

If an attempt were made to recount in detail the cruel actions and the massacres the Christians have perpetrated and each day are perpetrating in Peru, that relation would be such that all we have recounted of their actions in other parts of the Indies would seem as nothing, by comparison, both in quality and quantity.

The New Kingdom of Granada

In the year one thousand five hundred and thirty-nine many tyrants combined forces and went from Venezuela and Santa Marta and Cartagena in Peru and from Peru itself to invade and overrun the country adjacent to Santa Marta and Cartagena, which is called The New Kingdom of Granada. They took three hundred leagues of the interior land comprised of flourishing and admirable provinces, inhabited by peaceable and good people like the others elsewhere, and very rich in gold and the precious stones called emeralds. To these provinces the Spaniards applied the name The New Kingdom of Granada, because the first tyrant to arrive there was a native of Granada in Castile.

• • • •

"Give me a quarter of that rascal hanging there, to feed my dogs until I can kill another one for them." As if buying a quarter of a hog or other meat.

Other Spaniards go hunting with their dogs in the mornings and when one of them returns at noon and is asked "Did you have good hunting?" he will reply, "Very good! I killed fifteen or twenty rascals and left them with my dogs."

I will finish at this point and shall write no more until more news comes of still more egregious wickedness (if that is possible) or until we return to the Indies and see these things with our own eyes as we constantly did for twenty-two years, constantly protesting before God and my conscience. For I believe, no, I am sure that what I have said about such perditions, injuries, and horrible cruelties and all kinds of ugliness, violence, injustice, thefts, and massacres that those men have perpetrated in these parts of the Indies (and are still perpetrating), I am sure that what I have described is only the ten-thousandth part of what has been done, in quality and quantity, by the Spaniards in the Indies, from the beginning until today.

And so that any Christian may have more compassion for those innocent and ruined nations and their plight, so they may feel the pain of guilt and detest still more the greed and ambition and cruelty of the Spaniards in the Indies, let all that I have said be taken for the real truth, along with what I have affirmed, which is that from the discovery of the Indies until today, never in any part of that New World have the Indians done wrong to the Christians without first having been hurt and robbed and betrayed by them. For in the beginning they thought the Christians were immortals who had come down from Heaven, and they welcomed them, until they saw by their works what these Christians were and what they wanted.

Another thing must be added: from the beginning to the present time the Spaniards have taken no more care to have the Faith of Jesus Christ preached to those nations than they would to have it preached to dogs or other beasts. Instead, they have prohibited the religious from carrying out this intention, and have afflicted them and persecuted them in many ways, because such preaching would, they deemed, have hindered them from acquiring gold and other wealth they coveted. And today in all the Indies there is no more knowledge of God, whether He be of wood or sky, or earth, and this after one hundred years in the New World, except in New Spain, where some religious have gone, and which is but a very small part of the Indies. And thus all the nations have perished and are perishing without the sacraments of the Faith.

I, Fray Bartolomé de Las Casas (or Casaus), a Dominican friar, through the mercy of God, was induced to come to this court of Spain to bring about the ending of that inferno in the Indies and the irremediable destruction of souls that were redeemed by the blood of Jesus Christ; and to set up a work that would bring those souls to know their Creator and Savior. I am also here because of the compassion I have for my native land, Castile, that it not be destroyed by God as punishment for the great sins committed by Spaniards devoid of faith. I am also here because there reside in this court certain persons who are Zealous for the honor of God and have compassion for the afflictions of their fellow men.

Finished in Valencia this eighth day of December, one thousand five hundred and forty-two, when actually all the force and violence are at their peak, when conditions in the Indies are at their worst, with all the anguish and disasters, all the massacres, looting, and destruction, outrages, and exterminations I have described. They are the lot of the native peoples in every part of the Indies where there are Christian conquerors. Although in some parts the Christian Spaniards are more ferocious and abominable in their behavior, they are a little less so in Mexico, or at least there they dare not commit their vile acts as openly as in other parts of the Indies. And although some justice does prevail there, all the same, an infernal amount of killing is done. I have great hope that our Emperor Charles V will harken to and comprehend the evils and betrayals that afflict that land and its peoples, against the will of God and against the will of His Majesty, deeds still being perpetrated, because until now the truth has industriously been concealed, and it is my hope that His Majesty will abolish the evils and remedy conditions in the New World that God has entrusted to him, as the lover and motivator of justice that he is, and may God protect his glorious and felicitous life and the Imperial State that all-powerful God has given him, to heal the universal Church. And may his royal soul be saved at last, and may he prosper for many years to come on this earth. Amen.

After writing the above, there were promulgated certain laws and ordinances which His Majesty issued from the city of Barcelona, in the year one thousand five hundred and forty-two, the month of November, and from the palace in Madrid, the following year, by which it was ordained that henceforth such evil deeds and sins against God and our fellow men would cease in the New World. And finally, after having made these laws, His Majesty held many councils and conferences with persons of great authority, learning, and conscience and there were debates in the palace of Valladolid and the votes cast were set down in writing, the Counselors keeping close to the law of Jesus Christ, being good Christians. It was ordained that the Spanish conquerors should cease the corruption and the soiling of their hands and souls in robbing the Indians of their treasures.

The laws being published, the makers of the tyrants who were at the court had many transcriptions made of them, and these were sent to diverse parts of the Indies. (They did this unwillingly, for the laws seemed to shut them out of participating in the robberies and tyrannies.)

And those who, in the Indies, had charge of the ruin and the robberies have continued, as if no orders had been issued, being inspired by Lucifer, when they saw the transcriptions, to engage in still more disorders before the new judges should arrive to execute the laws. And the tyrants noted and rebelled when the new judges did come to supplant those who had aided and abetted the tyrants since they had lost all love and all fear of God, and lost all shame and all obedience to the King). And thus they agreed to adopt the fame of traitors, their extreme cruelties and tyrannies were now unleashed, especially in the kingdom of Peru, where today in the year one thousand five hundred and forty-six they are committing such horrible, frightful, nefarious acts as were never before committed in the Indies or anywhere else in the world.

And these acts were committed not only against the Indians, most of the Indians having been killed and their lands destroyed, but against each other, and since the laws of the King no longer operated, punishment came from Heaven, allowing each tyrant to be the executioner of the other.

In imitation of this rebellion against the King in this part of the Indies, the tyrants in other parts of the New World have disregarded the new laws and are behaving in the same way. For they cannot bring themselves to relinquish the estates and properties they have usurped, or let go their hold on the Indians, whom they maintain in perpetual subjection. And wherever killing with the sword has come to an end, they are killing the Indians little by little through subjecting them to servitude. And until now the King has been powerless to check them, for all the Spaniards, young and old, in the Indies, are occupied in pillage, some openly, others secretly and stealthily. And with the pretense of serving the King they are dishonoring God and robbing and destroying the King.

Concerning Christian Liberty

Martin Luther

Translated by R. S. Grignon

Part 1: Letter of Martin Luther to Pope Leo X

Letter of Martin Luther to Pope Leo X

Among those monstrous evils of this age with which I have now for three years been waging war, I am sometimes compelled to look to you and to call you to mind, most blessed father Leo. In truth, since you alone are everywhere considered as being the cause of my engaging in war, I cannot at any time fail to remember you; and although I have been compelled by the causeless raging of your impious flatterers against me to appeal from your seat to a future council — fearless of the futile decrees of your predecessors Pius and Julius, who in their foolish tyranny prohibited such an action — yet I have never been so alienated in feeling from your Blessedness as not to have sought with all my might, in diligent prayer and crying to God, all the best gifts for you and for your see. But those who have hitherto endeavoured to terrify me with the majesty of your name and authority, I have begun quite to despise and triumph over. One thing I see remaining which I cannot despise, and this has been the reason of my writing anew to your Blessedness: namely, that I find that blame is cast on me, and that it is imputed to me as a great offence, that in my rashness I am judged to have spared not even your person.

Now, to confess the truth openly, I am conscious that, whenever I have had to mention your person, I have said nothing of you but what was honourable and good. If I had done otherwise, I could by no means have approved my own conduct, but should have supported with all my power the judgment of those men concerning me, nor would anything have pleased me better, than to recant such rashness and impiety. I have called you Daniel in Babylon; and every reader thoroughly knows with what distinguished zeal I defended your conspicuous innocence against Silvester, who tried to stain it. Indeed, the published opinion of so many great men and the repute of your blameless life are too widely famed and too much reverenced throughout the world to be assailable by any man, of however great name, or by any arts. I am not so foolish as to attack one whom everybody praises; nay, it has been and always will be my desire not to attack even those whom public repute disgraces. I am not delighted at the faults of any man, since I am very conscious myself of the great beam in my own eye, nor can I be the first to cast a stone at the adulteress.

I have indeed inveighed sharply against impious doctrines, and I have not been slack to censure my adversaries on account, not of their bad morals, but of their impiety. And for this I am so far from being sorry that I have brought my mind to despise the judgments of men and to persevere in this vehement zeal, according to the example of Christ, who, in His zeal, calls His adversaries a generation of vipers, blind, hypocrites, and children of the devil. Paul, too, charges the sorcerer with being a child of the devil, full of all subtlety and all malice; and defames certain persons as evil workers, dogs, and deceivers. In the opinion of those

From *Concerning Christian Liberty* (1520) by Project Wittenberg, R.S. Grignon, Translator.

delicate-eared persons, nothing could be more bitter or intemperate than Paul's language. What can be more bitter than the words of the prophets? The ears of our generation have been made so delicate by the senseless multitude of flatterers that, as soon as we perceive that anything of ours is not approved of, we cry out that we are being bitterly assailed; and when we can repel the truth by no other pretence, we escape by attributing bitterness, impatience, intemperance, to our adversaries. What would be the use of salt if it were not pungent, or of the edge of the sword if it did not slay? Accursed is the man who does the work of the Lord deceitfully.

Wherefore, most excellent Leo, I beseech you to accept my vindication, made in this letter, and to persuade yourself that I have never thought any evil concerning your person; further, that I am one who desires that eternal blessing may fall to your lot, and that I have no dispute with any man concerning morals, but only concerning the word of truth. In all other things I will yield to any one, but I neither can nor will forsake and deny the word. He who thinks otherwise of me, or has taken in my words in another sense, does not think rightly, and has not taken in the truth.

Your see, however, which is called the Court of Rome, and which neither you nor any man can deny to be more corrupt than any Babylon or Sodom, and quite, as I believe, of a lost, desperate, and hopeless impiety, this I have verily abominated, and have felt indignant that the people of Christ should be cheated under your name and the pretext of the Church of Rome; and so I have resisted, and will resist, as long as the spirit of faith shall live in me. Not that I am striving after impossibilities, or hoping that by my labours alone, against the furious opposition of so many flatterers, any good can be done in that most disordered Babylon; but that I feel myself a debtor to my brethren, and am bound to take thought for them, that fewer of them may be ruined, or that their ruin may be less complete, by the plagues of Rome. For many years now, nothing else has overflowed from Rome into the world — as you are not ignorant — than the laying waste of goods, of bodies, and of souls, and the worst examples of all the worst things. These things are clearer than the light to all men; and the Church of Rome, formerly the most holy of all Churches, has become the most lawless den of thieves, the most shameless of all brothels, the very kingdom of sin, death, and hell; so that not even antichrist, if he were to come, could devise any addition to its wickedness.

Meanwhile you, Leo, are sitting like a lamb, like Daniel in the midst of lions, and, with Ezekiel, you dwell among scorpions. What opposition can you alone make to these monstrous evils? Take to yourself three or four of the most learned and best of the cardinals. What are these among so many? You would all perish by poison before you could undertake to decide on a remedy. It is all over with the Court of Rome; the wrath of God has come upon her to the uttermost. She hates councils; she dreads to be reformed; she cannot restrain the madness of her impiety; she fills up the sentence passed on her mother, of whom it is said, "We would have healed Babylon, but she is not healed; let us forsake her." It had been your duty and that of your cardinals to apply a remedy to these evils, but this gout laughs at the physician's hand, and the chariot does not obey the reins. Under the influence of these feelings, I have always grieved that you, most excellent Leo, who were worthy of a better age, have been made pontiff in this. For the Roman Court is not worthy of you and those like you, but of Satan himself, who in truth is more the ruler in that Babylon than you are.

Oh, would that, having laid aside that glory which your most abandoned enemies declare to be yours, you were living rather in the office of a private priest or on your paternal inheritance! In that glory none are worthy to glory, except the race of Iscariot, the children of perdition. For what happens in your court, Leo, except that, the more wicked and execrable any man is, the more prosperously he can use your name and authority for the ruin of the property and souls of men, for the multiplication of crimes, for the oppression of faith and truth and of the whole Church of God? Oh, Leo! in reality most unfortunate, and sitting on a most perilous throne, I tell you the truth, because I wish you well; for if Bernard felt compassion for Eugenius III, formerly abbot of St. Anastasius his Anastasius at a time when the Roman see, though even then most corrupt, was as yet ruling with better hope than now, why should not we lament, to whom so much further corruption and ruin has been added in three hundred years?

Is it not true that there is nothing under the vast heavens more corrupt, more pestilential, more hateful, than the Court of Rome? She incomparably surpasses the impiety of the Turks, so that in very truth she, who was formerly the gate of heaven, is now a sort of open mouth of hell, and such a mouth as, under the urgent wrath of God, cannot be blocked up; one course alone being left to us wretched men: to call back and save some few, if we can, from that Roman gulf.

Behold, Leo, my father, with what purpose and on what principle it is that I have stormed against that seat of pestilence. I am so far from having felt any rage against your person that I even hoped to gain favour with you and to aid you in your welfare by striking actively and vigorously at that your prison, nay, your hell. For whatever the efforts of all minds can contrive against the confusion of that impious Court will be advantageous to you and to your welfare, and to many others with you. Those who do harm to her are doing your office; those who in every way abhor her are glorifying Christ; in short, those are Christians who are not Romans.

But, to say yet more, even this never entered my heart: to inveigh against the Court of Rome or to dispute at all about her. For, seeing all remedies for her health to be desperate, I looked on her with contempt, and, giving her a bill of divorcement, said to her, "He that is unjust, let him be unjust still; and he that is filthy, let him be filthy still," giving myself up to the peaceful and quiet study of sacred literature, that by this I might be of use to the brethren living about me.

While I was making some advance in these studies, Satan opened his eyes and goaded on his servant John Eccius, that notorious adversary of Christ, by the unchecked lust for fame, to drag me unexpectedly into the arena, trying to catch me in one little word concerning the primacy of the Church of Rome, which had fallen from me in passing. That boastful Thraso, foaming and gnashing his teeth, proclaimed that he would dare all things for the glory of God and for the honour of the holy apostolic seat; and, being puffed up respecting your power, which he was about to misuse, he looked forward with all certainty to victory; seeking to promote, not so much the primacy of Peter, as his own pre-eminence among the theologians of this age; for he thought it would contribute in no slight degree to this, if he were to lead Luther in triumph. The result having proved unfortunate for the sophist, an incredible rage torments him; for he feels that whatever discredit to Rome has arisen through me has been caused by the fault of himself alone.

Suffer me, I pray you, most excellent Leo, both to plead my own cause, and to accuse your true enemies. I believe it is known to you in what way Cardinal Cajetan, your imprudent and unfortunate, nay unfaithful, legate, acted towards me. When, on account of my reverence for your name, I had placed myself and all that was mine in his hands, he did not so act as to establish peace, which he could easily have established by one little word, since I at that time promised to be silent and to make an end of my case, if he would command adversaries to do the same. But that man of pride, not content with this agreement, began to justify my adversaries, to give them free licence, and to order me to recant, a thing which was certainly not in his commission. Thus indeed, when the case was in the best position, it came through his vexatious tyranny into a much worse one. Therefore whatever has followed upon this is the fault not of Luther, but entirely of Cajetan, since he did not suffer me to be silent and remain quiet, which at that time I was entreating for with all my might. What more was it my duty to do?

Next came Charles Miltitz, also a nuncio from your Blessedness. He, though he went up and down with much and varied exertion, and omitted nothing which could tend to restore the position of the cause thrown into confusion by the rashness and pride of Cajetan, had difficulty, even with the help of that very illustrious prince the Elector Frederick, in at last bringing about more than one familiar conference with me. In these I again yielded to your great name, and was prepared to keep silence, and to accept as my judge either the Archbishop of Treves, or the Bishop of Naumburg; and thus it was done and concluded. While this was being done with good hope of success, lo! that other and greater enemy of yours, Eccius, rushed in with his Leipsic disputation, which he had undertaken against Carlstadt, and, having taken up a new question concerning the primacy of the Pope, turned his arms unexpectedly against me, and completely overthrew the plan for peace. Meanwhile Charles Miltitz was waiting, disputations were held, judges were being chosen, but no decision was arrived at. And no wonder! for by the falsehoods, pretences, and arts of Eccius the whole business was brought into such thorough disorder, confusion, and festering soreness, that, whichever way the sentence might lean, a greater conflagration was sure to arise; for he was seeking, not after truth, but after his own credit. In this case too I omitted nothing which it was right that I should do.

I confess that on this occasion no small part of the corruptions of Rome came to light; but, if there was any offence in this, it was the fault of Eccius, who, in taking on him a burden beyond his strength, and in furiously aiming at credit for himself, unveiled to the whole world the disgrace of Rome.

Here is that enemy of yours, Leo, or rather of your Court; by his example alone we may learn that an enemy is not more baneful than a flatterer. For what did he bring about by his flattery, except evils which no king could have brought about? At this day the name of the Court of Rome stinks in the nostrils of the world, the papal authority is growing weak, and its notorious ignorance is evil spoken of. We should hear none of these things, if Eccius had not disturbed the plans of Miltitz and myself for peace. He feels this clearly enough himself in the indignation he shows, too late and in vain, against the publication of my books. He ought to have reflected on this at the time when he was all mad for renown, and was seeking in your cause nothing but his own objects, and that with the greatest peril to you. The foolish man hoped that, from fear of your name, I should yield and keep silence; for I do not think he presumed on his talents and learning. Now, when he sees that I am very confident and speak aloud, he repents too late of his rashness, and sees — if indeed he does see it — that there is One in heaven who resists the proud, and humbles the presumptuous.

Since then we were bringing about by this disputation nothing but the greater confusion of the cause of Rome, Charles Miltitz for the third time addressed the Fathers of the Order, assembled in chapter, and sought their advice for the settlement of the case, as being now in a most troubled and perilous state. Since, by the favour of God, there was no hope of proceeding against me by force, some of the more noted of their number were sent to me, and begged me at least to show respect to your person and to vindicate in a humble letter both your innocence and my own. They said that the affair was not as yet in a position of extreme hopelessness, if Leo X., in his inborn kindliness, would put his hand to it. On this I, who have always offered and wished for peace, in order that I might devote myself to calmer and more useful pursuits, and who for this very purpose have acted with so much spirit and vehemence, in order to put down by the strength and impetuosity of my words, as well as of my feelings, men whom I saw to be very far from equal to myself — I, I say, not only gladly yielded, but even accepted it with joy and gratitude, as the greatest kindness and benefit, if you should think it right to satisfy my hopes.

Thus I come, most blessed Father, and in all abasement beseech you to put to your hand, if it is possible, and impose a curb to those flatterers who are enemies of peace, while they pretend peace. But there is no reason, most blessed Father, why any one should assume that I am to utter a recantation, unless he prefers to involve the case in still greater confusion. Moreover, I cannot bear with laws for the interpretation of the word of God, since the word of God, which teaches liberty in all other things, ought not to be bound. Saving these two things, there is nothing which I am not able, and most heartily willing, to do or to suffer. I hate contention; I will challenge no one; in return I wish not to be challenged; but, being challenged, I will not be dumb in the cause of Christ my Master. For your Blessedness will be able by one short and easy word to call these controversies before you and suppress them, and to impose silence and peace on both sides — a word which I have ever longed to hear.

Therefore, Leo, my Father, beware of listening to those sirens who make you out to be not simply a man, but partly a god, so that you can command and require whatever you will. It will not happen so, nor will you prevail. You are the servant of servants, and more than any other man, in a most pitiable and perilous position. Let not those men deceive you who pretend that you are lord of the world; who will not allow any one to be a Christian without your authority; who babble of your having power over heaven, hell, and purgatory. These men are your enemies and are seeking your soul to destroy it, as Isaiah says, "My people, they that call thee blessed are themselves deceiving thee." They are in error who raise you above councils and the universal Church; they are in error who attribute to you alone the right of interpreting Scripture. All these men are seeking to set up their own impieties in the Church under your name, and alas! Satan has gained much through them in the time of your predecessors.

In brief, trust not in any who exalt you, but in those who humiliate you. For this is the judgment of God: "He hath cast down the mighty from their seat, and hath exalted the humble." See how unlike Christ was to His successors, though all will have it that they are His vicars. I fear that in truth very many of them have been in too serious a sense His vicars, for a vicar represents a prince who is absent. Now if a pontiff rules while Christ is absent and does not dwell in his heart, what else is he but a vicar of Christ? And then what is that Church but a multitude without Christ? What indeed is such a vicar but antichrist and an idol? How much more rightly did the Apostles speak, who call themselves servants of a present Christ, not the vicars of an absent one!

Perhaps I am shamelessly bold in seeming to teach so great a head, by whom all men ought to be taught, and from whom, as those plagues of yours boast, the thrones of judges receive their sentence; but I imitate St. Bernard in his book concerning *Considerations* addressed to Eugenius, a book which ought to be known by heart by every pontiff. I do this, not from any desire to teach, but as a duty, from that simple and faithful solicitude which teaches us to be anxious for all that is safe for our neighbours, and does not allow considerations of worthiness or unworthiness to be entertained, being intent only on the dangers or advantage of others. For since I know that your Blessedness is driven and tossed by the waves at Rome, so that the depths of the sea press on you with infinite perils, and that you are labouring under such a condition of misery that you need even the least help from any the least brother, I do not seem to myself to be acting unsuitably if I forget your majesty till I shall have fulfilled the office of charity. I will not flatter in so serious and perilous a matter; and if in this you do not see that I am your friend and most thoroughly your subject, there is One to see and judge.

In fine, that I may not approach you empty-handed, blessed Father, I bring with me this little treatise, published under your name, as a good omen of the establishment of peace and of good hope. By this you may perceive in what pursuits I should prefer and be able to occupy myself to more profit, if I were allowed, or had been hitherto allowed, by your impious flatterers. It is a small matter, if you look to its exterior, but, unless I mistake, it is a summary of the Christian life put together in small compass, if you apprehend its meaning. I, in my poverty, have no other present to make you, nor do you need anything else than to be enriched by a spiritual gift. I commend myself to your Paternity and Blessedness, whom may the Lord Jesus preserve for ever. Amen.

Wittenberg, 6th September, 1520.

Part 2: Beginning of the Treatise

Concerning Christian Liberty

Christian faith has appeared to many an easy thing; nay, not a few even reckon it among the social virtues, as it were; and this they do because they have not made proof of it experimentally, and have never tasted of what efficacy it is. For it is not possible for any man to write well about it, or to understand well what is rightly written, who has not at some time tasted of its spirit, under the pressure of tribulation; while he who has tasted of it, even to a very small extent, can never write, speak, think, or hear about it sufficiently. For it is a living fountain, springing up into eternal life, as Christ calls it in John iv.

Now, though I cannot boast of my abundance, and though I know how poorly I am furnished, yet I hope that, after having been vexed by various temptations, I have attained some little drop of faith, and that I can speak of this matter, if not with more elegance, certainly with more solidity, than those literal and too subtle disputants who have hitherto discoursed upon it without understanding their own words. That I may open then an easier way for the ignorant — for these alone I am trying to serve — I first lay down these two propositions, concerning spiritual liberty and servitude: —

A Christian man is the most free lord of all, and subject to none; a Christian man is the most dutiful servant of all, and subject to every one.

Although these statements appear contradictory, yet, when they are found to agree together, they will make excellently for my purpose. They are both the statements of Paul himself, who says, "Though I be free from all men, yet have I made myself servant unto all" (1 Cor. ix. 19), and "Owe no man anything, but to love one another" (Rom. xiii. 8). Now love is by its own nature dutiful and obedient to the beloved object. Thus even Christ, though Lord of all things, was yet made of a woman; made under the law; at once free and a servant; at once in the form of God and in the form of a servant.

Let us examine the subject on a deeper and less simple principle. Man is composed of a twofold nature, a spiritual and a bodily. As regards the spiritual nature, which they name the soul, he is called the spiritual, inward, new man; as regards the bodily nature, which they name the flesh, he is called the fleshly, outward, old man. The Apostle speaks of this: "Though our outward man perish, yet the inward man is renewed day by day" (2 Cor. iv. 16). The result of this diversity is that in the Scriptures opposing statements are made concerning the same man, the fact being that in the same man these two men are opposed to one another; the flesh lusting against the spirit, and the spirit against the flesh (Gal. v. 17).

We first approach the subject of the inward man, that we may see by what means a man becomes justified, free, and a true Christian; that is, a spiritual, new, and inward man. It is certain that absolutely none among outward things, under whatever name they may be reckoned, has any influence in producing Christian righteousness or liberty, nor, on the other hand, unrighteousness or slavery. This can be shown by an easy argument.

What can it profit the soul that the body should be in good condition, free, and full of life; that it should eat, drink, and act according to its pleasure; when even the most impious slaves of every kind of vice are prosperous in these matters? Again, what harm can ill-health, bondage, hunger, thirst, or any other outward evil, do to the soul, when even the most pious of men and the freest in the purity of their conscience, are harassed by these things? Neither of these states of things has to do with the liberty or the slavery of the soul.

And so it will profit nothing that the body should be adorned with sacred vestments, or dwell in holy places, or be occupied in sacred offices, or pray, fast, and abstain from certain meats, or do whatever works can be done through the body and in the body. Something widely different will be necessary for the justification and liberty of the soul, since the things I have spoken of can be done by any impious person, and only hypocrites are produced by devotion to these things. On the other hand, it will not at all injure the soul that the body should be clothed in profane raiment, should dwell in profane places, should eat and drink in the ordinary fashion, should not pray aloud, and should leave undone all the things above mentioned, which may be done by hypocrites.

And, to cast everything aside, even speculation, meditations, and whatever things can be performed by the exertions of the soul itself, are of no profit. One thing, and one alone, is necessary for life, justification, and Christian liberty; and that is the most holy word of God, the Gospel of Christ, as He says, "I am the resurrection and the life; he that believeth in Me shall not die eternally" (John xi. 25), and also, "If the Son shall make you free, ye shall be free indeed" (John viii. 36), and, "Man shall not live by bread alone, but by every word that proceedeth out of the mouth of God" (Matt. iv. 4).

Let us therefore hold it for certain and firmly established that the soul can do without everything except the word of God, without which none at all of its wants are provided for. But, having the word, it is rich and wants for nothing, since that is the word of life, of truth, of light, of peace, of justification, of salvation, of joy, of liberty, of wisdom, of virtue, of grace, of glory, and of every good thing. It is on this account that the prophet in a whole Psalm (Psalm cxix, and in many other places), sighs for and calls upon the word of God with so many groanings and words.

Again, there is no more cruel stroke of the wrath of God than when He sends a famine of hearing His words (Amos viii. 11), just as there is no greater favour from Him than the sending forth of His word, as it is said, "He sent His word and healed them, and delivered them from their destruction" (Psalm cvii. 20). Christ was sent for no other office than that of the word; and the order of Apostles, that of bishops, and that of the whole body of the clergy, have been called and instituted for no object but the ministry of the word.

But you will ask, What is this word, and by what means is it to be used, since there are so many words of God? I answer, The Apostle Paul (Rom. i.) explains what it is, namely the Gospel of God, concerning His Son, incarnate, suffering, risen, and glorified, through the Spirit, the Sanctifier. To preach Christ is to feed the soul, to justify it, to set it free, and to save it, if it believes the preaching. For faith alone and the efficacious use of the word of God, bring salvation. "If thou shalt confess with thy mouth the Lord Jesus, and shalt believe in thine heart that God hath raised Him from the dead, thou shalt be saved" (Rom. x. 9); and again, "Christ is the end of the law for righteousness to every one that believeth" (Rom. x. 4), and "The just shall live by faith" (Rom. i. 17). For the word of God cannot be received and honoured by any works, but by faith alone. Hence it is clear that as the soul needs the word alone for life and justification, so it is justified by faith alone, and not by any works. For if it could be justified by any other means, it would have no need of the word, nor consequently of faith.

But this faith cannot consist at all with works; that is, if you imagine that you can be justified by those works, whatever they are, along with it. For this would be to halt between two opinions, to worship Baal, and to kiss the hand to him, which is a very great iniquity, as Job says. Therefore, when you begin to believe, you learn at the same time that all that is in you is utterly guilty, sinful, and damnable, according to that saying, "All have sinned, and come short of the glory of God" (Rom. iii. 23), and also: "There is none righteous, no, not one; they are all gone out of the way; they are together become unprofitable: there is none that doeth good, no, not one" (Rom. iii. 10612). When you have learnt this, you will know that Christ is necessary for you, since He has suffered and risen again for you, that, believing on Him, you might by this faith become another man, all your sins being remitted, and you being justified by the merits of another, namely of Christ alone.

Since then this faith can reign only in the inward man, as it is said, "With the heart man believeth unto righteousness" (Rom. x. 10); and since it alone justifies, it is evident that by no outward work or labour can the inward man be at all justified, made free, and saved; and that no works whatever have any relation to him. And so, on the other hand, it is solely by impiety and incredulity of heart that he becomes guilty and a slave of sin, deserving condemnation, not by any outward sin or work. Therefore the first care of every Christian ought to be to lay aside all reliance on works, and strengthen his faith alone more and more, and by it grow in the knowledge, not of works, but of Christ Jesus, who has suffered and risen again for him, as Peter teaches (1 Peter v.) when he makes no other work to be a Christian one. Thus Christ, when the Jews asked Him what they should do that they might work the works of God, rejected the multitude of works, with which He saw that they were puffed up, and commanded them one thing only, saying, "This is the work of God: that ye believe on Him whom He hath sent, for Him hath God the Father sealed" (John vi. 27, 29).

Hence a right faith in Christ is an incomparable treasure, carrying with it universal salvation and preserving from all evil, as it is said, "He that believeth and is baptised shall be saved; but he that believeth not shall be damned" (Mark xvi. 16). Isaiah, looking to this treasure, predicted, "The consumption decreed shall overflow with righteousness. For the Lord God of hosts shall make a consumption, even determined (*verbum abbreviatum et consummans*), in the midst of the land" (Isa. x. 22, 23). As if he said, "Faith, which is the brief and complete fulfilling of the law, will fill those who believe with such righteousness that they will need nothing else for justification." Thus, too, Paul says, "For with the heart man believeth unto righteousness" (Rom. x. 10).

But you ask how it can be the fact that faith alone justifies, and affords without works so great a treasure of good things, when so many works, ceremonies, and laws are prescribed to us in the Scriptures? I answer, Before all things bear in mind what I have said: that faith alone without works justifies, sets free, and saves, as I shall show more clearly below.

Meanwhile it is to be noted that the whole Scripture of God is divided into two parts: precepts and promises. The precepts certainly teach us what is good, but what they teach is not forthwith done. For they show us what we ought to do, but do not give us the power to do it. They were ordained, however, for the purpose of showing man to himself, that through them he may learn his own impotence for good and may despair of his own strength. For this reason they are called the Old Testament, and are so.

For example, "Thou shalt not covet," is a precept by which we are all convicted of sin, since no man can help coveting, whatever efforts to the contrary he may make. In order therefore that he may fulfil the precept, and not covet, he is constrained to despair of himself and to seek elsewhere and through another the help which he cannot find in himself; as it is said, "O Israel, thou hast destroyed thyself; but in Me is thine help" (Hosea xiii. 9). Now what is done by this one precept is done by all; for all are equally impossible of fulfilment by us.

Now when a man has through the precepts been taught his own impotence, and become anxious by what means he may satisfy the law — for the law must be satisfied, so that no jot or tittle of it may pass away, otherwise he must be hopelessly condemned — then, being truly humbled and brought to nothing in his own eyes, he finds in himself no resource for justification and salvation.

Then comes in that other part of Scripture, the promises of God, which declare the glory of God, and say, "If you wish to fulfil the law, and, as the law requires, not to covet, lo! believe in Christ, in whom are promised to you grace, justification, peace, and liberty." All these things you shall have, if you believe, and shall be without them if you do not believe. For what is impossible for you by all the works of the law, which are many and yet useless, you shall fulfil in an easy and summary way through faith, because God the Father has made everything to depend on faith, so that whosoever has it has all things, and he who has it not has nothing. "For God hath concluded them all in unbelief, that He might have mercy upon all" (Rom. xi. 32). Thus the promises of God give that which the precepts exact, and fulfil what the law commands; so that all is of God alone, both the precepts and their fulfilment. He alone commands; He alone also fulfils. Hence the promises of God belong to the New Testament; nay, are the New Testament.

Now, since these promises of God are words of holiness, truth, righteousness, liberty, and peace, and are full of universal goodness, the soul, which cleaves to them with a firm faith, is so united to them, nay, thoroughly absorbed by them, that it not only partakes in, but is penetrated and saturated by, all their virtues. For if the touch of Christ was healing, how much more does that most tender spiritual touch, nay, absorption of the word, communicate to the soul all that belongs to the word! In this way therefore the soul, through faith alone, without works, is from the word of God justified, sanctified, endued with truth, peace, and liberty, and filled full with every good thing, and is truly made the child of God, as it is said, "To them gave He power to become the sons of God, even to them that believe in His name" (John i. 12).

From all this it is easy to understand why faith has such great power, and why no good works, nor even all good works put together, can compare with it, since no work can cleave to the word of God or be in the soul. Faith alone and the word reign in it; and such as is the word, such is the soul made by it, just as iron exposed to fire glows like fire, on account of its union with the fire. It is clear then that to a Christian man his faith suffices for everything, and that he has no need of works for justification. But if he has no need of works, neither has he need of the law; and if he has no need of the law, he is certainly free from the law, and the saying is true, "The law is not made for a righteous man" (1 Tim. i. 9). This is that Christian liberty, our faith, the effect of which is, not that we should be careless or lead a bad life, but that no one should need the law or works for justification and salvation.

Let us consider this as the first virtue of faith; and let us look also to the second. This also is an office of faith: that it honours with the utmost veneration and the highest reputation Him in whom it believes, inasmuch as it holds Him to be truthful and worthy of belief. For there is no honour like that reputation of truth and righteousness with which we honour Him in whom we believe. What higher credit can we attribute to any one than truth and righteousness, and absolute goodness? On the other hand, it is the greatest insult to brand any one with the reputation of falsehood and unrighteousness, or to suspect him of these, as we do when we disbelieve him.

Thus the soul, in firmly believing the promises of God, holds Him to be true and righteous; and it can attribute to God no higher glory than the credit of being so. The highest worship of God is to ascribe to Him truth, righteousness, and whatever qualities we must ascribe to one in whom we believe. In doing this the soul shows itself prepared to do His whole will; in doing this it hallows His name, and gives itself up to be dealt with as it may please God. For it cleaves to His promises, and never doubts that He is true, just, and wise, and will do, dispose, and provide for all things in the best way. Is not such a soul, in this its faith, most obedient to God in all things? What commandment does there remain which has not been amply fulfilled by such an obedience? What fulfilment can be more full than universal obedience? Now this is not accomplished by works, but by faith alone.

On the other hand, what greater rebellion, impiety, or insult to God can there be, than not to believe His promises? What else is this, than either to make God a liar, or to doubt His truth — that is, to attribute truth to ourselves, but to God falsehood and levity? In doing this, is not a man denying God and setting himself up as an idol in his own heart? What then can works, done in such a state of impiety, profit us, were they even angelic or apostolic works? Rightly hath God shut up all, not in wrath nor in lust, but in unbelief, in order that those who pretend that they are fulfilling the law by works of purity and benevolence (which are social and human virtues) may not presume that they will therefore be saved, but, being included in the sin of unbelief, may either seek mercy, or be justly condemned.

But when God sees that truth is ascribed to Him, and that in the faith of our hearts He is honoured with all the honour of which He is worthy, then in return He honours us on account of that faith, attributing to us truth and righteousness. For faith does truth and righteousness in rendering to God what is His; and therefore in return God gives glory to our righteousness. It is true and righteous that God is true and righteous; and to confess this and ascribe these attributes to Him, this it is to be true and righteous. Thus He says, "Them that honour Me I will honour, and they that despise Me shall be lightly esteemed" (1 Sam. ii. 30). And so Paul says that Abraham's faith was imputed to him for righteousness, because by it he gave glory to God; and that to us also, for the same reason, it shall be imputed for righteousness, if we believe (Rom. iv.).

The third incomparable grace of faith is this: that it unites the soul to Christ, as the wife to the husband, by which mystery, as the Apostle teaches, Christ and the soul are made one flesh. Now if they are one flesh, and if a true marriage — nay, by far the most perfect of all marriages — is accomplished between them (for human marriages are but feeble types of this one great marriage), then it follows that all they have becomes theirs in common, as well good things as evil things; so that whatsoever Christ possesses, that the believing soul may take to itself and boast of as its own, and whatever belongs to the soul, that Christ claims as His.

If we compare these possessions, we shall see how inestimable is the gain. Christ is full of grace, life, and salvation; the soul is full of sin, death, and condemnation. Let faith step in, and then sin, death, and hell will belong to Christ, and grace, life, and salvation to the soul. For, if He is a Husband, He must needs take to Himself that which is His wife's, and at the same time, impart to His wife that which is His. For, in giving her His own body and Himself, how can He but give her all that is His? And, in taking to Himself the body of His wife, how can He but take to Himself all that is hers?

In this is displayed the delightful sight, not only of communion, but of a prosperous warfare, of victory, salvation, and redemption. For, since Christ is God and man, and is such a Person as neither has sinned, nor dies, nor is condemned, nay, cannot sin, die, or be condemned, and since His righteousness, life, and salvation are invincible, eternal, and almighty, — when I say, such a Person, by the wedding-ring of faith, takes a share in the sins, death, and hell of

His wife, nay, makes them His own, and deals with them no otherwise than as if they were His, and as if He Himself had sinned; and when He suffers, dies, and descends to hell, that He may overcome all things, and since sin, death, and hell cannot swallow Him up, they must needs be swallowed up by Him in stupendous conflict. For His righteousness rises above the sins of all men; His life is more powerful than all death; His salvation is more unconquerable than all hell.

Thus the believing soul, by the pledge of its faith in Christ, becomes free from all sin, fearless of death, safe from hell, and endowed with the eternal righteousness, life, and salvation of its Husband Christ. Thus He presents to Himself a glorious bride, without spot or wrinkle, cleansing her with the washing of water by the word; that is, by faith in the word of life, righteousness, and salvation. Thus He betrothes her unto Himself "in faithfulness, in righteousness, and in judgment, and in lovingkindness, and in mercies" (Hosea ii. 19, 20).

Who then can value highly enough these royal nuptials? Who can comprehend the riches of the glory of this grace? Christ, that rich and pious Husband, takes as a wife a needy and impious harlot, redeeming her from all her evils and supplying her with all His good things. It is impossible now that her sins should destroy her, since they have been laid upon Christ and swallowed up in Him, and since she has in her Husband Christ a righteousness which she may claim as her own, and which she can set up with confidence against all her sins, against death and hell, saying, "If I have sinned, my Christ, in whom I believe, has not sinned; all mine is His, and all His is mine," as it is written, "My beloved is mine, and I am His" (Cant. ii. 16). This is what Paul says: "Thanks be to God, which giveth us the victory through our Lord Jesus Christ," victory over sin and death, as he says, "The sting of death is sin, and the strength of sin is the law" (1 Cor. xv. 56, 57).

From all this you will again understand why so much importance is attributed to faith, so that it alone can fulfil the law and justify without any works. For you see that the First Commandment, which says, "Thou shalt worship one God only," is fulfilled by faith alone. If you were nothing but good works from the soles of your feet to the crown of your head, you would not be worshipping God, nor fulfilling the First Commandment, since it is impossible to worship God without ascribing to Him the glory of truth and of universal goodness, as it ought in truth to be ascribed. Now this is not done by works, but only by faith of heart. It is not by working, but by believing, that we glorify God, and confess Him to be true. On this ground faith alone is the righteousness of a Christian man, and the fulfilling of all the commandments. For to him who fulfils the first the task of fulfilling all the rest is easy.

Works, since they are irrational things, cannot glorify God, although they may be done to the glory of God, if faith be present. But at present we are inquiring, not into the quality of the works done, but into him who does them, who glorifies God, and brings forth good works. This is faith of heart, the head and the substance of all our righteousness. Hence that is a blind and perilous doctrine which teaches that the commandments are fulfilled by works. The commandments must have been fulfilled previous to any good works, and good works follow their fulfillment, as we shall see.

But, that we may have a wider view of that grace which our inner man has in Christ, we must know that in the Old Testament God sanctified to Himself every first-born male. The birthright was of great value, giving a superiority over the rest by the double honour of priesthood and kingship. For the first-born brother was priest and lord of all the rest.

Under this figure was foreshown Christ, the true and only First-born of God the Father and of the Virgin Mary, and a true King and Priest, not in a fleshly and earthly sense. For His kingdom is not of this world; it is in heavenly and spiritual things that He reigns and acts as Priest; and these are righteousness, truth, wisdom, peace, salvation, etc. Not but that all things, even those of earth and hell, are subject to Him — for otherwise how could He defend and save us from them? — but it is not in these, nor by these, that His kingdom stands.

So, too, His priesthood does not consist in the outward display of vestments and gestures, as did the human priesthood of Aaron and our ecclesiastical priesthood at this day, but in spiritual things, wherein, in His invisible office, He intercedes for us with God in heaven, and there offers Himself, and performs all the duties of a priest, as Paul describes Him to the Hebrews under the figure of Melchizedek. Nor does He only pray and intercede for us; He also teaches us inwardly in the spirit with the living teachings of His Spirit. Now these are the two special offices of a priest, as is figured to us in the case of fleshly priests by visible prayers and sermons.

As Christ by His birthright has obtained these two dignities, so He imparts and communicates them to every believer in Him, under that law of matrimony of which we have spoken above, by which all that is the husband's is also the wife's. Hence all we who believe in Christ are kings and priests in Christ, as it is said, "Ye are a chosen generation, a royal priesthood, a holy nation, a peculiar people, that ye should show forth the praises of Him who hath called you out of darkness into His marvellous light" (1 Peter ii. 9).

These two things stand thus. First, as regards kingship, every Christian is by faith so exalted above all things that, in spiritual power, he is completely lord of all things, so that nothing whatever can do him any hurt; yea, all things are subject to him, and are compelled to be subservient to his salvation. Thus Paul says, "All things work together for good to them who are the called" (Rom. viii. 28), and also, "Whether life, or death, or things present, or things to come, all are yours; and ye are Christ's" (1 Cor. iii. 22, 23).

Not that in the sense of corporeal power any one among Christians has been appointed to possess and rule all things, according to the mad and senseless idea of certain ecclesiastics. That is the office of kings, princes, and men upon earth. In the experience of life we see that we are subjected to all things, and suffer many things, even death. Yea, the more of a Christian any man is, to so many the more evils, sufferings, and deaths is he subject, as we see in the first place in Christ the First-born, and in all His holy brethren.

This is a spiritual power, which rules in the midst of enemies, and is powerful in the midst of distresses. And this is nothing else than that strength is made perfect in my weakness, and that I can turn all things to the profit of my salvation; so that even the cross and death are compelled to serve me and to work together for my salvation. This is a lofty and eminent dignity, a true and almighty dominion, a spiritual empire, in which there is nothing so good, nothing so bad, as not to work together for my good, if only I believe. And yet there is nothing of which I have need — for faith alone suffices for my salvation — unless that in it faith may exercise the power and empire of its liberty. This is the inestimable power and liberty of Christians.

Nor are we only kings and the freest of all men, but also priests for ever, a dignity far higher than kingship, because by that priesthood we are worthy to appear before God, to pray for others, and to teach one another mutually the things which are of God. For these are the duties of priests, and they cannot possibly be permitted to any unbeliever. Christ has obtained for us this favour, if we believe in Him: that just as we are His brethren and co-heirs and fellow-kings with Him, so we should be also fellow-priests with Him, and venture with confidence, through the spirit of faith, to come into the presence of God, and cry, "Abba, Father!" and to pray for one another, and to do all things which we see done and figured in the visible and corporeal office of priesthood. But to an unbelieving person nothing renders service or work for good. He himself is in servitude to all things, and all things turn out for evil to him, because he uses all things in an impious way for his own advantage, and not for the glory of God. And thus he is not a priest, but a profane person, whose prayers are turned into sin, nor does he ever appear in the presence of God, because God does not hear sinners.

Who then can comprehend the loftiness of that Christian dignity which, by its royal power, rules over all things, even over death, life, and sin, and, by its priestly glory, is all-powerful with God, since God does what He Himself seeks and wishes, as it is written, "He will fulfil the desire of them that fear Him; He also will hear their cry, and will save them"? (Psalm cxlv. 19). This glory certainly cannot be attained by any works, but by faith only.

From these considerations any one may clearly see how a Christian man is free from all things; so that he needs no works in order to be justified and saved, but receives these gifts in abundance from faith alone. Nay, were he so foolish as to pretend to be justified, set free, saved, and made a Christian, by means of any good work, he would immediately lose faith, with all its benefits. Such folly is prettily represented in the fable where a dog, running along in the water and carrying in his mouth a real piece of meat, is deceived by the reflection of the meat in the water, and, in trying with open mouth to seize it, loses the meat and its image at the same time.

Here you will ask, "If all who are in the Church are priests, by what character are those whom we now call priests to be distinguished from the laity?" I reply, By the use of these words, "priest," "clergy," "spiritual person," "ecclesiastic," an injustice has been done, since they have been transferred from the remaining body of Christians to those few who are now, by hurtful custom, called ecclesiastics. For Holy Scripture makes no distinction between them, except that those who are now boastfully called popes, bishops, and lords, it calls ministers, servants, and stewards, who are to serve the rest in the ministry of the word, for teaching the faith of Christ and the liberty of believers. For though it is true that we are all equally priests, yet we cannot, nor, if we could, ought we all to, minister and teach publicly. Thus Paul says, "Let a man so account of us as of the ministers of Christ and stewards of the mysteries of God" (1 Cor. iv. 1).

This bad system has now issued in such a pompous display of power and such a terrible tyranny that no earthly government can be compared to it, as if the laity were something else than Christians. Through this perversion of things it has happened that the knowledge of Christian grace, of faith, of liberty, and altogether of Christ, has utterly perished, and has been succeeded by an intolerable bondage to human works and laws; and, according to the Lamentations of Jeremiah, we have become the slaves of the vilest men on earth, who abuse our misery to all the disgraceful and ignominious purposes of their own will.

Returning to the subject which we had begun, I think it is made clear by these considerations that it is not sufficient, nor a Christian course, to preach the works, life, and words of Christ in a historic manner, as facts which it suffices to know as an example how to frame our life, as do those who are now held the best preachers, and much less so to keep silence altogether on these things and to teach in their stead the laws of men and the decrees of the Fathers. There are now not a few persons who preach and read about Christ with the object of moving the human affections to sympathise with Christ, to indignation against the Jews, and other childish and womanish absurdities of that kind.

Now preaching ought to have the object of promoting faith in Him, so that He may not only be Christ, but a Christ for you and for me, and that what is said of Him, and what He is called, may work in us. And this faith is produced and is maintained by preaching why Christ came, what He has brought us and given to us, and to what profit and advantage He is to be received. This is done when the Christian liberty which we have from Christ Himself is rightly taught, and we are shown in what manner all we Christians are kings and priests, and how we are lords of all things, and may be confident that whatever we do in the presence of God is pleasing and acceptable to Him.

Whose heart would not rejoice in its inmost core at hearing these things? Whose heart, on receiving so great a consolation, would not become sweet with the love of Christ, a love to which it can never attain by any laws or works? Who can injure such a heart, or make it afraid? If the consciousness of sin or the horror of death rush in upon it, it is prepared to hope in the Lord, and is fearless of such evils, and undisturbed, until it shall look down upon its enemies. For it believes that the righteousness of Christ is its own, and that its sin is no longer its own, but that of Christ; but, on account of its faith in Christ, all its sin must needs be swallowed up from before the face of the righteousness of Christ, as I have said above. It learns, too, with the Apostle, to scoff at death and sin, and to say, "O death, where is thy sting? O grave, where is thy victory? The sting of death is sin, and the strength of sin is the law. But thanks be to God, which giveth us the victory through our Lord Jesus Christ" (1 Cor. xv. 55–57). For death is swallowed up in victory, not only the victory of Christ, but ours also, since by faith it becomes ours, and in it we too conquer.

Let it suffice to say this concerning the inner man and its liberty, and concerning that righteousness of faith which needs neither laws nor good works; they are even hurtful to it, if any one pretends to be justified by them.

Part 3: Conclusion of the Treatise

And now let us turn to the other part: to the outward man. Here we shall give an answer to all those who, taking offence at the word of faith and at what I have asserted, say, "If faith does everything, and by itself suffices for justification, why then are good works commanded? Are we then to take our ease and do no works, content with faith?" Not so, impious men, I reply; not so. That would indeed really be the case, if we were thoroughly and completely inner and spiritual persons; but that will not happen until the last day, when the dead shall be raised. As long as we live in the flesh, we are but beginning and making advances in that which shall be completed in a future life. On this account the Apostle calls that which we have in this life the firstfruits of the Spirit (Rom. viii. 23). In future we shall have the tenths, and the fullness of the Spirit. To this part belongs the fact I have stated before: that the Christian is the servant of all and subject to all. For in that part in which he is free he does no works, but in that in which he is a servant he does all works. Let us see on what principle this is so.

Although, as I have said, inwardly, and according to the spirit, a man is amply enough justified by faith, having all that he requires to have, except that this very faith and abundance ought to increase from day to day, even till the future life, still he remains in this mortal life upon earth, in which it is necessary that he should rule his own body and have intercourse with men. Here then works begin; here he must not take his ease; here he must give heed to exercise his body by fastings, watchings, labour, and other regular discipline, so that it may be subdued to the spirit, and obey and conform itself to the inner man and faith, and not rebel against them nor hinder them, as is its nature to do if it is not kept under. For the inner man, being conformed to God and created after the image of God through faith, rejoices and delights itself in Christ, in whom such blessings have been conferred on it, and hence has only this task before it: to serve God with joy and for nought in free love.

But in doing this he comes into collision with that contrary will in his own flesh, which is striving to serve the world and to seek its own gratification. This the spirit of faith cannot and will not bear, but applies itself with cheerfulness and zeal to keep it down and restrain it, as Paul says, "I delight in the law of God after the inward man; but I see another law in my members, warring against the law of my mind and bringing me into captivity to the law of sin" (Rom. vii. 22, 23), and again, "I keep under my body, and bring it unto subjection, lest that by any means, when I have preached to others, I myself should be a castaway" (1 Cor. ix. 27), and "They that are Christ's have crucified the flesh, with the affections and lusts" (Gal. v. 24).

These works, however, must not be done with any notion that by them a man can be justified before God — for faith, which alone is righteousness before God, will not bear with this false notion — but solely with this purpose: that the body may be brought into subjection, and be purified from its evil lusts, so that our eyes may be turned only to purging away those lusts. For when the soul has been cleansed by faith and made to love God, it would have all things to be cleansed in like manner, and especially its own body, so that all things might unite with it in the love and praise of God. Thus it comes that, from the requirements of his own body, a man cannot take his ease, but is compelled on its account to do many good works, that he may bring it into subjection. Yet these works are not the means of his justification before God; he does them out of disinterested love to the service of God; looking to no other end than to do what is well-pleasing to Him whom he desires to obey most dutifully in all things.

On this principle every man may easily instruct himself in what measure, and with what distinctions, he ought to chasten his own body. He will fast, watch, and labour, just as much as he sees to suffice for keeping down the wantonness and concupiscence of the body. But those who pretend to be justified by works are looking, not to the mortification of their lusts, but only to the works themselves; thinking that, if they can accomplish as many works and as great ones as possible, all is well with them, and they are justified. Sometimes they even injure their brain, and extinguish nature, or at least make it useless. This is enormous folly, and ignorance of Christian life and faith, when a man seeks, without faith, to be justified and saved by works.

To make what we have said more easily understood, let us set it forth under a figure. The works of a Christian man, who is justified and saved by his faith out of the pure and unbought mercy of God, ought to be regarded in the same light as would have been those of Adam and Eve in paradise and of all their posterity if they had not sinned. Of them it is said, "The Lord God took the man and put him into the garden of Eden to dress it and to keep it" (Gen. ii. 15). Now Adam had been created by God just and righteous, so that he could not have needed to be justified and made righteous by keeping the garden and working in it; but, that he might not be unemployed, God gave him the business of keeping and cultivating paradise. These would have indeed been works of perfect freedom, being done for no object but that of pleasing God, and not in order to obtain justification, which he already had to the full, and which would have been innate in us all.

So it is with the works of a believer. Being by his faith afresh in paradise and created anew, he does not need works for his justification, but that he may not be idle, but may exercise his own body and preserve it. His works are to be done freely, with the sole object of pleasing God. Only we are not yet fully created anew in perfect faith and love; these require to be increased, not, however, through works, but through themselves.

A bishop, when he consecrates a church, confirms children, or performs any other duty of his office, is not consecrated as bishop by these works; nay, unless he had been previously consecrated as bishop, not one of those works would have any validity; they would be foolish, childish, and ridiculous. Thus a Christian, being consecrated by his faith, does good works; but he is not by these works made a more sacred person, or more a Christian. That is the effect of faith alone; nay, unless he were previously a believer and a Christian, none of his works would have any value at all; they would really be impious and damnable sins.

True, then, are these two sayings: "Good works do not make a good man, but a good man does good works"; "Bad works do not make a bad man, but a bad man does bad works." Thus it is always necessary that the substance or person should be good before any good works can be done, and that good works should follow and proceed from a good person. As Christ says, "A good tree cannot bring forth evil fruit, neither can a corrupt tree bring forth good fruit" (Matt. vii. 18). Now it is clear that the fruit does not bear the tree, nor does the tree grow on the fruit; but, on the contrary, the trees bear the fruit, and the fruit grows on the trees.

As then trees must exist before their fruit, and as the fruit does not make the tree either good or bad, but on the contrary, a tree of either kind produces fruit of the same kind, so must first the person of the man be good or bad before he can do either a good or a bad work; and his works do not make him bad or good, but he himself makes his works either bad or good.

We may see the same thing in all handicrafts. A bad or good house does not make a bad or good builder, but a good or bad builder makes a good or bad house. And in general no work makes the workman such as it is itself; but the workman makes the work such as he is himself. Such is the case, too, with the works of men. Such as the man himself is, whether in faith or in unbelief, such is his work: good if it be done in faith; bad if in unbelief. But the converse is not true that, such as the work is, such the man becomes in faith or in unbelief. For as works do not make a believing man, so neither do they make a justified man; but faith, as it makes a man a believer and justified, so also it makes his works good.

Since then works justify no man, but a man must be justified before he can do any good work, it is most evident that it is faith alone which, by the mere mercy of God through Christ, and by means of His word, can worthily and sufficiently justify and save the person; and that a Christian man needs no work, no law, for his salvation; for by faith he is free from all law, and in perfect freedom does gratuitously all that he does, seeking nothing either of profit or of salvation — since by the grace of God he is already saved and rich in all things through his faith — but solely that which is well-pleasing to God.

So, too, no good work can profit an unbeliever to justification and salvation; and, on the other hand, no evil work makes him an evil and condemned person, but that unbelief, which makes the person and the tree bad, makes his works evil and condemned. Wherefore, when any man is made good or bad, this does not arise from his works, but from his faith or unbelief, as the wise man says, "The beginning of sin is to fall away from God"; that is, not to believe. Paul says, "He that cometh to God must believe" (Heb. xi. 6); and Christ says the same thing: "Either make the tree good and his fruit good; or else make the tree corrupt, and his fruit corrupt" (Matt. xii. 33), — as much as to say, He who wishes to have good fruit will begin with the tree, and plant a good one; even so he who wishes to do good works must begin, not by working, but by believing, since it is this which makes the person good. For nothing makes the person good but faith, nor bad but unbelief.

It is certainly true that, in the sight of men, a man becomes good or evil by his works; but here "becoming" means that it is thus shown and recognised who is good or evil, as Christ says, "By their fruit ye shall know them" (Matt. vii. 20). But all this stops at appearances and externals; and in this matter very many deceive themselves, when they presume to write and teach that we are to be justified by good works, and meanwhile make no mention even of faith, walking in their own ways, ever deceived and deceiving, going from bad to worse, blind leaders of the blind, wearying themselves with many works, and yet never attaining to true righteousness, of whom Paul says, "Having a form of godliness, but denying the power thereof, ever learning and never able to come to the knowledge of the truth" (2 Tim. iii. 5, 7).

He then who does not wish to go astray, with these blind ones, must look further than to the works of the law or the doctrine of works; nay, must turn away his sight from works, and look to the person, and to the manner in which it may be justified. Now it is justified and saved, not by works or laws, but by the word of God — that is, by the promise of His grace — so that the glory may be to the Divine majesty, which has saved us who believe, not by works of righteousness which we have done, but according to His mercy, by the word of His grace.

From all this it is easy to perceive on what principle good works are to be cast aside or embraced, and by what rule all teachings put forth concerning works are to be understood. For if works are brought forward as grounds of justification, and are done under the false persuasion that we can pretend to be justified by them, they lay on us the yoke of necessity, and extinguish liberty along with faith, and by this very addition to their use they become no longer good, but really worthy of condemnation. For such works are not free, but blaspheme the grace of God, to which alone it belongs to justify and save through faith. Works cannot accomplish this, and yet, with impious presumption, through our folly, they take it on themselves to do so; and thus break in with violence upon the office and glory of grace.

We do not then reject good works; nay, we embrace them and teach them in the highest degree. It is not on their own account that we condemn them, but on account of this impious addition to them and the perverse notion of seeking justification by them. These things cause them to be only good in outward show, but in reality not good, since by them men are deceived and deceive others, like ravening wolves in sheep's clothing.

Now this leviathan, this perverted notion about works, is invincible when sincere faith is wanting. For those sanctified doers of works cannot but hold it till faith, which destroys it, comes and reigns in the heart. Nature cannot expel it by her own power; nay, cannot even see it for what it is, but considers it as a most holy will. And when custom steps in besides, and strengthens this pravity of nature, as has happened by means of impious teachers, then the evil is incurable, and leads astray multitudes to irreparable ruin. Therefore, though it is good to preach and write about penitence, confession, and satisfaction, yet if we stop there, and do not go on to teach faith, such teaching is without doubt deceitful and devilish. For Christ, speaking by His servant John, not only said, "Repent ye," but added, "for the kingdom of heaven is at hand" (Matt. iii. 2).

For not one word of God only, but both, should be preached; new and old things should be brought out of the treasury, as well the voice of the law as the word of grace. The voice of the law should be brought forward, that men may be terrified and brought to a knowledge of their sins, and thence be converted to penitence and to a better manner of life. But we must not stop here; that would be to wound only and not to bind up, to strike and not to heal, to kill and not to make alive, to bring down to hell and not to bring back, to humble and not to exalt. Therefore the word of grace and of the promised remission of sin must also be preached, in order to teach and set up faith, since without that word contrition, penitence, and all other duties, are performed and taught in vain.

There still remain, it is true, preachers of repentance and grace, but they do not explain the law and the promises of God to such an end, and in such a spirit, that men may learn whence repentance and grace are to come. For repentance comes from the law of God, but faith or grace from the promises of God, as it is said, "Faith cometh by hearing, and hearing by the word of God" (Rom. x. 17), whence it comes that a man, when humbled and brought to the knowledge of himself by the threatenings and terrors of the law, is consoled and raised up by faith in the Divine promise. Thus "weeping may endure for a night, but joy cometh in the morning" (Psalm xxx. 5). Thus much we say concerning works in general, and also concerning those which the Christian practises with regard to his own body.

Lastly, we will speak also of those works which he performs towards his neighbour. For man does not live for himself alone in this mortal body, in order to work on its account, but also for all men on earth; nay, he lives only for others, and not for himself. For it is to this end that he brings his own body into subjection, that he may be able to serve others more sincerely and more freely, as Paul says, "None of us liveth to himself, and no man dieth to himself. For whether we live, we live unto the Lord; and whether we die, we die unto the Lord" (Rom. xiv. 7, 8). Thus it is impossible that he should take his ease in this life, and not work for the good of his neighbours, since he must needs speak, act, and converse among men, just as Christ was made in the likeness of men and found in fashion as a man, and had His conversation among men.

Yet a Christian has need of none of these things for justification and salvation, but in all his works he ought to entertain this view and look only to this object — that he may serve and be useful to others in all that he does; having nothing before his eyes but the necessities and the advantage of his neighbour. Thus the Apostle commands us to work with our own hands, that we may have to give to those that need. He might have said, that we may support ourselves; but he tells us to give to those that need. It is the part of a Christian to take care of his own body for the very purpose that, by its soundness and well-being, he may be enabled to labour, and to acquire and preserve property, for the aid of those who are in want, that thus the stronger member may serve the weaker member, and we may be children of God, thoughtful and busy one for another, bearing one another's burdens, and so fulfilling the law of Christ.

Here is the truly Christian life, here is faith really working by love, when a man applies himself with joy and love to the works of that freest servitude in which he serves others voluntarily and for nought, himself abundantly satisfied in the fulness and riches of his own faith.

Thus, when Paul had taught the Philippians how they had been made rich by that faith in Christ in which they had obtained all things, he teaches them further in these words: "If there be therefore any consolation in Christ, if any comfort of love, if any fellowship of the Spirit, if any bowels and mercies, fulfil ye my joy, that ye be like-minded, having the same love, being of one accord, of one mind. Let nothing be done through strife or vainglory; but in lowliness of mind let each esteem other better than themselves. Look not every man on his own things, but every man also on the things of others" (Phil. ii. 1–4).

In this we see clearly that the Apostle lays down this rule for a Christian life: that all our works should be directed to the advantage of others, since every Christian has such abundance through his faith that all his other works and his whole life remain over and above wherewith to serve and benefit his neighbour of spontaneous goodwill.

To this end he brings forward Christ as an example, saying, "Let this mind be in you, which was also in Christ Jesus, who, being in the form of God, thought it not robbery to be equal with God, but made Himself of no reputation, and took upon Him the form of a servant, and was made in the likeness of men; and being found in fashion as a man, He humbled Himself, and became obedient unto death" (Phil. ii. 5–8). This most wholesome saying of the Apostle has been darkened to us by men who, totally misunderstanding the expressions "form of God," "form of a servant," "fashion," "likeness of men," have transferred them to the natures of Godhead and manhood. Paul's meaning is this: Christ, when He was full of the form of God and abounded in all good things, so that He had no need of works or sufferings to be just and saved — for all these things He had from the very beginning — yet was not puffed up with these things, and did not raise Himself above us and arrogate to Himself power over us, though He might lawfully have done so, but, on the contrary, so acted in labouring, working, suffering, and dying, as to be like the rest of men, and no otherwise than a man in fashion and in conduct, as if He were in want of all things and had nothing of the form of God; and yet all this He did for our sakes, that He might serve us, and that all the works He should do under that form of a servant might become ours.

Thus a Christian, like Christ his Head, being full and in abundance through his faith, ought to be content with this form of God, obtained by faith; except that, as I have said, he ought to increase this faith till it be perfected. For this faith is his life, justification, and salvation, preserving his person itself and making it pleasing to God, and bestowing on him all that Christ has, as I have said above, and as Paul affirms: "The life which I now live in the flesh I live by the faith of the Son of God" (Gal. ii. 20). Though he is thus free from all works, yet he ought to empty himself of this liberty, take on him the form of a servant, be made in the likeness of men, be found in fashion as a man, serve, help, and in every way act towards his neighbour as he sees that God through Christ has acted and is acting towards him. All this he should do freely, and with regard to nothing but the good pleasure of God, and he should reason thus: —

Lo! my God, without merit on my part, of His pure and free mercy, has given to me, an unworthy, condemned, and contemptible creature all the riches of justification and salvation in Christ, so that I no longer am in want of anything, except of faith to believe that this is so. For such a Father, then, who has overwhelmed me with these inestimable riches of His, why should I not freely, cheerfully, and with my whole heart, and from voluntary zeal, do all that I know will be pleasing to Him and acceptable in His sight? I will therefore give myself as a sort of Christ, to my neighbour, as Christ has given Himself to me; and will do nothing in this life except what I see will be needful, advantageous, and wholesome for my neighbour, since by faith I abound in all good things in Christ.

Thus from faith flow forth love and joy in the Lord, and from love a cheerful, willing, free spirit, disposed to serve our neighbour voluntarily, without taking any account of gratitude or ingratitude, praise or blame, gain or loss. Its object is not to lay men under obligations, nor does it distinguish between friends and enemies, or look to gratitude or ingratitude, but most freely and willingly spends itself and its goods, whether it loses them through ingratitude, or gains goodwill. For thus did its Father, distributing all things to all men abundantly and freely, making His sun to rise upon the just and the unjust. Thus, too, the child does and endures nothing except from the free joy with which it delights through Christ in God, the Giver of such great gifts.

You see, then, that, if we recognize those great and precious gifts, as Peter says, which have been given to us, love is quickly diffused in our hearts through the Spirit, and by love we are made free, joyful, all-powerful, active workers, victors over all our tribulations, servants to our neighbour, and nevertheless lords of all things. But, for those who do not recognise the good things given to them through Christ, Christ has been born in vain; such persons walk by works, and will never attain the taste and feeling of these great things. Therefore just as our neighbour is in want, and has need of our abundance, so we too in the sight of God were in want, and had need of His mercy. And as our heavenly Father has freely helped us in Christ, so ought we freely to help our neighbour by our body and works, and each should become to other a sort of Christ, so that we may be mutually Christs, and that the same Christ may be in all of us; that is, that we may be truly Christians.

Who then can comprehend the riches and glory of the Christian life? It can do all things, has all things, and is in want of nothing; is lord over sin, death, and hell, and at the same time is the obedient and useful servant of all. But alas! it is at this day unknown throughout the world; it is neither preached nor sought after, so that we are quite ignorant about our own name, why we are and are called Christians. We are certainly called so from Christ, who is not absent, but dwells among us — provided, that is, that we believe in Him and are reciprocally and mutually one the Christ of the other, doing to our neighbour as Christ does to us. But now, in the doctrine of men, we are taught only to seek after merits, rewards, and things which are already ours, and we have made of Christ a taskmaster far more severe than Moses.

The Blessed Virgin beyond all others, affords us an example of the same faith, in that she was purified according to the law of Moses, and like all other women, though she was bound by no such law and had no need of purification. Still she submitted to the law voluntarily and of free love, making herself like the rest of women, that she might not offend or throw contempt on them. She was not justified by doing this; but, being already justified, she did it freely and gratuitously. Thus ought our works too to be done, and not in order to be justified by them; for, being first justified by faith, we ought to do all our works freely and cheerfully for the sake of others.

St. Paul circumcised his disciple Timothy, not because he needed circumcision for his justification, but that he might not offend or contemn those Jews, weak in the faith, who had not yet been able to comprehend the liberty of faith. On the other hand, when they contemned liberty and urged that circumcision was necessary for justification, he resisted them, and would not allow Titus to be circumcised. For, as he would not offend or contemn any one's weakness in faith, but yielded for the time to their will, so, again, he would not have the liberty of faith offended or contemned by hardened self-justifiers, but walked in a middle path, sparing the weak for the time, and always resisting the hardened, that he might convert all to the liberty of faith. On the same principle we ought to act, receiving those that are weak in the faith, but boldly resisting these hardened teachers of works, of whom we shall hereafter speak at more length.

Christ also, when His disciples were asked for the tribute money, asked of Peter whether the children of a king were not free from taxes. Peter agreed to this; yet Jesus commanded him to go to the sea, saying, "Lest we should offend them, go thou to the sea, and cast a hook, and take up the fish that first cometh up; and when thou hast opened his mouth thou shalt find a piece of money; that take, and give unto them for Me and thee" (Matt. xvii. 27).

This example is very much to our purpose; for here Christ calls Himself and His disciples free men and children of a King, in want of nothing; and yet He voluntarily submits and pays the tax. Just as far, then, as this work was necessary or useful to Christ for justification or salvation, so far do all His other works or those of His disciples avail for justification. They are really free and subsequent to justification, and only done to serve others and set them an example.

Such are the works which Paul inculcated, that Christians should be subject to principalities and powers and ready to every good work (Titus iii. 1), not that they may be justified by these things — for they are already justified by faith — but that in liberty of spirit they may thus be the servants of others and subject to powers, obeying their will out of gratuitous love.

Such, too, ought to have been the works of all colleges, monasteries, and priests; every one doing the works of his own profession and state of life, not in order to be justified by them, but in order to bring his own body into subjection, as an example to others, who themselves also need to keep under their bodies, and also in order to accommodate himself to the will of others, out of free love. But we must always guard most carefully against any vain confidence or presumption of being justified, gaining merit, or being saved by these works, this being the part of faith alone, as I have so often said.

Any man possessing this knowledge may easily keep clear of danger among those innumerable commands and precepts of the Pope, of bishops, of monasteries, of churches, of princes, and of magistrates, which some foolish pastors urge on us as being necessary for justification and salvation, calling them precepts of the Church, when they are not so at all. For the Christian freeman will speak thus: I will fast, I will pray, I will do this or that which is commanded me by men, not as having any need of these things for justification or salvation, but that I may thus comply with the will of the Pope, of the bishop, of such a community or such a magistrate, or of my neighbour as an example to him; for this cause I will do and suffer all things, just as Christ did and suffered much more for me, though He needed not at all to do so on His own account, and made Himself for my sake under the law, when He was not under the law. And although tyrants may do me violence or wrong in requiring obedience to these things, yet it will not hurt me to do them, so long as they are not done against God.

From all this every man will be able to attain a sure judgment and faithful discrimination between all works and laws, and to know who are blind and foolish pastors, and who are true and good ones. For whatsoever work is not directed to the sole end either of keeping under the body, or of doing service to our neighbour — provided he require nothing contrary to the will of God — is no good or Christian work. Hence I greatly fear that at this day few or no colleges, monasteries, altars, or ecclesiastical functions are Christian ones; and the same may be said of fasts and special prayers to certain saints. I fear that in all these nothing is being sought but what is already ours; while we fancy that by these things our sins are purged away and salvation is attained, and thus utterly do away with Christian liberty. This comes from ignorance of Christian faith and liberty.

This ignorance and this crushing of liberty are diligently promoted by the teaching of very many blind pastors, who stir up and urge the people to a zeal for these things, praising them and puffing them up with their indulgences, but never teaching faith. Now I would advise you, if you have any wish to pray, to fast, or to make foundations in churches, as they call it, to take care not to do so with the object of gaining any advantage, either temporal or eternal. You will thus wrong your faith, which alone bestows all things on you, and the increase of which, either by working or by suffering, is alone to be cared for. What you give, give freely and without price, that others may prosper and have increase from you and your goodness. Thus you will be a truly good man and a Christian. For what to you are your goods and your works, which are done over and above for the subjection of the body, since you have abundance for yourself through your faith, in which God has given you all things?

We give this rule: the good things which we have from God ought to flow from one to another and become common to all, so that every one of us may, as it were, put on his neighbour, and so behave towards him as if he were himself in his place. They flowed and do flow from Christ to us; He put us on, and acted for us as if He Himself were what we are. From us they flow to those who have need of them; so that my faith and righteousness ought to be laid down before God as a covering and intercession for the sins of my neighbour, which I am to take on myself, and so labour and endure servitude in them, as if they were my own; for thus has Christ done for us. This is true love and the genuine truth of Christian life. But only there is it true and genuine where there is true and genuine faith. Hence the Apostle attributes to charity this quality: that she seeketh not her own.

We conclude therefore that a Christian man does not live in himself, but in Christ and in his neighbour, or else is no Christian: in Christ by faith; in his neighbour by love. By faith he is carried upwards above himself to God, and by love he sinks back below himself to his neighbour, still always abiding in God and His love, as Christ says, "Verily I say unto you, Hereafter ye shall see heaven open, and the angels of God ascending and descending upon the Son of man" (John i. 51).

Thus much concerning liberty, which, as you see, is a true and spiritual liberty, making our hearts free from all sins, laws, and commandments, as Paul says, "The law is not made for a righteous man" (1 Tim. i. 9), and one which surpasses all other external liberties, as far as heaven is above earth. May Christ make us to understand and preserve this liberty. Amen.

Finally, for the sake of those to whom nothing can be stated so well but that they misunderstand and distort it, we must add a word, in case they can understand even that. There are very many persons who, when they hear of this liberty of faith, straightway turn it into an occasion of licence. They think that everything is now lawful for them, and do not choose to show themselves free men and Christians in any other way than by their contempt and reprehension of ceremonies, of traditions, of human laws; as if they were Christians merely because they refuse to fast on stated days, or eat flesh when others fast, or omit the customary prayers; scoffing at the precepts of men, but utterly passing over all the rest that belongs to the Christian religion. On the other hand, they are most pertinaciously resisted by those who strive after salvation solely by their observance of and reverence for ceremonies, as if they would be saved merely because they fast on stated days, or abstain from flesh, or make formal prayers; talking loudly of the precepts of the Church and of the Fathers, and not caring a straw about those things which belong to our genuine faith. Both these parties are plainly culpable, in that, while they neglect matters which are of weight and necessary for salvation, they contend noisily about such as are without weight and not necessary.

How much more rightly does the Apostle Paul teach us to walk in the middle path, condemning either extreme and saying, "Let not him that eateth despise him that eateth not; and let not him which eateth not judge him that eateth" (Rom. xiv. 3)! You see here how the Apostle blames those who, not from religious feeling, but in mere contempt, neglect and rail at ceremonial observances, and teaches them not to despise, since this "knowledge puffeth up." Again, he teaches the pertinacious upholders of these things not to judge their opponents. For neither party observes towards the other that charity which edifieth. In this matter we must listen to Scripture, which teaches us to turn aside neither to the right hand nor to the left, but to follow those right precepts of the Lord which rejoice the heart. For just as a man is not righteous merely because he serves and is devoted to works and ceremonial rites, so neither will he be accounted righteous merely because he neglects and despises them.

It is not from works that we are set free by the faith of Christ, but from the belief in works, that is from foolishly presuming to seek justification through works. Faith redeems our consciences, makes them upright, and preserves them, since by it we recognise the truth that justification does not depend on our works, although good works neither can nor ought to be absent, just as we cannot exist without food and drink and all the functions of this mortal body. Still it is not on them that our justification is based, but on faith; and yet they ought not on that account to be despised or neglected. Thus in this world we are compelled by the needs of this bodily life; but we are not hereby justified. "My kingdom is not hence, nor of this world," says Christ; but He does not say, "My kingdom is not here, nor in this world." Paul, too, says, "Though we walk in the flesh, we do not war after the flesh" (2 Cor. x. 3), and "The life which I now live in the flesh I live by the faith of the Son of God" (Gal. ii. 20). Thus our doings, life, and being, in works and ceremonies, are done from the necessities of this life, and with the motive of governing our bodies; but yet we are not justified by these things, but by the faith of the Son of God.

The Christian must therefore walk in the middle path, and set these two classes of men before his eyes. He may meet with hardened and obstinate ceremonialists, who, like deaf adders, refuse to listen to the truth of liberty, and cry up, enjoin, and urge on us their ceremonies, as if they could justify us without faith. Such were the Jews of old, who would not understand, that they might act well. These men we must resist, do just the contrary to what they do, and be bold to give them offence, lest by this impious notion of theirs they should deceive many along with themselves. Before the eyes of these men it is expedient to eat flesh, to break fasts, and to do on behalf of the liberty of faith things which they hold to be the greatest sins. We must say of them, "Let them alone; they be blind leaders of the blind" (Matt. xv. 14). In this way Paul also would not have Titus circumcised, though these men urged it; and Christ defended the Apostles, who had plucked ears of corn on the Sabbath day; and many like instances.

Or else we may meet with simple-minded and ignorant persons, weak in the faith, as the Apostle calls them, who are as yet unable to apprehend that liberty of faith, even if willing to do so. These we must spare, lest they should be offended. We must bear with their infirmity, till they shall be more fully instructed. For since these men do not act thus from hardened malice, but only from weakness of faith, therefore, in order to avoid giving them offence, we must keep fasts and do other things which they consider necessary. This is required of us by charity, which injures no one, but serves all men. It is not the fault of these persons that they are weak, but that of their pastors, who by the snares and weapons of their own traditions have brought them into bondage and wounded their souls when they ought to have been set free and healed by the teaching of faith and liberty. Thus the Apostle says, "If meat make my brother to offend, I will eat no flesh while the world standeth" (1 Cor. viii. 13); and again, "I know, and am persuaded by the Lord Jesus, that there is nothing unclean of itself; but to him that esteemeth anything to be unclean, to him it is unclean. It is evil for that man who eateth with offence" (Rom. xiv. 14, 20).

Thus, though we ought boldly to resist those teachers of tradition, and though the laws of the pontiffs, by which they make aggressions on the people of God, deserve sharp reproof, yet we must spare the timid crowd, who are held captive by the laws of those impious tyrants, till they are set free. Fight vigorously against the wolves, but on behalf of the sheep, not against the sheep. And this you may do by inveighing against the laws and lawgivers, and yet at the same time observing these laws with the weak, lest they be offended, until they shall themselves recognise the tyranny, and understand their own liberty. If you wish to use your liberty, do it secretly, as Paul says, "Hast thou faith? have it to thyself before God" (Rom. xiv. 22). But take care not to use it in the presence of the weak. On the other hand, in the presence of tyrants and obstinate opposers, use your liberty in their despite, and with the utmost pertinacity, that they too may understand that they are tyrants, and their laws useless for justification, nay that they had no right to establish such laws.

Since then we cannot live in this world without ceremonies and works, since the hot and inexperienced period of youth has need of being restrained and protected by such bonds, and since every one is bound to keep under his own body by attention to these things, therefore the minister of Christ must be prudent and faithful in so ruling and teaching the people of Christ, in all these matters, that no root of bitterness may spring up among them, and so many be defiled, as Paul warned the Hebrews; that is, that they may not lose the faith, and begin to be defiled by a belief in works as the means of justification. This is a thing which easily happens, and defiles very many, unless faith be constantly inculcated along with works. It is impossible to avoid this evil, when faith is passed over in silence, and only the ordinances of men are taught, as has been done hitherto by the pestilent, impious, and soul-destroying traditions of our pontiffs and opinions of our theologians. An infinite number of souls have been drawn down to hell by these snares, so that you may recognise the work of antichrist.

In brief, as poverty is imperilled amid riches, honesty amid business, humility amid honours, abstinence amid feasting, purity amid pleasures, so is justification by faith imperilled among ceremonies. Solomon says, "Can a man take fire in his bosom, and his clothes not be burned?" (Prov. vi. 27). And yet as we must live among riches, business, honours, pleasures, feastings, so must we among ceremonies, that is among perils. Just as infant boys have the greatest need of being cherished in the bosoms and by the care of girls, that they may not die, and yet, when they are grown, there is peril to their salvation in living among girls, so inexperienced and fervid young men require to be kept in and restrained by the barriers of ceremonies, even were they of iron, lest their weak minds should rush headlong into vice. And yet it would be death to them to persevere in believing that they can be justified by these things. They must rather be taught that they have been thus imprisoned, not with the purpose of their being justified or gaining merit in this way, but in order that they might avoid wrong-doing, and be more easily instructed in that righteousness which is by faith, a thing which the headlong character of youth would not bear unless it were put under restraint.

Hence in the Christian life ceremonies are to be no otherwise looked upon than as builders and workmen look upon those preparations for building or working which are not made with any view of being permanent or anything in themselves, but only because without them there could be no building and no work. When the structure is completed, they are laid aside. Here you see that we do not contemn these preparations, but set the highest value on them; a belief in them we do contemn, because no one thinks that they constitute a real and permanent structure. If any one were so manifestly out of his senses as to have no other object in life but that of setting up these preparations with all possible expense, diligence, and perseverance, while he never thought of the structure itself, but pleased himself and made his boast of these useless preparations and props, should we not all pity his madness and think that, at the cost thus thrown away, some great building might have been raised?

Thus, too, we do not contemn works and ceremonies — nay, we set the highest value on them; but we contemn the belief in works, which no one should consider to constitute true righteousness, as do those hypocrites who employ and throw away their whole life in the pursuit of works, and yet never attain to that for the sake of which the works are done. As the Apostle says, they are "ever learning and never able to come to the knowledge of the truth" (2 Tim. iii. 7). They appear to wish to build, they make preparations, and yet they never do build; and thus they continue in a show of godliness, but never attain to its power.

Meanwhile they please themselves with this zealous pursuit, and even dare to judge all others, whom they do not see adorned with such a glittering display of works; while, if they had been imbued with faith, they might have done great things for their own and others' salvation, at the same cost which they now waste in abuse of the gifts of God. But since human nature and natural reason, as they call it, are naturally superstitious, and quick to believe that justification can be attained by any laws or works proposed to them, and since nature is also exercised and confirmed in the same view by the practice of all earthly lawgivers, she can never of her own power free herself from this bondage to works, and come to a recognition of the liberty of faith.

We have therefore need to pray that God will lead us and make us taught of God, that is, ready to learn from God; and will Himself, as He has promised, write His law in our hearts; otherwise there is no hope for us. For unless He himself teach us inwardly this wisdom hidden in a mystery, nature cannot but condemn it and judge it to be heretical. She takes offence at it, and it seems folly to her, just as we see that it happened of old in the case of the prophets and Apostles, and just as blind and impious pontiffs, with their flatterers, do now in my case and that of those who are like me, upon whom, together with ourselves, may God at length have mercy, and lift up the light of His countenance upon them, that we may know His way upon earth and His saving health among all nations, who is blessed for evermore. Amen. In the year of the Lord MDXX.

Dear Christians, One and All, Rejoice

Martin Luther

Translated by Richard Massie

1. Dear christians, one and all, rejoice,
   With exultation springing,
   And, with united heart and voice,
   And holy rapture singing,
   Proclaim the wonders God hath done,
   How His right arm the victory won;
   Right dearly it hath cost him.

2. Fast bound in Satan's chains I lay.
   Death brooded darkly o'er me.
   Sin was my torment night and day.
   In sin my mother bore me.
   Yea, deep and deeper still I fell.
   Life had become a living hell,
   So firmly sin possessed me.

3. My own good works availed me naught,
   No merit they attaining.
   Free will against God's judgment fought,
   Dead to all good remaining.
   My fears increased till sheer despair
   Left naught but death to be my share.
   The pains of hell I suffered.

4. But God beheld my wretched state
   Before the world's foundation.
   And, mindful of His mercies great,
   He planned my soul's salvation.
   A father's heart He turned to me,
   Sought my redemption fervently.
   He gave His dearest Treasure.

5. He spoke to His beloved Son:
   'Tis time to have compassion.
   Then go, bright Jewel of My crown,
   And bring to man salvation;
   From sin and sorrow set him free.
   Slay bitter death for him that he
   May live with Thee forever.

From *Dear Christians, One and All, Rejoice* (1523) by Project Wittenberg, Richard Massie, Translator.

6. This Son obeyed His Father's will,
   Was born of virgin mother.
   And God's good pleasure to fulfil,
   He came to be my Brother.
   No garb of pomp or power He wore,
   A servant's form, like mine, He bore,
   To lead the devil captive.

7. To me He spake: Hold fast to Me,
   I am thy Rock and Castle;
   Thy ransom I Myself will be,
   For thee I strive and wrestle;
   For I am with thee, I am thine,
   And evermore thou shalt be mine.
   The foe shall not divide us.

8. The foe shall shed my precious blood,
   Me of My life bereaving.
   All this I suffer for thy good
   Be steadfast and believing.
   Life shall from death the victory win.
   My innocence shall bear thy sin;
   So art thou blest forever.

9. Now to My Father I depart,
   The Holy Spirit sending
   And heavenly wisdom to impart
   My help to thee extending.
   He shall in trouble comfort thee,
   Teach thee to know and follow Me,
   And in all truth shall guide thee.

10. What I have done and taught, teach thou,
    My ways forsake thou never.
    So shall My kingdom flourish now
    And God be praised forever.
    Take heed lest men with base alloy
    The heavenly treasure should destroy.
    This counsel I bequeath thee.

Of Cannibals

Michel de Montaigne

When King Pyrrhus invaded Italy, having viewed and considered the order of the army the Romans sent out to meet him; "I know not," said he, "what kind of barbarians" (for so the Greeks called all other nations) "these may be; but the disposition of this army that I see has nothing of barbarism in it." As much said the Greeks of that which Flaminius brought into their country; and Philip, beholding from an eminence the order and distribution of the Roman camp formed in his kingdom by Publius Sulpicius Galba, spake to the same effect. By which it appears how cautious men ought to be of taking things upon trust from vulgar opinion, and that we are to judge by the eye of reason, and not from common report.

I long had a man in my house that lived ten or twelve years in the New World, discovered in these latter days, and in that part of it where Villegaignon landed, which he called Antarctic France. This discovery of so vast a country seems to be of very great consideration. I cannot be sure, that hereafter there may not be another, so many wiser men than we having been deceived in this. I am afraid our eyes are bigger than our bellies, and that we have more curiosity than capacity; for we grasp at all, but catch nothing but wind.

Plato brings in Solon, telling a story that he had heard from the priests of Sais in Egypt, that of old, and before the Deluge, there was a great island called Atlantis, situated directly at the mouth of the straits of Gibraltar, which contained more countries than both Africa and Asia put together; and that the kings of that country, who not only possessed that Isle, but extended their dominion so far into the continent that they had a country of Africa as far as Egypt, and extending in Europe to Tuscany, attempted to encroach even upon Asia, and to subjugate all the nations that border upon the Mediterranean Sea, as far as the Black Sea; and to that effect overran all Spain, the Gauls, and Italy, so far as to penetrate into Greece, where the Athenians stopped them: but that some time after, both the Athenians, and they and their island, were swallowed by the Flood.

It is very likely that this extreme irruption and inundation of water made wonderful changes and alterations in the habitations of the earth, as 'tis said that the sea then divided Sicily from Italy:—

> *"Hæc loca, vi quondam et vastâ convulsa ruina,*
> *Dissiluisse ferunt, quum protenus utraque tellus*
> *Una foret"*

— Cyprus from Syria, the isle of Negropont from the continent of Boeotia, and elsewhere united lands that were separate before, by filling up the channel betwixt them with sand and mud:—

> *"Sterilisque diu palus, aptaque remis,*
> *Vicinas urbes alit, et grave sentit aratrum."*

But there is no great appearance that this isle was this New World so lately discovered: for that almost touched upon Spain, and it were an incredible effect of an inundation, to have tumbled back so prodigious a mass, above twelve hundred leagues: besides that our modern navigators have already almost discovered it to be no island, but *terra firma*, and continent with the East Indies on the one side, and with the lands under the two poles on

From *Essays of Montaigne*, 1902, Translated by Charles Cotton.

the other side; or, if it be separate from them, it is by so narrow a strait and channel, that it none the more deserves the name of an island for that.

It should seem, that in this great body, there are two sorts of motions, the one natural and the other febrific, as there are in ours. When I consider the impression that our river of Dordogne has made in my time on the right bank of its descent, and that in twenty years it has gained so much, and undermined the foundations of so many houses, I perceive it to be an extraordinary agitation: for had it always followed this course, or were hereafter to do it, the aspect of the world would be totally changed. But rivers alter their course, sometimes beating against the one side, and sometimes the other, and sometimes quietly keeping the channel. I do not speak of sudden inundations, the causes of which everybody understands. In Medoc, by the seashore, the Sieur d'Arsac, my brother, sees an estate he had there, buried under the sands which the sea vomits before it: where the tops of some houses are yet to be seen, and where his rents and domains are converted into pitiful barren pasturage. The inhabitants of this place affirm, that of late years the sea has driven so vehemently upon them, that they have lost above four leagues of land. These sands are her harbingers: and we now see great heaps of moving sand, that march half a league before her, and occupy the land.

The other testimony from antiquity, to which some would apply this discovery of the New World, is in Aristotle; at least, if that little book of Unheard-of Miracles be his. He there tells us, that certain Carthaginians, having crossed the Atlantic Sea without the Straits of Gibraltar, and sailed a very long time, discovered at last a great and fruitful island, all covered over with wood, and watered with several broad and deep rivers, far remote from all *terra firma*; and that they, and others after them, allured by the goodness and fertility of the soil, went thither with their wives and children, and began to plant a colony. But the senate of Carthage perceiving their people by little and little to diminish, issued out an express prohibition, that none, upon pain of death, should transport themselves thither; and also drove out these new inhabitants; fearing, 'tis said, lest in process of time they should so multiply as to supplant themselves and ruin their state. But this relation of Aristotle no more agrees with our new-found lands than the other.

This man that I had was a plain ignorant fellow, and therefore the more likely to tell truth: for your better-bred sort of men are much more curious in their observation, 'tis true, and discover a great deal more; but then they gloss upon it, and to give the greater weight to what they deliver, and allure your belief, they cannot forbear a little to alter the story; they never represent things to you simply as they are, but rather as they appeared to them, or as they would have them appear to you, and to gain the reputation of men of judgment, and the better to induce your faith, are willing to help out the business with something more than is really true, of their own invention. Now in this case, we should either have a man of irreproachable veracity, or so simple that he has not wherewithal to contrive, and to give a colour of truth to false relations, and who can have no ends in forging an untruth. Such a one was mine; and besides, he has at divers times brought to me several seamen and merchants who at the same time went the same voyage. I shall therefore content myself with his information, without inquiring what the cosmographers say to the business. We should have topographers to trace out to us the particular places where they have been; but for having had this advantage over us, to have seen the Holy Land, they would have the privilege, forsooth, to tell us stories of all the other parts of the world beside. I would have every one write what he knows, and as much as he knows, but no more; and that not in this only but in all other subjects; for such a person may have some particular knowledge and experience of the nature of such a river, or such a fountain, who, as to other things, knows no more than what everybody does, and yet to give a currency to his little pittance of learning, will undertake to write the whole body of physics: a vice from which great inconveniences derive their original.

Now, to return to my subject, I find that there is nothing barbarous and savage in this nation, by anything that I can gather, excepting, that every one gives the title of barbarism to everything that is not in use in his own country. As, indeed, we have no other level of truth and reason than the example and idea of the opinions and customs of the place wherein we live: there is always the perfect religion, there the perfect government, there the most exact and accomplished usage of all things. They are savages at the same rate that we say fruits are wild, which nature produces of herself and by her own ordinary progress; whereas, in truth, we ought rather to call those wild whose natures we have changed by our artifice and diverted from the common order. In those, the genuine, most useful, and natural virtues and properties are vigorous and sprightly, which we have helped to degenerate in these, by accommodating them to the pleasure of our own corrupted palate. And yet for all this, our taste confesses a flavour and delicacy excellent even to emulation of the beat of ours, in several fruits wherein those countries abound without art or culture. Neither is it reasonable that art should gain the pre-eminence of our great and powerful mother nature. We have so surcharged her with the additional ornaments and graces we have added to the beauty and riches of her own works by our inventions, that we have almost smothered her; yet in other places, where she shines in her own purity and proper lustre, she marvellously baffles and disgraces all our vain and frivolous attempts:—

> *"Et veniunt hederæ sponte suà melius;*
> *Surgit et in solis formosior arbutus antris;*
> *Et volucres nullâ dulcius arte canunt."*

Our utmost endeavours cannot arrive at so much as to imitate the nest of the least of birds, its contexture, beauty, and convenience: not so much as the web of a poor spider.

All things, says Plato, are produced either by nature, by fortune, or by art; the greatest and most beautiful by the one or the other of the former, the least and the most imperfect by the last.

These nations then seem to me to be so far barbarous, as having received but very little form and fashion from art and human invention, and consequently to be not much remote from their original simplicity. The laws of nature, however, govern them still, not as yet much vitiated with any mixture of ours: but 'tis in such purity, that I am sometimes troubled we were not sooner acquainted with these people, and that they were not discovered in those better times, when there were men much more able to judge of them than we are. I am sorry that Lycurgus and Plato had no knowledge of them; for to my apprehension, what we now see in those nations, does not only surpass all the pictures with which the poets have adorned the golden age, and all their inventions in feigning a happy state of man, but, moreover, the fancy and even the wish and desire of philosophy itself; so native and so pure a simplicity, as we by experience see to be in them, could never enter into their imagination, nor could they ever believe that human society could have been maintained with so little artifice and human patchwork. I should tell Plato that it is a nation wherein there is no manner of traffic, no knowledge of letters, no science of numbers, no name of magistrate or political superiority; no use of service, riches or poverty, no contracts, no successions, no dividends, no properties, no employments, but those of leisure, no respect of kindred, but common, no clothing, no agriculture, no metal, no use of corn or wine; the very words that signify lying, treachery, dissimulation, avarice, envy, detraction, pardon, never heard of. How much would he find his imaginary Republic short of his perfection?—

"Viri a diis recentes."

"Hos natura modos primum dedit."

As to the rest, they live in a country very pleasant and temperate, so that, as my witnesses inform me, 'tis rare to hear of a sick person, and they moreover assure me, that they never saw any of the natives, either paralytic, bleareyed, toothless, or crooked with age. The situation of their country is along the sea-shore, enclosed on the other side towards the land, with great and high mountains, having about a hundred leagues in breadth between. They have great store of fish and flesh, that have no resemblance to those of ours; which they eat without any other cookery, than plain boiling, roasting, and broiling. The first that rode a horse thither, though in several other voyages he had contracted an acquaintance and familiarity with them, put them into so terrible a fright, with his centaur appearance, that they killed him with their arrows before they could come to discover who he was. Their buildings are very long, and of capacity to hold two or three hundred people, made of the barks of tall trees, reared with one end upon the ground, and leaning to and supporting one another at the top, like some of our barns, of which the covering hangs down to the very ground, and serves for the side walls. They have wood so hard, that they cut with it, and make their swords of it, and their grills of it to broil their meat. Their beds are of cotton, hung swinging from the roof, like our seamen's hammocks, every man his own, for the wives lie apart from their husbands. They rise with the sun, and so soon as they are up, eat for all day, for they have no more meals but that; they do not then drink, as Suidas reports of some other people of the East that never drank at their meals; but drink very often all day after, and sometimes to a rousing pitch. Their drink is made of a certain root, and is of the colour of our claret, and they never drink it but lukewarm. It will not keep above two or three days; it has a somewhat sharp, brisk taste, is nothing heady, but very comfortable to the stomach; laxative to strangers, but a very pleasant beverage to such as are accustomed to it. They make use, instead of bread, of a certain white compound, like coriander seeds; I have tasted of it; the taste is sweet and a little flat. The whole day is spent in dancing. Their young men go a-hunting after wild beasts with bows and arrows; one part of their women are employed in preparing their drink the while, which is their chief employment. One of their old men, in the morning before they fall to eating, preaches to the whole family, walking from the one end of the house to the other, and several times repeating the same sentence, till he has finished the round, for their houses are at least a hundred yards long. Valour towards their enemies and love towards their wives, are the two heads of his discourse, never failing in the close, to put them in mind, that 'tis their wives who provide them their drink warm and well seasoned. The fashion of their beds, ropes, swords, and of the wooden bracelets they tie about their wrists, when they go to fight, and of the great canes, bored hollow at one end, by the sound of which they keep the cadence of their dances, are to be seen in several places, and amongst others, at my house. They shave all over, and much more neatly than we, without other razor than one of wood or stone. They believe in the immortality of the soul, and that those who have merited well of the gods are lodged in that part of heaven where the sun rises, and the accursed in the west.

They have I know not what kind of priests and prophets, who very rarely present themselves to the people, having their abode in the mountains. At their arrival, there is a great feast, and solemn assembly of many villages: each house, as I have described, makes a village, and they are about a French league distant from one another. This prophet declaims to them in public, exhorting them to virtue and their duty: but all their ethics are comprised in these two articles, resolution in war, and affection to their wives. He also prophesies to them events to come, and the issues they are to expect from their enterprises, and prompts them to or diverts them from war: but let him look to't; for if he fail in his divination, and anything happen otherwise than he has foretold, he is cut into a thousand pieces, if he be caught, and condemned for a false prophet: for that reason, if any of them has been mistaken, he is no more heard of.

Divination is a gift of God, and therefore to abuse it, ought to be a punishable imposture. Amongst the Scythians, where their diviners failed in the promised effect, they were laid, bound hand and foot, upon carts loaded with firs and bavins, and drawn by oxen, on which they were burned to death. Such as only meddle with things subject to the conduct of human capacity, are excusable in doing the best they can: but those other fellows that come to delude us with assurances of an extraordinary faculty, beyond our understanding, ought they not to be punished, when they do not make good the effect of their promise, and for the temerity of their imposture?

They have continual war with the nations that live further within the mainland, beyond their mountains, to which they go naked, and without other arms than their bows and wooden swords, fashioned at one end like the head of our javelins. The obstinacy of their battles is wonderful, and they never end without great effusion of blood: for as to running away, they know not what it is. Every one for a trophy brings home the head of an enemy he has killed, which he fixes over the door of his house. After having a long time treated their prisoners very well, and given them all the regales they can think of, he to whom the prisoner belongs, invites a great assembly of his friends. They being come, he ties a rope to one of the arms of the prisoner, of which, at a distance, out of his reach, he holds the one end himself, and gives to the friend he loves best the other arm to hold after the same manner; which being done, they two, in the presence of all the assembly, despatch him with their swords. After that, they roast him, eat him amongst them, and send some chops to their absent friends. They do not do this, as some think, for nourishment, as the Scythians anciently did, but as a representation of an extreme revenge; as will appear by this: that having observed the Portuguese, who were in league with their enemies, to inflict another sort of death upon any of, them they took prisoners, which was to set them up to the girdle in the earth, to shoot at the remaining part till it was stuck full of arrows, and then to hang them, they thought those people of the other world (as being men who had sown the knowledge of a great many vices amongst their neighbours, and who were much greater masters in all sorts of mischief than they) did not exercise this sort of revenge without a meaning, and that it must needs be more painful than theirs, they began to leave their old way, and to follow this. I am not sorry that we should here take notice of the barbarous horror of so cruel an action, but that, seeing so clearly into their faults, we should be so blind to our own. I conceive there is more barbarity in eating a man alive, than when he is dead; in tearing a body limb from limb by racks and torments, that is yet in perfect sense; in roasting it by degrees; in causing it to be bitten and worried by dogs and swine (as we have not only read, by lately seen, not amongst inveterate and mortal enemies, but among neighbours and fellow-citizens, and, which is worse, under colour of piety and religion), than to roast and eat him after he is dead.

Chrysippus and Zeno, the two heads of the Stoic sect, were of opinion that there was no hurt in making use of our dead carcasses, in what way soever for our necessity, and in feeding upon them too; as our own ancestors, who being besieged by Cæsar in the city Alexia, resolved to sustain the famine of the siege with the bodies of their old men, women, and other persons who were incapable of bearing arms:—

> *"Vascones, ut fama est, alimentis talibus usi*
> *Produxere animas."*

And the physicians make no bones of employing it to all sorts of use, either to apply it outwardly; or to give it inwardly for the health of the patient. But there never was any opinion so irregular, as to excuse treachery, disloyalty, tyranny, and cruelty, which are our familiar vices. We may then call these people barbarous, in respect to the rules of reason: but not in respect to ourselves, who in all sorts of barbarity exceed them. Their wars are throughout noble and generous, and carry as much excuse and fair pretence, as that human malady is capable of; having with them no other foundation than the sole jealousy of valour. Their disputes are not for the conquest of new lands, for these they already possess are so fruitful by nature, as to supply them without labour or concern, with all things necessary, in such abundance that they have no need to enlarge their borders. And they are, moreover, happy in this, that they only covet so much as their natural necessities require: all beyond that is superfluous to them: men of the same age call one another generally brothers, those who are younger, children; and the old men are fathers to all. These leave to their heirs in common the full possession of goods, without any manner of division, or other title than what nature bestows upon her creatures, in bringing them into the world. If their neighbours pass over the mountains to assault them, and obtain a victory, all the victors gain by it is glory only, and the advantage of having proved themselves the better in valour and virtue: for they never meddle with the goods of the conquered, but presently return into their own country, where they have no want of anything necessary, nor of this greatest of all goods, to know happily how to enjoy their condition and to be content. And those in turn do the same; they demand of their prisoners no other ransom, than acknowledgment that they are overcome: but there is not one found in an age, who will not rather choose to die than make such a confession, or either by word or look recede form the entire grandeur of an invincible courage. There is not a man amongst them who had not rather be killed and eaten, than so much as to open his mouth to entreat he may not. They use them with all liberality and freedom, to the end their lives may be so much the dearer to them; but frequently entertain them with menaces of their approaching death, of the torments they are to suffer, of the preparations making in order to it, of the mangling their limbs, and of the feast that is to be made, where their carcass is to be the only dish. All which they do, to no other end, but only to extort some gentle or submissive word from them, or to frighten them so as to make them run away, to obtain this advantage that they were terrified, and that their constancy was shaken; and indeed, if rightly taken, it is. in this point only that a true victory consists:—

> "Victoria nulla est,
> Quam quæ confessos animo quoque subjugate hostes."

The Hungarians, a very warlike people, never pretend further than to reduce the enemy to their discretion; for having forced this confession from them, they let them go without injury or ransom, excepting, at the most, to make them engage their word never to bear arms against them again. We have sufficient advantages over our enemies that are borrowed and not truly our own; it is the quality of a porter, and no effect of virtue, to have stronger arms and legs; it is a dead and corporeal quality to set in array; 'tis a turn of fortune to make our enemy stumble, or to dazzle him with the light of the sun; 'tis a trick of science and art, and that may happen in a mean base fellow, to be a good fencer. The estimate and value of a man consist in the heart and in the will: there his true honour lies. Valour is stability, not of legs and arms, but of the courage and the soul; it does not lie in the goodness of our horse or our arms: but in our own. He that falls obstinate in his courage:—

> "Si succiderit, de genu pugnat"

— he who, for any danger of imminent death, abates nothing of his assurance; who, dying, yet darts at his enemy a fierce and disdainful look, is overcome not by us, but by fortune; he is killed, not conquered; the most valiant are sometimes the most unfortunate. There are defeats more triumphant than victories. Never could those for sister victories, the fairest the sun ever beheld, of Salamis, Platæa, Mycale, and Sicily, venture to oppose all their united glories, to the single glory of the discomfiture of King Leonidas and his men, at the pass of Thermopylæ. Whoever ran with more glorious desire and greater ambition, to the winning, than Captain Iscolas to the certain loss of a battle? Who could have found out a more subtle invention to secure his safety, than he did to assure his destruction? He was set to defend a certain pass of Peloponnesus against the Arcadians, which, considering the nature of the place and the inequality of forces, finding it utterly impossible for him to do, and seeing that all who were presented to the enemy, must certainly be left upon the place; and on the other side, reputing it unworthy of his own virtue and magnanimity and of the Lacedæmonian name to fail in any part of his duty, he chose a mean betwixt these two extremes after this manner; the youngest and most active of his men, he preserved for the service and defence of their country, and sent them back; and with the rest, whose loss would be of less consideration, he resolved to make good the pass, and with the death of them, to make the enemy buy their entry as dear as possibly he could; as it fell out, for being presently environed on all sides by the Arcadians, after having made a great slaughter of the enemy, he and his were all cut in pieces. Is there any trophy dedicated to the conquerors which was not much more due to these who were overcome? The part that true conquering is to play, lies in the encounter, not in the coming off; and the honour of valour consists in fighting, not in subduing.

But to return to my story: these prisoners are so far from discovering the least weakness, for all the terrors that can be represented to them that, on the contrary, during the two or three months they are kept, they always appear with a cheerful countenance; importune their masters to make haste to bring them to the test, defy, rail at them, and reproach them with cowardice, and the number of battles they have lost against those of their country. I have a song made by one of these prisoners, wherein he bids them "come all, and dine upon him, and welcome, for they shall withal eat their own fathers and grandfathers, whose flesh has served to feed and nourish him. These muscles," says he, "this flesh and these veins, are your own: poor silly souls as you are, you little think that the substance of your ancestors' limbs is here yet; notice what you eat, and you will find in it the taste of your own flesh:" in which song there is to be observed an invention that nothing relishes of the barbarian. Those that paint these people dying after this manner, represent the prisoner spitting in the faces of his executioners and making wry mouths at them. And 'tis most certain, that to the very last gasp, they never cease to brave and defy them both in word and gesture. In plain truth, these men are very savage in comparison of us; of necessity, they must either be absolutely so or else we are savages; for there is a vast difference between their manners and ours.

The men there have several wives, and so much the greater number, by how much they have the greater reputation for valor. And it is one very remarkable feature in their marriages, that the same jealousy our wives have to hinder and divert us from the friendship and familiarity of other women, those employ to promote their husbands' desires, and to procure them many spouses; for being above all things solicitous of their husbands' honour, 'tis their chiefest care to seek out, and to bring in the most companions they can, forasmuch as it is a testimony of the husband's virtue. Most of our ladies will cry out, that 'tis monstrous; whereas in truth it is not so, but a truly matrimonial virtue, and of the highest form. In the Bible, Sarah, with Leah and Rachel, the two wives of Jacob, gave the most beautiful of their handmaids to their husbands; Livia preferred the passions of Augustus to her own interest; and the wife of King Deiotarus, Stratonice, did not only give up a fair young maid that served her to her husband's embraces, but moreover carefully brought up the children he had by her, and assisted them in the succession to their father's crown.

And that it may not be supposed, that all this is done by a simple and servile obligation to their common practice, or by any authoritative impression of their ancient custom, without judgment or reasoning, and from having a soul so stupid that it cannot contrive what else to do, I must here give you some touches of their sufficiency in point of understanding. Besides what I repeated to you before, which was one of their songs of war, I have another, a love-song, that begins thus: "Stay, adder, stay, that by thy pattern my sister may draw the fashion and work of a rich ribbon, that I may present to my beloved, by which means thy beauty and the excellent order of thy scales shall for ever be preferred before all other serpents." Wherein the first couplet, "Stay, adder," &c., makes the burden of the song. Now I have conversed enough with poetry to judge thus much: that not only there is nothing barbarous in this invention, but, moreover, that it is perfectly Anacreontic. To which may be added, that their language is soft, of a pleasing accent, and something bordering upon the Greek termination.

Three of these people, not foreseeing how dear their knowledge of the corruptions of this part of the world will one day cost their happiness and repose, and that the effect of this commerce will be their ruin, as I presuppose it is in a very fair way (miserable men to suffer themselves to be deluded with desire of novelty and to have left the serenity of their own heaven to come so far to gaze at ours!), were at Rouen at the time that the late King Charles IX. was there. The king himself talked to them a good while, and they were made to see our fashions, our pomp, and the form of a great city. After which, some one asked their opinion, and would know of them, what of all things they had seen, they found most to be admired? To which they made answer, three things, of which I have forgotten the third, and am troubled at it, but two I yet remember. They said, that in the first place they thought it very strange that so many tall men, wearing beards, strong, and well armed, who were about the king ('tis likely they meant the Swiss of the guard), should submit to obey a child, and that they did not rather choose out one amongst themselves to command. Secondly (they have a way of speaking in their language to call men the half to one another), that they had observed that there were amongst us men full and crammed with all manner of commodities, whilst, in the meantime, their halves were begging at their doors, lean and half-starved with hunger and poverty; and they thought it strange that these necessitous halves were able to suffer so great an inequality and injustice, and that they did not take the others by the throats, or set fire to their houses.

I talked to one of them a great while together, but I had so ill an interpreter, and one who was so perplexed by his own ignorance to apprehend my meaning, that I could get nothing out of him of any moment. Asking him what advantages he reaped from the superiority he had amongst his own people (for he was a captain, and our mariners called him king), he told me, to march at the head of them to war. Demanding of him further how many men he had to follow him, he showed me a space of ground, to signify as many as could march in such a compass, which might be four or five thousand men; and putting the question to him whether or no his authority expired with the war, he told me this remained: that when he went to visit the villages of his dependence, they planned him paths through the thick of their woods, by which he might pass at his ease. All this does not sound very ill, and the last was not at all amiss, for they wear no breeches.

The Social Contract

Jean-Jacques Rousseau

Translated by Lowell Bair

Taking men as they are and laws as they can be, I propose to inquire whether there can be any legitimate and reliable rule of administration in the civil order. In this inquiry I shall try always to combine *what right permits with what interest prescribes*, so that justice and utility will not be divided.

I shall go directly to my subject without first demonstrating its importance. I may be asked if I am a ruler or a lawmaker, since I am writing on politics. I answer that I am neither, and that that is why I am writing on politics. If I were a ruler or a lawmaker, I would not waste time saying what ought to be done; I would either do it or remain silent.

Having been born a citizen of a free state and a member of its sovereign, I feel that however slightly my vote may affect public affairs, the right to vote on them is enough to make it my duty to inquire into them. When I reflect on governments, I am always happy to discover that my studies have given me new reasons to love the government of my own country.

Man is born free, and is everywhere in chains. This or that man may regard himself as the master of others, but he is more of a slave than they. How did this change come about? I do not know. *What can make it legitimate?* I believe I can answer that question.

If I were to consider only force and the effects it produces, I would say, "As long as a people is compelled to obey and does so, it does well; as soon as it is able to throw off its yoke and does so, it does even better, for it has recovered its freedom by the same right as that by which it was taken away, so either it is justified in recovering it or there was no justification for taking it away." But the social order is a sacred right that serves as the basis of all others. Yet this right does not come from nature; it is therefore founded on agreements. The problem is to determine what those agreements are. First, however, I must substantiate what I have just stated.

The First Societies

The oldest of all societies, and the only natural one, is that of the family; yet even in it, children remain bound to their father only so long as they need him in order to survive. As soon as that need ceases, the natural bond is dissolved. The children are released from the duty of obeying the father, he is released from the duty of taking care of them, and they all become independent. If they continue to be united, it is no longer naturally, but voluntarily, and the family itself is maintained only by agreement.

This common freedom results from the nature of man. His first law is to look after his own preservation, his first concerns are those that he owes to himself. As soon as he reaches the age of reason, he is the sole judge of the proper means of preserving himself, and he thereby becomes his own master.

It can thus be said that the family is the first model of political societies: The father corresponds to the ruler, the children to the people; and all, having been born free and equal, give up their freedom only for their own advantage. The only difference is that in the family, the father's love for his children rewards him for the care he gives them, while in the state, the pleasure of commanding takes the place of love, which the ruler does not feel for his people.

Grotius denies that all human power is established in favor of those who are governed. He cites slavery as an example. His usual procedure is to establish right on the basis of fact. It is possible to use a more logical method of reasoning, but not one more favorable to tyrants.

It is an open question, according to Grotius, whether the human race belongs to a hundred men, or whether those hundred men belong to the human race. All through his book he seems to lean toward the first view, which is also Hobbes's. Thus the human race is divided into herds of cattle, each with a ruler who watches over it in order to devour it.

Since a herder is of a nature superior to that of his herd, the herders of men, their rulers, are of a nature superior to that of their peoples. Such was the reasoning of the Emperor Caligula, as reported by Philo. He concluded from this analogy that either kings were gods or peoples were animals.

Caligula's reasoning is equivalent to that of Hobbes and Grotius. Before any of them, Aristotle had also said that men were not naturally equal, but that some were born to be slaves and others to be masters.

Aristotle was right, but he mistook effect for cause. Nothing is more certain than that any man born in slavery is born to be a slave. Slaves lose everything in their chains, even the desire to be free of them; they love their servitude as Ulysses' companions loved their brutishness. If, then, there are slaves by nature, it is because there were once slaves against nature. Force made the first slaves, and their cowardice perpetuated slavery.

I have said nothing of King Adam or the Emperor Noah, father of three great monarchs who divided the world among themselves, like Saturn's children, with whom some have identified them. I hope my moderation will be appreciated, for I am a direct descendant of one of those monarchs, perhaps of the eldest branch, and who knows but what a verification of titles might establish me as the lawful king of the human race? Be that as it may, it cannot be denied that Adam was the sovereign of the world as Robinson Crusoe was of his island, as long as he was its only inhabitant; and the advantage of that empire was that the monarch was secure on his throne, with no rebellions, wars, or conspirators to fear.

The Right of the Strongest

The strongest man is never strong enough to maintain his mastery at all times unless he transforms his strength into right and obedience into a duty. Hence the right of the strongest, a right that is taken ironically in appearance and established as a principle in reality. But will anyone ever explain what the term means? I do not see what morality can be derived from physical force. Yielding to force is an act of necessity, not of will; at the very most, it is an act of prudence. In what sense could it be a duty?

Let us suppose for a moment that this alleged right exists. I say that nothing results from it but a mass of nonsense. For if might makes right, the effect changes with the cause: Any might greater than the first will take over its right. As soon as one can disobey with impunity, one can disobey legitimately, and since the strongest is always in the right, one has only to act in such a way as to be the strongest. But what kind of right is it that ceases to exist when strength perishes? If a man is forced to obey, he no longer has any obligation to do so. It is clear that the word "right" adds nothing to force; in that connection, it means nothing at all.

"Obey the powers that be." If that means "Yield to force," it is a good precept, but superfluous, and I can guarantee that it will never be violated. All power comes from God.

I acknowledge that; but all disease comes from him also. Does this mean that it is forbidden to call the doctor? If a bandit waylays me in the forest, I am forced to give him my money, but if it were possible for me to keep it, would I have a moral obligation to give it to him any way? After all, the pistol he points at me is also a form of force.

Let us agree, then, that might does not make right, and that we are obligated to obey only legitimate powers. Thus my original question returns.

Slavery

Since no man has natural authority over any other, and since force creates no right, we can only conclude that agreements are the basis of all legitimate authority among men.

If, asks Grotius, an individual can alienate his freedom and make himself the slave of a master, why cannot an entire people alienate its freedom and make itself subject to a king? There are many ambiguous words here that need explanation, but let us confine ourselves to "alienate." In this context, it can mean only "give" or "sell." Now a man who makes himself another's slave does not give himself; he sells himself, at least for his subsistence. But for what does a people sell itself? Far from giving his subjects their subsistence, a king draws his own only from them, and as Rabelais says, a king does not live on little. Do his subjects give themselves to him on condition that he will also take their property? If so, I do not see what they have left to preserve.

It will be said that a despot guarantees his subjects civil peace. Granted, but what do they gain if the wars in which his ambition involves them, his insatiable greed, and the harassments inflicted on them by his ministers distress them more than their dissensions would do? What do they gain if that civil peace is one of their miseries? Life in a dungeon is also peaceful; is that enough to make it desirable? The Greeks imprisoned in the Cyclops' cave lived peacefully, while waiting their turn to be devoured.

To say that a man gives himself for nothing is to say something absurd and incomprehensible. Such an act is illegitimate and invalid, from the mere fact that the man who does it is not in possession of his reason. To say the same thing of an entire people is to assume a people composed of madmen, and madness does not make right.

Even if a man can alienate his own freedom, he cannot alienate that of his children. They are born human and free; their freedom belongs to them, and no one else has a right to dispose of it. Before they have reached the age of reason, their father can, in their name, stipulate conditions for their preservation, but he cannot give them to someone else irrevocably and unconditionally, for such an act is contrary to the ends of nature and goes beyond the rights of fatherhood. In order, then, for an arbitrary government to be legitimate, each generation of the people would have to be free to accept or reject it; but then the government would no longer be arbitrary.

A man who renounces his freedom renounces his humanity, along with the rights of humanity, and even its duties. There is no possible compensation for someone who renounces everything. Such a renunciation is incompatible with the nature of man, and to remove all freedom from his will is to remove all morality from his acts. And finally, an agreement that stipulates absolute authority on one side and unlimited obedience on the other is vain and contradictory. Is it not clear that one has no obligation toward someone from whom one is entitled to demand everything, and does not that single condition, without reciprocity or compensation, nullify the agreement? What right could my slave have against me, since everything he has belongs to me? His rights are mine, and the idea of my rights against myself is meaningless.

Grotius and others see war as another origin of the supposed right of enslavement. Since the victor has the right to kill the vanquished, they say, the latter can save his life at the expense of his freedom, an agreement that is all the more legitimate because it is advantageous to both parties.

But it is clear that this supposed right to kill the vanquished does not result in any way from the state of war. Since men living in their original independence have no mutual relations stable enough to constitute either a state of peace or a state of war, they are not naturally enemies. It is a relation of things, not of men, that constitutes war, and since the state of war cannot arise from simple personal relations, but only from material relations, private war, or war between man and man, cannot exist, either in the state of nature, where there is no stable property, or in the social state, where everything is under the authority of law.

Individual combats, such as duels and other fights, are acts that do not constitute a state. As for the private wars authorized by the Establishments of Saint Louis and suspended by the Peace of God, they were abuses of feudal government, an absurd system if ever there was one, contrary to the principles of natural right and all good political administration.

War is therefore not a relation of man to man, but a relation of state to state, in which individuals are enemies only accidentally, not as men or even as citizens, but as soldiers; not as members of their nation, but as its defenders. Finally, the enemies of a state can only be other states, not men, because there can be no real relation between things of different natures.

This principle is in conformity with the established rules of all times and the uniform practice of all civilized nations. Declarations of war are notifications not so much to rulers as to their subjects. A foreigner, whether a king, a private individual, or a people, who robs, kills, or imprisons a ruler's subjects without addressing a declaration of war to him is not an enemy, but a brigand. Even in the midst of a war, a just ruler takes possession of all public property in the enemy country, but respects the lives and property of individuals; he respects the rights on which his own are founded. Since the goal of war is the destruction of the enemy state, one has a right to kill its defenders as long as they bear arms, but as soon as they lay down their arms and surrender, they cease to be enemies or instruments of the enemy; they are now simply men again, and the right to kill them no longer exists. Sometimes it is possible to kill a state without killing a single one of its members, and war gives no right that is not necessary to the achievement of its goal. These principles are not those of Grotius; they are not founded on the authority of poets: They derive from the nature of things, and are founded on reason.

As for the right of conquest, it has no other foundation than the power of the strongest. If war does not give the victor the right to massacre conquered peoples, this nonexistent right cannot be used as the basis of a right to enslave them. One has a right to kill an enemy only when one cannot enslave him; the right to enslave him therefore does not come from the right to kill him, and it is an unjust bargain to make him pay for his life, over which the victor has no right, with his freedom. Is it not clear that there is a vicious circle in founding the right of life and death on the right of enslavement, and the right of enslavement on the right of life and death?

Even assuming that terrible right to kill everyone, I say that men enslaved in war, or conquered peoples, are under no obligation to their master; they must obey him only as long as they are forced to do so. In taking an equivalent of their life, the victor has not spared them: Rather than killing them unprofitably, he has killed them profitably. He is so far from having acquired any authority over them, in addition to force, that the state of war continues between them as before; their relation to each other is an effect of it, and use of the right of war does not imply a treaty of peace. It is true that an agreement has been made between the victor and the vanquished, but far from destroying the state of war, that agreement presupposes its continuation.

Thus no matter how we look at it, the right of enslavement is invalid, not only because it is illegitimate, but also because it is absurd and meaningless. The words "enslavement" and "right" are mutually contradictory; they exclude each other. It will always be nonsensical for a man to say to another man or to a people, "I make with you an agreement entirely at your expense and entirely to my advantage. I will keep it as long as I please, and you will keep it as long as I please."

We Must Always Go Back to a First Agreement

Even if I were to grant everything that I have so far refuted, supporters of despotism would be no better off. There will always be a great difference between subduing a multitude and governing a society. If separate individuals are successively subjugated to the domination of one man, whatever their number may be, I see only a master and his slaves, not a people and its ruler. The result can be called an aggregation, but not an association; there is no public good or body politic. Even if the man in question has enslaved half the world, he is still only a private individual, and his interest, separate from that of others, is still only a private interest. If he dies, his empire is left scattered and without cohesion, as an oak disintegrates and falls into a heap of ashes when it has been consumed by fire.

A people, says Grotius, can give itself to a king. According to Grotius, then, a people is a people before giving itself to a king. That gift is itself a civil act and presupposes a collective agreement. Therefore, before examining the act by which a people elects a king, it would be good to examine the agreement by which a people is a people. Since the latter necessarily precedes the former, it is the true foundation of society.

If there were no prior agreement, why — assuming that the election was not unanimous — should the minority be obligated to submit to the choice of the majority? Why should a hundred men who want a master have the right to vote on behalf of ten who do not? The rule of accepting the decision of the majority is itself established by agreement and presupposes unanimity on at least one occasion.

The Social Pact

I suppose men to have reached the point where the obstacles to their survival in the state of nature have a resistance that cannot be overcome by the forces each individual has at his disposal for preserving himself in that state. The time has thus come when that original state can subsist no longer, and the human race will perish if it does not change its way of living.

Since men cannot engender new forces, but can only unite and direct existing ones, they now have only one means of preserving themselves: to form by aggregation a sum of forces capable of overcoming the resistance, then direct them toward a single goal and make them act together.

Such a sum of forces can be produced only by the collaboration of a group of men. But since each man's strength and freedom are his primary means of self-preservation, how can he pledge them without harming himself, without neglecting the care he owes to himself? The problem that arises here can be stated as follows:

"To devise a form of association which will defend and protect the person and possessions of each associate with all the collective strength, and in which each is united with all, yet obeys only himself and remains as free as before." Such is the fundamental problem that the social contract solves.

The terms of this contract are so determined by the nature of the agreement that the slightest alternation would make them null and void, so that even though they may never have been formally enunciated, they are everywhere the same, everywhere tacitly accepted and acknowledged, as long as the social pact is not violated, in which case each man regains his original rights and returns to his natural freedom, losing the contractual freedom for which he renounced it.

These terms, properly understood, can all be reduced to one, namely, the complete surrender of each associate, with all his rights, to the whole community. For in the first place, since each man gives himself entirely, the condition is equal for all; and since the condition is equal for all, it is to no one's interest to make it burdensome for others.

Furthermore, since the surrender is made without reserve, the union is as perfect as it can be and no associate has anything more to demand, for if individuals retained any rights, each would soon be his own judge on some point or other, there being no common superior to decide between him and the public; then eventually everyone would set himself up as his own judge on all points, the state of nature would subsist, and the association would necessarily become either tyrannical or ineffectual.

Finally, in giving himself to all, each man gives himself to no one, and since he acquires the same right over all the other associates as they acquire over him, he gains the equivalent of everything he loses, plus greater power to preserve what he has.

If, then, we exclude from the social pact everything that is not essential to it, we find that it reduces itself to his formulation: "Each of us puts his person and all his power in common under the supreme control of the general will, and we collectively receive each member as an indivisible part of the whole."

In place of the individual persons of the contracting parties, the act of association immediately creates a collective, artificial body, composed of as many members as the assembly has voters, and the same act gives this body its unity, its collective self, its life, and its will. Such a public person, formed by the union of all other persons, was formerly called as *city*, and is now known as a *republic* or a *body politic*. Its members call it in the *state* when it is passive, this *sovereign* when it is active and a *power* when they compare it with others of its kind. They themselves collectively take the name of the *people*, and are individually called *citizens* as sharing in the sovereign authority, and *subjects* as owing obedience to the laws of the state. But these terms are often used indiscriminately, one in place of another; it is enough to know how to distinguish them when they are used precisely.

The Sovereign

This formulation shows that the act of association involves a reciprocal commitment between the public and the individuals who compose it, and that each individual, contracting with himself, so to speak, is under a double obligation: toward other individuals, as a member of the sovereign, and toward the sovereign, as a member of the state. But the principle of common law which says that a man cannot be held to a commitment he has made to himself does not apply here, for there is a great difference between assuming an obligation toward himself and assuming one toward a whole of which he is a part.

It should also be pointed out that while public decisions can obligate all subjects toward the sovereign, because of the two capacities in which each subject is considered, they cannot obligate the sovereign toward itself. It is therefore contrary to the nature of the body politic for the sovereign to impose a law on itself that it cannot infringe. Since it can be considered only in a single capacity, it is in the position of an individual contracting with himself. Hence we see that there neither is nor can be any kind of fundamental law binding on the people as a body — not even the social contract. This does not mean that the body politic cannot assume obligations toward others, insofar as they do not violate that contract, for in relation to outsiders it is an indivisible being, an individual.

But since the body politic or the sovereign draws its being only from the sanctity of the contract, it can never obligate itself, even to an outsider, to do anything contrary to that original agreement, such as alienating some portion of itself, or placing itself under the authority of another sovereign. To violate the agreement by which it exists would be to annihilate itself, and that which is nothing can do nothing.

Once a multitude is thus united in a body, no one can offend one of its members without attacking the body, much less offend the body without affecting its members. Duty and interest therefore equally oblige the two contracting parties to help each other, and the same men must seek to combine, in their double capacity, all the advantages that pertain to it.

The sovereign, being formed only by the individuals who compose it, neither has nor can have any interest contrary to theirs; consequently there is no need for the sovereign power to give guarantees to the subjects, because it is impossible for the body to want to harm all its members, and as we shall see later, it cannot harm any one of them in particular. Merely by virtue of existing, the sovereign is always what it should be.

This, however, is not true of the subjects in relation to the sovereign, which, despite the common interest, could not count on them to fulfill their obligations unless it devised means of making sure of their fidelity.

Each individual can, as a man, have a private will different from or even contrary to the general will which he has as a citizen. His private interest may speak to him quite differently from the common interest; his absolute and naturally independent existence may make him regard what he owes to the common cause as a gratuitous contribution, loss of which would be less harmful to others than payment of it is burdensome to him, and considering that the artificial person that constitutes the state is an imaginary being because it is not a man, he may want to enjoy the rights of a citizen without fulfilling the duties of a subject, an injustice that would bring about the ruin of the body politic if it were to spread.

In order, therefore, that the social pact shall not be an empty formality, it tacitly includes one stipulation without which all the others would be ineffectual: that anyone who refuses to obey the general will shall be compelled to do so by the whole body. This means nothing else than that he shall be forced to be free, for such is the condition which gives each citizen to his country and thus secures him against all personal dependence. This condition is essential to the functioning of the political machine, and it alone legitimizes civil obligations, which would otherwise be absurd, tyrannical, and subject to the most outrageous abuses.

The Civil State

The passage from the state of nature to the civil state produces a remarkable change in man by substituting justice for instinct in his conduct and giving his acts the morality they previously lacked. Only then, when physical impulses have yielded to the voice of duty, and appetite to right, does man, who so far had considered only himself, find that he is forced to act according to different principles and to consult his reason before listening to his inclinations. In this state he is deprived of some advantages given to him by nature, but he gains others so great — his faculties are exercised and developed, his ideas are broadened, his feelings are ennobled, his whole soul is uplifted — that if the abuses of this new state did not often degrade him below his previous level, he would constantly have reason to bless the happy moment when he was drawn out of the state of nature forever and changed from a stupid, shortsighted animal into intelligent being and a man.

Let us reduce the balance to terms that can be easily compared. What man loses by the social contract is his natural freedom and an unlimited right to anything he wants and can get. What he gains is civil freedom and ownership of everything he possesses. To avoid error in evaluating this exchange, we must make two clear distinctions: first, between natural freedom, which is limited only by the individual's power, and civil freedom, which is limited by the general will; and second, between possession, which results only from force or the right of first occupancy, and ownership, which can be based only on juridical title.

Another gain can be added to those that come with the civil state: moral freedom, which alone makes man truly his own master, for impulsion by appetite alone is slavery, and obedience to self-imposed law is freedom. But I have already said too much on this point, and the philosophical meaning of the word "freedom" is not part of my subject here.

Real Property

When the community is formed, each member gives himself to it as he is at that time, with all his resources, including the goods he possesses. This act does not make possessions change their nature in changing hands; they do not become property in the hands of the sovereign. But just as the might of the state is incomparably greater than the individual's public possession is, *de facto*, stronger and more irrevocable, though not more legitimate, at least so far as foreigners are concerned. For the state, in relation to its members, has control of all their goods by virtue of the social contract, which, within the state, is the basis of all rights; but it has control of them in relation to other powers only by virtue of the right of first occupancy, which it derives from individuals.

The right of first occupancy, though more real than the right of the strongest, does not become a true right until the right of property has been established. Every man has a natural right to everything that is necessary to him, but the juridical title that makes him the owner of one piece of property excludes him from all others. Having received his share, he must limit himself to it and can name no further claim to what is held in common. That is why the right of first occupancy, so weak in the state of nature, is deemed worthy of respect by every man in the civil state. In this right we respect less what belongs to others than what does not belong to us.

In general, to authorize the right of first occupancy to a certain piece of land, the following conditions are necessary. First, the land must not yet be inhabited by anyone; second, one must occupy only so much of it as one needs for one's subsistence; third, one must take possession of it not by a vain ceremony, but by work and cultivation, the only sign of ownership that must be respected by others in the absence of a juridical title.

In granting the right of first occupancy to need and work, are we not carrying it as far as it can go? Is it possible to leave that right without limits? In order for a man to lay claim to a piece of land held in common, shall it be enough for him to set foot on it? If he has the strength to expel others from it for a short time, shall that be enough to divest them forever of the right to return to it? If a man or a people seizes a vast territory and deprives the rest of the human race of it, is this not a punishable usurpation, since it robs other men of the habitation and food that nature had given them in common? When Nuñez Balboa stood on the shore and took possession of the Pacific Ocean and all of South America in the name of the Castilian crown, was that sufficient to dispossess all the inhabitants and exclude all of the world's other rulers? If so, such ceremonies were repeated unnecessarily, for the Catholic King could have sat in his study and taken possession of the whole world all at once, later deducting from his empire what was already in the possession of other monarchs.

It is easy to understand how adjoining parcels of land held by individuals are united and become public territory, and how the right of sovereignty, extending from subjects to the land they occupy, becomes real and personal. This places the possessors in greater dependency and makes their resources themselves a guarantee of their fidelity. Ancient monarchs apparently did not realize the advantage of this: They called themselves King of the Persians, Scythians, or Macedonians, and seemed to regard themselves as rulers of men rather than masters of a given country. Today's monarchs are clever enough to call themselves King of France, Spain, England, etc. By thus holding the land, they are sure of being able to hold its inhabitants.

Oddly enough, when an individual surrenders his goods to the community, the latter does not deprive him of them, but on the contrary, assures him of their legitimate possession. It changes usurpation into a genuine right, and tenure into ownership. He is then regarded as a depositary of public wealth; his rights are respected by all members of the state and upheld against foreigners by all its strength, so that by a transfer that is advantageous to the public and still more so to himself, he has, so to speak, acquired everything that he has given up. This paradox is easily explained by the distinction between the sovereign's and the owner's rights to the same piece of property, as we shall see later.

It may also happen that men begin to unite before they possess anything, then afterward occupy a territory large enough for all of them and either use it in common or divide it among themselves, the shares being either equal or of different sizes established by the sovereign. No matter how this acquisition is made, each individual's right over his own piece of land is always subordinate to the community's right over all the land, for otherwise there would be no strength in the social bond and no real power in the exercise of sovereignty.

I shall end his chapter and this book by pointing out something that should be the basis of the whole social system: Rather than destroying natural equality, the fundamental pact substitutes a moral and legitimate equality for whatever physical inequality nature has produced among men, so that while they may be unequal in strength or intelligence, they all become equal by agreement and rights.

Sovereignty is Inalienable

The first and most important consequence of the principles established above is that only the general will can direct the forces of the state in such a way as to achieve the goal for which it was instituted, namely, the common good; for while the creation of societies was made necessary by the clash of individual interests, it was made possible by the fact that those same interests also coincide. It is what they have in common that forms the social bond, and if there were no point at which all interests coincided, no society could exist. It is solely on the basis of this common interest that society should be governed.

I therefore say that sovereignty, being only the exercise of the general will, can never be alienated and that the sovereign, which is only a collective being, can be represented only by itself; power can be transferred, but will cannot.

While it is not impossible for an individual will to concur with the general will on a particular point, it is at least impossible for such a concurrence to be lasting and constant, for an individual will, by its nature, tends toward partiality, and the general will tends toward equality. It is still more impossible to have any guarantee of this concurrence; even if it were always to exist, it would be by accident and not by design. The sovereign can say, "I now will what this man wills, or at least what he says he wills," but it cannot say, "Tomorrow I shall still will what he wills," because it is absurd for the will to bind itself with regard to the future, and because no will can consent to anything contrary to the good of the being that wills. If, therefore, a people promises to obey unconditionally, it thereby dissolves itself and ceases to be a people; as soon as there is a master, there is no longer a sovereign, and the body politic is then destroyed.

This is not to say that the commands of rulers cannot pass for general ills; they can, as long as the sovereign is free to oppose them and does not do so. In that case, universal silence must be assumed to indicate the people's consent. This will later be explained at greater length.

Sovereignty is Indivisible

For the same reason that it is inalienable, sovereignty is indivisible. For either a will is general or it is not; it is either the will of the whole people or of only a part of it. In the first case, when the will is declared, it is an act of sovereignty and constitutes law. In the second, it is only an individual will, or an act of administration, or at the very most, a decree.

But our political theorists, unable to divide sovereignty in its source, divide it in its object. They divide it into force and will; into legislative power and executive power; into the rights of taxation, justice, and war; into internal administration and the power to negotiate with foreigners. Sometimes they mingle all these parts and sometimes they separate them. They make the sovereign a fantastic being put together from various bits and pieces; it is as if they composed man of several bodies, each one with eyes, arms, or feet, and nothing more. Japanese conjurers are said to dismember a child before spectators, throw all the pieces into the air one after the other, then make the child fall to the ground, alive and whole. This is essentially the same as the legerdemain of our political theorists: After having dismembered the social body by a sleight-of-hand trick worthy of a fair, they reassemble the pieces in a manner known only to themselves.

This error comes from not having formed precise ideas concerning sovereign authority, and from mistaking mere manifestations of it for parts of it. Thus, for example, declaring war and making peace have been regarded as acts of sovereignty, which they are not. Each of these acts is not a law, but only an application of the law, a particular act which determines how the law applies in a given case, as will be seen clearly when the idea attached to the word "law" has been delineated.

If the other divisions were examined in the same way, it would be found that anyone who thinks he sees sovereignty divided is always mistaken, that all the rights taken for parts of it are subordinate to it and always presuppose supreme wills which they merely put into execution.

This lack of precision has introduced vast amounts of obscurity into the conclusions of political philosophers when they try to judge the respective rights of kings and peoples on the basis of the principles they have previously established. Everyone can see, in Chapters III and IV of the first book of Grotius, how that learned man and his translator Barbeyrac become entangled and embroiled in their own sophistries, for fear of saying too much or too little to suit their purposes, and of offending the interests they set out to conciliate. Grotius, a refugee in France, dissatisfied with his own country and wishing to win the favor of Louis XIII, to whom his book is dedicated, spares no effort to strip peoples of all their rights and bestow them on kings as artfully as possible. That would also have been very much to the liking of Barbeyrac, who dedicated his translation to the king of England, George I. But unfortunately the expulsion of James II, which he calls an abdication, forced him to maintain an attitude of reserve, to equivocate and be evasive, in order to avoid making William out to be a usurper. If those two writers had adopted the right principles, all their difficulties would have been removed and they would always have been consistent; but they would have sadly told the truth and won favor only with the people. Telling the truth is not a way to make one's fortune; the people appoints no ambassadors or professors, and grants no pensions.

Whether the General Will Can Err

It follows from what has been said above that the general will is always well-meaning and always tends toward the public good; but it does not follow that all decisions made by the people are equally sound. We always will our own good, but we do not always see what it is. The people is never corrupted, but it is often misled, and only then does it seem to will what is bad.

There is often a great difference between the will of all and the general will. The latter looks only to the common interest, while the former looks to private interest and is only a sum of individual wills. But take away from those same wills the pluses and minuses that cancel each other out, and the general will remains as the sum of the differences.

If the people always decided on the basis of adequate information, and with no discussion among the citizens beforehand, the general will would always result from the larger number of small differences and the decision would always be right. But when there are factions, lesser associations detrimental to the greater one, the will of each of them becomes general in relation to its members and particular in relation to the state. It can then be said that there are no longer as many voters as there are men, but only as many as there are associations. The differences become less numerous and give a less general result. Finally, when one of these associations is so large that it prevails over all the others, the result is no longer a sum of small differences, but a single difference; there is then no longer a general will, and the opinion that prevails is only a particular one.

Therefore, if the general will is to be clearly expressed, it is important that there be no partial societies within the state, and that each citizen form his opinion independently. Such was the unique and sublime system established by the great Lycurgus. When partial societies do exist, they must be made numerous and prevented from being unequal, as was done by Solon, Numa, and Servius. These are the only effective precautions that can be taken to ensure that the general will is always enlightened and the people never mistaken.

Limits of the Sovereign Power

If the state or body politic is only an artificial person whose life is in the union of its members, and if its most important concern is its own preservation, it must have a universal coercive power in order to move and direct each part in the manner most advantageous to the whole. Just as nature gives each man absolute power over the parts of his body, the social pact gives the body politic absolute power over its members, and it is this same power which, under the direction of the general will, bears the name of sovereignty, as I have already said.

But besides this public person, we must also consider the private persons who compose it, and whose life and freedom are naturally independent of it. We must therefore distinguish between the respective rights of the citizens and the sovereign, as well as between the duties which the citizens must fulfill as subjects and the natural rights they should enjoy as men.

It is acknowledged that the social pact requires each individual to relinquish only that part of his power, possessions, and freedom which it is important for the community to control; but it must also be acknowledged that the sovereign is the sole judge of that importance.

If a citizen is able to render certain services to the state, it is his duty to render them as soon as the sovereign requests them. But the sovereign, for its part, cannot place the subjects under any constraint useless to the community; it cannot even will to do so, for under the law of reason, as under the law of nature, nothing can occur without a cause.

The commitments that bind us to the social body are obligatory only because they are mutual, and their nature is such that, in fulfilling them, one cannot work for others without also working for oneself. Why is the general will always well-meaning, and why does everyone constantly will the happiness of each individual, if not because everyone applies the word "each" to himself and thinks of himself when he votes for the good of all? This proves that equality of rights, and the notion of justice it produces, stem from the preference that each man gives to himself, and therefore from the nature of man. It proves that in order to be truly general, the general will must be general in its object as well as in its essence, that it must come from everyone if it is to apply to everyone, and that it loses its natural rectitude when it tends toward a specific individual object, for we are then judging something alien to us, with no true principle of equity to guide us.

As soon as a question of particular fact or right arises on a point that has not been settled by a prior general agreement, the matter becomes contentious. It is a lawsuit in which the individuals concerned are one party and the public is the other, but I do not see which law should be followed, or which judge should hand down the decision. It would be ridiculous to try to resolve the question by an express decision of the general will, which could be only the conclusion of one of the parties, and would consequently be for the other party only an alien, particular will, inclined in this case toward injustice, and subject to error. Thus, just as a particular will cannot represent the general will, the general will in turn changes its nature when it has a particular object, and cannot, in its capacity as the general will, pronounce judgment on either a man or a fact. When the people of Athens, for example, appointed and removed its leaders, bestowed honors on some and inflicted punishment on others, and by multitudes of decrees indiscriminately exercised all functions of government, it no longer had a general will in the true sense of the term; it was no longer acting as a sovereign, but as a magistrate. This will seem contrary to generally accepted ideas, but I must be given time to set forth my own views.

From the above it should be apparent that what makes a will general is not so much the number of individuals involved as the common interest that unites them, for under this system each man necessarily submits to the conditions he imposes on others. This admirable concordance between self-interest and justice gives collective deliberations an equitable character that vanishes in a discussion of any particular matter in which there is no common interest to unite and identify the criteria of the judge with those of the party.

By whatever direction we approach the principle, we always reach the same conclusion, namely, that the social pact establishes such equality among citizens that they all bind themselves under the same conditions and should all enjoy the same rights. Thus by the nature of the pact, any act of sovereignty, that is, any genuine act of the general will, obligates or favors all citizens equally, so that the sovereign recognizes only the nation as a whole and does not distinguish any of the individuals who compose it. What, then, strictly speaking, is an act of sovereignty? It is an agreement not between a superior and an inferior, but between the body politic and each of its members. It is a legitimate agreement because it is based on the social contract; it is equitable because it is common to all; it is useful because it can have no other object than the general good; and it is binding because it is backed by public force and supreme power. As long as the subjects are bound only by such agreements, they obey no one; they obey only their own will, and to ask how far the respective rights of the sovereign and the citizens extend is to ask how far the citizens can go in imposing obligations on themselves, each committing himself to all, and all to each.

From this it can be seen that the power of the sovereign, absolute, sacred, and inviolable though it is, does not and cannot go beyond the bounds of general agreements, and that each man has full control of such goods and freedom as have been left to him by those agreements, so that the sovereign never has a right to burden one subject more than another, because the matter then becomes particular and therefore lies beyond the competency of the sovereign power.

Once these distinctions have been accepted, it becomes obvious that individuals do not really give up anything when they enter into the social contract. Their new situation is genuinely preferable to their old one, before the contract. Rather than depriving themselves of anything, they have made an advantageous exchange: Instead of an uncertain and precarious way of life, they now have one that is better and more secure; instead of natural independence, they now have freedom; instead of the power to harm others, they now have their own security; and instead of their individual strength, which others might overcome, they now have rights which the social union makes invincible. Their lives themselves, which they have devoted to the state, are constantly protected by it, and when they risk them to defend it, are they not simply returning to it what they have received from it? Are they not doing what they would have to do more often and with greater danger in the state of nature, in which they would inevitably have to risk their lives in fights to defend their means of preserving them? It is true that everyone must fight for his country when necessary, but it is also true that no one ever has to fight for himself. Are we not better off in running a risk to defend what gives us our security, rather than running the greater risk that would be imposed on us if we lost that security?

The Right of Life and Death

It may be asked how individuals, having no right to dispose of their own lives, can transfer such a right to the sovereign. The question seems difficult to answer only because it is wrongly formulated. Everyone has the right to risk his life in order to preserve it. Has it ever been said that a man who jumps from a window to escape a fire is guilty of suicide? Has that crime ever been imputed to a man who died in a storm at sea, having been aware of the danger when he boarded the ship?

The purpose of the social contract is the preservation of the contracting parties. He who wills the end also wills the means, and in this case the means are inseparable from certain risks, and even certain losses. Anyone who wants to preserve his life at the expense of others must be willing to give it for them when necessary. When the law requires a citizen to expose himself to a danger, he is no longer his own judge of it, and when the government says to him, "It is expedient for the state that you die," he must die, since it is only on that condition that he has so far lived in security, and since his life is no longer merely a gift of nature, but a conditional grant from the state.

The death penalty imposed on criminals can be viewed in much the same light: It is to avoid being a murderer's victim that each man consents to die if he should become a murderer himself. Far from disposing of his life, he thinks only of making it more secure; we may assume that none of the parties to the agreement intends to get himself hanged.

Moreover, every criminal attacks social rights, and by his crimes, becomes a rebel and a traitor to his country. In violating its laws, he ceases to be a member of it, and even wages war against it. The preservation of the state is then incompatible with his, and one of the two must perish. When a criminal is put to death, it is less as a citizen than as an enemy. His trial and judgment prove and declare that he has broken the social contract and is therefore no longer a member of the state. Since he has acknowledged himself to be a member of it, at the very least by living within its boundaries, he must be cut off from it, either by banishment as a violator of the pact, or by death as a public enemy; for such an enemy is not an artificial person, but a man, and in that case the right of war is to kill the vanquished.

But, it will be said, the condemnation of a criminal is a particular act. Granted, and that is why it is outside the competence of the sovereign; it is a right that the sovereign can confer but cannot exercise. My ideas are all consistent, but I cannot expound them all at once.

Frequent executions are always a sign of weakness of laziness on the part of a government. There is no evildoer who could not be made good for something. No man can rightfully be put to death, even as a deterrent example, unless he cannot be spared without danger.

As for the right to grant pardon, to exempt a guilty man from a punishment specified by law and imposed by a judge, it belongs only to what is above judges and the law, that is, the sovereign. But this right is not very clearly defined, and occasions for using it are quite rare. In a well-governed state there are few punishments, not because pardon is granted often, but because there are few criminals. When a state is decaying, crimes are so numerous that most of them go unpunished. Under the Roman Republic, neither the Senate nor the consuls ever tried to grant pardon; the people itself did not do it, although it sometimes revoked its own judgments. Frequent pardons announce that soon criminals will no longer need them, and everyone knows where that leads. But I feel my heart protesting and restraining my pen; let us leave these questions to be discussed by a righteous man who, having never done wrong, has never been in need of pardon for himself.

Law

By the social pact we have given existence and life to the body politic; we must now give it movement and will by legislation, for the original agreement by which it is formed and unified has not yet determined what it must do to preserve itself.

What is proper and in conformity with order is such by the nature of things, independently of human agreements. All justice comes from God, and only from him; but if we were able to receive it directly from that exalted source, we would have no need of either government or laws. There is, no doubt, a universal justice emanating from reason alone, but in order to be accepted among us, this justice must be reciprocal. Looking at things from a human standpoint, it is evident that, lacking natural sanctions, the laws of justice are ineffectual among men; they serve only to reward evil and penalize good when the righteous man always observes them in his dealings with others and others never observe them in their dealings with him. Agreements and laws are therefore needed to join rights to duties and direct justice toward its object. In the state of nature, where everything is held in common, I owe nothing to those to whom I have promised nothing; I recognize as belonging to others only what is useless to me. This is not the case in the civil state, where all rights are fixed by law.

What, then, is a law? Those who content themselves with attaching metaphysical ideas to the word will go on discussing it without ever reaching agreement, and when they have defined a law of nature, they will still have no better understanding of what a law of the state is.

I have already said that there can be no general will with a particular object. Any such object must be either within the state or outside it. If it is outside, a will that is alien to the state is not general with respect to it; if the object is within the state, it is part of it, and there is then a relation between whole and part which makes them two separate entities, of which the part is one and the whole minus that part is the other. But the whole minus a part is not the whole, and as long as that relation subsists there is no longer a whole but two unequal parts. Hence it follows that the will of one is not general with respect to the other.

But when the whole people establishes a rule for the whole people, it considers only itself. If a relation is then formed, it is between the entire object from one viewpoint and the entire object from another viewpoint, with no division of the whole. In this case the matter to which the rule applies is general, like the will that establishes the rule. It is such an act that I call a law.

When I say that the object of a law is always general, I mean that a law always considers the subjects collectively and actions abstractly, never an individual person or a particular action. Thus the law can declare that there will be privileges, but it cannot give them to anyone by name; it can create different classes of citizens, and even stipulate qualifications for membership in them, but it cannot assign specific persons to a given class; it can establish a monarchical government with hereditary succession, but it cannot choose a king or designate a royal family. In short, no function relating to an individual object is within the legislative power.

In this view, it is readily apparent that there is no longer any need to ask who has the power to make laws, since they are acts of the general will; or whether a ruler is above the law, since he is a member of the state; or whether the law can be unjust, since no one is unjust to himself; or how we can be both free and subject to the law, since it is only a declaration of our will.

It can also be seen that since the law combines generality of will with generality of object, no order that any man gives on his own initiative is a law. Even an order given by the sovereign with regard to a particular object is not a law, but a decree, and it is an act not of sovereignty, but of administration.

I therefore give the name of republic to any state controlled by laws, no matter what its form of administration may be, for only in such states does the public interest govern, and only in them is there a genuine "public thing" [*res publica*]. Every legitimate government is republican, I will later explain what government is.

Laws are properly speaking, only the terms of the civil association. A people bound by laws should be the author of them; only those who come together to form a society are entitled to specify the conditions under which they do so. But how are they to specify them? Shall it be by spontaneous assent, by a sudden inspiration? Does the body politic have a voice to declare its will? Who will give it the foresight to formulate and announce its decisions in advance? Or how will it announce them at the moment of need? How can a blind multitude, which often does not know what it wants because it seldom knows what is good for it, accomplish on its own such a great and difficult undertaking as the promulgation of a system of law? Of itself, the people always wills the good, but does not always see it. The general will is always well-meaning, but the judgment that guides it is not always enlightened. It must be made to see things as they are, and sometimes as they ought to appear to it; it must be shown the right path that it is seeking, protected from being led astray by particular wills, made to see places and times in closer relation to one another, taught to weigh the attraction of present and perceptible advantages against remote and hidden evils. Individuals can see a good but reject it;

the public can will a good but not see it. Both need guides. Individuals must be made to bring their will into conformity with their reason; the public must be taught to perceive what it wills. Public enlightenment then leads to the union of understanding and will in the social body, which in turn leads to precise coordination among the parts, and finally to maximum strength of the whole. All this is the origin of the need for a lawgiver.

The Lawgiver

To discover the rules of society best suited to nations, a superior intelligence would be required. Such an intelligence would have to see all human passions without feeling any of them; it would have to be completely unrelated to our nature, yet know it thoroughly; it would have to be independent of us for its happiness, yet willing to concern itself with ours; and finally, it would have to seek its glory in the distant reaches of the future, working in one century to enjoy the results in another.

In seeking to define the political or kingly man in his dialogue *The statesman*, Plato used the same line or reasoning with regard to right as Caligula used with regard to fact; but if it is true that a great ruler is a rare man, what are we to say of a great lawgiver? The lawgiver must draw up a plan; the ruler has only to follow it. The lawgiver is the engineer who invents the machine; the ruler is only the workman who assembles it and keeps it running. When societies are born, says Montesquieu, the leaders of republics establish institutions, and afterward the institutions form the leaders of republics.

Anyone who dares to undertake the task of instituting a nation must feel himself capable of changing human nature, so to speak; of transforming each individual, who by himself is a complete and solitary whole, into a part of a greater whole from which he, in a sense, receives his life and his being; of marring man's constitution in order to strengthen it; of substituting a partial and moral existence for the physical and independent existence that we have all received from nature. He must, in short, take away man's resources to give him others that are foreign to him and cannot be used without the help of other men. The more completely these natural resources are annihilated, the greater and more durable are the acquired ones and the stronger and more perfect are the new institutions. If, then, each citizen is nothing, and can do nothing, without all the others, and if the resources acquired by the whole are equal or superior to the sum of all the individual's natural resources, legislation can be said to have reached its highest possible degree of perfection.

The lawgiver is in every respect an extraordinary man in the state, by the talents he should have, as well as by his function. This function is neither administrative nor sovereign. It institutes the republic but has no place in its institutions. It is a private and superior function which has nothing in common with human dominion, for while it is true that he who controls men must not control laws, it is also true that he who controls laws must not control men; otherwise, his laws would serve his passions, often doing nothing but perpetuating his injustices, and he could never prevent his personal aims from tainting the purity of his work.

When Lycurgus gave laws to his country, he began by abdicating the kingship. Most Greek towns customarily called on outsiders to draw up their laws. The republics of modern Italy often followed that example; Geneva did the same, and found it advantageous. At the height of its glow, Rome suffered a resurgence of all the crimes of tyranny, and was on the verge of perishing, because it had placed legislative authority and sovereign power in the same hands.

The deceivers themselves, however, never claimed the right to establish any law on their own authority. "Nothing that we propose to you," they said to the people, "can become a law without your consent. Romans, you yourselves must be the authors of the laws that assure your well-being."

He who formulates laws has, or should have, no right to legislate. Even if it should want to do so, the people cannot divest itself of that nontransferable right, because, according to the fundamental pact, only the general will is binding on individuals, and the only way to determine whether a particular will coincides with the general will is to submit it to a free vote of the people. I have said this before, but it is not useless to repeat it.

Thus in the task of the lawgiver we find two things that seem incompatible: an enterprise beyond human capability, and a lack of authority to put it into execution.

There is another difficulty that deserves attention. If a wise man tries to speak to ordinary people in his own language rather than theirs, he cannot make them understand him. There are all sorts of ideas that cannot be translated into their language. Concepts too general and aims too remote are beyond their comprehension. Each individual, having no inclination toward any plan of government unrelated to his private interest, finds it difficult to see the advantages he is to derive from the constant privations imposed by good laws. In order for a people in the process of formation to value sound political principles and follow the fundamental rules of statecraft, the effect would have to become the cause: The social spirit that is to be produced by the new institutions would have to preside over their creation, and before the laws exist, men would have to be what they are to become by means of those same laws. Therefore, since the lawgiver can use neither force nor reasoning, he must resort to another kind of authority which can lead without compelling and persuade without convincing.

This is what has forced the founders of nations in all ages to appeal to divine intervention and attribute their own wisdom to the gods, so that their peoples, submitting to the laws of the state as to those of nature, and acknowledging the same power in the formation of man as in that of the body politic, will obey with freedom and bear the yoke of public well-being with docility.

The lawgiver puts the demands of this sublime purpose, beyond the grasp of ordinary men, into the mouths of the immortals in order to lead by divine authority those who could not be moved by considerations of human prudence. But it is not given to everyone to make the gods speak, or to be believed when he announces that he is their interpreter. The lawgiver's greatness of soul is the real miracle that must validate his mission. Anyone can carve stone tablets, or bribe an oracle, or pretend to be in secret communication with some divinity, or train a bird to speak in his ear, or find other crude means of beguiling the people. A man whose resources are limited to such things may happen to assemble a band of fools, but he will never found an empire, and his ludicrous creation will soon perish with him. Inane tricks may form a momentary bond; only wisdom can make it last. Judaic law, which has survived to the present, and the law of the child of Ishmael, which has ruled half the world for ten centuries, still bear witness to the greatness of the men who drafted them; and while proud philosophy and blind partisan spirit see those men only as lucky impostors, true political understanding admires in their institutions the great and powerful genius that presides over lasting achievements.

The People

Before building a large edifice, an architect studies and tests the ground to determine whether it can bear the weight. Similarly, the wise lawgiver does not begin by drafting laws good in themselves, but first examines the question of whether the people for which they are intended is capable of supporting them. That was why Plato refused to give laws to the Arcadians and the Cyrenians, knowing that those two peoples were rich and could not tolerate equality; and in Crete there were good laws and bad men because Minos had only disciplined a people laden with vices.

There have been a thousand successful nations on earth that could not have tolerated good laws, and even those that could have done so had only a brief period in their whole history when they were capable of it. Most peoples, like most individuals, are malleable only in youth and become incorrigible as they grow older. Once their customs are established and their prejudices have taken root, trying to reform them is a dangerous and futile enterprise; like those foolish and cowardly invalids who tremble at the sight of a doctor, they cannot bear to let anyone touch their infirmities, even to cure them.

It is true that, just as some illnesses unhinge a man's mind and take away his memory of the past, there are sometimes violent periods in the history of a state when revolutions do to the people what certain afflictions do to individuals, when horror of the past corresponds to loss of memory, and when the state, consumed by civil warfare, is reborn from its ashes, so to speak, and regains the vigor of youth in freeing itself from the embrace of death. This was the case with Sparta in the time of Lycurgus, Rome after the Tarquins, and in our own time, Holland and Switzerland after the expulsion of their tyrants.

But such events are rare; they are exceptions whose explanation is always found in the special constitution of the state involved. They cannot even happen twice to the same people, for a people can make itself free as long as it is still uncivilized, but not when its civil energies have been exhausted. It can then be destroyed by upheavals but cannot be restored by revolutions; as soon as its chains have been broken, it disintegrates and ceases to exist. From that point onward, it needs a master, not a liberator. Free peoples, remember this maxim: Freedom can be acquired, but never regained.

Youth is not childhood. With nations as with individuals, there is a time of youth, or maturity if you prefer, which must be awaited before they are made subject to laws. But a people's maturity is not always easy to recognize, and assuming its existence too soon will result in failure. One people may be amenable to discipline at birth, another may still not be amenable to it after ten centuries. The Russians will never be truly civilized, because the attempt to civilize them was made prematurely. Peter the Great had a genius for imitation; he did not have true genius, which is creative and makes everything from nothing. He did some good things, but most of his efforts were misguided. He saw that his subjects were barbarous, but he did not see that they were not ripe for civilization; he tried to civilize them when they should only have been trained. He first tried to turn them into Germans or Englishmen when he should have begun by turning them into Russians. By persuading them that they were something they were not, he prevented them from ever becoming what they could have been. That is how a French tutor educates his pupil to shine briefly during his childhood, then never do anything worthwhile for the rest of his life. The Russian empire will try to subjugate Europe and will itself be subjugated. The Tartars, its subjects or neighbors, will become its masters, and ours. That revolution seems inevitable to me. All the kings of Europe are working together to hasten it.

Nature has set upper and lower limits to the height of a well-built man, and produces only giants or dwarfs outside them. Similarly, with regard to the best constitution for a state, there are limits to the size it can have if it is to be neither too large to be well governed nor too small to maintain itself. Every body politic has a maximum strength which it cannot exceed. Expansion often makes it fall below this maximum. The more the social bond is stretched, the slacker it becomes, and a small state is usually stronger in proportion to its size than a large one.

There are many reasons for this. First of all, administration becomes more difficult over great distances, as a weight becomes heavier at the end of a long lever. It also becomes more expensive as the number of administrative levels is increased: Each town has an administration which the people pays for; each district has one, also paid for by the people; then each province; then the larger governments, such as satrapies and viceroyalties, each costing more than the one below it, and all paid for by the unfortunate people; and finally the supreme administration, which overwhelms everything. All these accumulated charges are a constant drain on the subjects, and far from being better governed by those different authorities, they are not governed as well as they would be if they were under only one. Meanwhile there are hardly any resources for emergencies, and the state is always on the verge of ruin when it must draw on those that remain.

Nor is that all: Not only is the government less swift and vigorous in enforcing its laws, preventing nuisances, correcting abuses, and forestalling seditious activities that may occur in distant places, but the citizens have less affection for their leaders, whom they never see, for their country, which to them seems to be the whole world, and for their fellow citizens, most of whom are strangers. The same laws cannot suit so many various provinces, which have different customs and contrasting climates and cannot all tolerate the same form of government. But differing laws only give rise to disorder and confusion among peoples which live under the same rulers, are in constant communication, intermarry, and travel freely among one another's territories; forced to accept other customs, they never know if their heritage is really their own. When a multitude of strangers are brought together at the seat of the supreme administration, talents are buried, virtues are unrecognized, and vices go unpunished. The rulers are so busy that they see nothing for themselves, and clerks govern the state. Finally, the measures that must be taken to maintain the general authority, which so many distant officials try to evade or deceive, absorb all governmental concern, so that none is left for the happiness of the people, and scarcely any for its defense, when necessary. It is thus that a body too large for its constitution collapses and perishes, crushed by its own weight.

On the other hand, a state must give itself a certain base if it is to be solid enough to withstand the jolts it is sure to receive and the efforts it will have to make to sustain itself, for all peoples have a kind of centrifugal force by which they continually act against each other and strive to expand at the expense of their neighbors, like Descartes's vortices. The weak are therefore always in danger of being swallowed up, and it is hardly possible for any state to survive unless it forms with others a kind of balance which more or less equalizes the pressure on all of them.

From this it can be seen that there are some reasons for expansion and others for contraction, and finding the proportion between these two sets of reasons best suited to the preservation of the state is not the least important of political talents. In general it can be said that the reasons for expansion, being only external and relative, must be subordinate to those for contraction, which are internal and absolute. A strong, sound constitution is the first thing to be sought, and the vigor that comes from good government is more likely to create it than the resources provided by a large territory.

There have been states so constituted that a need for conquest was an integral part of their constitution, so that they were forced to expand constantly in order to maintain themselves. They may have been glad to be under that necessity, but it meant that their downfall was inevitable as soon as their greatness came to an end.

A body politic can be measured in two ways: by the area of its territory and by the number of its people. The optimum size of a state depends on the relation between these two factors. Men make the state, and land sustains them. The proper relation is therefore achieved when the land is able to feed all its inhabitants and there are as many inhabitants as the land can feed. This proportion ensures the maximum strength of a given number of people, for if there is too much territory, it is expensive to maintain, its cultivation is inadequate, its produce is excessive, and it soon gives rise to defensive wars; but if there is not enough, the state must rely on the willingness of its neighbors to supply it with what it lacks, and this soon leads to offensive wars. Any people in a situation that allows it only a choice between commerce and war is weak in itself: It depends on its neighbors, it depends on events, and its existence can only be uncertain and short. It will either conquer and change its situation, or be conquered and cease to exist. It can remain free only by becoming smaller or larger.

There can be no fixed, mathematically precise ratio between a given area of land and the ideal number of inhabitants for it, because of differences not only in the quality of the soil, its fertility, the nature of its produce, and the influence of climate, but also in the temperaments of its inhabitants, for some people consume little in a fertile region, while others consume much in a barren one. We must also consider the fecundity of the women, the features of the country that are favorable or unfavorable to population growth, and the extent to which the lawgiver can expect to further that growth by his institutions, for he must base his judgment not on what he sees, but on what he foresees, and he must consider not so much the present size of the population as the size it should naturally reach. Finally, there are many situations where special features of the terrain make it necessary or possible to take in more land than might seem to be needed. The population will be more thinly spread in mountainous country, for example, where the natural products, namely, timber and grazing animals, require less work, where experience shows that women are more fecund than in the plains, and where the great area occupied by slopes leaves only a small amount of level ground, which is all that can be relied on for vegetation. Along the seashore, however, population can be denser, even where there are rocks and almost sterile sand, because fishing can to a large extent compensate for the inadequacy of agriculture, because people need to be closer together in order to repulse pirates, and because it is easier to get rid of excess population by means of colonies.

To these conditions for the founding of a people, we must add one which can take the place of no other, but without which all the others would be useless: There must be peace and abundance, for a state is like a battalion, in that the time when it is being formed is the time when it is least capable of offering resistance and easiest to destroy. It could defend itself better in total disorder than in a period of ferment when everyone is concerned with his personal position and not with the common danger. If there is a war, a famine, or a rebellion during that critical time, the state will inevitably be overthrown.

Not that there have not been many governments established during such storms; but then it is the governments themselves that destroy the state. Taking advantage of public panic, usurpers always choose or foment troubled times to enact destructive laws that the people would never adopt in its normal frame of mind. Noting the time chosen for establishing a people's institutions is one of the surest ways to distinguish the work of a lawgiver from that of a tyrant.

What kind of a people, then, is fit to receive laws? One that is already bound together by some tie of origin, interest, or agreement, but has not yet borne the real yoke of law; one that has no deeply rooted customs or superstitions; one that has no fear of being overwhelmed by a sudden invasion, and while remaining aloof from the quarrels of its neighbors, is capable of withstanding any of them alone, or of enlisting the aid of one to repel another; one in which each man can be known to all, and in which there is no need to place a larger burden on anyone than he can bear; one that can do without other peoples, and that all other peoples can do without; one that is neither rich nor poor and can be self-sufficient; and finally, one that combines the stability of an ancient people with the malleability of a new one. What makes the work of the lawgiver difficult is not so much what must be established as what must be destroyed; and what makes success so rare is the impossibility of finding the simplicity of nature together with the needs that arise in society. All these conditions, it is true, cannot easily be combined, which is why there are so few well-constituted states.

There is still one European country capable of receiving laws: the island of Corsica. The valor and steadfastness with which that brave people has recovered and defended its freedom make it deserve to be taught by some wise man how to preserve that freedom. I have a presentiment that some day that little island will astonish Europe.

Various Systems of Law

If we seek to determine precisely what constitutes the greatest good of all, which should be the goal of every system of law, we find that it can be reduced to these two main elements: *freedom* and *equality*. Freedom, because any individual dependence is so much strength taken away from the state; equality, because there can be no freedom without it.

I have already said what civil freedom is. As for equality, the word must not be taken to imply that power and wealth are to be exactly the same for everyone, but rather that power shall not reach the point of violence and shall never be exercised except by virtue of rank and law, and that, so far as wealth is concerned, no citizen shall be rich enough to be able to buy another, and none poor enough to be forced to sell himself. This presupposes moderation with regard to property and influence on the part of those in high positions, and moderation with regard to avarice and covetousness on the part of those in humbler circumstances.

It will be said that such equality is a speculative fancy which cannot exist in reality. But if abuse is inevitable, does it follow that it should not at least be controlled? Precisely because the force of events always tends to destroy equality, the force of law should always tend to uphold it.

But these general objectives of all good institutions must be modified in each country to fit the relations arising from the local situation and the character of the inhabitants, and it is on the basis of these relations that each people must be given the particular system of institutions that will be best, not perhaps in itself, but for the country for which it is intended. For example, is your soil unproductive, or is your territory too small for the number of inhabitants? Then turn to crafts and industry, so that you exchange your products for the foodstuffs you lack. Or, on the other hand, do you live on rich plains and fertile slopes, with good land and too few inhabitants? Then direct all your efforts to agriculture, which increases population, and banish manufacturing, which would further depopulate the countryside by draining off its inhabitants and concentrating them in towns. Do you have a long and accessible coastline? Then cover the sea with vessels, develop trade and shipping; you will have a glorious and short existence. Does the sea along your shores wash against nothing but forbidding rocks? Then remain fish-eating barbarians; you will live more peacefully, perhaps better, and certainly more happily. In short, besides the principles that are common to all, each people has within itself something that orders those principles in a special way and makes its system of law suitable for it alone. Thus long ago the Hebrews, and more recently the Arabs, took religion as their main object; for the

Athenians, it was literature; for Carthage and Tyre, commerce; for Rhodes, seafaring; for Sparta, war; and for Rome, virtue. The author of *The Spirit of the Laws* has shown with abundant examples how the art of the lawgiver directs institutions toward each of these objects.

The constitution of a state is truly strong and durable when there is such close observance of what is proper that natural relations are in harmony with law on every point, and law serves only, so to speak, to assure, accompany, and rectify them. But if the lawgiver mistakes his object and adopts a principle different from the one that is called for by circumstances — if one tends toward servitude and the other toward freedom, or one toward wealth and the other toward population growth, or one toward peace and the other toward conquest — then the laws will gradually be weakened, the constitution will deteriorate, and the state will be in constant turmoil until it is either destroyed or changed, and invincible nature regains its dominion.

Classification of Laws

To bring order to the whole, or give the best possible form to the state, various relations must be considered. First, there is the action of the entire body on itself, that is, the relation of the whole to the whole, or of the sovereign to the state, and this relation is composed of relations among intermediate terms, as we shall see later.

The laws governing this relation are known as political laws, and are also called fundamental laws, not without reason if they are wisely conceived. For if there is in each state only one good way of ordering it, the people that has found it should hold to it, but if the established order is bad, why should the laws that prevent it from being good be considered fundamental? In any case, moreover, the people is always free to change its laws, even the best ones, for if it chooses to harm itself, who has a right to prevent it?

The second relation is that of the members among themselves, or with the entire body politic. This relation should be as small as possible in the first case and as great as possible in the second, so that each citizen will be completely independent of all the others and extremely dependent on the state. This is always done by the same means, since only the power of the state makes its members free. It is from this second relation that civil laws arise.

We may consider a third kind of relation between the individual and the law: that of disobedience and punishment. It gives rise to criminal laws, which are actually less a specific type of law than the sanction of all others.

In addition to these three kinds of law, there is a fourth, the most important of all. It is engraved in neither marble nor brass, but in the hearts of the citizens; it forms the true constitution of the state; it renews its vigor every day, and when other laws become obsolete or ineffective, it restores or replaces them; it keeps the people in the spirit of its institutions, and gradually substitutes the force of habit for that of authority. I am referring to morals, customs, and above all, public opinion. This category of laws is unknown to our political theorists, but it is essential to the success of all the others; the great lawgiver concerns himself with it in secret, while seeming to limit himself to specific regulations that are only the sides of the arch, whereas morals, slower to develop, eventually form its unshakable keystone.

Of these various classes, only political law, which constitute the form of government, are relevant to my subject.

What is Enlightenment?

Immanuel Kant

Enlightenment is man's emergence from his self-imposed immaturity. Immaturity is the inability to use one's understanding without guidance from another. This immaturity is self-imposed when its cause lies not in lack of understanding, but in lack of resolve and courage to use it without guidance from another. *Sapere Aude*! [dare to know] "Have courage to use your own understanding!" — that is the motto of enlightenment.

Laziness and cowardice are the reasons why so great a proportion of men, long after nature has released them from alien guidance (natura-liter maiorennes), nonetheless gladly remain in lifelong immaturity, and why it is so easy for others to establish themselves as their guardians. It is so easy to be immature. If I have a book to serve as my understanding, a pastor to serve as my conscience, a physician to determine my diet for me, and so on, I need not exert myself at all. I need not think, if only I can pay: others will readily undertake the irksome work for me. The guardians who have so benevolently taken over the supervision of men have carefully seen to it that the far greatest part of them (including the entire fair sex) regard taking the step to maturity as very dangerous, not to mention difficult. Having first made their domestic livestock dumb, and having carefully made sure that these docile creatures will not take a single step without the gocart to which they are harnessed, these guardians then show them the danger that threatens them, should they attempt to walk alone. Now this danger is not actually so great, for after falling a few times they would in the end certainly learn to walk; but an example of this kind makes men timid and usually frightens them out of all further attempts.

Thus, it is difficult for any individual man to work himself out of the immaturity that has all but become his nature. He has even become fond of this state and for the time being is actually incapable of using his own understanding, for no one has ever allowed him to attempt it. Rules and formulas, those mechanical aids to the rational use, or rather misuse, of his natural gifts, are the shackles of a permanent immaturity. Whoever threw them off would still make only an uncertain leap over the smallest ditch, since he is unaccustomed to this kind of free movement. Consequently, only a few have succeeded, by cultivating their own minds, in freeing themselves from immaturity and pursuing a secure course.

But that the public should enlighten itself is more likely; indeed, if it is only allowed freedom, enlightenment is almost inevitable. For even among the entrenched guardians of the great masses a few will always think for themselves, a few who, after having themselves thrown off the yoke of immaturity, will spread the spirit of a rational appreciation for both their own worth and for each person's calling to think for himself. But it should be particularly noted that if a public that was first placed in this yoke by the guardians is suitably aroused by some of those who are altogether incapable of enlightenment, it may force the guardians themselves to remain under the yoke — so pernicious is it to instill prejudices, for they finally take revenge upon their originators, or on their descendants. Thus a public can only attain enlightenment slowly. Perhaps a revolution can overthrow autocratic despotism and profiteering or power-grabbing oppression, but it can never truly reform a manner of thinking; instead, new prejudices, just like the old ones they replace, will serve as a leash for the great unthinking mass.

From *Konigsberg in Prussia*, 1784 by I. Kant.

Nothing is required for this enlightenment, however, except freedom; and the freedom in question is the least harmful of all, namely, the freedom to use reason publicly in all matters. But on all sides I hear: "Do not argue!" The officer says, "Do not argue, drill!" The tax man says, "Do not argue, pay!" The pastor says, "Do not argue, believe!" (Only one ruler in the World says, "Argue as much as you want and about what you want, but obey!") In this we have examples of pervasive restrictions on freedom. But which restriction hinders enlightenment and which does not, but instead actually advances it? I reply: The public use of one's reason must always be free, and it alone can bring about enlightenment among mankind; the private use of reason may, however, often be very narrowly restricted, without otherwise hindering the progress of enlightenment. By the public use of one's own reason I understand the use that anyone as a scholar makes of reason before the entire literate world. I call the private use of reason that which a person may make in a civic post or office that has been entrusted to him. Now in many affairs conducted in the interests of a community, a certain mechanism is required by means of which some of its members must conduct themselves in an entirely passive manner so that through an artificial unanimity the government may guide them toward public ends, or at least prevent them from destroying such ends. Here one certainly must not argue, instead one must obey. However, insofar as this part of the machine also regards himself as a member of the community as a whole, or even of the world community, and as a consequence addresses the public in the role of a scholar, in the proper sense of that term, he can most certainly argue, without thereby harming the affairs for which as a passive member he is partly responsible. Thus it would be disastrous if an officer on duty who was given a command by his superior were to question the appropriateness or utility of the order. He must obey. But as a scholar he cannot be justly constrained from making comments about errors in military service, or from placing them before the public for its judgment. The citizen cannot refuse to pay the taxes imposed on him; indeed, impertinent criticism of such levies, when they should be paid by him, can be punished as a scandal (since it can lead to widespread insubordination). But the same person does not act contrary to civic duty when, as a scholar, he publicly expresses his thoughts regarding the impropriety or even injustice of such taxes. Likewise a pastor is bound to instruct his catecumens and congregation in accordance with the symbol of the church he serves, for he was appointed on that condition. But as a scholar he has complete freedom, indeed even the calling, to impart to the public all of his carefully considered and well-intentioned thoughts concerning mistaken aspects of that symbol, as well as his suggestions for the better arrangement of religious and church matters. Nothing in this can weigh on his conscience. What he teaches in consequence of his office as a servant of the church he sets out as something with regard to which he has no discretion to teach in accord with his own lights; rather, he offers it under the direction and in the name of another. He will say, "Our church teaches this or that and these are the demonstrations it uses." He thereby extracts for his congregation all practical uses from precepts to which he would not himself subscribe with complete conviction, but whose presentation he can nonetheless undertake, since it is not entirely impossible that truth lies hidden in them, and, in any case, nothing contrary to the very nature of religion is to be found in them. If he believed he could find anything of the latter sort in them, he could not in good conscience serve in his position; he would have to resign. Thus an appointed teacher's use of his reason for the sake of his congregation is merely private, because, however large the congregation is, this use is always only domestic; in this regard, as a priest, he is not free and cannot be such because he is acting under instructions from someone else. By contrast, the cleric — as a scholar who speaks through his writings to the public as such, i.e., the world — enjoys in this public use of reason an unrestricted freedom to use his own rational capacities and to speak his own mind.

For that the (spiritual) guardians of a people should themselves be immature is an absurdity that would insure the perpetuation of absurdities.

But would a society of pastors, perhaps a church assembly or venerable presbytery (as those among the Dutch call themselves), not be justified in binding itself by oath to a certain unalterable symbol in order to secure a constant guardianship over each of its members and through them over the people, and this for all time: I say that this is wholly impossible. Such a contract, whose intention is to preclude forever all further enlightenment of the human race, is absolutely null and void, even if it should be ratified by the supreme power, by parliaments, and by the most solemn peace treaties. One age cannot bind itself, and thus conspire, to place a succeeding one in a condition whereby it would be impossible for the later age to expand its knowledge (particularly where it is so very important), to rid itself of errors, and generally to increase its enlightenment. That would be a crime against human nature, whose essential destiny lies precisely in such progress; subsequent generations are thus completely justified in dismissing such agreements as unauthorized and criminal. The criterion of everything that can be agreed upon as a law by a people lies in this question: Can a people impose such a law on itself? Now it might be possible, in anticipation of a better state of affairs, to introduce a provisional order for a specific, short time, all the while giving all citizens, especially clergy, in their role as scholars, the freedom to comment publicly, i.e., in writing, on the present institution's shortcomings. The provisional order might last until insight into the nature of these matters had become so widespread and obvious that the combined (if not unanimous) voices of the populace could propose to the crown that it take under its protection those congregations that, in accord with their newly gained insight, had organized themselves under altered religious institutions, but without interfering with those wishing to allow matters to remain as before. However, it is absolutely forbidden that they unite into a religious organization that nobody may for the duration of a man's lifetime publicly question, for so doing would deny, render fruitless, and make detrimental to succeeding generations an era in man's progress toward improvement. A man may put off enlightenment with regard to what he ought to know, though only for a short time and for his own person; but to renounce it for himself, or, even more, for subsequent generations, is to violate and trample man's divine rights underfoot. And what a people may not decree for itself may still less be imposed on it by a monarch, for his lawgiving authority rests on his unification of the people's collective will in his own. If he only sees to it that all genuine or purported improvement is consonant with civil order, he can allow his subjects to do what they find necessary to their spiritual well-being, which is not his affair. However, he must prevent anyone from forcibly interfering with another's working as best he can to determine and promote his well-being. It detracts from his own majesty when he interferes in these matters, since the writings in which his subjects attempt to clarify their insights lend value to his conception of governance. This holds whether he acts from his own highest insight — whereby he calls upon himself the reproach, "Caesar non eat supra grammaticos." — as well as, indeed even more, when he despoils his highest authority by supporting the spiritual despotism of some tyrants in his state over his other subjects.

If it is now asked, "Do we presently live in an enlightened age?" the answer is, "No, but we do live in an age of enlightenment." As matters now stand, a great deal is still lacking in order for men as a whole to be, or even to put themselves into a position to be able without external guidance to apply understanding confidently to religious issues. But we do have clear indications that the way is now being opened for men to proceed freely in this direction and that the obstacles to general enlightenment — to their release from their self-imposed immaturity — are gradually diminishing. In this regard, this age is the age of enlightenment, the century of Frederick.

A prince who does not find it beneath him to say that he takes it to be his duty to prescribe nothing, but rather to allow men complete freedom in religious matters — who thereby renounces the arrogant title of tolerance — is himself enlightened and deserves to be praised by a grateful present and by posterity as the first, at least where the government is concerned, to release the human race from immaturity and to leave everyone free to use his own reason in all matters of conscience. Under his rule, venerable pastors, in their role as scholars and without prejudice to their official duties, may freely and openly set out for the world's scrutiny their judgments and views, even where these occasionally differ from the accepted symbol. Still greater freedom is afforded to those who are not restricted by an official post. This spirit of freedom is expanding even where it must struggle against the external obstacles of governments that misunderstand their own function. Such governments are illuminated by the example that the existence of freedom need not give cause for the least concern regarding public order and harmony in the commonwealth. If only they refrain from inventing artifices to keep themselves in it, men will gradually raise themselves from barbarism.

I have focused on religious matters in setting out my main point concerning enlightenment, i.e., man's emergence from self-imposed immaturity, first because our rulers have no interest in assuming the role of their subjects' guardians with respect to the arts and sciences, and secondly because that form of immaturity is both the most pernicious and disgraceful of all. But the manner of thinking of a head of state who favors religious enlightenment goes even further, for he realizes that there is no danger to his legislation in allowing his subjects to use reason publicly and to set before the world their thoughts concerning better formulations of his laws, even if this involves frank criticism of legislation currently in effect. We have before us a shining example, with respect to which no monarch surpasses the one whom we honor.

But only a ruler who is himself enlightened and has no dread of shadows, yet who likewise has a well-disciplined, numerous army to guarantee public peace, can say what no republic may dare, namely: "Argue as much as you want and about what you want, but obey!" Here as elsewhere, when things are considered in broad perspective, a strange, unexpected pattern in human affairs reveals itself, one in which almost everything is paradoxical. A greater degree of civil freedom seems advantageous to a people's spiritual freedom; yet the former established impassable boundaries for the latter; conversely, a lesser degree of civil freedom provides enough room for all fully to expand their abilities. Thus, once nature has removed the hard shell from this kernel for which she has most fondly cared, namely, the inclination to and vocation for free thinking, the kernel gradually reacts on a people's mentality (whereby they become increasingly able to act freely), and it finally even influences the principles of government, which finds that it can profit by treating men, who are now more than machines, in accord with their dignity.

I. Kant
Konigsberg in Prussia, 30 September 1784

The Interesting Narrative of the Life of Olaudah Equiano, or Gustavus Vassa, the African

Olaudah Equiano

Edited by Robert J. Allison

Olaudah Equiano

or

GUSTAVUS VASSA,

the African

Daniel Orme after William Denton, *Olaudah Equiano, or Gustavus Vassa, the African.*
Frontispiece, Volume I. Engraving, 1789. **Library of Congress.**

From *The Interesting Narrative of the Life of Olaudah Equiano* by Olaudah Equiano, 1789.

THE

INTERESTING NARRATIVE

OF

THE LIFE

OF

OLAUDAH EQUIANO,

OR

GUSTAVUS VASSA,

THE AFRICAN.

WRITTEN BY HIMSELF.

VOL I.

Behold, God is my salvation; I will trust and not be afraid, for the Lord Jehovah is my strength and my song; he also is become my salvation.

And in that day shall ye say, Praise the Lord, call upon his name, declare his doings among the people. Isaiah xii. 2, 4.

LONDON:

Printed for and sold by the AUTHOR, No. 10, Union-Street, Middlesex Hospital;

Sold also by Mr. Johnson, St. Paul's Church-Yard; Mr. Murray, Fleet-Street; Messrs. Robson and Clark, Bond-Street; Mr. Davis, opposite Gray's Inn, Holborn; Messrs. Shepperson and Reynolds, and Mr. Jackson, Oxford-Street; Mr. Lackington, Chiswell-Street; Mr. Mathews, Strand; Mr. Murray, Prince's-Street, Soho; Mess. Taylor and Co. South Arch, Royal Exchange; Mr. Button, Newington-Causeway; Mr. Parsons, Paternoster-Row; and may be had of all the Booksellers in Town and Country.

[Entered at Stationer's Hall.]

Title Page of the First Edition, London, 1789. **Courtesy of the Senate House Library, University of London.**

TO THE LORDS SPIRITUAL AND TEMPORAL, AND THE
COMMONS OF THE PARLIAMENT OF GREAT BRITAIN.

My Lords and Gentlemen,

Permit me, with the greatest deference and respect, to lay at your feet the following genuine Narrative; the chief design of which is to excite in your august assemblies a sense of compassion for the miseries which the Slave-Trade has entailed on my unfortunate countrymen. By the horrors of that trade was I first torn away from all the tender connexions that were naturally dear to my heart; but these, through the mysterious ways of Providence, I ought to regard as infinitely more than compensated by the introduction I have thence obtained to the knowledge of the Christian religion, and of a nation which, by its liberal sentiments, its humanity, the glorious freedom of its government, and its proficiency in arts and sciences, has exalted the dignity of human nature.

I am sensible I ought to entreat your pardon for addressing to you a work so wholly devoid of literary merit; but, as the production of an unlettered African, who is actuated by the hope of becoming an instrument towards the relief of his suffering countrymen, I trust that *such a man*, pleading in *such a cause*, will be acquitted of boldness and presumption.

May the God of heaven inspire your hearts with peculiar benevolence on that important day when the question of Abolition is to be discussed, when thousands, in consequence of your Determination, are to look for Happiness or Misery!

I am, My Lords and Gentlemen,
Your most obedient,
And devoted humble Servant,

OLAUDAH EQUIANO,
or
GUSTAVUS VASSA.

Union-Street, Mary-le-bone,
March 24, 1789.

Note: The following text maintains the sometimes antiquated and irregular spelling of the 1789 edition.

I believe it is difficult for those who publish their own memoirs to escape the imputation of vanity; nor is this the only disadvantage under which they labour: it is also their misfortune, that what is uncommon is rarely, if ever, believed, and what is obvious we are apt to turn from with disgust, and to charge the writer with impertinence. People generally think those memoirs only worthy to be read or remembered which abound in great or striking events, those, in short, which in a high degree excite either admiration or pity: all others they consign to contempt and oblivion. It is therefore, I confess, not a little hazardous in a private and obscure individual, and a stranger too, thus to solicit the indulgent attention of the public; especially when I own I offer here the history of neither a saint, a hero, nor a tyrant. I believe there are few events in my life, which have not happened to many: it is true the incidents of it are numerous; and, did I consider myself an European, I might say my sufferings were great: but when I compare my lot with that of most of my countrymen, I regard myself as a *particular favourite of Heaven*, and acknowledge the mercies of Providence in every occurrence of my life. If then the following narrative does not appear sufficiently interesting to engage general attention, let my motive be some excuse for its publication. I am not so foolishly vain as to expect from it either immortality or literary reputation. If it affords any satisfaction to my numerous friends, at whose request it has been written, or in the smallest degree promotes the interests of humanity, the ends for which it was undertaken will be fully attained, and every wish of my heart gratified. Let it therefore be remembered, that, in wishing to avoid censure, I do not aspire to praise.

That part of Africa, known by the name of Guinea, to which the trade for slaves is carried on, extends along the coast above 3400 miles, from the Senegal to Angola, and includes a variety of kingdoms. Of these the most considerable is the kingdom of Benen, both as to extent and wealth, the richness and cultivation of the soil, the power of its king, and the number and warlike disposition of the inhabitants. It is situated nearly under the line, and extends along the coast about 170 miles, but runs back into the interior part of Africa to a distance hitherto I believe unexplored by any traveller; and seems only terminated at length by the empire of Abyssinia, near 1500 miles from its beginning. This kingdom is divided into many provinces or districts: in one of the most remote and fertile of which, called Eboe, I was born, in the year 1745, in a charming fruitful vale, named Essaka. The distance of this province from the capital of Benin and the sea coast must be very considerable; for I had never heard of white men or Europeans, nor of the sea: and our subjection to the king of Benin was little more than nominal; for every transaction of the government, as far as my slender observation extended, was conducted by the chiefs or elders of the place. The manners and government of a people who have little commerce with other countries are generally very simple; and the history of what passes in one family or village may serve as a specimen of a nation. My father was one of those elders or chiefs I have spoken of, and was styled Embrenche, a term, as I remember, importing the highest distinction, and signifying in our language a *mark* of grandeur. This mark is conferred on the person entitled to it, by cutting the skin across at the top of the forehead, and drawing it down to the eye-brows; and while it is in this situation applying a warm hand, and rubbing it until it shrinks up into a thick *weal* across the lower part of the forehead. Most of the judges and senators were thus marked, my father had long born it: I had seen it conferred on one of my brothers, and I was also *destined* to receive it by my parents. Those Embrenche, or chief men, decided disputes and punished crimes; for which purpose they always assembled together. The proceedings were generally short; and in most cases the law of retaliation prevailed. I remember a man was brought before my father, and the other judges, for kidnapping a boy; and, although he was the son of a chief or senator, he was condemned to make recompense by a man or woman slave. Adultery, however, was sometimes punished with slavery or death; a punishment which I believe is inflicted on it throughout most of the nations of Africa. so sacred among them is the honour of the marriage bed, and so jealous are they of the fidelity of their wives. Of this I recollect an instance: — a woman was convicted before the judges of adultery, and delivered over, as the custom was, to her husband to be punished. Accordingly he determined to put her to death: but it being found, just before her execution, that she had an infant at her breast; and no woman being prevailed on to perform the part of a nurse, she was spared on account of the child. The men, however, do not preserve the same constancy to their wives, which they expect from them; for they indulge in a plurality, though seldom in more than two. Their mode of marriage is thus: — both parties are usually betrothed when young by their parents, (though I have known the males to betroth themselves). On this occasion a feast is prepared, and the bride and bridegroom stand up in the midst of all their friends, who are assembled for the purpose, while he declares she is thenceforth to be looked upon as his wife, and that no other person is to pay any addresses to her. This is also immediately proclaimed in the vicinity, on which the bride retires from the assembly. Some time after she is brought home to her husband, and then another feast is made, to which the relations of both parties are invited: her parents then deliver her to the bridegroom, accompanied with a number of blessings, and at the same time they tie round her waist a cotton string of the thickness of a goose-quill, which none but married women are permitted to wear: she is now considered as completely his wife; and at this time the dowry is given to the new married pair, which generally consists of portions of land, slaves, and cattle, house-hold goods, and implements of husbandry. These are offered by the friends of both parties; besides which the parents of the bridegroom present gifts to those of the bride, whose property she is looked upon before marriage; but after it she is esteemed the sole property of her husband. The ceremony being now ended the festival begins, which is celebrated with bonfires, and loud acclamations of joy, accompanied with music and dancing.

We are almost a nation of dancers, musicians, and poets. Thus every great event, such as a triumphant return from battle, or other cause of public rejoicing is celebrated in public dances, which are accompanied with songs and music suited to the occasion. The assembly is separated into four divisions, which dance either apart or in succession, and each with a character peculiar to itself. The first division contains the married men, who in their dances frequently exhibit feats of arms, and the representation of a battle. To these succeed the married women, who dance in the second division. The young men occupy the third; and the maidens the fourth. Each represents some interesting scene of real life, such as a great achievement, domestic employment, a pathetic story or some rural sport; and as the subject is generally founded on some recent event, it is therefore ever new. This gives our dances a spirit and variety which I have scarcely seen elsewhere. We have many musical instruments, particularly drums of different kinds, a piece of music which resembles a guitar, and another much like a stickado. These last are chiefly used by betrothed virgins, who play on them on all grand festivals.

As our manners are simple, our luxuries are few. The dress of both sexes is nearly the same. It generally consists of a long piece of calico, or muslin, wrapped loosely round the body, somewhat in the form of a highland plaid. This is usually dyed blue, which is our favourite colour. It is extracted from a berry, and is brighter and richer than any I have seen in Europe. Besides this, our women of distinction wear golden ornaments; which they dispose with some profusion on their arms and legs. When our women are not employed with the men in tillage, their usual occupation is spinning and weaving cotton, which they afterwards dye, and make it into garments. They also manufacture earthen vessels, of which we have many kinds. Among the rest tobacco pipes, made after the same fashion, and used in the same manner, as those in Turkey.

Our manner of living is entirely plain; for as yet the natives are unacquainted with those refinements in cookery which debauch the taste: bullocks, goats, and poultry, supply the greatest part of their food. These constitute likewise the principal wealth of the country, and the chief articles of its commerce. The flesh is usually stewed in a pan; to make it savoury we sometimes use also pepper, and other spices, and we have salt made of wood ashes. Our vegetables are mostly plantains, eadas, yams, beans, and Indian corn. The head of the family usually eats alone; his wives and slaves have also their separate tables. Before we taste the food we always wash our hands: indeed our cleanliness on all occasions is extreme; but on this it is an indispensable ceremony. After washing, libation is made, by pouring out a small portion of the food, in a certain place, for the spirits of departed relations, which the natives suppose to preside over their conduct, and guard them from evil. They are totally unacquainted with strong or spirituous liquours; and their principal beverage is palm wine. This is gotten from a tree of that name by tapping it at the top, and fastening a large gourd to it; and sometimes one tree will yield three or four gallons in a night. When just drawn it is of a most delicious sweetness; but in a few days it acquires a tartish and more spirituous flavour: though I never saw any one intoxicated by it. The same tree also produces nuts and oil. Our principal luxury is in perfumes; one sort of these is an odoriferous wood of delicious fragrance: the other a kind of earth; a small portion of which thrown into the fire diffuses a most powerful odour. We beat this wood into powder, and mix it with palm oil; with which both men and women perfume themselves.

In our buildings we study convenience rather than ornament. Each master of a family has a large square piece of ground, surrounded with a moat or fence, or enclosed with a wall made of red earth tempered; which, when dry, is as hard as brick. Within this are his houses to accommodate his family and slaves; which, if numerous, frequently present the appearance of a village. In the middle stands the principal building, appropriated to the sole use of the master, and consisting of two apartments; in one of which he sits in the day with his family, the other is left apart for the reception of his friends. He has besides these a distinct apartment in which he sleeps, together with his male children. On each side their families, are distributed the apartments of his wives, who have also their families are distributed throughout the rest of the enclosure. These houses never exceed one story in height: they are always built of wood, or stakes driven into the ground, crossed with wattles, and neatly plastered within, and without. The roof is thatched with reeds. Our day-houses are left open at the sides; but those in which we sleep are always covered, and plastered in the inside, with a composition mixed with cow-dung, to keep off the different insects, which annoy us during the night. The walls and floors also of these are generally covered with mats. Our beds consist of a platform, raised three or four feet from the ground, on which are laid skins, and different parts of spungy tree called plaintain. Our covering is calico or muslin, the same as our dress. The usual seats are a few logs of wood; but we have benches, which are generally perfumed, to accommodate strangers: these compose the greater part of our household furniture. Houses so constructed and furnished require but little skill to erect them. Every man is a sufficient architect for the purpose. The whole neighbourhood afford their unanimous assistance in building them and in return receive, and expect no other recompose than a feast.

As we live in a country where nature is prodigal of her favours, our wants are few and easily supplied; of course we have few manufactures. They consist for the most part of calicoes, earthern ware, ornaments, and instruments of war and husbandry. But these make no part of our commerce, the principal articles of which, as I have observed, are provisions. In such a state money is of little use; however we have some small pieces of coin, if I may call them such. They are made something like an anchor; but I do not remember either their value or denomination. We have also markets, at which I have been frequently with my mother. These are sometimes visited by stout mahogany-coloured men from the south west of us: we call them Oye-Eboe, which term signifies red men living at a distance. They generally bring us firearms, gunpowder, hats, beads, and dried fish. The last we esteemed a great rarity, as our waters were only brooks and springs. These articles they barter with us for odoriferous woods and earth, and our salt of wood ashes. They always carry slaves through our land; but the strictest account is exacted of their manner of procuring them, before they are suffered to pass. Sometimes indeed we sold slaves to them, but they were only prisoners of war, or such among us as had been convicted of kidnapping, or adultery, and some other crimes, which we esteemed heinous. This practice of kidnapping induces me to think, that, notwithstanding all our strictness, their principal business among us was to trepan our people. I remember too they carried great sacks along with them, which not long after I had an opportunity of fatally seeing applied to that infamous purpose.

Our land is uncommonly rich and fruitful, and produces all kinds of vegetables in great abundance. We have plenty of Indian corn, and vast quantities of cotton and tobacco. Our pine apples grow without culture; they are about the size of the largest sugar-loaf, and finely flavoured. We have also spices of different kinds, particularly pepper; and a variety of delicious fruits which I have never seen in Europe; together with gums of various kinds, and honey in abundance. All our industry is exerted to improve those blessings of nature. Agriculture is our chief employment; and every one, even the children and women, are engaged in it. Thus we are all habituated to labour from our earliest years. Every one contributes something to the common stock; and as we are unacquainted with idleness, we have no beggars. The benefits of such a mode of living are obvious. The West India planters prefer the slaves of Benin or Eboe to those of any other part of Guinea, for their hardiness, intelligence, integrity, and zeal. Those benefits are felt by us in the general healthiness of the people, and in their vigour and activity; I might have added too in their comeliness. Deformity is indeed unknown amongst us, I mean that of shape. Numbers of the natives of Eboe now in London might be brought in support of this assertion: for, in regard to complexion, ideas of beauty are wholly relative. I remember while in Africa to have seen three negro children, who were tawny, and another quite white, who were universally regarded by myself, and the natives in general, as far as related to their complexions, as deformed. Our women too were in my eyes at least uncommonly graceful, alert, and modest to a degree of bashfulness; nor do I remember to have ever heard of an instance of incontinence amongst them before marriage. They are also remarkably cheerful. Indeed cheerfulness and affability are two of the leading characteristics of our nation.

Our tillage is exercised in a large plain or common, some hours' walk from our dwellings, and all the neighbours resort thither in a body. They use no beasts of husbandry, and their only instruments are hoes, axes, shovels, and beaks, or pointed iron to dig with. Sometimes we are visited by locusts, which come in large clouds, so as to darken the air, and destroy our harvest. This however happens rarely, but when it does, a famine is produced by it. I remember an instance or two wherein this happened. This common is often the theatre of war; and therefore when our people go out to till their land, they not only go in a body, but generally take their arms with them for fear of a surprise; and when they apprehend an invasion they guard the avenues to their dwellings, by driving sticks into the ground, which are so sharp at one end as to pierce the foot, and are generally dipt in poison. From what I can recollect of these battles, they appear to have been irruptions of one little state or district on the other, to obtain prisoners to booty. Perhaps they were incited to this by those traders who brought the European goods I mentioned amongst us. Such a mode of obtaining slaves in Africa is common; and I believe more are procured this way and by kidnapping, than any other. When a trader wants slaves, he applies to a chief for them, and tempts him with his wares. It is not extraordinary, if on this occasion he yields to the temptation with as little firmness, and accepts the price of his fellow creatures' liberty with as little reluctance as the enlightened merchant. Accordingly he falls on his neighbours, and a desperate battle ensues. If he prevails and takes prisoners, he gratifies his avarice by selling them; but, if his party be vanquished, and he falls into the hands of the enemy, he is put to death: for, as he has been known to foment their quarrels, it is thought dangerous to let him survive, and no ransom can save him, though all other prisoners may be redeemed. We have fire-arms, bows and arrows, broad two-edged swords and javelins: we have shields also which cover a man from head to foot. All are taught the use of these weapons; even our women are warriors, and march boldly out to fight along with the men. Our whole district is a kind of militia: on a certain signal given, such as the firing of a gun at night, they all rise in arms and rush upon their enemy. It is perhaps something remarkable, that when our people march to the field a red flag or banner is borne before them. I was once a witness to a battle in our common. We had been all at work in it one day as usual, when our people were suddenly attacked. I climbed a tree at some distance, from which I beheld the fight. There were many women as well as men on both sides; among others my mother was there, and armed with a broad sword. After fighting for a considerable time with great fury, and after many had been killed our people obtained the victory, and took their enemy's Chief prisoner. He was carried off in great triumph, and, though he offered a large ransom for his life, he was put to death. A virgin of note among our enemies had been slain in the battle, and her arm was exposed in our market-place, where our trophies were always exhibited. The spoils were divided according to the merit of the warriors. Those prisoners which were not sold or redeemed we kept as slaves: but how different was their condition from that of the slaves in the West Indies! With us they do no more work than other members of the community, even their masters; their food, clothing and lodging were nearly the same as theirs, (except that they were not permitted to eat with those who were free-born); and there was scarce any other difference between them, than a superior degree of importance which the head of a family possesses in our state, and that authority which, as such, he exercises over every part of his household. Some of these slaves have even slaves under them as their own property, and for their own use.

As to religion, the natives believe that there is one Creator of all things, and that he lives in the sun, and is girted round with a belt that he may never eat or drink; but, according to some, he smokes a pipe, which is our own favourite luxury. They believe he governs events, especially our deaths or captivity; but, as for the doctrine of eternity, I do not remember to have ever heard of it: some however believe in the transmigration of souls in a certain degree. Those spirits, which are not transmigrated, such as our dear friends or relations, they believe always attend them, and guard them from the bad spirits or their foes. For this reason they always before eating, as I have observed, put some small portion of the meat, and pour some of their drink, on the ground for them; and they often make oblations of the blood of beasts or fowls at their graves. I was very fond of my mother, and almost constantly with her. When she went to make these oblations at her mother's tomb, which was a kind of small solitary thatched house, I sometimes attended her. There she made her libations, and spent most of the night in cries and lamentations. I have been often extremely terrified on these occasions. The loneliness of the place, the darkness of the night, and the ceremony of libation, naturally awful and gloomy, were heightened by my mother's lamentations, and these, concurring with the cries of doleful birds, by which these places were frequented, gave an inexpressible terror to the scene.

We compute the year from the day on which the sun crosses the line, and on its setting that evening there is a general shout throughout the land; at least I can speak from my own knowledge throughout our vicinity. The people at the same time make a great noise with rattles, not unlike the basket rattles used by children here, though much larger, and hold up their hands to heaven for a blessing. It is then the greatest offerings are made; and those children whom our wise men foretell will be fortunate are then presented to different people. I remember many used to come to see me, and I was carried about to others for that purpose. They have many offerings, particularly at full moons; generally two at harvest before the fruits are taken out of the ground: and when any young animals are killed, sometimes they offer up part of them as a sacrifice. These offerings, when made by one of the heads of a family, serve for the whole. I remember we often had them at my father's and my uncle's, and their families have been present. Some of our offerings are eaten with bitter herbs. We had a saying among us to any one of a cross temper, "That if they were to be eaten, they should be eaten with bitter herbs."

We practiced circumcision like the Jews, and made offerings and feasts on that occasion in the same manner as they did. Like them also, our children were named from some event, some circumstance, or fancied foreboding at the time of their birth. I was named *Olaudah*, which, in our language, signifies vicissitude or fortune also, one favoured, and having a loud voice and well spoken. I remember we never polluted the name of the object of our adoration; on the contrary, it was always mentioned with the greatest reverence; and we were totally unacquainted with swearing, and all those terms of abuse and reproach which find their way so readily and copiously into the languages of more civilized people. The only expressions of that kind I remember were "May you not, or may you swell, or may a beast take you."

I have before remarked that the natives of this part of Africa are extremely cleanly. This necessary habit of decency was with us a part of religion, and therefore we had many purifications and washings; indeed almost as many, and used on the same occasions, if my recollection does not fail me, as the Jews. Those that touched the dead at any time were obliged to wash and purify themselves before they could enter a dwelling-house. Every woman too, at certain times, was forbidden to come into a dwelling-house, or touch any person, or any thing we ate. I was so fond of my mother I could not keep from her, or avoid touching her at some of those periods, in consequence of which I was obliged to be kept out with her, in a little house made for that purpose, till offering was made, and then we were purified.

Though we had no places of public worship, we had priests and magicians, or wise men. I do not remember whether they had different offices, or whether they were united in the same persons, but they were held in great reverence by the people. They calculated our time, and foretold events, as their name imported, for we called them Ahaffoe-way-cah, which signifies calculators or yearly men, our year being called Ahaffoe. They wore their beards, and when they died they were succeeded by their sons. Most of their implements and things of value were interred along with them. Pipes and tobacco were also put into the grave with the corpse, which was always perfumed and ornamented, and animals were offered in sacrifice to them. None accompanied their funerals but those of the same profession or tribe. These buried them after sunset, and always returned from the grave by a different way from that which they went.

These magicians were also our doctors or physicians. They practiced bleeding by cupping; and were very successful in healing wounds and expelling poisons. They had likewise some extraordinary method of discovering jealousy, theft, and poisoning; the success of which no doubt they derived from their unbounded influence over the credulity and superstition of the people. I do not remember what those methods were, except that as to poisoning: I recollect an instance or two, which I hope it will not be deemed impertinent here to insert, as it may serve as a kind of specimen of the rest, and is still used by the negroes in the West Indies. A virgin had been poisoned, but it was not known by whom: the doctors ordered the corpse to be taken up by some persons, and carried to the grave. As soon as the bearers had raised it on their shoulders, they seemed seized with some, sudden impulse, and ran to and fro unable to stop themselves. At last, after having passed through a number of thorns and prickly bushes unhurt, the corpse fell from them close to a house, and defaced it in the fall; and, the owner being taken up, he immediately confessed the poisoning.

The natives are extremely cautious about poison. When they buy any capable seller kisses it all round before the buyer, to shew him it is not poisoned; and the same is done when any meat or drink is presented, particularly to a stranger. We have serpents of different kinds, some of which are esteemed ominous when they appear in our houses, and these we never molest. I remember two of those ominous snakes, each of which was as thick as the calf of a man's leg, and in colour resembling a dolphin in the water, crept at different times into my mother's night-house, where I always lay with her, and coiled themselves into folds, and each time they crowed like a cock. I was desired by some of our wise men to touch these, that I might be interested in the good omens, which I did, for they were quite harmless, and would tamely suffer themselves to be handled; and then they were put into a large open earthen pan, and set on one side of the highway. Some of our snakes, however, were poisonous: one of them crossed the road one day when I was standing on it, and passed between my feet without offering to touch me, to the great surprise of many who saw it; and these incidents were accounted by the wise men, and therefore by my mother and the rest of the people, as remarkable omens in my favour.

Such is the imperfect sketch my memory has furnished me with of the manners and customs of a people among whom I first drew my breath. And here I cannot forbear suggesting what has long struck me very forcibly, namely, the strong analogy which even by this sketch, imperfect as it is, appears to prevail in the manners and customs of my countrymen and those of the Jews, before they reached the Land of Promise, and particularly the partriarchs while they were yet in that pastoral state which is described in Genesis — an analogy, which alone would induce me to think that the one people had sprung from the other. Indeed this is the opinion of Dr. Gill, who, in his commentary on Genesis, very ably deduces the pedigree of the Africans from Afer and Afra, the descendants of Abraham by Keturah his wife and concubine (for both these titles are applied to her). It is also conformable to the sentiments of Dr. John Clarke, formerly Dean of Sarum, in his Truth of the Christian Religion: both these authors concur in ascribing to us this origin. The reasonings of these gentlemen are still further confirmed by the scripture chronology; and if any further corroboration were required, this resemblance in so many respects is a strong evidence in support of the opinion. Like the Israelites in their primitive state, our government was conducted by our chiefs or judges, our wise men and elders; and the head of a family with us enjoyed a similar authority over his household with that which is ascribed to Abraham and the other patriarchs. The law of retaliation obtained almost universally with us as with them: and even their religion appeared to have shed upon us a ray of its glory, though broken and spent in its passage, or eclipsed by the cloud with which time, tradition, and ignorance might have enveloped it; for we had our circumcision (a rule I believe peculiar to that people): we had also our sacrifices and burnt-offerings, our washings and purifications on the same occasions as they had.

As to the difference of colour between the Eboan Africans and the modern Jews, I shall not presume to account for it. It is a subject which has engaged the pens of men of both genius and learning, and is far above my strength. The most able and Reverend Mr. T. Clarkson, however, in his much admired Essay on the Slavery and Commerce of the Human Species, has ascertained the cause, in a manner that at once solves every objection on that account, and, on my mind at least, has produced the fullest conviction. I shall therefore refer to that performance for the theory, contenting myself with extracting a fact as related by Dr. Mitchel. "The Spaniards, who have inhabited America, under the torrid zone, for any time, are become as dark coloured as our native Indians of Virginia; of which *I myself have been a witness.*" There is also another instance of a Portuguese settlement at Mitomba, a river in Sierra Leona; where the inhabitants are bred from a mixture of the first Portuguese discoverers with the natives, and are now become in their complexion, and in the woolly quality of their hair, *perfect negroes*, retaining however a smattering of the Portuguese language.

These instances, and a great many more which might be adduced, while they shew how the complexions of the same persons vary in different climates, it is hoped may tend also to remove the prejudice that some conceive against the natives of Africa on account to their colour. Surely the minds of the Spaniards did not change with their complexions! Are there not causes enough to which the apparent inferiority of an African may be ascribed, without limiting the goodness of God, and supposing he forbore to stamp understanding on certainly his own image, because "carved in ebony," Might it not naturally be ascribed to their situation? When they come among Europeans, they are ignorant of their language, religion, manners, and customs. Are any pains taken to teach them these? Are they treated as men? Does not slavery itself depress the mind, and extinguish all its fire and every noble sentiment? But, above all, what advantages do not a refined people possess over those who are rude and uncultivated. Let the polished and haughty European recollect that his ancestors were once, like the Africans, uncivilized, and even barbarous. Did Nature make *them* inferior to their sons? And should *they* too have been made slaves? Every rational mind answers, No. Let such reflections as these melt the pride of their superiority into sympathy for the wants and miseries of their sable brethren, and compel them to acknowledge, that understanding is not confined to feature of color. If, when they look round the world, they feel exultation, let it be tempered with benevolence to others and gratitude to God, "who hath made of one blood all nations of men for to dwell on all the face of the earth, and whose wisdom is nor our wisdom, neither are our ways his ways."

> *The author's birth and parentage—His being kidnapped with his sister—Their separation—Surprise at meeting again—Are finally separated—Account of the different places and incidents the author met with till his arrival on the coast—The effect the sight of a slave ship had on him—He sails for the West Indies—Horrors of a slave ship—Arrives at Barbadoes, where the cargo is sold and dispersed.*

I hope the reader will not think I have trespassed on his patience in introducing myself to him with some account of the manners and customs of my country. They had been implanted in me with great care, and made an impression on my mind, which time could not erase, and which all the adversity and variety of fortune I have since experienced served only to rivet and record; for, whether the love of one's country be real or imaginary, of a lesson of reason, or an instinct of nature, I still look back with pleasure on the first scenes of my life, though that pleasure has been for the most part mingled with sorrow.

I have already acquainted the reader with the time and place of my birth. My father, besides many slaves, had a numerous family, of which seven lived to grow up, including myself and a sister, who was the only daughter. As I was the youngest of the sons, I became, of course, the greatest favourite with my mother, and was always with her; and she used to take particular pains to form my mind. I was trained up from my earliest years in the art of war; my daily exercise was shooting and throwing javelins; and my mother adorned me with emblems, after the manner of our greatest warriors. In this way I grew up till I was turned the age of eleven, when an end was put to my happiness in the following manner: — Generally when the grown people in the neighborhood were gone far in the fields to labour, the children assembled together in some of the neighbours' premises to play; and commonly some of us used to get up a tree to look out for any assailant, or kidnapper, that might come upon us; for they sometimes took those opportunities of our parents' absence to attack and carry off as any as they could seize. One day, as I was watching at the top of a tree in our yard, I saw one of those people come into the yard of our next neighbour but one, to kidnap, there being many stout young people in it. Immediately on this I gave the alarm of the rogue, and he was surrounded by the stoutest of them, who entangled him with cords, so that he could not escape till some of the grown people came and secured him. But alas! ere long it was my fate to be thus attacked, and to be carried off, when none of the grown people were nigh. One day, when all our people were gone out to their works as usual, and only I and my dear sister were left to mind the house, two men and a woman got over our walls, and in a moment seized us both, and without giving us time to cry out, or make resistance, they stopped our mouths, and ran off with us into the nearest wood. Here they tied our hands, and continued to carry us as far as they could, till night came on, when we reached a small house, where the robbers halted for refreshment, and spent the night. We were then unbound, but were unable to take any food; and, being quite overpowered by fatigue and grief, our only relief was some sleep, which allayed our misfortune for a short time. The next morning we left the house, and continued traveling all the day. For a long time we had kept the woods, but at last we came into a road which I believed I knew. I had now some hopes of being delivered; for we had advanced but a little way before I discovered some people at a distance, on which I began to cry out for their assistance: but my cries had no other effect than to make them tie me faster and stop my mouth, and then they put me into a large sack. They also stopped my sister's mouth, and tied her hands; and in this manner we proceeded till we were out of the sight of these people. When we went to rest the following night they offered us some victuals; but we refused it; and the only comfort we had in being in one another's arms all that night, and bathing each other with our tears. But alas! we were soon deprived of even the small comfort of weeping together. The next day proved a day of greater sorrow than I had yet experienced; for my sister and I were then separated, while we lay clasped in each other's arms. It was in vain that we besought them not to part us; she was torn from me, and immediately carried away, while I was left in a state of distraction not to be described. I cried and grieved continually; and for several days I did not eat any thing but what they forced into my mouth. At length, after many days travel-ing, during which I had often changed masters, I got into the hands of a chieftain, in a very pleasant country. This man had two wives and some children, and they all used me extremely well, and did all they could to comfort me; particularly the first wife, who was something like my mother. Although I was a great many days' journey from my father's house, yet these people spoke exactly the same language with us. This first master of mine, as I may call him, was a smith, and my principal employment was working his bellows, which were the same kind a I had seen in my vicinity. They were in some respects not unlike the stoves here in gentlemen's kitchens, and were covered over with leather, and in the middle of that leather a stick was fixed, and a person stood up, and worked it, in the same manner as is done to pump water out of a cask with a hand pump. I believe it was gold he worked, for it was of a lovely bright yellow colour, and was worn by the women in their wrists and ancles. I was there I sup-pose about a month, and they at last used to trust me some little distance from the house. This was liberty I used in embracing every opportunity to inquire the way to my own home: and I also sometimes, for the same purpose, went with the maidens, in the cool of the evenings, to bring pitchers of water from the springs for the use of the house. I had also remarked where the sun rose in the morning, and set in the evening, a I had travelled along, and I had observed that my father's house was towards the rising of the sun. I therefore determined to seize the first opportunity of making my escape, and to shape my course for that quarter; for I was quite oppressed and weighed down by grief after my mother and friends; and my love of lib-erty, ever great, was strengthened by the mortifying circumstance of not daring to eat with the free-born children, although I was mostly their companion. While I was projecting my escape, one day an unlucky event happened, which quite disconcerted my plan, and put an end to my hopes. I used to be sometimes employed in assisting an elderly woman slave to cook and take care of the poultry; and one morning, while I was feeding some chickens, I happened to toss a small pebble at one of them, which hit it on the middle and directly killed it. The old slave, having soon after missed the chicken, inquired after it; and on my relating the accident (for I told her the truth, because my mother would never suffer me to tell a lie) she flew into a violent passion, threatened that I should suffer for it; and, my master being out, she immedi-ately went and told her mistress what I had done. This alarmed me very much, and I expected an instant flogging, which to me was uncommonly dreadful; for I had seldom been beaten at home. I therefore resolved to fly; and accordingly I ran into a thicket that was hard by, and hid myself in the bushes. Soon afterwards my mistress and the slave returned, and, not seeing me, they searched all the house, but not finding me, and I not making answer when they called to me, they thought I had run away, and the whole neighborhood was raised in the pursuit of me. In that part of the country (as in ours) the houses and villages were skirted with woods, or shrubberies, and the bushes were so thick that a man could readily conceal himself in them, so as to elude the strictest search. The neighbors continued the whole day looking for me, and several times many of them came within a few yards of the place where I lay hid. I then gave myself up for lost entirely, and expected every moment, when I heard a rustling among the trees, to be found out, and punished by my master: but they never discovered me, though they were often so near that I even heard their conjectures as they were looking about for me; and I now learned from them, that any attempt to return home would be hopeless. Most of them supposed I had fled towards home, but the distance was so great, and the way so intricate, that they thought I could never reach it, and that I should be lost in the woods. When I heard this I was seized with a violent panic, and abandoned myself to despair. Night too began to approach, and aggravated all my fears. I had before entertained hopes of getting home, and I had determined when it should be dark to make the attempt; but I was now convinced it was fruitless, and I began to consider that, if possibly I could escape all other animals, I could not those the human kind; and that, not knowing the way, I must perish in the words. Thus was I like the hunted deer:

> —"Ev'ry leaf and ev'ry whisp'ring breath
> Convey'd a foe, and ev'ry foe a death.

I heard frequent rustling among the leaves; and being pretty sure they were snakes I expected every instant to be stung by them. This increased my anguish, and the horror of my situation became now quite insupportable. I at length quitted the thicket, very faint and hungry, for I had not eaten or drank any thing all the day; and crept to my master's kitchen, from whence I set out at first, and which was an open shed, and laid myself down in the ashes with an anxious wish for death to relieve me from all my pains. I was scarcely awake in the morning when the old woman slave, who was the first up, came to light the fire, and saw me in the fire place. She was very much surprised to see me, and could scarcely believe her own eyes. She now promised to intercede for me, and went for her master, who soon after came, and, having slightly reprimanded me, ordered me to be taken care of, and not to be ill-treated.

Soon after this my master's only daughter, and child by his first wife, sickened and died, which affected him so much that for some time he was almost frantic, and really would have killed himself, and he not been watched and prevented. However, in a small time after wards he recovered, and I was again sold. I was now carried to the left of the sun's rising, through many different countries, and a number of large woods. The people I was sold to used to carry me very often, when I was tired, either on their shoulders *or* on their backs. I saw many convenient well-built sheds along the roads, at proper distances, to accommodate the merchants and travelers, who lay in those building along with their wives, who often accompany them; and they always go well armed.

From the time I left my own nation I always found somebody that understood me till I came to the sea coast. The languages of different nations did not totally differ, nor were they so copious as those of the Europeans, particularly the English. They were therefore easily learned; and, while I was journeying thus through Africa, I acquired two or three different tongues. In this manner I had been traveling for a considerable time, when one evening, to my great surprise, whom should I see brought to the house where I was but my dear sister! As soon as she saw me she gave a loud shriek, and ran into my arms — I was quite overpowered: neither of us could speak; but, for a considerable time, clung to each other in mutual embraces unable to do any thing but weep. Our meeting affected all who saw us; and indeed I must acknowledge, in honour of those sable destroyers of human rights, that I never met with any ill treatment, or saw any offered to their slaves, except tying them, when necessary, to keep them from running away. When these people knew we were brother and sister they indulged us together; and the man, to whom I supposed we belonged, lay with us, he in the middle, while she and I held one another by the hands across his breast all night; and thus for a while we forgot our misfortunes in the joy of being together: but even this small comfort was soon to have an end; for scarcely had the fatal morning appeared, when she was again torn from me for ever! I was now more miserable, if possible, than before. The small relief which her presence gave me from pain was gone, and the wretchedness of the situation was redoubled by my anxiety after her fate, and my apprehensions lest her sufferings should be greater than mine, when I could not be with her to alleviate them. Yes, thou dear partner of all my child-ish sports! thou sharer of my joys and sorrows! happy should I have ever esteemed myself to encounter every misery for you, and to procure your freedom by the sacrifice of my own. Though you were early forced from my arms, your image has been always rivetted in my heart, from which neither *time nor fortune* have been able to remove it; so that, while the thoughts of your sufferings have damped my prosperity, they have mingled with adversity and increased its bitterness. To that Heaven which protects the weak from the strong, I commit the care of your innocence and virtues, if they have not already received their full reward, and if your youth and delicacy have not long since fallen victims to the violence of the African trader, the pestilential stench of a Guinea ship, the seasoning in the European colonies, or the lash and lust of a brutal and unrelenting overseer.

I did not long remain after my sister. I was again sold, and carried though a number of places, till, after traveling a considerable time, I came to a town called Tinmah, in the most beautiful country I had yet seen in Africa. It was extremely rich, and there were many rivulets which flowed through it, and supplied a large pond in the centre of the town, where the people washed. Here I first saw and tasted cocoanuts, which I thought superior to any nuts I had ever tasted before; and the trees, which were loaded, were also interspersed amongst the houses, which had commodious shades adjoining, and were in the same manner as ours, the insides being neatly plastered and whitewashed. Here I also saw and tasted for the first time sugar-cane. Their money consisted of little white shells, the size of the finger nail. I was sold here for one hundred and seventy-two of them by a merchant who lived and brought me there. I had been about two or three days at his house, when a wealthy widow, a neighbour of his, came there one evening, and brought with her an only son, a young gentleman about my own age and size. Here they saw me; and, having taken a fancy to me, I was bought of the merchant, and went home with them. Her house and premises were situated close to one of those rivu-lets I have mentioned, and were the finest I ever saw in Africa: they were very extensive, and she had a number of slaves to attend her. The next day I was washed and perfumed, and when meal-time came I was led into the presence of my mistress, and ate and drank before her with her son. This filled me with astonishment; and I could scarce help expressing my surprise that the young gentleman should suffer me, who was bound, to eat with him who was free; and not only so, but that he would not at any time either eat or drink till I had taken first, because I was the eldest, which was agreeable to our custom. Indeed every thing here, and all their treatment of me, made me forget that I was a slave. The language of these people resembled ours so nearly, that we understood each other perfectly. They had also the very same customs as we. There were likewise slaves daily to attend us, while my young master and I with other boys sported with our darts and bows and arrows, as I had been used to do at home. In this resemblance to my former happy state I passed about two months; and I now began to think I was to be adopted into the family, and was beginning to the reconciled to my situation, and to forget by degrees my misfortunes, when all at once the delusion vanished; for, without the least previous knowledge, one morning early, while my dear master and companion was still asleep, I was wakened out of my reverie to fresh sorrow, and hurried away even amongst the uncircumcised.

Thus, at the very moment I dreamed of the greatest happiness, I found myself most miserable; and it seemed as if fortune wished to give me this taste of joy, only to render the reverse more poignant. The change I now experienced was as painful as it was sudden and unexpected. It was a change indeed from a state of bliss to a scene which is inexpressible by me, as it discovered to me an element I had never before beheld, and till then had no idea of, and wherein such instances of hardship and cruelty continually occurred as I can never reflect on but with horror.

All the nations and people I had hitherto passed through resembled our own in their manners, customs, and language: but I came at length to a country, the inhabitants of which differed from us in all those particulars. I was very much struck with this difference, especially when I came among a people who did not circumcise, and ate without washing their hands. They cooked also in iron pots and had European cutlasses and cross bows, which were unknown to us, and fought with their fists amongst themselves. Their women were not so modest as ours, for they ate, and drank, and slept, with their men. But, above all, I was amazed to see no sacrifices or offerings among them. In some of those places the people ornamented themselves with scars, and likewise filed their teeth very sharp. They wanted sometimes to ornament me in the same manner, but I would not suffer them; hoping that I might some time be among a people who did not thus disfigure themselves, as I thought they did. At last I came to the banks of a large river, which was covered with canoes, in which the people appeared to live with their household utensils and provisions of all kinds. I was beyond measure astonished at this, as I had never before seen any water larger that a pond or a rivulet: and my surprise was mingled with no small fear when I was put into one of these canoes, and we began to paddle and move along the river. We continued going on thus till night, and when we came to land, and made fires on the banks, each family by themselves, some dragged their canoes on shore, others stayed and cooked in theirs, and laid in them all night. Those on the land had mats, of which they made tents, some in the shape of little houses: in these we slept; and after the morning meal we embarked again and proceeded as before. I was often very much astonished to see some of the women as well as the men, jump into the water, dive to the bottom, come up again, and swim about. Thus I continued to travel, sometimes by land, sometimes by water, through different countries and various nations till, at the end of six or seven months after I had been kidnapped, I arrived at the sea coast. It would be tedious and uninteresting to relate all the incidents which befell me during this journey, and which I have not yet forgotten; of the various hands I passed through, and the manners and customs of all the different people among whom I lived: I shall therefore only observe, that in all the places where I was the soil was exceedingly rich; the pumpkins, eadas plantains, yams, &c. &c. were in great abundance, and of incredible size. There were also vast quantities of different gums, though not used for any purpose; and every where a great deal of tobacco. The cotton even grew quite wild and there was plenty of redwood. I saw no mechanics whatever in all the way, except such as I have mentioned. The chief employment in all these countries was agriculture, and both the males and females, as with us, were brought up to it, and trained in the arts of war.

The first object which saluted my eyes when I arrived on the coast was the sea, and a slave ship, which was then riding at anchor, and waiting for its cargo. These filled me with astonishment, which was soon converted into terror when I was carried on board. I was immediately handled and tossed up to see if I were sound by some of the crew; and I was now persuaded that I had gotten into a world of bad spirits, and that they were going to kill me. Their complexions too differing so much from ours, their long hair, and the language they spoke, (which was very different from any I had ever heard) united to confirm me in this belief. Indeed such were the horrors of my views and fears at the moment, that, if ten thousand worlds had been my own, I would have freely parted with them all to have exchanged my condition with that of the meanest slave in my own country. When I looked round the ship too and saw a large furnace or copper boiling, and a multitude of black people of every description chained together, every one of their countenances expressing dejection and sorrow, I no longer doubted of my fate; and, quite overpowered with horror and anguish, I fell motionless on the deck and fainted. When I recovered a little I found some black people about me, who I believed were some of those who brought me on board, and had been receiving their pay; they talked to me in order to cheer me, but all in vain. I asked them if we were not to be eaten by those white men with horrible looks, red faces, and loose hair. They told me I was not; and one of the crew brought me a small portion of spirituous liquor in a wine glass; but; being afraid of him, I would not take it out of his hand. One of the blacks therefore took it from him and gave it to me, and I took a little down my palate, which, instead of reviving me, as they thought it would, threw me into the greatest consternation at the strange feeling it produced, having never tasted any such liquor before. Soon after this the blacks who brought me on board went off, and left me abandoned to despair. I now saw myself deprived of all chance of returning to my native country, or even the least glimpse of hope of gaining the shore, which I now considered as friendly; and I even wished for my former slavery in preference to my present situation, which was filled with horrors of every kind, still heightened by my ignorance of what I was to undergo. I was not long suffered to indulge my grief; I was soon put down under the decks, and there I received such a salutation in my nostrils as I had never experienced in my life: so that, with the loathsomeness of the stench, and crying together, I became so sick and low that I was not able to eat, nor had the least desire to taste any thing. I now wished for the last friend, death, to relieve me; but soon, to my grief, two of the white men offered me eatables; and, on my refusing to eat, one of them held me fast by the hands, and laid me across I think the windlass, and tied my feet, while the other flogged me severely. I had never experienced any thing of this kind before; and although, not being used to the water, I naturally feared that element the first time I saw it, yet nevertheless could I have got over the nettings, I would have jumped over the side but I could not, and, besides, the crew used to watch us very closely who were not chained down to the decks, lest we should leap into the water: and I have seen some of these poor African prisoners most severely cut for attempting to do so, and hourly whipped for not eating. This indeed was often the case with myself. In a little time after amongst the poor chained men, I found some of my own nation, which in a small degree gave ease to my mind. I inquired of these what was to be done with us; they gave me to understand we were to be carried to these white people's country to work for them. I then was a little revived, and thought, if it were no worse than working, my situation was not so desperate: but still I feared I should be put to death, the white people looked and acted, as I thought, in so savage a manner; for I had never seen among any people such instances of brutal cruelty; and this not only shewn towards us blacks, but also to some of the whites themselves. One white man in particular I saw, when we were permitted to be on deck, flogged so unmercifully with a large rope near the foremast, that he died in consequence of it; and they tossed him over the side as they would have done a brute. This made me fear these people the more; and I expected nothing less than to be treated in the same manner. I could not help expressing my fears and apprehensions to some of my countrymen: I asked them if these people had no country, but lived in this hollow place (the ship): they told me they did not, but came from a distant one. "Then," said I, "how comes it in all our country we never heard of them?" They told me because they lived so very far off. I then asked where were their women? had they any like them-selves? I was told they had: "and why," said I, "do we not see them?" they answered, because they were left behind. I asked how the vessel could go? they told me they could not tell; but that there were cloths put upon the masts by the help of the ropes I saw, and then the vessel went on; and the white men had some spell or magic they put in the water when they liked in order to stop the vessel. I was exceedingly amazed at this account, and really thought they were spirits. I therefore wished much to be from amongst them, for I expected they would sacrifice me: but my wishes were vain; for we were so quartered that it was impossible for any of us to make our escape. While we stayed on the coast I was mostly on deck; and one day, to my great astonishment, I saw one of these vessels coming in with the sails up. As soon as the whites saw it, they gave a great shout, at which we were amazed; and the more so as the vessel appeared larger by approaching nearer. At last she came to an anchor in my sight, and when the anchor was let go I and my countrymen who saw it were lost in astonishment to observe the vessel stop; and were now convinced it was done by magic. Soon after this the other ship got her boats out, and they came on board of us, and the people of both ships seemed very glad to see each other. Several of the strangers also shook hands with us black people, and made motions with their hands, signifying I suppose we were to go to their country; but we did not understand them. At last, when the ship we were in had got in all her cargo, they made ready with many fearful noises, and we were all put under deck, so that we could not see how they managed the vessel. But this disappointment was the least of my sorrow. The stench of the hold while we were on the coast was so intolerably loathsome, that it was dangerous to remain there for any time, and some of us had been permitted to stay on the deck for the fresh air; but now that the whole ship's cargo were confined together, it became absolutely pestilential. The closeness of the place, and the heat of the climate, added to the number in the ship, which was so crowded that each had scarcely room to turn himself, almost suffocated us. This produced copious perspirations, so that the air soon became unfit for respiration, from the variety of loathsome smells, and brought on a sickness among the slaves, of which many died, thus falling victims to the improvident avarice, as I may call it, of their purchasers. This wretched situation was again aggravated by the galling of the chains, now become insupportable; and the filth of the necessary tubs, into which the children often fell, and were almost suffocated. The shrieks of the women, and the groans of the dying, rendered the whole a scene of horror almost inconceivable. Happily perhaps for myself I was soon reduced so low here that it was thought necessary to keep me almost always on deck; and from my extreme youth I was not put in fetters. In this situation I expected every hour to share the fate of my companions, some of whom were almost daily brought upon deck at the point of death, which I began to hope would soon put an end to my miseries. Often did I think many of the inhabitants of the deep much more happy than myself. I envied them the freedom they enjoyed, and as often wished I could change my condition for theirs. Every circumstance I met with served only to render my state more painful, and heighten my apprehensions, and my opinion of the cruelty of the whites. One day they had taken a number of fishes; and when they had killed and satisfied themselves with as many as they thought fit, to our astonishment who were on the deck, rather than give any of them to us to eat as we expected, they tossed the remaining fish into the sea again, although we begged and prayed for some as well as we could, but in vain; and some of my countrymen, being pressed by hunger, took an opportunity, when they thought no one saw them, of trying to get a little privately; but they were discovered, and the attempt procured them some very severe floggings. One day, when we had a smooth sea and moderate wind, two of my wearied countrymen who were chained together (I was near them at the time), preferring death to such a life of misery, somehow made through the nettings and jumped into the sea: immediately another quite dejected fellow, who, on one account of his illness, was suffered to be out of irons, also followed their example; and I believe many more would very soon have done the same if they had not been prevented by the ship's crew, who were instantly alarmed. Those of us that were the most active were in a moment put down under the deck, and here was such a noise and confusion amongst the people of the ship as I never heard before, to stop her, and get the boat out to go after the slaves. However two of the wretches were drowned, but they got the other, and afterwards flogged him unmercifully for thus attempting to prefer death to slavery. In this manner we continued to undergo more hardships than I can now relate, hardships which are inseparable from this accursed trade. Many a time we were near suffocation from the want of fresh air, which we were often without for whole days together. This, and the stench of the necessary tubs, carried off many. During our passage I first saw flying fishes, which surprised me very much: they used frequently to fly across the ship, and many of them fell on the deck. I also now first saw the use of the quadrant; I had often with astonishment seen the mariners make observations with it, and I could not think what it meant. They at last took notice of my surprise; and one of them, willing to increase it, as well as to gratify my curiosity, made me one day look through it. The clouds appeared to me to be land, which disappeared as they passed along. This heightened my wonder; and I was now more persuaded than ever that I was in another world, and that every thing about me was magic. At last we came in sight of the island of Barbadoes, at which the whites on board gave a great shout, and made many signs of joy to us. We did not know what to think of this; but as the vessel drew nearer we plainly saw the harbour, and other ships of different kinds and sizes; and we soon anchored amongst them off Bridge Town. Many merchants and planters now came on board, though it was in the evening. They put us in separate parcels, and examined us attentively. They also made us jump, and pointed to the land, signifying we were to go there. We thought by this we should be eaten by these ugly men, as they appeared to us; and, when soon after we were all put down under the deck again, there was much dread and trembling among us, and nothing but bitter cries to be heard all the night from these apprehensions, insomuch that at last the white people got some old slaves from the land to pacify us. They told us we were not to be eaten, but to work, and were soon to go on land, where we should see many of our country people. This report eased as much; and sure enough, soon after we were landed, there came to us Africans of all languages. We were conducted immediately to the merchant's yard, where we were all pent up together like so many sheep in a fold, without regard to sex or age. As every object was new to me every thing I saw filled me with surprise. What struck me first was that the houses were built with stories, and in every other respect different from those in Africa: but I was still more astonished on seeing people on horseback. I did not know what this could mean; and indeed I thought these people were full nothing but magical arts. While I was in this astonishment one of my fellow prisoners spoke to a countryman of his about the horses, who said they were the same kind they had in their country. I understood them, though they were from a distant part of Africa, and I thought it odd I had not seen any horses there; but afterwards, when I came to converse with different Africans, I found they had many horses amongst them, and much larger than those I then saw. We were not many days in the merchant's custody before we were sold after their usual manner, which is this: — On a signal given, (as the beat of a drum) the buyers rush at once into the yard where the slaves are confined, and make choice of that parcel they like best. The noise and clamour with which this is attended, and the eagerness visible in the countenances of the buyers, serve not a little to increase the apprehensions of the terrified Africans, who may well be supposed to consider them as the ministers of that destruction to which they think themselves devoted. In this manner, without scruple, are relations and friends separated most of them never to see each other again. I remember in the vessel in which I was brought over, in the men's apartment, there were several brothers, who, in the sale, were sold in different lots; and it was very moving on this occasion to see and hear their cries at parting. O, ye nominal Christians! Might not an African ask you, learned you this from your God, who says unto you, Do unto all men as you would men should do unto you? Is it not enough that we are torn from our country and friends to toil for your luxury and lust of gain? Must every tender feeling be likewise sacrificed to your avarice? Are the dearest friends and relations, now rendered more dear by their separation from their kindred, still to be parted from each other, and thus prevented from cheering the gloom of slavery with the small comfort of being together and mingling their sufferings and sorrows? Why are parents to lose their children, brothers and sisters, or husbands and their wives? Surely this is a new refinement in cruelty, which, while it has no advantage to atone for it, thus aggravates distress, and adds fresh horrors even to the wretchedness of slavery.

. . . .

To the Queen's most Excellent Majesty.

MADAM,

Your Majesty's well known benevolence and humanity emboldens me to approach your royal presence, trusting that the obscurity of my situation will not prevent your Majesty from attending to the sufferings for which I plead.

Yet I do not solicit your royal pity for my own distress; my sufferings, although numerous, are in a measure forgotten. I supplicate your Majesty's compassion for millions of my African countrymen, who groan under the lash of tyranny in the West Indies.

The oppression and cruelty exercised to the unhappy negroes there, have at length reached the British legislature, and they are now deliberating on its redress; even several persons of property in slaves in the West Indies, have petitioned parliament against its continuance, sensible that it is as impolitic as it is unjust — and what is inhuman must ever be unwise.

Your Majesty's reign has been hitherto distinguished by private acts of benevolence and bounty; surely the more extended the misery is, the greater claim it has to your Majesty's compassion, and the greater must be your Majesty's pleasure in administering to its relief.

I presume, therefore, gracious Queen, to implore your interposition with your royal consort, in favour of the wretched Africans; that, by your Majesty's benevolent influence, a period may now be put to their misery; and that they may be raised from the condition of brutes, to which they are at present degraded, to the rights and situation of freemen, and admitted to partake of the blessings of your Majesty's happy government; so shall your Majesty enjoy the heart-felt pleasure of procuring happiness to millions, and be rewarded in the grateful prayers of themselves, and of their posterity.

And may the all-bountiful Creator shower on your Majesty, and the Royal Family, every blessing that this world can afford, and every fulness of joy which divine revelation has promised us in the next.

I am your Majesty's
most dutiful and devoted servant to command,

GUSTAVUS VASSA,
The Oppressed Ethiopean.

NO. 53, BALDWIN'S GARDENS.

The negro consolidated act, made by the assembly of Jamaica last year, and the new act of amendment now in agitation there, contain a proof of the existence of those charges that have been made against the planters relative to the treatment of their slaves.

I hope to have the satisfaction of seeing the renovation of liberty and justice resting on the British government, to vindicate the honour of our common nature. These are concerns which do not perhaps belong to any particular office: but, to speak more seriously to every man of sentiment, actions like these are the just and sure foundation of future fame; a reversion, though remote, is coveted by some noble minds as a substantial good. It is upon these grounds that I hope and expect the attention of gentlemen in power. These are designs consonant to the elevation of their rank, and the dignity of their stations: they are ends suitable to the nature of a free and generous government; and, connected with views of empire and dominion, suited to the benevolence and solid merit of the legislature. It is a pursuit of substantial greatness. — May the time come — at least the speculation to me is pleasing — when the sable people shall gratefully commemorate the auspicious era of extensive freedom. Then shall those persons particularly be named with praise and honour, who generously proposed and stood forth in the cause of humanity, liberty, and good policy; and brought to the ear of the legislature designs worthy of royal patronage and adoption. May Heaven make the British senators the dispersers of light, liberty, and science, to the uttermost parts of the earth: then will be glory to God in the highest, on earth peace, and good-will to men: — Glory, honour, peace, &c. to every soul of man that worketh good, to the Britons first, (because to them the Gospel is preached) and also to the nations. 'Those that honour their Maker have mercy on the poor.' 'It is righteousness exalteth a nation; but sin is a reproach to any people; destruction shall be to the workers of iniquity, and the wicked shall fall by their own wickedness.' May the blessings of the Lord be upon the heads of all those who commiserated the cases of the oppressed negroes, and the fear of God prolong their days; and may their expectations be filled with gladness! 'The liberal devise liberal things, and by liberal things shall stand,' Isaiah xxxii. 8. They can say with pious Job, 'Did not I weep for him that was in trouble? Was not my soul grieved for the poor?' Job xxx. 25.

As the inhuman traffic of slavery is to be taken into the consideration of the British legislature, I doubt not, if a system of commerce was established in Africa, the demand for manufactures would most rapidly augment, as the native inhabitants will insensibly adopt the British fashions, manners, customs, &c. In proportion to the civilization, so will be the consumption of British manufactures.

The wear and tear of a continent, nearly twice as large as Europe, and rich in vegetable and mineral productions, is much easier conceived than calculated.

A case in point. — It cost the Aborigines of Britain little or nothing in clothing, &c. The difference between their forefathers and the present generation, in point of consumption, is literally infinite. The supposition is most obvious. It will be equally immense in Africa — The same cause, viz. civilization, will ever have the same effect.

It is trading upon safe grounds. A commercial intercourse with Africa opens an inexhaustible source of wealth to the manufacturing interests of Great Britain, and to all which the slave trade is an objection.

If I am not misinformed, the manufacturing interest is equal, if not superior, to the landed interest, as to the value, for reasons which will soon appear. The abolition of slavery, so diabolical, will give a most rapid extension of manufactures, which is totally and diametrically opposite to what some interested people assert.

The manufacturers of this country must and will, in the nature and reason of things, have a full and constant employ by supplying the African markets.

Population, the bowels and surface of Africa, abound in valuable and useful returns; the hidden treasures of centuries will be brought to light and into circulation. Industry, enterprize, and mining, will have their full scope, proportionably as they civilize. In a word, it lays open an endless field of commerce to the British manufactures and merchant adventurer. The manufacturing interest and the general interests are synonymous. The abolition of slavery would be in reality as universal good.

Tortures, murder, and every other imaginable barbarity and iniquity, are practised upon the poor slaves with impunity. I hope the slave trade will be abolished. I pray it may be an event at hand. The great body of manufacturers, uniting in the cause, will considerably facilitate and expedite it; and, as I have already stated, it is most substantially their interest and advantage, and as such the nation's at large, (expect those persons concerned in the manufacturing neck-yokes, collars, chains, hand-cuffs, leg-bolts, drags, thumbscrews, iron muzzles, and coffins; cats, scourges, and other instruments of torture used in the slave trade). In a short time one sentiment alone will prevail, from motives of interest as well as justice and humanity. Europe contains one hundred and twenty millions of inhabitants. Query — How many millions doth Africa contain? Supposing the Africans, collectively and individually, to expend £5 a head in raiment and furniture yearly when civilized, &c. an immensity beyond the reach of imagination!

This I conceive to be a theory founded upon facts, and therefore an infallible one. If the blacks were permitted to remain in their own country, they would double themselves every fifteen years. In proportion to such increase will be the demand for manufactures. Cotton and indigo grow spontaneously in most parts of Africa; a consideration this of no small consequence to the manufacturing towns of Great Britain. It opens a most immense, glorious, and happy prospect — the clothing, &c. of a continent ten thousand miles in circumference, and immensely rich in productions of every denomination in return for manufactures.

I have only therefore to request the reader's indulgence and conclude. I am far from the vanity of thinking there is any merit in this narrative: I hope censure will be suspended, when it is considered that it was written by one who was as unwilling as unable to adorn the plainness of truth by the colouring of imagination. My life and fortune have been extremely chequered, and my adventures various. Even those I have related are considerably abridged. If any incident in this little work should appear uninteresting and trifling to most readers, I can only say, as my excuse for mentioning it, that almost every event of my life made an impression on my mind and influenced my conduct. I early accustomed myself to look for the hand of God in the minutest occurrence, and to learn from it a lesson of morality and religion; and in this light every circumstance I have related was to me of importance. After all, what makes any event important, unless by its observation we become better and wiser, and learn 'to do justly, to love mercy, and to walk humbly before God?' To those who are possessed of this spirit, there is scarcely any book or incident so trifling that does not afford some profit, while to others the experience of ages seems of no use; and even to pour out to them the treasures of wisdom is throwing the jewels of instruction away.

THE END.

The Condition of the Working Class in England

Friedrich Engels

WORKING MEN!

To you I dedicate a work, in which I have tried to lay before my German Countrymen a faithful picture of your condition, of your sufferings and struggles, of your hopes and prospects. I have lived long enough amidst you to know something about your circumstances; I have devoted to their knowledge my most serious attention, I have studied the various official and non-official documents as far as I was able to get hold of them — I have not been satisfied with this, I wanted more than a mere *abstract* knowledge of my subject, I wanted to see you in your own homes, to observe you in your everyday life, to chat with you on your condition and grievances, to witness your struggles against the social and political power of your oppressors. I have done so: I forsook the company and the dinner-parties, the port wine and champagne of the middle classes, and devoted my leisure hours almost exclusively to the intercourse with plain Working Men; I am both glad and proud of having done so. Glad, because thus I was induced to spend many a happy hour in obtaining a knowledge of the realities of life — many an hour, which else would have been wasted in fashionable talk and tiresome etiquette; proud, because thus I got an opportunity of doing justice to an oppressed and calumniated class of men who, with all their faults and under all the disadvantages of their situation, yet command the respect of everyone but an English money-monger; proud, too, because thus I was placed in a position to save the English people from the growing contempt which on the Continent has been the necessary consequence of the brutally selfish policy and general behaviour of your ruling middle class.

Having, at the same time, ample opportunity to watch the middle classes, your opponents, I soon came to the conclusion that you are right, perfectly right in expecting no support whatever from them. Their interest is diametrically opposed to yours, though they always will try to maintain the contrary and to make you believe in their most hearty sympathy with your fates. Their doings give them the lie. I hope to have collected more than sufficient evidence of the fact that — be their words what they please — the middle classes intend in reality nothing else but to enrich themselves by your labour while they can sell its produce, and to abandon you to starvation as soon as they cannot make a profit by this indirect trade in human flesh. What have they done to prove their professed goodwill towards you? Have they ever paid any serious attention to your grievances? Have they done more than paying the expenses of half a dozen commissions of inquiry, whose voluminous reports are damned to everlasting slumber among heaps of waste paper on the shelves of the Home Office? Have they even done as much as to compile from those rotting Blue Books a single readable book from which everybody might easily get some information on the condition of the great majority of 'freeborn Britons'? Not they indeed, those are things they do not like to speak of — they have left it to a foreigner to inform the civilized world of the degrading situation you have to live in.

A foreigner to *them*, not to *you*, I hope. Though my English may not be pure, yet, I hope, you will find it *plain* English. No working man in England — nor in France either, by the by — ever treated me as a foreigner. With the greatest pleasure I observed you

From *The Condition of the Working Class in England* by Friedrich Engels, 1845.

103

to be free from that blasting curse, national prejudice and national pride, which after all means nothing but *wholesale selfishness* — I observed you to sympathize with everyone who earnestly applies his powers to human progress — may he be an Englishman or not — to admire everything great and good, whether nursed on your native soil or not — I found you to be more than mere *English*men, members of a single, isolated nation, I found you to be *Men*, members of the great and universal family of Mankind, who know, their interests and that of all the human race to be the same. And as such, as members of the Family of 'One and Indivisible' Mankind, as Human Beings in the most emphatic meaning of the word, as such I, as many others on the Continent, hail your progress in every direction and wish you speedy success. Go on then, as you have done hitherto. Much remains to be undergone; be firm, be undaunted — your success is certain, and no step you will have to take in your onward march will be lost to our common cause, the cause of Humanity!

Friedrich Engels

Barmen (Rhenan Prussia)
15 March 1845

. . . .

The history of the proletariat in England begins with the second half of the last century, with the invention of the steam-engine and of machinery for working cotton. These inventions gave rise, as is well known, to an industrial revolution, a revolution which altered the whole civil society; one, the historical importance of which is only now beginning to be recognized. England is the classic soil of this transformation, which was all the mightier, the more silently it proceeded; and England is, therefore, the classic land of its chief product also, the proletariat. Only in England can the proletariat be studied in all its relations and from all sides.

We have not, here and now, to deal with the history of this revolution, nor with its vast importance for the present and the future. Such a delineation must be reserved for a future, more comprehensive work. For the moment, we must limit ourselves to the little that is necessary for understanding the facts that follow, for comprehending the present state of the English proletariat.

Before the introduction of machinery, the spinning and weaving of raw materials was carried on in the working man's home. Wife and daughter spun the yarn that the father wove or that they sold, if he did not work it up himself. These weaver families lived in the country in the neighbourhood of the towns, and could get on fairly well with their wages, because the home market was almost the only one, and the crushing power of competition that came later, the conquest of foreign markets and the extension of trade, did not yet press upon wages. There was, further, a constant increase in the demand for the home market, keeping pace with the slow increase in population and employing all the workers; and there was also the impossibility of vigorous competition of the workers among themselves, consequent upon the rural dispersion of their homes. So it was that the weaver was usually in a position to lay by something, and rent a little piece of land, that he cultivated in his leisure hours, of which he had as many as he chose to take, since he could weave whenever and as long as he pleased. True, he was a bad farmer and managed his land inefficiently, often obtaining but poor crops; nevertheless, he was no proletarian, he had a stake in the country, he was permanently settled, and stood one step higher in society than the English workman of to-day.

So the workers vegetated throughout a passably comfortable existence, leading a righteous and peaceful life in all piety and probity; and their material position was far better than that of their successors. They did not need to overwork; they did no more than they chose to do, and yet earned what they needed. They had leisure for healthful work in garden or field, work which, in itself, was recreation for them, and they could take part besides in the recreations and games of their neighbours, and all these games — bowling, cricket, football, etc., contributed to their physical health and vigour. They were, for the most part, strong, well-built people, in whose physique little or no difference from that of their peasant neighbours was discoverable. Their children grew up in the fresh country air, and, if they could help their parents at work, it was only occasionally; while of eight or twelve hours work for them there was no question.

What the moral and intellectual character of this class was may be guessed. Shut off from the towns, which they never entered, their yarn and woven stuff being delivered to travelling agents for payment of wages — so shut off that old people who lived quite in the neighbourhood of the town never went thither until they were robbed of their trade by the introduction of machinery and obliged to look about them in the towns for work — the weavers stood upon the moral and intellectual plane of the yeomen with whom they were usually immediately connected through their little holdings. They regarded their squire, the greatest landholder of the region, as their natural superior; they asked advice of him, laid their small disputes before him for settlement, and gave him all honour, as this patriarchal relation involved. They were 'respectable' people, good husbands and fathers, led moral lives because they had no temptation to be immoral, there being no gin palaces or low houses in their vicinity, and because the host, at whose inn they now and then quenched their thirst, was also a respectable man, usually a large tenant farmer who took pride in his good order, good beer, and early hours. They had their children the whole day at home, and brought them up in obedience and the fear of God; the patriarchal relationship remained undisturbed so long as the children were unmarried. The young people grew up in idyllic simplicity and intimacy with their playmates until they married; and even though sexual intercourse before marriage almost unfailingly took place, this happened only when the moral obligation of marriage was recognized on both sides, and a subsequent wedding made everything good. In short, the English industrial workers of those days lived and thought after the fashion still to be found here and there in Germany, in retirement and seclusion, without mental activity and without violent fluctuations in their position in life. They could rarely read and far more rarely write; went regularly to church, never talked politics, never conspired, never thought, delighted in physical exercises, listened with inherited reverence when the Bible was read, and were, in their unquestioning humility, exceedingly well-disposed towards the 'superior' classes. But intellectually, they were dead; lived only for their petty, private interest, for their looms and gardens, and knew nothing of the mighty movement which, beyond their horizon, was sweeping through mankind. They were comfortable in their silent vegetation, and but for the industrial revolution they would never have emerged from this existence, which, cosily romantic as it was, was nevertheless not worthy of human beings. In truth, they were not human beings; they were merely toiling machines in the service of the few aristocrats who had guided history down to that time. The industrial revolution has simply carried this out to its logical end by making the workers machines pure and simple, taking from them the last trace of independent activity, and so forcing them to think and demand a position worthy of men. As in France politics, so in England manufacture, and the movement of civil society in general drew into the whirl of history the last classes which had remained sunk in apathetic indifference to the universal interests of mankind.

The first invention which gave rise to a radical change in the state of the English workers was the jenny, invented in the year 1764 by a weaver, James Hargreaves, of Standhill, near Blackburn, in North Lancashire. This machine was the rough beginning of the later invented mule, and was moved by hand. Instead of one spindle like the ordinary spinning-wheel, it carried sixteen or eighteen manipulated by a single workman. This invention made it possible to deliver more yarn than heretofore. Whereas, though one weaver had employed three spinners, there had never been enough yarn, and the weaver had often been obliged to wait for it, there was now more yarn to be had than could be Woven by the available workers. The demand for woven goods, already increasing, rose yet more in consequence of the cheapness of these goods, which cheapness, in turn, was the outcome of the diminished cost of producing the yarn. More weavers were needed, and weavers' wages rose. Now that the weaver could earn more at his loom, he gradually abandoned his farming, and gave his whole time to weaving. At that tune a family of four grown persons and two children (who were set to spooling) could earn, with ten hours' daily work, £4 in a week, and often more if trade was good and work pressed. It happened often enough that a single weaver earned £2 a week at his loom. By degrees the class of farming weavers wholly disappeared, and was merged in the newly arising class of weavers who lived wholly upon wages, had no property whatever, not even the pretended property of a holding, and so became working men, proletarians. Moreover, the old relation between spinner and weaver was destroyed. Hitherto, so far as this had been possible, yarn had been spun and woven under one roof. Now that the jenny as well as the loom required a strong hand, men began to spin, and whole families lived by spinning, while others laid the antiquated, superseded spinning-wheel aside; and, if they had not means of purchasing a jenny, were forced to live upon the wages of the father alone. Thus began with spinning and weaving that division of labour which has since been so infinitely perfected.

While the industrial proletariat was thus developing with the first still very imperfect machine, the same machine gave rise to the agricultural proletariat. There had, hitherto, been a vast number of small landowners, yeomen, who had vegetated in the same unthinking quiet as their neighbours, the farming weavers. They cultivated their scraps of land quite after the ancient and inefficient fashion of their ancestors, and opposed every change with the obstinacy peculiar to such creatures of habit, after remaining stationary from generation to generation. Among them were many smallholders also, not tenants in the present sense of the word, but people who had their land handed down from their fathers, either by hereditary lease, or by force of ancient custom, and had hitherto held it as securely as if it had actually been their own property. When the industrial workers withdrew from agriculture, a great number of smallholdings fell idle, and upon these the new class of large tenants established themselves, tenants-at-will, holding fifty, one hundred, two hundred or more acres, liable to be turned out at the end of the year, but able by improved tillage and larger farming to increase the yield of the land. They could sell their produce more cheaply than the yeoman, for whom nothing remained when his farm no longer supported him but to sell it, procure a jenny or a loom, or take service as an agricultural labourer in the employ of a large farmer. His inherited slowness and the inefficient methods of cultivation bequeathed by his ancestors, and above which he could not rise, left him no alternative when forced to compete with men who managed their holdings on sounder principles and with all the advantages bestowed by farming on a large scale and the investment of capital for the improvement of the soil.

Meanwhile, the industrial movement did not stop here. Single capitalists began to set up spinning-jennies in great buildings and to use water-power for driving them, so placing themselves in a position to diminish the number of workers, and sell their yarn more cheaply than single spinners could do who moved their own machines by hand. There were constant improvements in the jenny, so that machines continually became antiquated, and must be altered or even laid aside; and though the capitalists could hold cut by the application of water-power even with the old machinery, for the single spinner this was impossible. And the factory system, the beginning of which was thus made, received a fresh extension in 1767, through the spinning throstle invented by Richard Arkwright, a barber, in Preston, in North Lancashire. After the steam-engine, this is the most important mechanical invention of the eighteenth century. It was calculated from the beginning for mechanical motive power, and was based upon wholly new principles. By the combination of the peculiarities of the jenny and throstle, Samuel Crompton, of Firwood, Lancashire, contrived the mule in 1785, and as Arkwright invented the carding engine, and preparatory ('slubbing and roving') frames about the same time, the factory system became the prevailing one for the spinning of cotton. By means of trifling modifications these machines were gradually adapted to the spinning of wool and later (in the first decade of the present century) also of flax, and so to the superseding of hand-work here, too. But even then, the end was not yet. In the closing years of the last century, Dr Cartwright, a country parson, had invented the power-loom and about 1804 had so far perfected it, that it could successfully compete with the hand-weaver; and all this machinery was made doubly important by James Watt's steam-engine, invented in 1764, and used for supplying motive power for spinning since 1785.

With these inventions, since improved from year to year, the victory of machine-work over hand-work in the chief branches of English industry was won; and the history of the latter from that time forward simply relates how the hand-workers have been driven by machinery from one position after another. The consequences of this were, on the one hand, a rapid fall in price of all manufactured commodities, prosperity of commerce and manufacture, the conquest of nearly all the unprotected foreign markets, the sudden multiplication of capital and national wealth; on the other hand, a still more rapid multiplication of the proletariat, the destruction of all property-holding and of all security of employment for the working class, demoralization, political excitement, and all those facts so highly repugnant to Englishmen in comfortable circumstances, which we shall have to consider in the following pages. Having already seen what a transformation in the social condition of the lower classes a single such clumsy machine as the jenny had wrought, there is no cause for surprise as to that which a complete and interdependent system of finely adjusted machinery has brought about, machinery which receives raw material and turns out woven goods.

Meanwhile, let us trace the development of English manufacture somewhat more minutely, beginning with the cotton industry. In the years 1771–5, there were annually imported into England rather less than 5,000,000 pounds of raw cotton; in the year 1841 there were imported 528,000,000 pounds, and the import for 1844 will reach at least 600,000,000 pounds. In 1834 England exported 556,000,000 yards of woven cotton goods, 76,500,000 pounds of cotton yarn, and cotton hosiery of the value of £1,200,000. In the same year over 8,000,000 mule spindles were at work, 110,000 power and 250,000 hand-looms, throstle spindles not included, in the service of the cotton industry; and, according to MacCulloch's reckoning, nearly a million and a half human beings were supported by this branch, of whom but 220,000 worked in the mills; the power used in these mills was steam, equivalent to 33,000 horse-power, and water, equivalent to 11,000 horse-power. At present these figures are far from adequate, and it may be safely assumed that, in the year 1845, the power and number of the machines and the number of the workers is greater by one-half than it was in 1834. The chief centre of this industry is Lancashire, where it originated; it has thoroughly revolutionized this county, converting it from an obscure, ill-cultivated swamp into a busy, lively region, multiplying its population tenfold in eighty years, and causing giant cities such as Liverpool and Manchester, containing together 700,000 inhabitants, and their neighbouring towns, Bolton with 60,000, Rochdale with 75,000, Oldham with 50,000, Preston with 60,000, Ashton and Stalybridge with 40,000, and a whole list of other manufacturing towns to spring up as if by a magic touch. The history of South Lancashire contains some of the greatest marvels of modern times, yet no one ever mentions them, and all these miracles are the product of the cotton industry. Glasgow, too, the centre for the cotton district of Scotland, for Lanarkshire and Renfrewshire, has increased in population, from 30,000 to 300,000, since the introdution of the industry. The hosiery manufacture of Nottingham and Derby also received one fresh impulse from the lower price of yarn, and a second one from an improvement of the stocking loom, by means of which two stockings could be woven at once. The manufacture of lace, too, became an important branch of industry after the invention of the lace machine in 1777; soon after that date Lindley invented the point-net machine, and in 1809 Heathcoat invented the bobbin-net machine, in consequence of which the production of lace was greatly simplified, and the demand increased proportionately in consequence of the diminished cost, so that now, at least 200,000 persons are supported by this industry. Its chief centres are Nottingham, Leicester, and the West of England, Wiltshire, Devonshire, etc. A corresponding extension has taken place in the branches dependent upon the cotton industry, in dyeing, bleaching, and printing. Bleaching by the application of chlorine in place of the oxygen of the atmosphere; dyeing and printing by the rapid development of chemistry, and printing by a series of most brilliant mechanical inventions, a yet greater advance which, with the extension of these branches caused by the growth of the cotton industry, raised them to a previously unknown degree of prosperity.

The same activity manifested itself in the manufacture of wool. This had hitherto been the leading department of English industry, but the quantities formerly produced are as nothing in comparison with that which is now manufactured. In 1782 the whole wool crop of the preceding three years lay unused for want of workers, and would have continued so to lie if the newly invented machinery had not come to its assistance and spun it. The adaptation of this machinery to the spinning of wool was most successfully accomplished. Then began the same sudden development in the wool districts which we have already seen in the cotton districts. In 1738 there were 75,000 pieces of woollen cloth produced in the West Riding of Yorkshire; in 1817 there were 490,000 pieces, and so rapid was the extension of the industry that in 1834, 450,000 more pieces were produced than in 1825. In 1801, 101,000,000 pounds of wool (7,000,000 pounds of it imported) were worked up; in 1835, 180,000,000, pounds were worked up; of which 42,000,000 pounds were imported. The principal centre of this industry is the West Riding of Yorkshire, where, especially at Bradford, long English wool is converted into worsted yarns, etc.; while in the other cities, Leeds, Halifax, Huddersfield etc., short wool is converted into hard-spun yarn and cloth. Then come the adjacent part of Lancashire, the region of Rochdale, where in addition to the cotton industry much flannel is produced, and the West of England which supplies the finest cloths. Here also the growth of population is worthy of observation [see Figure], a population which, since 1831, must have increased at least 20 to 25 per cent further.

Bradford		29,000		77,000	
Halifax		63,000		110,000	
Huddersfield	contained	15,000		34,000	
Leeds	in	53,000	and in	123,000	inhabitants
and the whole of the	1801		1831		
West Riding		564,000		980,000	

In 1835 the spinning of wool employed in the United Kingdom 1,313 mills, with 71,300 workers, these last being but a small portion of the multitude who are supported directly or indirectly by the manufacture of wool, and excluding nearly all weavers.

Progress in the linen trade developed later, because the nature of the raw material made the application of spinning machinery very difficult. Attempts had been made in the last years of the last century in Scotland, but the Frenchman, Girard, who introduced flax-spinning in 1810, was the first who succeeded practically, and even Girard's machines first attained on British soil the importance they deserved by means of improvements which they underwent in England, and of their universal application in Leeds, Dundee, and Belfast. From this time the British linen trade rapidly extended. In 1814, 3,000 tons of flax were imported; in 1833, nearly 19,000 tons of flax and 3,400 tons of hemp. The export of Irish linen to Great Britain rose from 32,000,000 yards in 1800 to 53,000,000 in 1825, of which a large part was re-exported. The export of English and Scottish woven linen goods rose from 24,000,000 yards in 1820 to 51,000,000 yards in 1833. The number of flax-spinning establishments in 1835 was 347, employing 33,000 workers, of which one-half were in the South of Scotland, more than 60 in the West Riding of Yorkshire, Leeds, and its environs, 25 in Belfast, Ireland, and the rest in Dorset and Lancashire. Weaving is carried on in the South of Scotland, here and there in England, but principally in Ireland.

With like success did the English turn their attention to the manufacture of silk. Raw material was imported from Southern Europe and Asia ready spun, and the chief labour lay in the twisting of fine threads. Until 1824 the heavy import duty, four shillings per pound on raw material, greatly retarded the development of the English silk industry, while only the markets of England and the Colonies were protected for it. In that year the duty was reduced to one penny, and the number of mills at once largely increased. In a single year the number of throwing spindles rose from 780,000 to 1,180,000; and, although the commercial crisis of 1825 crippled this branch of industry for the moment, yet in 1827 more was produced than ever, the mechanical skill and experience of the English having secured their twisting machinery the supremacy over the awkward devices of their competitors. In 1835 the British Empire possessed 263 twisting mills, employing 30,000 workers, located chiefly in Cheshire, in Macclesfield, Congleton, and the surrounding districts, and in Manchester and Somersetshire. Besides these, there are numerous mills for working up waste, from which a peculiar article known as spun silk is manufactured, with which the English supply even the Paris and Lyons weavers. The weaving of the silk so twisted and spun is carried on in Paisley and elsewhere in Scotland, and in Spitalfields, London, but also in Manchester and elsewhere. Nor is the gigantic advance achieved in English manufacture since 1760 restricted to the production of clothing materials. The impulse, once given, was communicated to all branches of industrial activity, and a multitude of inventions wholly unrelated to those here cited, received double importance from the fact that they were made in the midst of the universal movement. But as soon as the immeasurable importance of mechanical power was practically demonstrated, every energy was concentrated in the effort to exploit this power in all directions, and to exploit it in the interest of individual inventors and manufacturers; and the demand for machinery, fuel, and materials called a mass of workers and a number of trades into redoubled activity. The steam-engine first gave importance to the broad coalfields of England; the production of machinery began now for the first time, and with it arose a new interest in the iron mines which supplied raw material for it. The increased consumption of wool stimulated English sheep-breeding, and the growing importation of wool, flax, and silk called forth an extension of the British ocean carrying trade. Greatest of all was the growth of production of iron. The rich iron deposits of the English hills had hitherto been little developed; iron had always been smelted by means of charcoal, which became gradually more expensive as agriculture improved and forests were cut away. The beginning of the use of coke in iron smelting had been made in the last century, and in 1780 a new method was invented of converting into available wrought-iron coke-smelted iron, which up to that time had been convertible into cast iron only. This process, known as 'puddling', consists in withdrawing the carbon which had mixed with the iron during the process of smelting and opened a wholly new field for the production of English iron. Smelting furnaces were built fifty times larger than before, the process of smelting was simplified by the introduction of hot blasts, and iron could thus be produced so cheaply that a multitude of objects which had before been made of stone or wood were now made of iron.

In 1788 Thomas Paine, the famous democrat, built in Yorkshire the first iron bridge,* which was followed by a great number of others, so that now nearly all bridges, especially for railroad traffic, are built of cast iron, while in London itself a bridge across the Thames, the Southwark bridge, has been built of this material. Iron pillars, supports for machinery, etc., are universally used, and since the introduction of gas-lighting and railroads, new outlets for English iron products are opened. Nails and screws gradually came to be made by machinery. Huntsman, a Sheffielder, discovered in 1760 a method for casting steel, by which much labour was saved, and the production of wholly new cheap goods rendered practicable; and through the greater purity of the material placed at its disposal, and the more perfect tools, new machinery, and minute division of labour, the metal trade of England now first attained importance. The population of Birmingham grew from 73,000 in 1801 to 200,000 in 1844; that of Sheffield from 46,000 in 1801 to 110,000 in 1844, and the consumption of coal in the latter city alone reached in 1836, 515,000 tons. In 1805 there were exported 4,300 tons of iron products and 4,600 tons of pig-iron; in 1834, 16,200 tons of iron products and 107,000 tons of pig-iron, while the whole iron product reaching in 1740 but 17,000 tons, had risen in 1834 to nearly 700,000 tons. The smelting of pig-iron alone consumes yearly more than 3,000,000 tons of coal, and the importance which coal-mining has attained in the course of the last sixty years can scarcely be conceived. All the English and Scottish deposits are now worked, and the mines of Northumberland and Durham alone yield annually more than 5,000,000 tons for shipping, and employ from 40 to 50,000 men. According to the *Durham Chronicle*, there were worked in these two counties: In 1753, 14 mines; in 1800, 40 mines; in 1836, 76 mines; in 1843, 130 mines. Moreover, all mines are now much more energetically worked than formerly. A similarly increased activity was applied to the working of tin, copper and lead, and alongside of the extension of glass manufacture arose a new branch of industry in the production of pottery, rendered important by the efforts of Josiah Wedgwood, about 1763. This inventor placed the whole manufacture of stoneware on a scientific basis, introduced better taste, and founded the potteries of North Staffordshire, a district of eight English square miles, which, formerly a desert waste, is now sown with works and dwellings, and supports more than 60,000 people.

Into this universal whirl of activity everything was drawn. Agriculture made a corresponding advance. Not only did landed property pass, as we have already seen, into the hands of new owners and cultivators, agriculture was affected in still another way. The great holders applied capital to the improvement of the soil, tore down needless fences, drained, manured, employed better tools, and applied a rotation of crops. The progress of science came to their assistance also; Sir Humphry Davy applied chemistry to agriculture with success, and the development of mechanical science bestowed a multitude of advantages upon the large farmer. Further, in consequence of the increase of population, the demand for agricultural products increased in such measure that from 1760 to 1834, 6,840,540 acres of waste land were reclaimed; and, in spite of this, England was transformed from a grain exporting to a grain importing country.

The same activity was developed in the establishment of communication. From 1818 to 1829, there were built in England and Wales, 1,000 English miles of roadway of the width prescribed by law, 60 feet, and nearly all the old roads were reconstructed on the new system of McAdam. In Scotland, the Department of Public Works built since 1803 nearly 900 miles of roadway and more than 1,000 bridges, by which the population of the Highlands was suddenly placed within reach of civilization. The Highlanders had hitherto been chiefly poachers and smugglers; they now became farmers and hand-workers. And, though Gaelic schools were organized for the purpose of maintaining the Gaelic language, yet Gaelic-Celtic customs and speech are rapidly vanishing before the approach of English civilization. So, too, in Ireland; between the counties of Cork, Limerick, and Kerry lay hitherto a wilderness wholly without passable roads, and serving, by reason of its inaccessibility, as the refuge of all criminals and the chief protection of the Celtic Irish nationality in the South of Ireland. It has now been cut through by public roads, and civilization has thus gained admission even to this savage region. The whole British Empire, and especially England, which, sixty years ago, had as bad roads as Germany or France then had, is now covered by a network of the finest roadways; and these, too, like almost everything else in England, are the work of private enterprise, the State having done very little in this direction.

Before 1755 England possessed almost no canals. In that year a canal was built in Lancashire from Sankey Brook to St Helens; and in 1759 James Brindley built the first important one, the Duke of Bridgewater's canal from Manchester, and the coal-mines of the district to the mouth of the Mersey passing, near Barton, by aqueduct, over the river Irwell. From this achievement dates the canal building of England, to which Brindley first gave importance. Canals were now built, and rivers made navigable in all directions. In England alone, there are 2,200 miles of canals and 1,800 miles of navigable river. In Scotland, the Caledonian Canal was cut directly across the country, and in Ireland several canals were built. These improvements too, like the railroads and roadways, are nearly all the work of private individuals and companies.

The railroads have been only recently built. The first great one was opened from Liverpool to Manchester in 1830, since which all the great cities have been connected by rail. London with Southampton, Brighton, Dover, Colchester, Exeter, and Birmingham, Birmingham with Gloucester, Liverpool, Lancaster (via Newton and Wigan, and via Manchester and Bolton); also with Leeds (via Manchester and Halifax, and via Leicester, Derby, and Sheffield); Leeds with Hull and Newcastle (via York). There are also many minor lines building or projected, which will soon make it possible to travel from Edinburgh to London in one day.

As it had transformed the means of communication by land, so did the introduction of steam revolutionize travel by sea. The first steamboat was launched in 1807, in the Hudson, in North America; the first in the British Empire, in 1811, on the Clyde. Since then, more than 600 have been built in England; and in 1836 more than 500 were plying to and from British ports.

Such, in brief, is the history of English industrial development in the past sixty years, a history which has no counterpart in the annals of humanity. Sixty, eighty years ago, England was a country like every other, with small towns, few and simple industries, and a thin but *proportionally* large agricultural population. Today it is a country like *no* other, with a capital of two and a half million inhabitants; with vast manufacturing cities; with an industry that supplies the world, and produces almost everything by means of the most complex machinery; with an industrious, intelligent, dense population, of which two-thirds are employed in trade and commerce, and composed of classes wholly different; forming, in fact, with other customs and other needs, a different nation from the England of those days. The industrial revolution is of the same importance for England as the political revolution for France, and the philosophical revolution for Germany; and the difference between England in 1760 and in 1844 is at least as great as that between France, under the *ancien régime* and during the revolution of July. But the mightiest result of this industrial transformation is the English proletariat.

We have already seen how the proletariat was called into existence by the introduction of machinery. The rapid extension of manufacture demanded hands, wages rose, and troops of workmen migrated from the agricultural districts to the towns. Population multiplied enormously, and nearly all the increase took place in the proletariat. Further, Ireland had entered upon an orderly development only since the beginning of the eighteenth century. There, too, the population, more than decimated by English cruelty in earlier disturbances, now rapidly multiplied, especially after the advance in manufacture began to draw masses of Irishmen towards England. Thus arose the great manufacturing and commercial cities of the British Empire, in which at least three-fourths of the population belong to the working class, while the lower middle class consists only of small shopkeepers, and very very few handicraftsmen. For, though the rising manufacture first attained importance by transforming tools into machines, workrooms into factories, and consequently, the toiling lower middle class into the toiling proletariat, and the former large merchants into manufacturers, though the lower middle class was thus early crushed out, and the population reduced to the two opposing elements, workers and capitalists, this happened outside of the domain of manufacture proper, in the province of handicraft and retail trade as well. In the place of the former masters and apprentices, came great capitalists and working men who had no prospect of rising above their class. Hand-work was carried on after the fashion of factory work, the division of labour was strictly applied, and small employers who could not compete with great establishments were forced down into the proletariat. At the same time the destruction of the former organization of hand-work, and the disappearance of the lower middle class deprived the working man of all possibility of rising into the middle class himself. Hitherto he had always had the prospect of establishing himself somewhere as master artificer, perhaps employing journeymen and apprentices; but now, when master artificers were crowded out by manufacturers, when large capital had become necessary for carrying on work independently the working class became, for the first time, an integral, permanent class of the population, whereas it has formerly often been merely a transition leading to the bourgeoisie. Now, he who was born to toil had no other prospect than that of remaining a toiler all his life. Now, for the first time, therefore, the proletariat was in a position to undertake an independent movement.

In this way were brought together those vast masses of working men who now fill the whole British Empire, whose social condition forces itself every day more and more upon the attention of the civilized world. The condition of the working class is the condition of the vast majority of the English people. The question: What is to become of those destitute millions, who consume today what they earned yesterday; who have created the greatness of England by their inventions and their toil; who become with every passing day more conscious of their might, and demand, with daily increasing urgency, their share of the advantages of society? — This, since the Reform Bill,* has become the national question. All parliamentary debates of any importance may be reduced to this; and, though the English middle class will not as yet admit it, though they try to evade this great question, and to represent their own particular interests as the truly national ones, their action is utterly useless. With every session of Parliament the working class gains ground, the interests of the middle class diminish in importance and, in spite of the fact that the middle class is the chief, in fact, the only power in Parliament, the last session of 1844 was a continuous debate upon subjects affecting the working class, the Poor Relief Bill, the Factory Act, the Masters' and Servants' Act; and Thomas Duncombe, the representative of the working men in the House of Commons, was the great man of the session; while the Liberal middle class with its motion for repealing the Corn Laws, and the Radical middle class with its resolution for refusing the taxes, played pitiable roles. Even the debates about Ireland were at bottom debates about the Irish proletariat, and the means of coming to its assistance. It is high time, too, for the English middle class to make some concessions to the working men who no longer plead but threaten; for in a short time it may be too late.

In spite of all this, the English middle class, especially the manufacturing class, which is enriched directly by means of the poverty of the workers, persists in ignoring this poverty. This class, feeling itself the mighty representative class of the nation, is ashamed to lay the sore spot of England bare before the eyes of the world; will not confess, even to itself, that the workers are in distress, because it, the property-holding, manufacturing class, must bear the moral responsibility for this distress. Hence the scornful smile which intelligent Englishmen (and they, the middle class, alone are known on the Continent) assume when anyone begins to speak of the condition of the working class; hence the utter ignorance on the part of the whole middle class of everything which concerns the workers; hence the ridiculous blunders which men of this class, in and out of Parliament, make when the position of the proletariat comes under discussion; hence the absurd freedom from anxiety, with which the middle class dwells upon a soil that is honeycombed, and may any day collapse, the speedy collapse of which is as certain as a mathematical or mechanical demonstration; hence the miracle that the English have as yet no single book upon the condition of their workers, although they have been examining and mending the old state of things no one knows how many years. Hence also the deep wrath of the whole working class, from Glasgow to London, against the rich, by whom they are systematically plundered and mercilessly left to their fate, a wrath which before too long a time goes by, a time almost within the power of man to predict, must break out into a Revolution in comparison with which the French Revolution, and the year 1794, will prove to have been child's play.

The Industrial Proletariat

The order of our investigation of the different sections of the proletariat follows naturally from the foregoing history of its rise. The first proletarians were connected with manufacture, were engendered by it, and accordingly, those employed in manufacture, in the working up of raw materials, will first claim our attention. The production of raw materials and of fuel for manufacture attained importance only in consequence of the industrial change, and engendered a new proletariat, the coal and metal miners. Then, in the third place, manufacture influenced agriculture, and in the fourth, the conclusion of Ireland; and the fractions of the proletariat belonging to each, will find their place accordingly. We shall find, too, that with the possible exception of the Irish, the degree of intelligence of the various workers is in direct proportion to their relation to manufacture; and that the factory-hands are most enlightened as to their own interests, the miners somewhat less so, the agricultural labourers scarcely at all. We shall find the same order again among the industrial workers, and shall see how the factory-hands, eldest children of the industrial revolution, have from the beginning to the present day formed the nucleus of the Labour Movement, and how the others have joined this movement just in proportion as their handicraft has been invaded by the progress of machinery. We shall thus learn from the example which England offers, from the equal pace which the Labour Movement has kept with the movement of industrial development, the historical significance of manufacture.

Since, however, at the present moment, pretty much the whole industrial proletariat is involved in the movement, and the condition of the separate sections has much in common, because they all are industrial, we shall have first to examine the condition of the industrial proletariat as a whole, in order later to notice more particularly each separate division with its own peculiarities.

It has been already suggested that manufacture centralizes property in the hands of the few. It requires large capital with which to erect the colossal establishments that ruin the petty trading bourgeoisie and with which to press into its service the forces of Nature, so driving the hand-labour of the independent workman out of the market. The division of labour, the application of water and especially steam, and the application of machinery, are the three great levers with which manufacture, since the middle of the last century, has been busy putting the world out of joint. Manufacture, on a small scale, created the middle class; on a large scale, it created the working class, and raised the elect of the middle class to the throne, but only to overthrow them the more surely when the time comes. Meanwhile, it is an undenied and easily explained fact that the numerous petty middle class of the 'good old times' has been annihilated by manufacture, and resolved into rich capitalists on the one hand and poor workers on the other.

The centralizing tendency of manufacture does not, however, stop here. Population becomes centralized just as capital does; and, very naturally, since the human being, the worker, is regarded in manufacture simply as a piece of capital for the use of which the manufacturer pays interest under the name of wages. A manufacturing establishment requires many workers employed together in a single building, living near each other and forming a village of themselves in the case of a good-sized factory. They have needs for satisfying which other people are necessary; handicraftsmen, shoemakers, tailors, bakers, carpenters, stonemasons, settle at hand. The inhabitants of the village, especially the younger generation, accustom themselves to factory work, grow skilful in it, and when the first mill can no longer employ them all, wages fall, and the immigration of fresh manufacturers is the consequence. So the village grows into a small town, and the small town into a large one. The greater the town, the greater its advantages. It offers roads, railroads, canals; the choice of skilled labour increases constantly, new establishments can be built more cheaply because of the competition among builders and machinists who are at hand, than in remote country districts, whither timber, machinery, builders, and operatives must be brought; it offers a market to which buyers crowd, and direct communication with the markets supplying raw material or demanding finished goods. Hence the marvellously rapid growth of the great manufacturing towns. The country, on the other hand, has the advantage that wages are usually lower than in town, and so town and country are in constant competition; and, if the advantage is on the side of the town today, wages sink so low in the country tomorrow that new investments are most profitably made there. But the centralizing tendency of manufacture continues in full force, and every new factory built in the country bears in it the germ of a manufacturing town. If it were possible for this mad rush of manufacture to go on at this rate for another century, every manufacturing district of England would be one great manufacturing town, and, Manchester and Liverpool would meet at Warrington or Newton; for in commerce, too, this centralization of the population works in precisely the same way, and hence it is that one or two great harbours, such as Hull and Liverpool, Bristol and London, monopolize almost the whole maritime commerce of Great Britain.

Since commerce and manufacture attain their most complete development in these great towns, their influence upon the proletariat is also most clearly observable here. Here the centralization of property has reached the highest point; here the morals and customs of the good old times are most completely obliterated; here it has gone so far that the name Merry Old England conveys no meaning, for Old England itself is unknown to memory and to the tales of our grand fathers. Hence, too, there exist here only a rich and a poor class, for the lower middle class vanishes more completely with every passing day. Thus the class formerly most stable has become the most restless one. It consists today of a few remnants of a past time, and a number of people eager to make fortunes, industrial Micawbers* and speculators of whom one may amass a fortune, while ninety-nine become insolvent, and more than half of the ninety-nine live by perpetually repeated failure.

But in these towns the proletarians are the infinite majority, and how they fare, what influence the great town exercises upon them, we have now to investigate.

· · · ·

Meanwhile, let us proceed to a more detailed investigation of the position, in which the social war has placed the non-possessing class. Let us see what pay for his work society does give the working man in the form of dwelling, clothing, food, what sort of subsistence it grants those who contribute most to the maintenance of society; and, first, let us consider the dwellings.

Every great city has one or more slums, where the working class is crowded together. True, poverty often dwells in hidden alleys close to the palaces of the rich; but, in general, a separate territory has been assigned to it, where, removed from the sight of the happier classes, it may struggle along as it can. These slums are pretty equally arranged in all the great towns of England, the worst houses in the worst quarters of the towns; usually one- or two-storeyed cottages in long rows, perhaps with cellars used as dwellings, almost always irregularly built. These houses of three or four rooms and a kitchen form, throughout England, some parts of London excepted, the general dwellings of the working class. The streets are generally unpaved, rough, dirty, filled with vegetable and animal refuse, without sewers or gutters, but supplied with foul, stagnant pools instead. Moreover, ventilation is impeded by the bad, confused method of building of the whole quarter, and since many human beings here live crowded into a small space, the atmosphere that prevails in these working-men's quarters may readily be imagined. Further, the streets serve as drying grounds in fine weather; lines are stretched across from house to house, and hung with wet clothing.

Let us investigate some of the slums in their order. London comes first, and in London the famous rookery of St Giles which is now, at last, about to be penetrated by a couple of broad streets. St Giles is in the midst of the most populous part of the town, surrounded by broad, splendid avenues in which the gay world of London idles about, in the immediate neighbourhood of Oxford Street, Regent Street, of Trafalgar Square and the Strand. It is a disorderly collection of tall, three or four-storeyed houses, with narrow, crooked, filthy streets, in which there is quite as much life as in the great thoroughfares of the town, except that, here, people of the working class only are to be seen. A vegetable market is held in the street, baskets with vegetables and fruits, naturally all bad and hardly fit to use, obstruct the sidewalk still further, and from these, as well as from the fish-dealers' stalls, arises a horrible smell. The houses are occupied from cellar to garret, filthy within and without, and their appearance is such that no human being could possibly wish to live in them. But all this is nothing in comparison with the dwellings in the narrow courts and alleys between the streets, entered by covered passages between the houses, in which the filth and tottering ruin surpass all description. Scarcely a whole window-pane can be found, the walls are crumbling, door-posts and window-frames Loose and broken, doors of old boards nailed together, or altogether wanting in this thieves' quarter, where no doors are needed, there being nothing to steal. Heaps of garbage and ashes lie in all directions, and the foul liquids emptied before the doors gather in stinking pools. Here live the poorest of the poor, the worst paid workers with thieves and the victims of prostitution indiscriminately huddled together, the majority Irish, or of Irish extraction, and those who have not yet sunk in the whirlpool of moral ruin which surrounds them, sinking daily deeper, losing daily more and more of their power to resist the demoralizing influence of want, filth, and evil surroundings.

Nor is St Giles the only London slum. In the immense tangle of streets, there are hundreds and thousands of alleys and courts lined with houses too bad for anyone to live in, who can still spend anything whatsoever upon a dwelling fit for human beings. Close to the splendid houses of the rich such a lurking-place of the bitterest poverty may often be found. So, a short time ago, on the occasion of a coroner's inquest, a region close to Portman Square, one of the very respectable squares, was characterized as an abode 'of a multitude of Irish demoralized by poverty and filth'. So, too, may be found in streets, such as Long Acre and others, which, though not fashionable, are yet 'respectable', a great number of cellar dwellings out of which puny children and half-starved, ragged women emerge into the light of day. In the immediate neighbourhood of Drury Lane Theatre, the second in London, are some of the worst streets of the whole metropolis, Charles, King, and Park Streets, in which the houses are inhabited from cellar to garret exclusively by poor families. In the parishes of St John and St Margaret there lived in 1840, according to the *Journal of the Statistical Society*, 5,366 working-men's families in 5,294 'dwellings' (if they deserve the name!), men, women, and children thrown together without distinction of age or sex, 26,830 persons all told; and of these families three-fourths possessed but one room. In the aristocratic parish of St George, Hanover Square, there lived, according to the same authority, 1,465 working-men's families, nearly 6,000 persons, under similar conditions, and here, too, more than two-thirds of the whole number crowded together at the rate of one family in one room. And how the poverty of these unfortunates, among whom even thieves find nothing to steal, is exploited by the property-holding class in lawful ways! The abominable dwellings in Drury Lane, just mentioned, bring in the following rents: two cellar dwellings, 3s.; one room, ground-floor, 4s.; second-storey, 4s. 6d.; third-floor, 4s.; garret-room, 3s. weekly, so that the starving occupants of Charles Street alone pay the house-owners a yearly tribute of £2,000, and the 5,366 families above mentioned in Westminster, a yearly rent of £40,000.

The most extensive working-people's district lies east of the Tower in Whitechapel and Bethnal Green, where the greatest masses of London working people live. Let us hear Mr G. Alston, preacher of St Philip's, Bethnal Green, on the condition of his parish. He says:

> It contains 1,400 houses, inhabited by 2,795 families, or about 12,000 persons.
> The space upon which this large population dwells, is less than 400 yards (1,200

feet) square, and in this overcrowding it is nothing unusual to find a man, his wife, four or five children, and, sometimes, both grandparents, all in one single room of ten to twelve square feet, where they eat, sleep, and work. I believe that before the Bishop of London called attention to this most poverty-stricken parish, people at the West End knew as little of it as of the savages of Australia or the South Sea Isles. And if we make ourselves acquainted with these unfortunates, through personal observation, if we watch them at their scanty meal and see them bowed by illness and want of work, we shall find such a mass of helplessness and misery, that a nation like ours must blush that these things can be possible. I was rector near Huddersfield during the three years in which the mills were at their worst, but I have never seen such complete helplessness of the poor as since then in Bethnal Green. Not one father of a family in ten in the whole neighbourhood has other clothing than his working suit, and that is as bad and tattered as possible; many, indeed, have no other covering for the night than these rags, and no bed, save a sack of straw and shavings.

The foregoing description furnishes an idea of the aspect of the interior of the dwellings. But let us follow the English officials, who occasionally stray thither, into one or two of these working men's homes.

On the occasion of an inquest held on 14 November 1843 by Mr Carter, coroner for Surrey, upon the body of Ann Galway, aged 45 years, the newspapers related the following particulars concerning the deceased: She had lived at No. 3 White Lion Court, Bermondsey Street, London, with her husband and a 19-year-old son in a little room, in which neither a bedstead nor any other furniture was to be seen. She lay dead beside her son upon a heap of feathers which were scattered over her almost naked body, there being neither sheet nor coverlet. The feathers stuck so fast over the whole body that the physician could not examine the corpse until it was cleansed, and then found it starved and scarred from the bites of vermin. Part of the floor of the room was torn up, and the hole used by the family as a privy.

On Monday, 1 January 1844 two boys were brought before the police magistrate because, being in a starving condition, they had stolen and immediately devoured a half-cooked calf's foot from a shop. The magistrate felt called upon to investigate the case further, and received the following details from the policeman: The mother of the two boys was the widow of an ex-soldier, afterwards policeman, and had had a very hard time since the death of her husband, to provide for her nine children. She lived at No. 2 Pool's Place, Quaker Court, Spitalfields, in the utmost poverty. When the policeman came to her, he found her with six of her children literally huddled together in a little back room, with no furniture but two old rush-bottomed chairs with the seats gone, a small table with two legs broken, a broken cup, and a small dish. On the hearth was scarcely a spark of fire, and in one corner lay as many old rags as would fill a woman's apron, which served the whole family as a bed. For bed clothing they had only their scanty day clothing. The poor woman told him that she had been forced to sell her bedstead the year before to buy food. Her bedding she had pawned with the victualler for food. In short, everything had gone for food. The magistrate ordered the woman a considerable provision from the poor-box.

In February 1844 Theresa Bishop, a widow 60 years old, was recommended, with her sick daughter, aged 26, to the compassion of the police magistrate in Marlborough Street. She lived at No. 5 Brown Street, Grosvenor Square, in a small back room no larger than a closet, in which there was not one single piece of furniture. In one corner lay some rags upon which both slept; a chest served as table and chair. The mother earned a little by charring.

The owner of the house said that they had lived in this way since May 1843, had gradually sold or pawned everything that they had, and had still never paid any rent. The magistrate assigned them £1 from the poor-box.

I am far from asserting that *all* London working people live in such want as the foregoing three families. I know very well that ten are somewhat better off, where one is so totally trodden under foot by society; but I assert that thousands of industrious and worthy people — far worthier and more to be respected than all the rich of London — do find themselves in a condition unworthy of human beings; and that every proletarian, everyone, without exception, is exposed to a similar fate without any fault of his own and in spite of every possible effort.

But in spite of all this, they who have some kind of a shelter are fortunate, fortunate in comparison with the utterly homeless. In London 50,000 human beings get up every morning, not knowing where they are to lay their heads at night. The luckiest of this multitude, those who succeed in keeping a penny or two until evening, enter a lodging-house, such as abound in every great city, where they find a bed. But what a bed! These houses are filled with beds from cellar to garret, four, five, six beds in a room; as many as can he crowded in. Into every bed four, five, or six human beings are piled, as many as can be packed in, sick and well, young and old, drunk and sober, men and women, just as they come, indiscriminately. Then come strife, blows, wounds, or, if these bedfellows agree, so much the worse; thefts are arranged and things done which our language, grown more humane than our deeds, refuses to record. And those who cannot pay for such a refuge? They sleep where they find a place, in passages, arcades, in corners where the police and the owners leave them undisturbed. A few individuals find their way to the refuges which are managed, here and there, by private charity, others sleep on the benches in the parks close under the windows of Queen Victoria. Let us hear the London *Times*:

> *It appears from the report of the proceedings at Marlborough Street Police Court in our columns of yesterday, that there is an average number of 50 human beings of all ages, who huddle together in the parks every night, having no other shelter than what is supplied by the trees and a few hollows of the embankment. Of these, the majority are young girls who have been seduced from the country by the soldiers and turned loose on the world in all the destitution of friendless penury, and all the recklessness of early vice.*

> *This is truly horrible! Poor there must be everywhere. Indigence will find its way and set up its hideous state in the heart of a great and luxurious city. Amid the thousand narrow lanes and by-streets of a populous metropolis there must always, we fear, be much suffering—much that offends the eye—much that lurks unseen.*

> *But that within the precincts of wealth, gaiety, and fashion, nigh the regal grandeur of St. James, close on the palatial splendour of Bayswater, on the confines of the old and new aristocratic quarters, in a district where the cautious refinement of modern design has refrained from creating one single tenement for poverty; which seems, as it were, dedicated to the exclusive enjoyment of wealth, that there want, and famine, and disease, and vice should stalk in all their kindred horrors, consuming body by body, soul by soul!*

> *It is indeed a monstrous state of things! Enjoyment the most absolute, that bodily ease, intellectual excitement, or the more innocent pleasures of sense can supply to man's craving, brought in close contact with the most unmitigated misery! Wealth,*

from its bright saloons, laughing—an insolently heedless laugh—at the unknown wounds of want! Pleasure, cruelly but unconsciously mocking the pain that moans below! All contrary things mocking one another—all contrary, save the vice which tempts and the vice which is tempted!

But let all men remember this—that within the most courtly precincts of the richest city of God's earth, there may be found, night after night, winter after winter, women—young in years—old in sin and suffering—outcasts from society—ROTTING FROM FAMINE, FILTH, AND DISEASE. Let them remember this, and learn not to theorise but to act. God knows, there is much room for action nowadays.

I have referred to the refuges for the homeless. How greatly overcrowded these are, two examples may show. A newly erected Refuge for the Houseless in Upper Ogle Street, that can shelter 300 persons every night, has received since its opening, 27 January to 17 March 1844, 2,740 persons for one or more nights; and although the season was growing more favourable, the number of applicants in this, as well as in the asylums of Whitecross Street and Wapping, was strongly on the increase, and a crowd of the homeless had to be sent away every night for want of room. In another refuge, the Central Asylum in Playhouse Yard, there were supplied on an average 460 beds nightly, during the first three months of the year 1844, 6,681 persons being sheltered, and 96,141 portions of bread were distributed. Yet the committee of directors declare this institution began to meet the pressure of the needy to a limited extent only when the Eastern Asylum also was opened.

Let us leave London and examine the other great cities of the three kingdoms in their order. Let us take Dublin first, a city the approach to which from the sea is as charming as that of London is imposing. The Bay of Dublin is the most beautiful of the whole British Island Kingdom, and is even compared by the Irish with the Bay of Naples. The city, too, possesses great attractions, and its aristocratic districts are better and more tastefully laid out than those of any other.

· · · ·

Results

Having now investigated, somewhat in detail, the conditions under which the English working class lives, it is time to draw some further inferences from the facts presented, and then to compare our inferences with the actual state of things. Let us see what the workers themselves have become under the given circumstances, what sort of people they are, what their physical, mental, and moral status.

When one individual inflicts bodily injury upon another, such injury that death results, we call the deed manslaughter; when the assailant knew in advance that the injury would be fatal, we call his deed murder. But when society places hundreds of proletarians in such a position that they inevitably meet a too early and an unnatural death, one which is quite as much a death by violence as that by the sword or bullet; when it deprives thousands of the necessaries of life, places them under conditions in which they *cannot* live — forces them, through the strong arm of the law, to remain in such conditions until that death ensues which is the inevitable consequence — knows that these thousands of victims must perish, and yet permits these conditions to remain, its deed is murder just as surely as the deed of the single individual; disguised, malicious murder, murder against which none can defend himself, which does not seem what it is, because no man sees the murderer, because the death of the victim seems a natural one, since the offence is more one of omission than of commission. But murder it remains. I have now to prove that society in England daily and hourly commits what the working-men's organs, with perfect correctness, characterize as social murder, that it has placed the workers under conditions in which they can neither retain health nor live long; that it undermines the vital force of these workers gradually, little by little, and so hurries them to the grave before their time. I have further to proof that society knows how injurious such conditions are to the health and the life of the workers, and yet does nothing to improve these conditions. That it *knows* the consequences of its deeds; that its act is, therefore, not mere manslaughter, but murder, I shall have proved, when I cite official documents, reports of Parliament and of the Government, in substantiation of my charge.

That a class which lives under the conditions already sketched and is so ill-provided with the most necessary means of subsistence, cannot be healthy and can reach no advanced age, is self-evident. Let us review the circumstances once more with especial reference to the health of the workers. The centralization of population in great cities exercises of itself an unfavourable influence; the atmosphere of London can never be so pure, so rich in oxygen, as the air of the country; two and a half million pairs of lungs, two hundred and fifty thousand fires, crowded upon an area three to four miles square, consume an enormous amount of oxygen, which is replaced with difficulty, because the method of building cities in itself impedes ventilation. The carbonic acid gas, engendered by respiration and fire, remains in the streets by reason of its specific gravity, and the chief air current passes over the roofs of the city. The lungs of the inhabitants fail to receive the dire supply of oxygen, and the consequence is mental and physical lassitude and low vitality. For this reason, the dwellers in cities are far less exposed to acute, and especially to inflammatory, affections than rural populations, who live in a free, normal atmosphere; but they suffer the more from chronic affections. And if life in large cities is, in itself, injurious to health, how great must be the harmful influence of an abnormal atmosphere in the working-people's quarters, where, as we have seen, everything combines to poison the air. In the country, it may, perhaps, be comparatively innoxious to keep a dung-heap adjoining one's dwelling, because the air has free ingress from all sides; but in the midst of a large town, among closely built lanes and courts that shut out all movement of the atmosphere, the case is different. All putrefying vegetable and animal substances give off gases decidedly injurious to health, and if these gases have no free way of escape, they inevitably poison the atmosphere. The filth and stagnant pools of the working-people's quarters in the great cities have, therefore, the worst effect upon the public health, because they produce precisely those gases which engender disease; so, too, the exhalations from contaminated streams. But this is by no means all. The manner in which the great multitude of the poor is treated by society today is revolting. They are drawn into the large cities where they breathe a poorer atmosphere than in the country; they are relegated to districts which, by reason of the method of construction, are worse ventilated than any others; they are deprived of all means of cleanliness, of water itself, since pipes are laid only when paid for, and the rivers so polluted that they are useless for such purposes; they are obliged to throw all offal and garbage, all dirty water, often all disgusting drainage and excrement into the streets, being without other means of disposing of them; they are thus compelled to infect the region of their own dwellings. Nor is this enough. All conceivable evils are heaped upon the heads of the poor. If the population of great cities is too dense in general, it is they in particular who are packed into the least space. As though the vitiated atmosphere of the streets were not enough, they are penned in dozens into single rooms, so that the air which they breathe at night is enough in itself to stifle them. They are given damp dwellings, cellar dens that are not waterproof from below, or garrets that leak from above. Their houses are so built that the clammy air cannot escape. They are supplied bad, tattered, or rotten clothing, adulterated and indigestible food. They arc exposed to the most exciting changes of mental condition, the most violent vibrations between hope and fear; they are hunted like game, and not permitted to attain peace of mind and quiet enjoyment of life. They are deprived of all enjoyments except that of sexual indulgence and drunkenness, are worked every day to the point of complete exhaustion of their mental and physical energies, and are thus constantly spurred on to the maddest excess in the only two enjoyments at their command. And if they surmount all this, they fall victims to want of work in a crisis when all the little is taken from them that had hitherto been vouchsafed them.

How is it possible, under such conditions, for the lower class to be healthy and long lived? What else can he expected than an excessive mortality, an unbroken series of epidemics, a progressive deterioration in the physique of the working population? Let us see how the facts stand.

That the dwellings of the workers in the worst portions of the cities, together with the other conditions of life of this class, engender numerous diseases, is attested on all sides. The article already quoted from the *Artisan* asserts with perfect truth, that lung diseases must he the inevitable consequence of such conditions, and that, indeed, cases of this kind are disproportionately frequent in this class. That the bad air of London, and especially of the working-people's districts, is in the highest degree favourable to the development of consumption the hectic appearance of great numbers of persons sufficiently indicates. If one roams the streets a little in the early morning, when the multitudes are on their way to their work, one is amazed at the number of persons who look wholly or half-consumptive. Even in Manchester the people have not the same appearance; these pale, lank, narrow-chested, hollow-eyed ghosts, whom one passes at every step, these languid, flabby faces, incapable of the slightest energetic expression, I have seen in such startling numbers only in London, though consumption carries off a horde of victims annually in the factory towns of the North. In competition with consumption stands typhus, to say nothing of scarlet fever, a disease which brings most frightful devastation into the ranks of the working class. Typhus, that universally diffused affliction, is attributed by the official report on the sanitary condition of the working class directly to the bad state of the dwellings in the matters of ventilation, drainage, and cleanliness. This report, compiled, it must not be forgotten, by the leading physicians of England from the testimony of other physicians, asserts that a single ill-ventilated court, a single blind alley without drainage, is enough to engender fever, and usually does engender it, especially if the inhabitants are greatly crowded. This fever has the same character almost everywhere, and develops in nearly every case into specific typhus. It is to be found in the working-People's quarters of all great towns and cities, and in single ill-built, ill-kept streets of smaller places, though it naturally seeks out single victims in better districts also. In London it has now prevailed for a considerable time; its extraordinary violence in the year 1837 gave rise to the report already referred to. According to the annual report of Dr Southwood Smith on the London Fever Hospital, the number of patients in 1843 was 1,462, or 418 more than in any previous year. In the damp, dirty regions of the north, south, and east districts of London, this disease raged with extraordinary violence. Many of the patients were working people from the country, who had endured severest privation while migrating, and, after their arrival, had slept hungry and half-naked in the streets, and so fallen victims to the fever. These people were brought into the hospital in such a state of weakness, that unusual quantities of wine, cognac, and preparations of ammonia and other stimulants were required for their treatment; 16.5 per cent of all patients died.

This malignant fever is to be found in Manchester; in the worst quarters of the Old Town, Ancoats, Little Ireland, etc., it is rarely extinct; though here, as in the *English* towns generally, it prevails to a less extent than might be expected. In Scotland and Ireland, on the other hand, it rages with a violence that surpasses all conception. In Edinburgh and Glasgow it broke out in 1857, after the famine, and in 1826 and 1837 with especial violence, after the commercial crisis, subsiding somewhat each time after having raged about three years. In Edinburgh about 6,000 persons were attacked by the fever during the epidemic of 1817, and about 10,000 in that of 1837, and not only the number of persons attacked but the violence of the disease increased with each repetition.

But the fury of the epidemic in all former periods seems to have been child's play in comparison with its ravages after the crisis of 1842. One-sixth of the whole indigent population of Scotland was seized by the fever, and the infection was carried by wandering beggars with fearful rapidity from one locality to another. It did not reach the middle and upper classes of the population, yet in two months there were more fever cases than in twelve years before. In Glasgow, 12 per cent of the population were seized in the year 1843; 32,000 persons, of whom 32 per cent perished, while this mortality in Manchester and Liverpool does not ordinarily exceed 8 per cent. The illness reached a crisis on the seventh and fifteenth days; on the latter the patient usually became yellow, which our authority regards as an indication that the cause of the malady was to be sought in mental excitement and anxiety. In Ireland, too, these fever epidemics have become domesticated. During twenty-one months of the years 1817–18, 39,000 fever patients passed through the Dublin hospital; and in a more recent year, according to Sheriff Alison, 60,000. In Cork the fever hospital received one-seventh of the population in 1817–18, in Limerick in the same time one-fourth, and in the bad quarter of Waterford, nineteen-twentieths of the whole population were ill of the fever at one time.

When one remembers under what conditions the working people live, when one thinks how crowded their dwellings are, how every nook and corner swarms with human beings, how sick and well sleep in the same room, in the same bed, the only wonder is that a contagious disease like this fever does not spread yet further. And when one reflects how little medical assistance the sick have at command, how many are without any medical advice whatsoever, and ignorant of the most ordinary precautionary measures, the mortality seems actually small. Dr Alison, who has made a careful study of this disease, attributes it directly to the want and the wretched condition of the poor, as in the report already quoted. He asserts that privations and the insufficient satisfaction of vital needs are what prepare the frame for contagion and make the epidemic wide-spread and terrible. He proves that a period of privation, a commercial crisis or a bad harvest, has each time produced the typhus epidemic in Ireland as in Scotland, and that the fury of the plague has fallen almost exclusively on the working class. It is a noteworthy fact, that according to his testimony, the majority of persons who perish by typhus are fathers of families, precisely the persons who can least be spared by those dependent upon them; and several Irish physicians whom he quotes bear the same testimony.

Another category of diseases arises directly from the food rather than the dwellings of the workers. The food of the labourer, indigestible enough in itself, is utterly unfit for young children, and he has neither means nor time to get his children more suitable food. Moreover, the custom of giving children spirits, and even opium, is very general; and these two influences, with the rest of the conditions of life pre-judicial to bodily development, give rise to the most diverse affections of the digestive organs, leaving life-long traces behind them.

Nearly all workers have stomachs more or less weak, and are yet forced to adhere to the diet which is the root of the evil. How should they know what is to blame for it? And if they knew, how could they obtain a more suitable regimen so long as they cannot adopt a different way of living and are not better educated? But new disease arises during childhood from impaired digestion. Scrofula is almost universal among the working class, and scrofulous parents have scrofulous children, especially when the original influences continue in full force to operate upon the inherited tendency of the children. A second consequence of this insufficient bodily nourishment, during the years of growth and development, is rachitis, which is extremely common among the children of the working class. The hardening of the bones is delayed, the development of the skeleton in general is restricted, and deformities of the legs and spinal column are frequent in addition to the usual rachitic affections. How greatly all these evils are increased by the changes to which the workers are subject in consequence of fluctuations in trade, want of work, and the scanty wages in time of crisis, it is not necessary to dwell upon. Temporary want of sufficient food, to which almost every working man is exposed at least once in the course of his life, only contributes to intensify the effect of his usually sufficient but bad diet. Children who are half-starved, just when they most need ample and nutritious food — and how many such there are during every crisis and even when trade is at its best — must inevitably become weak, scrofulous, and rachitic in a high degree. And that they do become so, their appearance amply shows. The neglect to which the great mass of working-men's children are condemned leaves ineradicable traces and brings the enfeeblement of the whole race of workers with it. Add to this the unsuitable clothing of this class, the impossibility of precautions against colds, the necessity of toiling so long as health permits, want made more dire when sickness appears, and the only too common lack of all medical assistance; and we have a rough idea of the sanitary condition of the English working class. The injurious effects peculiar to single employments as now conducted, I shall not deal with here.

Besides these, there are other influences which enfeeble the health of a great number of workers, intemperance most of all. All possible temptations, all allurements combine to bring the workers to drunkenness. Liquor is almost their only source of pleasure, and all things conspire to make it accessible to them. The working man comes from his work tired, exhausted, finds his home comfortless, damp, dirty, repulsive; he has urgent need of recreation, he *must* have something to make work worth his trouble, to make the prospect of the next day endurable. His unnerved, uncomfortable, hypochondriac state of mind and body arising from his unhealthy condition, and especially from indigestion, is aggravated beyond endurance by the general conditions of his life, the uncertainty of his existence, his dependence upon all possible accidents and chances, and his inability to do anything towards gaining an assured position. His enfeebled frame, weakened by bad air and bad food, violently demands some external stimulus; his social need can be gratified only in the public house, he has absolutely no other place where he can meet his friends. How can he be expected to resist the temptation? It is morally and physically inevitable that, under such circumstances, a very large number of working men should fall into intemperance. And apart from the chiefly physical influences which drive the working man into drunkenness, there is the example of the great mass, the neglected education, the impossibility of protecting young from temptation, in many cases the direct influence of intemperate parents, who give their own children liquor, the certainty of forgetting for an hour or two the wretchedness and burden of life, and a hundred other circumstances so mighty that the workers can, in truth, hardly be blamed for yielding to such overwhelming pressure.

Drunkenness has here ceased to be a vice, for which the vicious can be held responsible; it becomes a phenomenon, the necessary, inevitable effect of certain conditions upon an object possessed of no volition in relation to those conditions. They who have degraded the working man to a mere object have the responsibility to bear. But as inevitably as a great number of working men fall prey to drink, just so inevitably does it manifest its ruinous influence upon the body and mind of its victims. All the tendencies to disease arising from the conditions of life of the workers are promoted by it, it stimulates in the highest degree the development of lung and digestive troubles, the rise and spread of typhus epidemics.

Another source of physical mischief to the working class lies in the impossibility of employing skilled physicians in cases of illness. It is true that a number of charitable institutions strive to supply this want, that the infirmary in Manchester, for instance, receives or gives advice and medicine to 22,000 patients annually. But what is that in a city in which, according to Gaskell's calculation, three-fourths of the population need medical aid every year? English doctors charge high fees, and working men are not in a position to pay them. They can therefore do nothing, or are compelled to call in cheap charlatans, and use quack remedies, which do more harm than good. An immense number of such quacks thrive in every English town, securing their clientele among the poor by means of advertisements, posters, and other such devices. Besides these, vast quantities of patent medicines are sold, for all conceivable ailments: Morrison's Pills, Parr's Life Pills, Dr Mainwaring's Pills, and a thousand other pills, essences, and balsams, all of which have the property of curing all the ills that flesh is heir to. These medicines rarely contain actually injurious substances, but, when taken freely and often, they affect the system prejudicially; and as the unwary purchasers are always recommended to take as much as possible, it is not to be wondered at that they swallow them wholesale whether wanted or not.

It is by no means unusual for the manufacture of Parr's life Pills to sell twenty to twenty-five thousand boxes of these salutary pills in a week, and they are taken for constipation by this one, for diarrhoea by that one, for fever, weakness, and all possible ailments. As our German peasants are cupped or bled at certain seasons, so do the English working people now consume patent medicines to their own injury and the great profit of the manufacturer. One of the most injurious of these patent medicines is a drink prepared with opiates, chiefly laudanum, under the name Godfrey's Cordial. Women who work at home, and have their own and other people's children to take care of, give them this drink to keep them quiet, and, as many believe, to strengthen them. They often begin to give this medicine to newly-born children, and continue, without knowing the effects of this 'heart's-ease', until the children die. The less susceptible the child's system to the action of the opium, the greater the quantities administered. When the cordial ceases to act, laudanum alone is given, often to the extent of fifteen to twenty drops at a dose. The Coroner of Nottingham testified before a Parliamentary Commission that one apothecary had, according to his own statement, used thirteen hundred-weight of laudanum in one year in the preparation of Godfrey's Cordial. The effects upon the children so treated may be readily imagined. They are pale, feeble, wilted, and usually die before completing the second year. The use of this cordial is very extensive in all great towns and industrial districts in the kingdom.

The result of all these influences is a general enfeeblement of the frame in the working class. There are few vigorous, well-built, healthy persons among the workers, i.e. among the factory operatives, who are employed in confined rooms, and we are here discussing these only. They are almost all weakly, of angular but not powerful build, lean, pale, and of relaxed fibre, with the exception of the muscles especially exercised in their work. Nearly all suffer from indigestion, and consequently from a more or less hypochondriac, melancholy, irritable, nervous condition. Their enfeebled constitutions are unable to resist disease, and are therefore seized by it on every occasion. Hence they age prematurely and die early. On this point the mortality statistics supply unquestionable testimony.

According to the Report of Registrar-General Graham, the annual death-rate of all England and Wales is something less than 2.25 per cent. That is to say, out of 45 persons, one dies every year. This was the average for the year 1839–40. In 1840–1 the mortality diminished somewhat, and the death-rate was but one in 46. But in the great cities the proportion is wholly different. I have before me official tables of mortality (*Manchester Guardian*, 31 July 1844), according to which the death-rate of several large towns is as follows: In Manchester, including Chorlton and Salford, one in 32.72; and excluding Chorlton and Salford, one in 30.75. In Liverpool, including West Derby (suburb), 31.90, and excluding West Derby, 29.90; while the average of all the districts of Cheshire, Lancashire, and Yorkshire cited, including a number of wholly or partially rural districts and many small towns, with a total population of 2,172,506 for the whole, is one death in 39.80 persons. How unfavourably the workers are placed in the great cities, the mortality for Prescott in Lancashire shows; a district inhabited by miners, and showing a lower sanitary condition than that of the agricultural districts, mining being by no means a healthful occupation. But these miners live in the country, and the death-rate among them is but one in 47.54, or nearly 2.5 per cent better than that for all England. All these statements are based upon the mortality tables for 1843. Still higher is the death-rate in the Scottish cities; in Edinburgh, in 1838–9, one in 29; in 1831, in the Old Town alone, one in 22. In Glasgow, according to Dr Cowen, the average has been, since 1830, one in 30; and in single years, one in 22 to 24. That this enormous shortening of life falls chiefly upon the working class, that the general average is improved by the smaller mortality of the upper and middle classes, is attested upon all sides. One of the most recent depositions is that of a physician, Dr P. N. Holland, in Manchester, who investigated Chorlton-on-Medlock, a suburb of Manchester, under official commission. He divided the houses and streets into three classes each, and ascertained the following variations in the death-rate [see Figure]. It is clear from other tables given by Holland that the mortality in the *streets* of the second class is 18 per cent greater, and in the streets of the third class 68 per cent greater than in those of the first class; that the mortality in the *houses* of the second class is 31 per cent greater, and in the third class 78 per cent greater than in those of the first class; that the mortality in those bad streets which were improved, decreased 25 per cent. He closes with the remark, very frank for an English bourgeois.

			Mortality 1 in	
First class of streets:	I			51
	II			45
houses, class	III			36
Second class of streets:	I			55
	II			38
houses, class	III			35
Third class of streets:	I			—
	II			35
houses, class	III			25

When we find the rate of mortality four times as high in some streets as in others, and twice as high in whole classes of streets as in other classes, and further find that it is all but invariably high in those streets which are in bad condition, and almost invariably low in those whose condition is good, we cannot resist the conclusion that multitudes of our fellow-creatures, hundreds of our immediate neighbours, are annually destroyed for want of the most evident precautions.

The Report on the Sanitary Condition of the Working Class contains information which attests the same fact. In Liverpool, in 1840, the average longevity of the upper classes, gentry, professional men, etc., was 35 years; that of the business men and better-placed handicraftsmen, 22 years; and that of the operatives, day-labourers, and serviceable class in general, but 15 years. The Parliamentary reports contain a mass of similar facts.

The death-rate is kept so high chiefly by the heavy mortality among young children in the working class. The tender frame of a child is least able to withstand the unfavourable influences of an inferior lot in life; the neglect to which they are often subjected, when both parents work or one is dead, avenges itself promptly, and no one need wonder that in Manchester, according to the report last quoted more than 57 per cent of the children of the working class perish before the fifth year, while but 20 per cent of the children of the higher classes, and not quite 32 per cent of the children of all classes in the country die under five years of age. The article of the *Artisan*, already several times referred to, furnishes exacter information on this point, by comparing the city death-rate in single diseases of children with the country death-rate, thus demonstrating that, in general, epidemics in Manchester and Liverpool are three times more fatal than in country districts; that affections of the nervous system are quintupled, and stomach troubles trebled, while deaths from affections of the lungs in cities are to those in the country as 2.5 to 1. Fatal cases of smallpox, measles, scarlet fever, and whooping cough, among small children, are four times more frequent; those of water on the brain are trebled, and convulsions ten times more frequent. To quote another acknowledged authority, I append the following table. Out of 10,000 persons, there die — [see Table]. Apart from the diverse diseases which are the necessary consequence of the present neglect and oppression of the poorer classes, there are other influences which contribute to, increase the mortality among small children. In many families the wife, like the husband, has to work away from home, and the

	Under 5 years	5–19	20–39	40–59	60–69	70–79	80–89	90–99	100+
In Ruthlandshire, a healthy agricultural district	2,865	891	1,275	1,299	1,189	1,428	938	112	3
Essex, marshy agricultural district	3,159	1,110	1,526	1,413	963	1,019	630	177	3
Town of Carlisle, 1779–87, before introduction of mills	4,408	911	1,006	1,201	940	826	533	153	22
Town of Carlisle, after the introduction of mills	4,738	930	1,261	1,134	677	727	452	80	1
Preston, factory town	4,947	1,136	1,379	1,114	553	532	298	38	3
Leeds, factory town	5,286	927	1,228	1,198	593	512	225	29	2

consequence is the total neglect of the children, who are either locked up or given out to be taken care of. It is, therefore, not to be wondered at if hundreds of them perish through all manner of accidents. Nowhere are so many children run over, nowhere are so many killed by falling, drowning, or burning, as in the great cities and towns of England. Deaths from burns and scalds are especially frequent, such a case occurring nearly every week during the winter months in Manchester, and very frequently in London, though little mention is made of them in the papers. I have at hand a copy of the *Weekly Dispatch* of 15 December 1844, according to which, in the week from 1 December to 7 December inclusive, *six* such cases occurred. These unhappy children, perishing in this terrible way, are victims of our social disorder, and of the property-holding classes interested in maintaining and prolonging this disorder. Yet one is left in doubt whether even this terribly torturing death is not a blessing for the children in rescuing them from a long life of toil and wretchedness, rich in suffering and poor in enjoyment. So far has it gone in England; and the bourgeoisie reads these things every day in newspapers and takes no further trouble in the matter. But it cannot complain if after the official and non-official testimony here cited which must be known to it, I broadly accuse it of social murder. Let the ruling class see to it that these frightful conditions are ameliorated, or let it surrender the administration of the common interests to the labouring class. To the latter course it is by no means inclined; for the former task, so long as it remains the bourgeoisie crippled by bourgeois prejudice, it has not the needed power. For if, at last, after hundreds of thousands of victims have perished, it manifests some little anxiety for the future, passing a 'Metropolitan Buildings Act',* under which the most unscrupulous overcrowding of dwellings is to be, at least in some slight degree, restricted; if it points with pride to measures which, far from attacking the root of the evil, do not by any means meet the demands of the commonest sanitary police, it cannot thus vindicate itself from the accusation. The English bourgeoisie has but one choice, either to continue its rule under the unanswerable charge murder and in spite of this charge, or to abdicate in favour of the labouring class. Hitherto it has chosen the former course.

Let us turn from the physical to the mental state of the workers. Since the bourgeoisie vouchsafes them only so much of life as is absolutely necessary, we need not wonder that it bestows upon them only so much education as lies in the interest of the bourgeoisie; and that, in truth, is not much. The means of education in England are restricted out of all proportion to the population. The few day schools at the command of the working class are available only for the smallest minority, and are bad besides. The teachers, worn-out workers, and other unsuitable persons who only turn to teaching in order to live, are usually without the indispensable elementary knowledge, without the moral discipline so needful for the teacher, and relieved of all public supervision. Here, too, free competition rules, and, as usual, the rich profit by it, and the poor, for whom competition is *not* free, who have not the knowledge needed to enable them to form a correct judgement, have the evil consequences to bear. Compulsory school attendance does not exist. In the mills it is, as we shall see, purely nominal; and when in the session of 1843 the Ministry was disposed to make this nominal compulsion effective, the manufacturing bourgeoisie opposed the measure with all its might, though the working class was outspokenly in favour of compulsory school attendance. Moreover, a mass of children work the whole week through in the mills or at home, and therefore cannot attend school. The evening schools, supposed to be attended by children who are employed during the day, are almost abandoned or attended without benefit. It is asking too much, that young workers who have been using themselves up twelve hours in the day should go to school from eight to ten at night. And those who try it usually fall asleep, as is testified by hundreds of witnesses in the Children's Employment Commission's Report. Sunday schools have been founded, it is true, but they, too, are most scantily supplied with teachers, and can be of use to those only who have already learnt something in the day schools. The interval from one Sunday to the next is too long for an ignorant child to remember in the second sitting what it learned in the first, a week before. The Children's Employment Commission's Report furnishes a hundred proofs, and the Commission itself most emphatically expresses the opinion, that neither the weekday nor the Sunday schools, in the least degree, meet the needs of the nation. This report gives evidence of ignorance in the working class of England, such as could hardly be expected in Spain or Italy. It cannot be otherwise; the bourgeoisie has little to hope, and much to fear, from the education of the working class. The Ministry, in its whole enormous budget of £55,000,000, has only the single trifling item of £40,000 for public education, and, but for the fanaticism of the religious sects which does at least as much harm as good, the means of education would be yet more scanty. As it is, the State Church manages its national schools and the various sects their sectarian schools for the sole purpose of keeping the children of the brethren of the faith within the congregation, and of winning away a poor childish soul here and there from some other sect. The consequence is that religion, and precisely the most unprofitable side of religion, polemical discussion, is made the principal subject of instruction, and the memory of the children overburdened with incomprehensible dogmas and theological distinctions; that sectarian hatred and bigotry are awakened as early as possible, and all rational mental and moral training shamefully neglected. The working class has repeatedly demanded of Parliament a system of strictly secular public education, leaving religion to the ministers of the sects; but, thus far, no Ministry has been induced to grant it. The Minister is the obedient servant of the bourgeoisie, and the bourgeoisie is divided into countless sects; but each would gladly grant the workers the otherwise dangerous education on the sole condition of their accepting, as an antidote, the dogmas peculiar to the especial sect in question. And as these sects are still quarrelling among themselves for supremacy, the workers remain for the present without education. It is true that the manufacturers boast of having enabled the majority to read, but the quality of the reading is appropriate to the source of the instruction, as the Children's Employment Commission proves. According to this report, he who knows his letters can read enough to satisfy the conscience of the manufacturers. And when one reflects upon the confused orthography of the English language which makes reading one of the arts, learned only under long instruction, this ignorance is readily understood. Very few working people write readily; and writing orthographically is beyond the powers even of many 'educated' persons. The Sunday schools of the State Church, of the Quakers, and, I think, of several other sects, do not teach writing, 'because it is too worldly an employment for Sunday'. The quality of the instruction offered the workers in other directions may be judged from a specimen or two, taken from the Children's Employment Commission's Report, which unfortunately does not embrace mill-work proper:

> 'In Birmingham,' says Commissioner Grainger, 'the children examined by me are, as a whole, utterly wanting in all that could be in the remotest degree called a useful education. Although in almost all the schools religious instruction alone is furnished, the profoundest ignorance even upon that subject prevailed.'—'In Wolverhampton,' says Commissioner Horne, 'I found, among others, the following example: A girl of eleven years had attended both day and Sunday school, "had never heard of another world, of Heaven, or another life." A boy, seventeen years old, did not know that twice two are four, nor how many farthings in two pence

even when the money was placed in his hand. Several boys had never heard of London nor of Willenhall, though the latter was but an hour's walk from their homes, and in the closest relations with Wolverhampton. Several had never heard the name of the Queen nor other names, such as Nelson, Wellington, Bonaparte; but it was noteworthy that those who had never heard even of St. Paul, Moses, or Solomon, were very well instructed as to the life, deeds, and character of Dick Turpin, the streetrobber, and especially of Jack Sheppard, the thief and gaol-breaker. A youth of sixteen did not know how many twice two are, nor how much four farthings make. A youth of seventeen asserted that four farthings are four half pence; a third, seventeen years old, answered several very simple questions with the brief statement, that he "was ne jedge o'nothin". These children who are crammed with religious doctrines four or five years at a stretch, know as little at the end as at the beginning. One child 'went to Sunday school regularly for five years; does not know who Jesus Christ is, but had heard the name; had never heard of the twelve Apostles, Samson, Moses, Aaron, etc. Another attended Sunday school regularly six years; knows who Jesus Christ was; he died on the cross to save our Saviour; had never heard of St. Peter or St. Paul'. A third, 'attended different Sunday schools seven years; can read only the thin, easy books with simple words of one syllable; has heard of the Apostles, but does not know whether St. Peter was one or St. John; the latter must have been St. John Wesley'. To the question who Christ was, Horne received the following answers among others: 'He was Adam', 'He was an Apostle', 'He was the Saviour's Lord's Son', and from a youth of sixteen: 'He was a king of London long ago'. In Sheffield, Commissioner Symons let the children from the Sunday school read aloud; they could not tell what they had read, or what sort of people the Apostles were, of whom they had just been reading. After he had asked them all one after the other about the Apostles without securing a single correct answer, one sly-looking little fellow, with great glee, called out: 'I know, mister; they were the lepers!' From the pottery districts and from Lancashire the reports are similar.

This is what the bourgeoisie and the State are doing for the education and improvement of the working class. Fortunately the conditions under which this class lives are such as give it a sort of practical training, which not only replaces school cramming, but renders harmless the confused religious notions connected with it, and even places the workers in the vanguard of the national movement of England. Necessity is the mother of invention, and what is still more important, of thought and action. The English working man, who can scarcely read and still less write, nevertheless knows very well where his own interest and that of the nation lies. He knows, too, what the especial interest of the bourgeoisie is, and what he has to expect of that bourgeoisie. If he cannot write he can speak, and speak in public; if he has no arithmetic, he can, nevertheless, reckon with the Political Economists enough to see through a Corn-Law-repealing bourgeois, and to get the better of him in argument; if celestial matters remain very mixed for him in spite of all the effort of the preachers, he sees all the more clearly into terrestrial, political, and social questions. We shall have occasion to refer again to this point; and pass now to the moral characteristics of our workers.

It is sufficiently clear that the instruction in morals can have no better effect than the religious teaching, with which in all English schools it is mixed up. The simple principles which, for plain human beings, regulate the relations of man to man, brought into the direst confusion by our social state, our war of each against all, necessarily remain confused and foreign to the working man when mixed with incomprehensible dogmas, and preached in the religious form of an arbitrary and dogmatic commandment. The schools contribute, according to the confession of all authorities, and especially of the Children's Employment Commission, almost nothing to the morality of the working class. So short-sighted, so stupidly narrow-minded is the English bourgeoisie in its egotism, that it does not even take the trouble to impress upon the workers the morality of the day, which the bourgeoisie has patched together in its own interest for its own protection! Even this precautionary measure is too great an effort for the enfeebled and sluggish bourgeoisie. A time must come when it will repent its neglect, too late. But it has no right to complain that the workers know nothing of its system of morals, and do not act in accordance with it.

Thus are the workers cast out and ignored by the class in power, morally as well as physically and mentally. The only provision made for them is the law, which fastens upon them when they become obnoxious to the bourgeoisie. Like the dullest of the brutes, they are treated to but one form of education, the whip, in the shape of force, not convincing but intimidating. There is, therefore, no cause for surprise if the workers, treated as brutes, actually become such; or if they can maintain their consciousness of manhood only by cherishing the most glowing hatred, the most unbroken inward rebellion against the bourgeoisie in power. They are men so long only as they burn with wrath against the reigning class. They become brutes the moment they bend in patience under the yoke, and merely strive to make life endurable while abandoning the effort to break the yoke.

This, then, is all that the bourgeoisie has done for the education of the proletariat — and when we take into consideration all the circumstances in which this class lives, we shall not think the worse of it for the resentment which it cherishes against the ruling class. The moral training which is not given to the worker in school is not supplied by the other conditions of his life; that moral training, at least, which alone has worth in the eyes of the bourgeoisie; his whole position and environment involves the strongest temptation to immorality. He is poor, life offers him no charm, almost every enjoyment is denied him, the penalties of the law have no further terrors for him; why should he restrain his desires, why leave to the rich the enjoyment of his birthright, why not seize a part of it for himself? What inducement has the proletarian not to steal? It is all very pretty and very agreeable to the ear of the bourgeois to hear the 'sacredness of property' asserted; but for him who has none, the sacredness of property dies out of itself. Money is the god of this world; the bourgeois takes the proletarian's money from him and so makes a practical atheist of him. No wonder, then, if the proletarian retains his atheism and no longer respects the sacredness and power of the earthly God. And when the poverty of the proletarian is intensified to the point of actual lack of the barest necessaries of life, to want and hunger, the temptation to disregard all social order does but gain power. This the bourgeoisie for the most part recognizes. Symons observes that poverty exercises the same ruinous influence upon the mind which drunkenness exercises upon the body; and Dr Alison explains to property-holding readers, with the greatest exactness, what the consequences of social oppression must be for the working class. Want leaves the working man the choice between starving slowly, killing himself speedily, or taking what he needs where he finds it — in plain English, stealing. And there is no cause for surprise that most of them prefer stealing to starvation and suicide.

True, there are, within the working class, numbers too moral to steal even when reduced to the utmost extremity, and these starve or commit suicide. For suicide, formerly the enviable privilege of the upper classes, has become fashionable among the English workers, and numbers of the poor kill themselves to avoid the misery from which they see no other means of escape.

But far more demoralizing than his poverty in its influence upon the English working man is the insecurity of his position, the necessity of living upon wages from hand to mouth, that in short which makes a proletarian of him. The smaller peasants in Germany are usually poor, and often suffer want, but they are less at the mercy of accident, they have at least something secure. The proletarian, who has nothing but his two hands, who consumes today what he earned yesterday, who is subject to every possible chance, and has not the slightest guarantee for being able to earn the barest necessities of life, whom every crisis, every whim of his employer may deprive of bread, this proletarian is placed in the most revolting, inhuman position conceivable for a human being. The slave is assured of a bare livelihood by the self-interest of his master, the serf has at least a scrap of land on which to live; each has at worst a guarantee for life itself. But the proletarian must depend upon himself alone, and is yet prevented from so applying his abilities as to be able to rely upon them. Everything that the proletarian can do to improve his position is but a drop in the ocean compared with the floods of varying chances to which he is exposed, over which he has not the slightest control. He is the passive subject of all possible combinations of circumstances, and must count himself fortunate when he has saved his life even for a short time; and his character and way of living are naturally shaped by these conditions. Either he seeks to keep his head above water in this whirlpool, to rescue his manhood, and this he can do solely in rebellion against the class which plunders him so mercilessly and then abandons him to his fate, which strives to hold him in this position so demoralizing to a human being; or he gives up the struggle against his fate as hopeless, and strives to profit, so far as he can, by the most favourable moment. To save is unavailing, for at the utmost he cannot save more than suffices to sustain life for a short time, while if he falls out of work, it is for no brief period. To accumulate lasting property for himself is impossible; and if it were not, he would only cease to be a working man and another would take his place. What better thing can he do, then, when he gets high wages, than live well upon them? The English bourgeoisie is violently scandalized at the extravagant living of the workers when wages are high; yet it is not only very natural but very sensible of them to enjoy life when they can, instead of laying up treasures which are of no lasting use to them, and which in the end moth and rust (i.e. the bourgeoisie) get possession of. Yet such a life is demoralizing beyond all others. What Carlyle says of the cotton spinners is true of all English industrial workers:

> *Their trade, now in plethoric prosperity, anon extenuated into inanition and 'short time', is of the nature of gambling; they live by it like gamblers, now in luxurious superfluity, now in starvation. Black, mutinous discontent devours them; simply the miserablest feeling that can inhabit the heart of man. English commerce, with its world-wide, convulsive fluctuations, with its immeasurable Proteus Steam demon, makes all paths uncertain for them, all life a bewilderment; society, steadfastness, peaceable continuance, the first blessings of man are not theirs.—This world is for them no home, but a dingy prison-house, of reckless unthrift, rebellion, rancour, indignation against themselves and against all men. Is it a green, flowery world, with azure everlasting sky stretched over it, the work and government of a god; or a murky, simmering Tophet, of copperas fumes, cotton fuzz, gin riot, wrath and toil, created by a Demon, governed by a Demon?*

And elsewhere:

> *Injustice, infidelity to truth and fact and Nature's order, being properly the one evil under the sun, and the feeling of injustice the one intolerable pain under the sun, our*

grand question as to the condition of these working-men would be: Is it just? And, first of all, what belief have they themselves formed about the justice of it? The words they promulgate are notable by way of answer; their actions are still more notable. Revolt, sullen revengeful humour of revolt against the upper classes, decreasing respect for what their temporal superiors command, decreasing faith for what their spiritual superiors teach, is more and more the universal spirit of the lower classes. Such spirit may be blamed, may be vindicated, but all men must recognise it as extant there, all may know that it is mournful, that unless altered it will be fatal.

Carlyle is perfectly right as to the facts and wrong only in censuring the wild rage of the workers against the higher classes. This rage, this passion, is rather the proof that the workers feel the inhumanity of their position, that they refuse to be degraded to the level of brutes, and that they will one day free themselves from servitude to the bourgeoisie. This may be seen in the case of those who do not share this wrath; they either bow humbly before the fate that overtakes them, live a respectful private life as well as they can, do not concern themselves as to the course of public affairs, help the bourgeoisie to forge the chains of the workers yet more securely, and stand upon the plane of intellectual nullity that prevailed before the industrial period began; or they are tossed about by fate, lose their moral hold upon themselves as they have already lost their economic hold, live along from day to day, drink and fall into licentiousness; and in both cases they are brutes. The last-named class contributes chiefly to the 'rapid increase of vice', at which the bourgeoisie is so horrified after itself setting in motion the causes which give rise to it.

Another source of demoralization among the workers is their being condemned to work. As voluntary, productive activity is the highest enjoyment known to us, so is compulsory toil the most cruel, degrading punishment. Nothing is more terrible than being constrained to do some one thing every day from morning until night against one's will. And the more a man the worker feels himself, the more hateful must his work be to him, because he feels the constraint, the aimlessness of it for himself. Why does he work? For love of work? From a natural impulse? Not at all! He works for money, for a thing which has nothing whatsoever to do with the work itself; and he works so long, moreover, and in such unbroken monotony, that this alone must make his work a torture in the first weeks if he has the least human feelings left. The division of labour has multiplied the brutalising influences of forced work. In most branches the line worker's activity is reduced to some paltry, purely mechanical manipulation, repeated minute after minute, unchanged year after year. How much human feeling, what abilities can a man retain in his thirtieth year, who has made needle points or filed toothed wheels twelve hours every day from his early childhood, living all the time under the conditions forced upon the English proletarian? It is still the same thing since the introduction of steam. The worker's activity is made easy, muscular effort is saved, but the work itself becomes unmeaning and monotonous to the last degree. It offers no field for mental activity, and claims just enough of his attention to keep him from thinking of anything else. And a sentence to such work, to work which takes his whole time for itself, leaving him scarcely time to eat and sleep, none for physical exercise in the open air, or the enjoyment of Nature, much less for mental activity, how can such a sentence help degrading a human being to the level of a brute? Once more the worker must choose, must either surrender himself to his fate, become a 'good' workman, heed 'faithfully' the interest of the bourgeoisie, in which case he most certainly becomes a brute, or else he must rebel, fight for his manhood to the last, and this he can only do in the fight against the bourgeoisie.

And when all these conditions have engendered vast demoralization among the workers, a new influence is added to the old, to spread this degradation more widely and carry it to the extremest point. This influence is the centralization of the population. The writers of the English bourgeoisie are crying murder at the demoralizing tendency of the great cities; like perverted Jeremiahs, they sing dirges, not over the destruction, but the growth of the cities. Sheriff Alison attributes almost everything, and Dr Vaughan, author of *The Age of Great Cities*, still more to this influence. And this is natural, for the propertied class has too direct an interest in the other conditions which tend to destroy the worker body and soul. If they should admit that 'poverty, insecurity, overwork, forced work, are the chief ruinous influences', they would have to draw the conclusion, 'then let us give the poor property, guarantee their subsistence, make laws against overwork', and this the bourgeoisie dare not formulate. But the great cities have grown up so spontaneously, the population has moved into them so wholly of its own motion, and the inference that manufacture and the middle class which profits from it alone have created the cities is so remote, that it is extremely convenient for the ruling class to ascribe all the evil to this apparently unavoidable source; whereas the great cities really only secure a more rapid and certain development for evils already existing in the germ. Alison is humane enough to admit this; he is no thoroughbred Liberal manufacturer, but only a half developed Tory bourgeois, and he has, therefore, an open eye, now and then, where full-fledged bourgeois is still stone blind. Let us hear him:

> It is in the great cities that vice has spread her temptations, and pleasure her seductions, and folly her allurements; that guilt is encouraged by the hope of impunity, and idleness fostered by the frequency of example. It is to these great marts of human corruption that the base and the profligate resort from the simplicity of country life; it is here that they find victims whereon to practise their iniquity, and gains to reward the dangers that attend them. Virtue is here depressed from the obscurity in which it is involved. Guilt is matured from the difficulty of its detection; licentiousness is rewarded by the immediate enjoyment which it promises. If any person will walk through St. Giles's, the crowded alleys of Dublin, or the poorer quarters of Glasgow by night, he will meet with ample proof of these observations; he will no longer wonder at the disorderly habits and profligate enjoyments of the lower orders; his astonishment will be, not that there is so much, but that there is so little crime in the world. The great cause of human corruption in these crowded situations is the contagious nature of bad example and the extreme difficulty of avoiding the seductions of vice when they are brought into close and daily proximity with the younger part of the people. Whatever we may think of the strength of virtue, experience proves that the higher orders are indebted for their exemption from atrocious crime or disorderly habits chiefly to their fortunate removal from the scene of temptation; and that where they are exposed to the seductions which assail their inferiors, they are noways behind them in yielding to their influence. It is the peculiar misfortune of the poor in great cities that they cannot fly from these irresistible temptations, but that, turn where they will, they are met by the alluring forms of vice, or the seductions of guilty enjoyment. It is the experienced impossibility of concealing the attractions of vice from the younger part of the poor in great cities which exposes them to so many causes of demoralisation. All this proceeds not from any unwonted or extraordinary depravity in the character of these victims of licentiousness, but from the almost irresistible nature of the temptations to which the poor are exposed. The rich, who censure their conduct, would in all probability yield as rapidly as they have done to the influence of similar causes. There is a certain degree of misery, a certain

proximity to sin, which virtue is rarely able to withstand, and which the young, in particular, are generally unable to resist. The progress of vice in such circumstances is almost as certain and often nearly as rapid as that of physical contagion.

And elsewhere:

When the higher orders for their own profit have drawn the labouring-classes in great numbers into a small space, the contagion of guilt becomes rapid and unavoidable. The lower orders, situated as they are in so far as regards moral or religious instruction, are frequently hardly more to be blamed for yielding to the temptations which surround them than for falling victims to the typhus fever.

Enough! The half-bourgeois Alison betrays to us, however narrow his manner of expressing himself, the evil effect of the great cities upon the moral development of the workers. Another, a bourgeois *pur sang,* * a man after the heart of the Anti-Corn Law League, Dr Andrew Ure, betrays the other side. He tells us that life in great cities facilitates cabals among the workers and confers power on the Plebs. If here the workers are not educated (i.e. to obedience to the bourgeoisie), they may view matters one-sidedly, from the standpoint of a sinister selfishness, and may readily permit themselves to be hoodwinked by sly demagogues; nay, they might even he capable of viewing their greatest benefactors, the frugal and enterprising capitalists, with a jealous and hostile eye. Here proper training alone can avail, or national bankruptcy and other horrors must follow, since a revolution of the workers could hardly fail to occur. And our bourgeois is perfectly justified in his fears. If the centralization of population stimulates and develops the property-holding class, it forces the development of the workers yet more rapidly. The workers begin to feel as a class, as a whole; they begin to perceive that, though feeble as individuals, they form a power united; their separation from the bourgeoisie, the development of views peculiar to the workers and corresponding to their position in life, is fostered, the consciousness of oppression awakens, and the workers attain social and political importance. The great cities are the birthplaces of labour movements; in them the workers first began to reflect upon their own condition, and to struggle against it; in them the opposition between proletariat and bourgeoisie first made itself manifest; from them proceeded the Trade Unions, Chartism, and Socialism. The great cities have transformed the disease of the social body, which appears in chronic form in the country, into an acute one, and so made manifest its real nature and the means of curing it. Without the great cities and their forcing influence upon the popular intelligence, the working class would be far less advanced than it is. Moreover, they have destroyed the last remnants of the patriarchal relation between working men and employers, a result to which manufacture on a large scale has contributed by multiplying the employees dependent upon a single employer. The bourgeoisie deplores all this, it is true, and has good reason to do so; for, under the old conditions, the bourgeois was comparatively secure against a revolt on the part of his hands. He could tyrannize over them and plunder them to his heart's content, and yet receive obedience, gratitude, and assent from these stupid people by bestowing a trifle of patronizing friendliness which cost him nothing, and perhaps some paltry present, all apparently out of pure, self-sacrificing uncalled-for goodness of heart, but really not one-tenth part of his duty. As an individual bourgeois, placed under conditions which he had not himself created, he might do his duty at least in part; but, as a member of the ruling class, which, by the mere fact of its ruling, is responsible for the condition of the whole nation, he did nothing of what his position involved. On the contrary, he plundered the whole nation for his own individual advantage. In the patriarchal relation that hypocritically concealed the slavery of the worker, the latter must have remained an intellectual zero, totally ignorant of his own interest, a mere private individual. Only when estranged from his employer, when convinced that the sole bond between employer and employee is the bond of pecuniary profit, when the sentimental bond between them, which stood not the slightest test, had wholly fallen away, then only did the worker begin to recognize his own interests and develop independently; then only did he cease to be the slave of the bourgeoisie in his thoughts, feelings, and the expression of his will. And to this end manufacture on a grand scale and in great cities has most largely contributed.

Another influence of great moment in forming the character of the English workers is the Irish immigration already referred to. On the one hand it has, as we have seen, degraded the English workers, removed them from civilization, and aggravated the hardship of their lot; but, on the other hand, it has thereby deepened the chasm between workers and bourgeoisie, and hastened the approaching crisis. For the course of the social disease from which England is suffering is the same as the course of a physical disease; it develops, according to certain laws, has its own crises, the last and most violent of which determines the fate of the patient. And as the English nation cannot succumb under the final crisis, but must go forth from it, born again, rejuvenated, we can but rejoice over everything which accelerates the course of the disease. And to this the Irish immigration further contributes by reason of the passionate, mercurial Irish temperament, which it imports into England and into the English working class. The Irish and English are to each other much as the French and the Germans; and the mixing of the more facile, excitable, fiery Irish temperament with the stable, reasoning, persevering English must, in the long run, be productive only of good for both. The rough egotism of the English bourgeoisie would have kept its hold upon the working class much more firmly if the Irish nature, generous to a fault, and ruled primarily by sentiment, had not intervened, and softened the cold, rational English character in part by a mixture of the races, and in part by the ordinary contact of life.

In view of all this, it is not surprising that the working class has gradually become a race wholly apart from the English bourgeoisie. The bourgeoisie has more in common with every other nation of the earth than with the workers in whose midst it lives. The workers speak other dialects, have other thoughts and ideals, other customs and moral principles, a different religion and other politics than those of the bourgeoisie. Thus they are two radically dissimilar nations, as unlike as difference of race could make them, of whom we on the Continent have known but one, the bourgeoisie. Yet it is precisely the other, the people, the proletariat, which is by far the more important for the future of England.

Of the public character of the English working man, as it finds expression in associations and political principles, we shall have occasion to speak later; let us here consider the results of the influences cited above, as they affect the private character of the worker. The workman is far more humane in ordinary life than the bourgeois. I have already mentioned the fact that the beggars are accustomed to turn almost exclusively to the workers, and that, in general, more is done by the workers than by the bourgeoisie for the maintenance of the poor. This fact, which any one may prove for himself any day, is confirmed, among others, by Dr Parkinson, Canon of Manchester, who says.

> *The poor give one another more than the rich give the poor. I can confirm my statement by the testimony of one of our eldest, most skilful, most observant, and humane physicians, Dr. Bardsley, who has often declared that the total sum which the poor yearly bestow upon one another, surpasses that which the rich contribute in the same time.*

In other ways, too, the humanity of the workers is constantly manifesting itself pleasantly. They have experienced hard times themselves, and can therefore feel for those in trouble; to them every person is a human being, while the worker is less than a human being to the bourgeois; whence they are more approachable, friendlier, and less greedy for money, though they need it far more than the property-holding class. For them money is worth only what it will buy, whereas for the bourgeois it has an especial inherent value, the value of a god, and makes the bourgeois the mean, low money-grubber that he is. The working man who knows nothing of this feeling of reverence for money is therefore less grasping than the bourgeois, whose whole activity is for the purpose of gain, who sees in the accumulations of his money-bags the end and aim of life. Hence the workman is much less prejudiced, has a clearer eye for facts as they are than the bourgeois, and does not look at everything through the spectacles of personal selfishness. His faulty education saves him from religious prepossessions, he does not understand religious questions, does not trouble himself about them, knows nothing of the fanaticism that holds the bourgeoisie bound; and if he chances to have any religion, he has it only in name, not even in theory. Practically he lives for this world, and strives to make himself at home in it. All the writers of the bourgeoisie are unanimous on this point, that the workers are not religious, and do not attend church. From the general statement are to be excepted the Irish, a few elderly people, and the half-bourgeois, the overlookers, foremen, and the like. But among the masses there prevails almost universally a total indifference to religion, or at the utmost, some trace of Deism too undeveloped to amount to more than mere words, or a vague dread of the words infidel atheist, etc. The clergy of all sects is in very bad odour with the working men, though the loss of its influence is recent. At present, however, the mere cry 'He's a parson!' is often enough to drive one of the clergy from the platform of a public meeting. And like the rest of the conditions under which he lives, his want of religious and other culture contributes to keep the working man more unconstrained, free from inherited stable tenets and cut-and-dried opinions, than the bourgeois who is saturated with the class prejudices poured into him from his earliest youth. There is nothing to be done with the bourgeois; he is essentially conservative in however liberal a guise, his interest is bound up with that of the property-holding class, he is dead to all active movement; he is losing his position in the forefront of England's historical development. The workers are taking his place, in rightful claim first, then in fact.

All this, together with the correspondent public action of the workers, with which we shall deal later, forms the favourable side of the character of this class; the unfavourable one may be quite as briefly summed up, and follows quite as naturally out of the given causes. Drunkenness, sexual irregularities, brutality, and disregard for the rights of property are the chief points with which the bourgeois charges them. That they drink heavily is to be expected. Sheriff Alison asserts that in Glasgow some 30,000 working men get drunk every Saturday night, and the estimate is certainly not exaggerated; and that in that city in 1830, one house in twelve, and in 1840, one house in ten, was a public house; that in Scotland, in 1823, excise was paid upon 2,300,000 gallons; in 1837, upon 6,620,000 gallons; in England, in 1823, upon 1,976,000 gallons, and in 1837, upon 7,875,000 gallons of spirits. The Beer Act of 1830, which facilitated the opening of beerhouses (jerry shops), whose keepers are licensed to sell beer to be drunk on the premises, facilitated the spread of intemperance by bringing a beerhouse, so to say, to everybody's door. In nearly every street there are several such beerhouses, and among two or three neighbouring houses in the country one is sure to be a jerry shop. Besides these, there are hush-shops in multitudes, i.e. secret drinking-places which are not licensed, and quite as many secret distilleries which produce great quantities of spirits in retired spots, rarely visited by the police, in the great cities. Gaskell estimates these secret distilleries in Manchester alone at more than a hundred, and their product at 156,000 gallons at the least. In Manchester there are, besides, more than a thousand public houses selling all sorts of alcoholic drinks, or quite as many in proportion to the number of inhabitants as in Glasgow. In all other great towns, the state of things is the same. And when one considers, apart from the usual consequences of intemperance, that men and women, even children, often mothers with babies in their arms, come into contact in these places with the most degraded victims of the bourgeois regime, with thieves, swindlers, and prostitutes; when one reflects that many a mother gives the baby on her arm gin to drink, the demoralizing effects of frequenting such places cannot be denied.

On Saturday evenings, especially when wages are paid and work stops somewhat earlier than usual, when the whole working class pours from its own poor quarters into the main thoroughfares, intemperance may be seen in all its brutality. I have rarely come out of Manchester on such an evening without meeting numbers of people staggering and seeing others lying in the gutter. On Sunday evening the same scene is usually repeated, only less noisily. And when their money is spent, the drunkards go to the nearest pawnshop, of which there are plenty in every city — over sixty in Manchester, and ten or twelve in a single street of Salford, Chapel Street — and pawn whatever they possess. Furniture, Sunday clothes where such exist, kitchen utensils in masses are fetched from the pawnbrokers on Saturday night only to wander back, almost without fail, before the next Wednesday, until at last some accident makes the final redemption impossible, and one article after another falls into the clutches of the usurer, or until he refuses to give a single farthing more upon the battered, used-up pledge. When one has seen the extent of intemperance among the workers in England, one readily believes Lord Ashley's statement that this class annually expends something like £25,000,000 upon intoxicating liquor; and the deterioration in external conditions, the frightful shattering of mental and physical health, the ruin of all domestic relations which follow may readily be imagined. True, the temperance societies have done much, but what are a few thousand teetotallers among the millions of workers? When Father Mathew, the Irish apostle of temperance, passes through the English cities, from thirty to sixty thousand workers take the pledge; but most of them break it again within a month. If one counts up the immense numbers who have taken the pledge in the last three or four years in Manchester, the total is greater than the whole population of the town — and still it is by no means evident that intemperance is diminishing.

Next to intemperance in the enjoyment of intoxicating liquors, one of the principal faults of English working men is sexual licence. But this, too, follows with relentless logic, with inevitable necessity out of the position of a class left to itself, with no means of making fitting use of its freedom. The bourgeoisie has left the working class only these two pleasures, while imposing upon it a multitude of labours and hardships, and the consequence is that the working men, in order to get something from life, concentrate their whole energy upon these two enjoyments, carry them to excess, surrender to them in the most unbridled manner. When people are placed under conditions which appeal to the brute only, what remains to them but to rebel or to succumb to utter brutality? And when, moreover, the bourgeoisie does its full share in maintaining prostitution — and how many of the 40,000 prostitutes who fill the streets of London every evening live upon the virtuous bourgeoisie! How many of them owe it to the seduction of a bourgeois, that they must offer their bodies to the passers-by in order to live? — surely it has least of all a right to reproach the workers with their sexual brutality.

The failings of the workers in general may be traced to an unbridled thirst for pleasure, to want of providence, and of flexibility in fitting into the social order, to the general inability to sacrifice the pleasure of the moment to a remoter advantage. But is that to be wondered at? When a class can purchase few and only the most sensual pleasures by its wearying toil, must it not give itself over blindly and madly to those pleasures? A class about whose education no one troubles himself, which is a play-ball to a thousand chances, knows no security in life — what incentives has such a class to providence, to 'respectability', to sacrifice the pleasure of the moment for a remoter enjoyment, most uncertain precisely by reason of the perpetually varying, shifting conditions under which the proletariat lives? A class which bears all the disadvantages of the social order without enjoying its advantages, one to which the social system appears in purely hostile aspects — who can demand that such a class respect this social order? Verily that is asking much! But the working man cannot escape the present arrangement of society so long as it exists, and when the individual worker resists it, the greatest injury falls upon himself.

Thus the social order makes family life almost impossible for the worker. In a comfortless, filthy house, hardly good enough for mere nightly shelter, ill-furnished, often neither rain-tight nor warm, a foul atmosphere filling rooms over-crowded with human beings, no domestic comfort is possible. The husband works the whole day through, perhaps the wife also and the elder children, all in different places; they meet night and morning only, all under perpetual temptation to drink; what family life is possible under such conditions? Yet the working man cannot escape from the family, must live in the family, and the consequence is a perpetual succession of family troubles, domestic quarrels, most demoralizing for parents and children alike. Neglect of all domestic duties, neglect of the children, especially, is only too common among the English working people, and only too vigorously fostered by the existing institutions of society. And children growing up in this savage way, amidst these demoralizing influences, are expected to turn out goody-goody and moral in the end! Verily the requirements are naïve, which the self-satisfied bourgeois makes upon the working man!

The contempt for the existing social order is most conspicuous in its extreme form — that of offences against the law. If the influences demoralizing to the working man act more powerfully, more concentratedly than usual, he becomes an offender as certainly as water abandons the fluid for the vaporous state at 80 degrees, Réaumur. Under the brutal and brutalizing treatment of the bourgeoisie, the working man becomes precisely as much a thing without volition as water, and is subject to the laws of Nature with precisely the same necessity; at a certain point all freedom ceases. Hence with the extension of the proletariat, crime bas increased in England, and the British nation has become the most criminal in the world. From the annual criminal tables of the Home Secretary, it is evident that the increase of crime in England has proceeded with incomprehensible rapidity. The numbers of arrests for *criminal* offences reached in the years: 1805, 4,605; 1810, 5,146; 1815, 7,898; 1820, 13,710; 1825, 14,437; 1830, 18,107; 1835, 20,731; 1840, 27,187; 1841, 27,760; 1842, 31,309 in England and Wales alone. That is to say, they increased sevenfold in thirty-seven years. Of these arrests, in 1842, 4,497 were made in Lancashire alone, or more than 14 per cent of the whole; and 4,094 in Middlesex, including London, or more than 13 per cent. So that two districts which include great cities with large proletarian populations, produced one-fourth of the total amount of crime, though their population is far from forming one-fourth of the whole. Moreover, the criminal tables prove directly that nearly all crime arises within the proletariat; for, in 1842, taking the average, out of 100 criminals, 32.35 could neither read nor write; 58.32 read and wrote imperfectly; 6.77 could read and write well; 0.22 had enjoyed a higher education, while the degree of education of 2.34 could not be ascertained. In Scotland, crime has increased yet more rapidly. There were but 89 arrests of criminal offences in 1819, and as early as 1837 the number had risen to 3,176, and in 1842 to 4,189. In Lanarkshire, where Sheriff Alison himself made out the official report, population has doubled once in thirty years, and crime once in five and a half, or six times more rapidly than the population. The offences, as in all civilized countries, are, in the great majority of cases, against property, and have, therefore, arisen from want in some form; for what a man has, he does not steal. The proportion of offences against property to the population, which in the Netherlands is as 1:7,140, and in France, as 1:804, was in England, when Gaskell wrote, as 1:799. The proportion of offences against persons to the population is, in the Netherlands, 1:28,904; in France, 1:17,573; in England, 1:23,395; that of crimes in general to the population in the agricultural districts, as 1:1,043 in the manufacturing districts as 1:840. In the whole of England today the proportion is 1:660, though it is scarcely ten years since Gaskell's book appeared!

These facts are certainly more than sufficient to bring any one, even a bourgeois, to pause and reflect upon the consequences of such a state of things. If demoralization and crime multiply twenty years longer in this proportion (and if English manufacture in these twenty years should be less prosperous than heretofore, the progressive multiplication of crime can only continue the more rapidly), what will the result be? Society is already in a state of visible dissolution; it is impossible to pick up a newspaper without seeing the most striking evidence of the giving way of all social ties. I look at random into a heap of English journals lying before me; there is the *Manchester Guardian* for 30 October 1844, which reports for three days. It no longer takes the trouble to give exact details as to Manchester, and merely relates the most interesting cases: that the workers in a mill have struck for higher wages without giving notice, and been condemned by a Justice of the Peace to resume work; that in Salford a couple of boys had been caught stealing, and a bankrupt tradesman tried to cheat his creditors. From the neighbouring towns the reports are more detailed: in Ashton, two thefts, one burglary, one suicide; in Bury, one theft; in Bolton, two thefts, one revenue fraud; in Leigh, one theft; in Oldham, one strike for wages, one theft, one fight between Irish women, one non-Union hatter assaulted by Union men, one mother beaten by her son, one attack upon the police, one robbery of a church; in Stockport, discontent of working men with wages, one theft, one fraud, one fight, one wife beaten by her husband; in Warrington, one theft, one fight; in Wigan, one theft, and one robbery of a church. The reports of the London papers are much worse; frauds, thefts, assaults, family quarrels crowd one another. A *Times* of 12 September 1844, falls into my hand, which gives a report of a single day, including a theft, an attack upon the police, a sentence upon a father requiring him to support his illegitimate son, the abandonment of a child by its parents, and the poisoning of a man by his wife. Similar reports are to be found in all the English papers. In this Country, social war is under full headway, every one stands for himself, and fights for himself against all comers, and whether or not he shall injure all the others who are his declared foes, depends upon a cynical calculation as to what is most advantageous for himself. It no longer occurs to any one to come to a peaceful understanding with his fellow-man; all differences are settled by threats, violence, or in a law-court. In short, every one sees in his neighbour an enemy to be got out of the way, or, at best, a tool to be used for his own advantage. And this war grows from year to year, as the criminal tables show, more violent, passionate, irreconcilable. The enemies are dividing gradually into two great camps — the bourgeoisie on the one hand, the workers on the other. This war of each against all, of the bourgeoisie against the proletariat, need cause us no surprise, for it is only the logical sequel of the principle involved in free competition. But it may very well surprise us that the bourgeoisie remains so quiet and composed in the face of the rapidly gathering storm-clouds, that it can read all these things daily in the papers without, we will not say indignation at such a social condition, but fear of its consequences, of a universal outburst of that which manifests itself symptomatically from day to day in the form of crime. But then it is the bourgeoisie, and from its standpoint it cannot even see the facts, much less perceive their consequences. One thing only is astounding, that class prejudice and preconceived opinions can hold a whole class of human beings in such perfect, I might almost say, such mad blindness. Meanwhile, the development of the nation goes its way whether the bourgeoisie has eyes for it or not, and will surprise the property-holding class one day with things not dreamed of in its philosophy.

Hard Times

Charles Dickens

Edited by Fred Kaplan and Sylvére Monod

The Key-Note

Coketown, to which Messrs. Bounderby and Gradgrind now walked, was a triumph of fact; it had no greater taint of fancy in it that Mrs. Gradgrind herself. Let us strike the key-note, Coketown, before pursuing our tune.

It was a town of red brick, or of brick that would have been red if the smoke and ashes had allowed it; but, as matters stood it was a town of unnatural red and black like the painted face of a savage. It was a town of machinery and tall chimneys, out of which interminable serpents of smoke trailed themselves for ever and ever, and never got uncoiled. It had a black canal in it, and a river that ran purple with ill-smelling dye, and vast piles of buildings full of windows where there was a rattling and a trembling all day long, and where the piston of the steam-engine worked monotonously up and down, like the heads of an elephant in a state of melancholy madness. It contained several large streets all very like one another, and many small streets still more like one another, inhabited by the people equally like one another, who all went in and out at the same hours, with the same sound upon the same pavements, to do the same work, and to whom every day was the same as yesterday and to-morrow, and every year the counterpart of the last and the next.

These attributes of Coketown were in the main inseparable from the work by which it was sustained; against them were to be set off, comforts of life which found their way all over the world, and elegancies of life which made, we will not ask how much of the fine lady, who could scarcely bear to hear the place mentioned. The rest of its features were voluntary, and they were these.

You saw nothing in Coketown but what was severely workful. If the members of a religious persuasion built a chapel there — as the members of eighteen religious persuasions had done — they made it a pious ware-house of red brick, with sometimes (but this only in highly ornamented examples) a bell in a bird-cage on the top of it. The solitary exception was the New Church; a stuccoed edifice with a square steeple over the door, terminating in four short pinnacles like florid wooden legs. All the public inscriptions in the town were painted alike, in severe characters of black and white. The jail might have been the infirmary, the infirmary might have been the jail, the town-hall might have been either, or both, or anything else, for anything that appeared to the contrary in the graces of their construction. Fact, fact, fact, everywhere in the material aspect of the town; fact, fact, fact, everywhere in the immaterial. The M'Choakumchild school was all fact, and the school of design was all fact, and the relations between master and man were all fact, and everything was fact between the lying-in hospital and the cemetery, and what you couldn't state in figures, or show to be purchasable in the cheapest market and saleable in the dearest, was not, and never should be, world without end, Amen.

A town so sacred to fact, and so triumphant in its assertion, of course got on well.? Why no, not quite well. No? Dear me!

No. Coketown did not come of its own furnaces, in all respects like gold that had stood the fire. First, the perplexing mystery of the place was, Who belonged to the eighteen denominations? Because, whoever did, the laboring people did not. It was very strange to walk through the streets on a Sunday morning, and note how few of *them* the barbarous jangling of bells that was driving the sick and nervous mad, called away from their own quarter, from their own close rooms, from the corners of their own streets, where they lounged listlessly, gazing at all the church and chapel going, as at a thing with which they had no manner of concern. Nor was it merely the stranger who noticed this, because there was a native organization in Coketown itself, whose members were to be heard of in the House of Commons every session, indignantly petitioning for acts of parliament that should make these people religious by main force. Then, came the Teetotal Society, who complained that these same people *would* get drunk, and showed in tabular statements that they did get drunk, and proved at tea parties that no inducement, human or Divine (except a medal), would induce them to forego their custom of getting drunk. Then, came the chemist and druggist, with other tabular statements, showing that when they didn't get drunk, they took opium. Then, came the experienced chaplain of the jail, with more tabular statements, outdoing all the previous tabular statements, and showing that the same people *would* resort to low haunts, hidden from the public eye, where they heard low singing and saw low dancing, and mayhap joined in it; and where A.B., aged twenty-four next birthday, and committed for eighteen month's solitary, had himself said(not that he had ever shown himself particularly worthy of belief) his ruin began, as he was perfectly sure and confident that otherwise he would have been a tip-top moral specimen. Then, came Mr. Gradgrind and Mr. Bounderby, the two gentlemen at this present moment walking through Coketown, and both eminently practical, who could, on occasion, furnish more tabular statements derived from their own personal experience, and illustrated by cases they had known and seen, from which it clearly appeared — in short it was the only clear thing in the case — that these same people were a bad lot altogether, gentlemen; that do what you would for them they were never thankful for it, gentlemen; that they were restless, gentlemen; that they never knew what they wanted; that they lived upon the best, and bought fresh butter, and instead in Mocha coffee, and rejected all but prime parts of meat, and yet were eternally dissatisfied and unmanageable. In short it was the morale of the old nursery fable:

> *There was an old woman, and what do you think?*
> *She lived upon nothing but victuals and drink;*
> *Victuals and drink were the whole of her diet,*
> *And yet this old woman would* NEVER *be quiet.*

Is it possible, I wonder, that there was any analogy between the case of the Coketown population and the case of the little Gradgrinds? Surely, none of us in our sober senses and acquainted with figures, are to be told at this time of day, that one of the foremost elements in the existence of the Coketown working people had been for scores of years, deliberately set as nought? That there was any Fancy in them demanding to be brought into healthy existence instead of struggling on in convulsions? That exactly in the ratio as they worked long and monotonously, the craving grew within them for some physical relief — some relaxation, encouraging good humour and good spirits, and giving them a vent — some recognized holiday, though it were but for an honest dance to a stirring band of music — some occasional light pie in which even M'Choakumchild had no finger — which craving must and would be satisfied aright, or must and would inevitably go wrong, until the laws of the Creation were repealed?

"This man lives at Pod's End, and I don't quite know Pod's End," said Mr. Gradgrind. "Which is it, Bounderby?"

Mr. Bounderby knew it was somewhere down town, but knew no more respecting it. So they stopped for a moment, looking about.

Almost as they did so, there came running round the corner of the street at a quick pace and with a frightened look, a girl whom Mr. Gradgrind recognised. "Halloa!" said he. "Stop! Where are you going? Stop!" Girl number twenty stopped then, palpitating, and made him a curtsey.

"Why are you tearing about the streets," said Mr. Gradgrind, "in this improper manner?"

"I was — I was run after, sir," the girl panted, "and I wanted to get away."

"Run after?" repeated Mr. Gradgrind. "Who would run after *you?*"

The question was unexpectedly and suddenly answered for her, by the colourless boy, Bitzer, who came round the corner with such blind speed and so little anticipating a stoppage on the pavement that he brought himself up against Mr. Gradgrind's waistcoat, and rebounded into the road.

"What do you mean, boy?" said Mr. Gradgrind. "What are you doing? How dare you dash against — everybody — in this manner?"

Bitzer picked up his cap, which the concussion had knocked off; and backing, and knuckling his forehead, pleaded that it was an accident.

"Was this boy running after you, Jupe?" asked Mr. Gradgrind.

"Yes, sir" said the girl reluctantly.

No, I wasn't sir!" cried Bitzer. "Not till she run away from me. But the horse-riders never mind what they say, sir; they're famous for it. You know the horse-riders are famous for never minding what they say," addressing Sissy. "It's as well known in the town as — please, sir, as the multiplication table isn't known to the horseriders." Bitzer tried Mr. Bounderby with this.

"He frightened me so", said the girl, "with his cruel faces!"

"Oh!" cried Bitzer. "Oh! An't you one of the rest! An't you a horserider! I never looked at her, sir. I asked her if she would know how to define a horse tomorrow, and offered to tell her again, and she ran away, and I ran after her, sir, that she might know how to answer when she was asked. You wouldn't have thought of saying such mischief if you hadn't been a horse-rider!"

"Her calling seems to be pretty well known among'em," observed Mr. Bounderby. "You'd have had the whole school peeping in a row, in a week."

"Truly, I think so," returned his friend. "Bitzer, turn you about and take yourself home. Jupe, stay here a moment. Let me hear of your running in this manner any more, boy, and you will hear of me through the master of the school. You understand what I mean. Go along."

The boy stopped in his rapid blinking, knuckled his forehead again, glanced at Sissy, turned about, and retreated.

"Now, girl," said Mr. Gradgrind, "take this gentleman and me to your father's; we are going there. What have you got in that bottle you are carrying?"

"Gin," said Mr. Bounderby.

"Dear, no sir! It's the nine oils."

"The what?" cried Mr. Bounderby.

"The nine oils, sir. To rub faster with," Then, said Mr. Bounderby, with a loud, short laugh, "what the devil do you rub your father with nine oils for?"

"It's what our people always use, sir, when they get any hurts in the ring," replied the girl, looking over her shoulder, to assure herself that her pursuer was gone. "They bruise themselves very bad sometimes."

"Serve 'em right," said Mr. Bounderby, "for being idle." She glanced up at his face, with mingled astonishment and dread.

"By George!" said Mr. Bounderby," when I was four or five years younger than you, I had worse bruises upon me than ten oils, twenty oils, forty oils, would have rubbed off. I didn't get 'em by posture-making, but by being banged about. There was no rope-dancing for me; I danced on the bare ground and was larruped with the rope."

Mr. Gradgrind, though hard enough, was by no means so rough a man as Mr. Bounderby. His character was not unkind, all things considered; it might have been a very kind one indeed, if he had only made some round mistake in the arithmetic that balanced it, years ago. He said, in what he meant for a re-assuring tone, as they turned down a narrow road, "And this is Pod's End; is it, Jupe?"

"This is it, sir, and — if you wouldn't mind, sir — this is the house."

She stopped, at twilight, at the door of a mean little public house, with dim red lights in it. As haggard and as shabby, as if, for want of custom, it had itself taken to drinking, and had gone the way all drunkards go, and was very near the end of it.

"It's only crossing the bar, sir, and up the stairs, if you wouldn't mind, and waiting there for a moment till I get a candle. If you should hear a dog, sir, it's only Merrylegs, and he only barks."

"Merrylegs and nine oils, eh!" said Mr. Bounderby, entering last with his metallic laugh. "Pretty well this, for a self-made man!"

. . . .

Stephen Blackpool

I entertain a weak idea that the English people are as hard-worked as any people upon whom the sun shines. I acknowledge to this ridiculous idiosyncrasy, as a reason why I would given them a little more play.

In the hardest working part of Coketown; in the innermost fortification of that ugly citadel, where Nature was as strongly bricked out as killing airs and gases were bricked in; at the heart of the labyrinth of narrow courts upon courts, and close streets upon streets, which had come into existence piecemeal, every piece in a violent hurry for some one man's purpose, and the whole unnatural family, shouldering, and trampling, and pressing one another to death; in the last close nook of this great exhausted receiver, where the chimneys, for want of air to make a draught, were built in an immense variety of stunted and crooked shapes, as though every house put out a sign of the kind of people who might be expected to be born in it; among the multitude of Coketown, generically called "the Hands," — a race who would have found more favor with some people, if Providence had seen fit to make them only hands, or, like the lower creatures of the sea-shore, only hands and stomachs — lived a certain Stephen Blackpool, forty years of age.

Stephen looked older, but he had had a hard life. It is said that every life has its roses and thorns; there seemed, however, to have been a misadventure or mistake in Stephen's case, whereby somebody else had become possessed of his roses, and he had become possessed of the same somebody else's thorns in addition to his own, He had known, to use his words, a peck of trouble. He was usually called Old Stephen, in a kind of rough homage to the fact.

A rather stooping man, with a knitted brow, a pondering expression of face, and a hard-looking head sufficiently capacious, on which his iron-grey hair lay long and thin, Old Stephen might have passed for a particularly intelligent man in his condition. Yet he was not. He took no place among those remarkable "Hands," who, piecing together their broken intervals of leisure through many years, had mastered difficult sciences, and acquired a knowledge of most unlikely things. He held no station among the Hands who could make speeches and carry on debates. Thousands of his compeers could talk much better than he, at any time. He was a good power-loom weaver, and a man of perfect integrity. What more he was, or what else he had in him, if anything let him show for himself.

The lights in the great factories, which looked, when they were illuminated, like Fairy palaces — or the travellers by express-train said so — were all extinguished; and the bells had rung for knocking off for the night, and had ceased again; and the Hands, men and women, boy and girl, were clattering home. Old Stephen was standing in the street, with the odd sensation upon him which the stoppage of the machinery always produced — the sensation of its having worked and stopped in his own head.

"Yet I don't see Racheal, still!" said he.

It was a wet night, and many groups of young women passed him, with their shawls drawn over their bare heads and held close under their chins to keep the rain out. He knew Rachael well, for a glance at any one of these groups was sufficient to show him that she was not there. At last, there were no more to come; and then he turned away, saying in a tone of disappointment, "Why, then, I ha' missed her!"

But, he had not gone the length of three streets, when he saw another of the shawled figures in advance of him, at which he looked so keenly that perhaps its mere shadow indistinctly reflected on the wet pavement — if he could have seen it without the figure itself moving along from lamp to lamp, brightening and fading as it went — would have been enough to tell him who was there. Making his pace at once much quicker and much softer, he darted on until he was very near this figure, then fell into his former walk, and called "Rachael!"

She turned, being then in the brightness of a lamp; and raising her hood a little, showed a quiet oval face, dark and rather delicate, irradiated by a pair of very gentle eyes, and further set off by the perfect order of her shining black hair. It was not a face in its bloom; she was a woman five and thirty years of age.

"Ah, lad! 'Tis thou?" When she had said this, with a smile which would have been quite expressed, though nothing of her had been seen but her pleasant eyes, she replaced her hood again, and they went on together.

"I thought thou wast ahind me, Racheal?"

"No."

"Early t'night, lass?"

"'Times I'm a little early, Stephen; 'times a little late. I'm never to be counted on, going home."

"Nor going t'other way, neither, t'seems to me, Racheal?"

"No, Stephen."

He looked at her with some disappointment in his face, but with a respectful and patient conviction that she must be right in whatever she did. The expression was not lost upon her; she laid her hand lightly on his arm a moment, as if to thank for it.

"We are such true friends, lad, and such old friends, and getting to be such old folk, now."

"No, Racheal, thou'rt as young as ever thou wast."

"One of us would be puzzled how to get old, Stephen, without t'other getting so too, both being alive," she answered, laughing; "but, any ways, we're such old friends, that t'hide a word of honest truth fro' one another would be a sin and a pity. 'Tis better not to walk too much together. 'Times, yes! 'Twould be hard, indeed, if 'twas not to be at all," she said with a cheerfulness she sought to communicate to him.

"'Tis hard, anyways, Racheal."

"Try to think not; and 'twill seem better."

"I've tried a long time, and 'ta'nt got better. But thou'rt right; 'tmight mak for talk, even of thee. Thou hast been that to me, Racheal, through so many year: thou hast done me so much good, and heartened of me in that cheering way, that thy word is a law to me. Ah lass, and a bright good law! Better than some real ones."

"Never fret about them, Stephen," she answered quickly, and not without an anxious glance at his face. "Let the laws be."

"Yes," he said, with a slow nod or two. "Let 'em be. Let everything be. Let all sorts alone. 'Tis a muddle, and that's aw."

"Always a muddle?" said Rachael, with another gentle touch upon his arm, as if to recall him out of the thoughtfulness, in which he was biting the long ends of his loose neckerchief as he walked along. The touch had its instantaneous effect. He let them fall, turned a smiling face upon her, and said, as he broke into a good-humoured laugh, "Ay, Rachael, lass, alwus a muddle. That's where I stick. I come to the muddle many times and agen, and I never get beyond it."

They had walked some distance, and were near their own homes. The woman's was the first reached. It was in one of the many small streets for which the favourite undertaker (who turned a handsome sum out of the one poor ghastly pomp of the neighbourhood) kept a black ladder, in order that those who had done their daily groping up and down the narrow stairs might slide out of this working world by the windows. She stopped at the corner, and putting her hand in his, wished him good night.

"Good night, dear lass; good night!"

She went, with her neat figure and her sober womanly step, down the dark street, and he stood looking after her until she turned into one of the small houses. There was not a flutter of her coarse shawl, perhaps, but had its interest in this man's eyes; not a tone of her voice but had its echo in his innermost heart.

When she was lost to his view, he pursued his homeward way, glancing up sometimes at the sky, where the clouds were sailing fast and wildly. But, they were broken now, and the rain had ceased, and the moon shone — looking down the high chimneys of Coketown on the deep furnaces below, and casting Titanic shadows of the steam engines at rest, upon the walls where they were lodged. The man seemed to have brightened with the night, as he went on.

His home, in such another street as the first, saving that it was narrower, was over a little shop. How it came to pass that any people found it worth their while to sell or buy the wretched little toys, mixed up in its window with cheap newspapers and pork (there was a leg to be raffled for to-morrow night), matters not here. He took his end of candle from a shelf, lighted it at another end of candle on the counter, without disturbing the mistress of the shop who was asleep in her little room, and went up stairs into his lodging.

It was a room, not unacquainted with the black ladder under various tenants; but as neat, at present, as such a room could be. A few books and writings were on an old bureau in a corner, the furniture was decent and sufficient, and, though the atmosphere was tainted, the room was clean.

Going to the hearth to set the candle down upon a round three-legged table standing there, he stumbled against something. As he recoiled, looking down at it, it raised itself up into the form of a woman in a sitting attitude.

"Heaven's mercy, woman!" he cried, falling farther off from the figure. "Hast thou come back again!"

Such a woman! A disable, drunken creature, barely able to preserve her sitting posture by steadying herself with one begrimed hand on the floor, while the other was so purposeless in trying to push away her tangled hair from her face, that it only blinded her the more with the dirt upon it. A creature so foul to look at, in her tatters, stains, and splashes, but so much fouler than that in her moral infamy, that it was a shameful thing even to see her.

After an impatient oath or two, and some stupid clawing of herself with the hand not necessary to her support, she got her hair away from her eyes sufficiently to obtain a sight of him. Then she sat swaying her body to and fro, and making gestures with her unnerved arm, which seemed intended as the accompaniment to a fit of laughter, though her face was stolid and drowsy.

"Eigh lad? What, yo'r there?" Some hoarse sounds meant for this, came mockingly out of her at last; and her head dropped forward on her breast.

"Back agen?" she screeched, after some minutes, as if he had that moment said it.

"Yes! And back agen. Back agen ever and ever so often. Back? Yes, back. Why not?" Roused by the unmeaning violence with which she cried it out, she scrambled up, and stood supporting herself with her shoulders against the wall; dangling in one hand by the string, a dunghill-fragment of a bonnet, and trying to look scornfully at him.

"I'll sell thee off again, and I'll sell thee off again, and I'll sell thee off a score of times!" she cried, with something between a furious menace and an effort at a defiant dance. "Come awa' from th' bed!" He was sitting on the side of it, with his face hidden in his hands. "Come awa' from't. 'Tis mine, and I've a right to 't!"

As she staggered to it, he avoided her with a shudder, and passed — his face still hidden — to the opposite end of the room. She threw herself upon the bed heavily, and soon was snoring hard. He sunk into a chair, and moved but once all that night. It was to throw a covering over her; as if his hands were not enough to hide her, even in the darkness.

No Way Out

The Fairy palaces burst into illumination, before pale morning showed the monstrous serpents of smoke trailing themselves over Coketown. A clattering of clogs upon the pavement; a rapid ringing of bells; and all the melancholy-mad elephants, polished and oiled up for the day's monotony, were at their heavy exercise again.

Stephen bent over his loom, quiet, watchful, and steady. A special contrast, as every man was in the forest of looms where Stephen worked, to the crashing, smashing, tearing piece of mechanism at which he laboured. Never fear, good people of an anxious turn of mind, that Art will consign Nature to oblivion. Set anywhere, side by side, the work of GOD and the work of man; and the former, even though it be a troop of Hands of very small account, will gain in dignity from the comparison.

So many hundred Hands in this Mill; so many hundred horse Steam Power. It is known, to the force of a single pound weight, what the engine will do; but, not all the calculators of the National Debt can tell me the capacity for good or evil, for love or hatred, for patriotism or discontent, for the decomposition of virtue into vice, or the reverse, at any single moment in the soul of one of these its quiet servants, with the composed faces and the regulated actions. There is no mystery in it; there is an unfathomable mystery in the meanest of them, for ever. — Supposing we were to reserve our arithmetic for material objects, and to govern these awful unknown quantities by other means!

The day grew strong, and showed itself outside, even against the flaming lights within. The lights were turned out, and the work went on. The rain fell, and the Smoke-serpents, submissive to the curse of all that tribe, trailed themselves upon the earth. In the waste-yard outside, the steam from the escape-pipe, the litter of barrels and old iron, the shining heaps of coals, the ashes everywhere, were shrouded in a veil of mist and rain.

The work went on, until the noon-bell rang. More clattering upon the pavements. The looms, and wheels, and Hands, all out of gear for an hour.

Stephen came out of the hot mill into the damp wind and cold wet streets, haggard and worn. He turned from his own class and his own quarter, taking nothing but a little bread as he walked along, towards the hill on which his principal employer lived, in a red house with black outside shutters, green inside blinds, a black street door, up two white steps, BOUNDERBY (in letters very like himself) upon a brazen plate, and a round brazen door-handle underneath it like a brazen full-stop.

Mr. Bounderby was at his lunch. So Stephen had expected. Would his servant say that one of the Hands begged leave to speak to him? Message in return, requiring name of such Hand. Stephen Blackpool. There was nothing troublesome against Stephen Blackpool; yes, he might come in.

Stephen Blackpool in the parlour. Mr. Bounderby (whom he just knew by sight), at lunch on chop and sherry. Mrs. Sparsit netting at the fire-side, in a side-saddle attitude, with one foot in a cotton stirrup. It was a part, at once of Mrs. Sparsit's dignity and service, not to lunch. She supervised the meal officially, but implied that in her own stately person she considered lunch a weakness.

"Now, Stephen," said Mr. Bounderby, "what's the matter with *you?*" Stephen made a bow. Not a servile one — these Hands will never do that! Lord bless you, sir, you'll never catch them at that, if they have been with you twenty years! — and, as a complimentary toilet for Mrs. Sparsit, tucked his neckerchief ends into his waistcoat.

"Now, you know," said Mr. Bounderby, taking some sherry, "we have never had any difficulty with you, and you have never been one of the unreasonable ones. You don't expect to be set up in a coach and six, and to be fed on turtle soup and venison, with a gold spoon, as a good many of' em do!" Mr. Bounderby always represented this to be the sole, immediate, and direct object of any Hand who was not entirely satisfied; "and therefore I know already that you have not come here to make a complaint. Now, you know, I am certain of that, beforehand."

"No, sir, sure I ha' not coom for nowt o' th' kind."

Mr. Bounderby seemed agreeably surprised, notwithstanding his previous strong conviction. "Very well," he returned. "You're a steady Hand, and I was not mistaken. Now, let me hear what it's all about. As it's not that, let me hear what it is. What have you got to say? Out with it, lad!"

Stephen happened to glance towards Mrs. Sparsit. "I can go, Mr. Bounderby, if you wish it," said that self-sacrificing lady, making a feint of taking her foot out of the stirrup.

Mr. Bounderby stayed her, by holding a mouthful of chop in suspension before swallowing it, and putting out his left hand. Then, withdrawing his hand and swallowing his mouthful of chop, he said to Stephen:

"Now, you know, this good lady is a born lady, a high lady. You are not to suppose because she keeps my house for me, that she hasn't been very high up the tree — ah, up at the top of the tree! Now, if you have got anything to say that can't be said before a born lady, this lady will leave the room. If what you have got to say *can* be said before a born lady, this lady will stay where she is."

"Sir, I hope I never had nowt to say, not fitten for a born lady to year, sin' I were born mysen,'" was the reply, accompanied with a slight flush.

"Very well," said Mr. Bounderby, pushing away his plate, and leaning back. "Fire away!"

"I ha' coom," Stephen began, raising his eyes from the floor, after a moment's consideration, "to ask yo yor advice. I need't overmuch. I were married on Eas'r Monday nineteen year sin, long and dree. She were a young lass — pretty enow — wi' good accounts of herseln. Well! She went bad — soon. Not along of me. Gonnows I were not a unkind husband to her."

"I have heard all this before," said Mr. Bounderby. "She took to drinking, left off working, sold the furniture, pawned the clothes, and played old Gooseberry.

"I were patient wi' her."

("The more fool you, I think," said Mr. Bounderby, in confidence to his wine-glass.)

"I were very patient wi' her. I tried to wean her fra't, ower and ower agen. I tried this, I tried that, I tried t'other. I ha' gone home, many's the time, and found all vanished as I had in the world, and her without a sense left to bless herseln lying on bare ground. I ha' dun't not once, not twice — twenty time!"

Every line in his face deepened as he said it, and put in its affecting evidence of the suffering he had undergone.

"From bad to worse, from worse to worsen. She left me. She disgraced herseln everyways, bitter and bad. She coom back, she coom back, she coom back. What could I do t' hinder her? I ha' walked the streets nights long, ere ever I'd go home. I ha' gone t' th' brigg, minded to fling myseln ower, and ha' no more on't. I ha' bore that much, that I were owd when I were young."

Mrs. Sparsit, easily ambling along with her netting-needles, raised the Coriolanian eyebrows and shook her head, as much as to say, "The great know trouble as well as the small. Please to turn your humble eye in My direction."

"I ha' paid her to keep awa' fra' me. These five year I ha' paid her. I ha' gotten decent fewtrils about me agen. I ha' lived hard and sad, but not ashamed and fearfo' a' the minnits o' my life. Last night, I went home. There she lay upon my har-stone! There she IS!"

In the strength of his misfortune, and the energy of his distress, he fired for the moment like a proud man. In another moment, he stood as he had stood all the time — his usual stoop upon him; his pondering face addressed to Mr. Bounderby, with a curious expression on it, half shrewd, half perplexed, as if his mind were set upon unraveling something very difficult; his hat held tight in his left hand, which rested on his hip; his right arm, with a rugged propriety and force of action, very earnestly emphasizing what he said: not least so when it always paused, a little bent, but not withdrawn, as he paused.

"I was acquainted with all this, you know," said Mr. Bounderby, "except the last clause, long ago. It's a bad job; that's what it is. You had better have been satisfied as you were, and not have got married. However, it's too late to say that."

"Was it an unequal marriage, sir, in point of years?" asked Mrs. Sparsit.

"You hear what this lady asks. Was it an unequal marriage in point of years, this unlucky job of yours?" said Mr. Bounderby.

"Not e'en so. I were one-and-twenty myseln; she were twenty nighbut."

"Indeed, sir?" said Mrs. Sparsit to her Chief, with great placidity. "I inferred, form its being so miserable a marriage, that it was probably an unequal one in point of years."

Mr. Bounderby looked very hard at the good lady in a sidelong way that had an odd sheepishness about it. He fortified himself with a little more sherry.

"Well? Why don't you go on?" he then asked, turning rather irritably on Stephen Blackpool.

"I ha' coom to ask yo, sir, how I am to be ridded o' this woman." Stephen infused a yet deeper gravity into the mixed expression of his attentive face. Mrs. Sparsit uttered a gentle ejaculation, as having received a moral shock.

"What do you mean?" said Bounderby, getting up to lean his back against the chimney-piece. "What are you talking about? You took her for better for worse."

"I mun' be ridden o' her. I cannot bear't nommore. I ha' lived under't so long, for that I ha' had'n the pity and comforting words o' th' best lass living or dead. Haply, but for her, I should ha' gone hottering mad."

"He wishes to be free, to marry the female of whom he speaks, I fear, sir," observed Mrs. Sparsit in an undertone, and much dejected by the immorality of the people.

"I do. The lady says what's right. I do. I were a coming to't. I ha' read I' th' papers that great fok (fair faw 'em a I wishes 'em no hurt!) are not bonded together for better for worse so fast, but that they can be set free fro' *their* misfortnet marriages, an marry ower agen. When they dunnot agree, for that their tempers is ill-sorted, they has rooms o' one kind an another in their houses, above a bit, and they can live asunders. We fok ha' only one room, an we can't. When that won't do, they ha' gowd an other cash, an they can say 'This for yo, an that for me,' an they can go their separate ways. We can't. Spite o' all that, they can be set free for smaller wrongs than mine. So, I mun be ridden o' this woman an I want t'know how?"

"No how," returned Mr. Bounderby.

"If I do her any hurt, sir, there's a law to punish me?"

"Of course there is."

"If I flee from her, there's a law to punish me?"

"Of course there is."

"If I marry t'oother dear lass, there's a law to punish me?"

"Of course there is."

"If I was to live wi' her an not marry her — saying such a thing could be, which it never could or would, an her so good — there's a law to punish me, in every innocent child belonging to me?"

"Of course there is."

"Now, a' God's name," said Stephen Blackpool, "show me the law to help me!"

"Hem! There's a sanctity in this relation of life," said Mr. Bounderby "and — and — it must be kept up."

"No no, dunnot say that, sir. 'Tan't kep' up that way. Not that way. 'Tis kep' down that way. I'm a weaver, I were in a fact'ry when a chilt, but I ha' gotten een to see wi' and eern to year wi'. I read in th' papers every 'Sizes, every Sessions — and you read too — I know it! — with dismay — how th' supposed unpossibility o' ever getting unchained from one another, at any price, on any terms, brings blood upon this land, and brings many common married fok to battle, murder, and sudden death. Let us ha' this, right understood. Mine's a grievous case, and want — if yo will be so good — t'know the law that helps me."

"Now, I tell you what!" said Mr. Bounderby, putting his hands in his pockets. "There *is* such a law."

Stephen, subsiding into his quiet manner, and never wandering in his attention, gave a nod.

"But it's not for you at all. It costs money. Its costs a mint of money." How much might that be? Stephen calmly asked.

"Why, you'd have to go to Doctor's Commons with a suit, and you'd have to go to a court of Common Law with a suit, and you'd have to go to the House of Lords with a suit, and you'd have to get an Act of Parliament to enable you to marry again, and it would cost you (if it was a case of very plain-sailing), I suppose from a thousand to fifteen hundred pound," said Mr. Bounderby. "Perhaps twice the money."

"There's no other law?"

"Certainly not."

"Why then, sir," said Stephen, turning white, and motioning with that right hand of his, as if he gave everything to the four winds, "'tis a muddle. 'Tis just a muddle a'toogether, an the sooner I am dead, the better."

(Mrs. Sparsit again dejected by the impiety of the people.)

"Pooh, pooh! Don't you talk nonsense, my good fellow," said Mr. Bounderby, "about things you don't understand; and don't you call the Institutions of your country a muddle, or you'll get yourself into a real muddle one of these fine mornings. The institutions of your country are not your piece-work, and the only thing you have got to do, is, to mind your piece-work. You didn't take your wife for fast and for loose; but for better for worse. If she has tuned out worse — why, all we have got to say is, she might have turned out better."

"'Tis a muddle," said Stephen, shaking his head as he moved to the door. "'Tis a' a muddle!"

"Now, I'll tell you what!" Mr. Bounderby resumed, as valedictory address. "With what I shall call your unhallowed opinions, you have been quite shocking this lady: who, as I have already told you, is a born lady and who, as I have not already told you, has had her own marriage misfortunes to the tune of tens of thousands of pounds — tens of Thousands of Pounds!" (he repeated it with great relish). "Now, you have always been a steady Hand hitherto; but my opinion is, and so I tell you plainly that you are turning into the wrong road. You have been listening to some mischievous stranger or other — they're always about — and the best thing you can do is, to come out of that. Now you know;" here his countenance expressed marvelous acuteness; "I can see as far into a grindstone as another man; farther than a good many, perhaps, because I had my nose well kept to it when I was young. I see traces of the turtle soup and venison, and gold spoon in this. Yes, I do!" cried Mr. Bounderby shaking his head with obstinate cunning. "By the Lord Harry, I do!"

With a very different shake of the head and a deep sigh, Stephen said, "Thank you, sir, I wish you good day." So he left Mr. Bounderby swelling at his own portrait on the wall, as if he were going to explode himself into it; and Mrs. Sparsit still ambling on with her foot in her stirrup, taking quite cast down by the popular vices.

Recollections: The French Revolution of 1848

Alexis de Tocqueville

Edited by J. P. Mayer and A. P. Kerr

My view of the reasons for the events of the 24th February, and my thoughts concerning its effects for the future

So the July Monarchy had fallen, fallen without a struggle, not under the victors' blows, but before they were struck; and the victors were as astonished at their success as the losers at their defeat. After the February Revolution I often heard M. Guizot and even M. Molé and M. Thiers say that it was all due to surprise and should be considered pure accident, a lucky stroke and nothing more. I have always felt tempted to answer them as Molière's Misanthrope answers Oronte: *"Pour en juger ainsi, vous avez vos raisons,"* for for eighteen years those three men had directed the affairs of France under Louis-Philippe, and it was hard for them to admit that that prince's bad government had prepared the way for the catastrophe that threw him from the throne.

Obviously I, not having the same reasons to believe it, was not quite of their opinion. I am not asserting that accidents played no part in the February Revolution, for they played a very great one; but they were not the only thing.

In my life I have come across literary men who wrote histories without taking part in public affairs, and politicians whose only concern was to control events without a thought of describing them. And I have invariably noticed that the former see general causes everywhere, whereas the latter, spending their lives amid the disconnected events of each day, freely attribute everything to particular incidents and think that all the little strings their hands are busy pulling daily are those that control the world's destiny. Probably both of them are mistaken.

For my part I hate all those absolute systems that make all the events of history depend on great first causes linked together by the chain of fate and thus succeed, so to speak, in banishing men form the history of the human race. Their boasted breadth seems to me narrow, and their mathematical exactness false. I believe, *pace* the writers who find these sublime theories to feed their vanity and lighten their labours, that many important historical facts can be explained only by accidental circumstances, while many others are inexplicable. Finally, that chance, or rather the concatenation of secondary causes, which we call by that name because we can't sort them all out, is a very important element in all that we see taking place in the world's theatre. But I am firmly convinced that chance can do nothing unless the ground has been prepared in advance. Antecedent facts, the nature of institutions, turns of mind and the state of mores are the materials from which chance composes those impromptu events that surprise and terrify us.

In common with all other great events of this sort, the February Revolution was born of general causes fertilized, if I may put it so, by accidents. And to make the whole thing depend on the former is as superficial as attributing it solely to the latter.

The industrial revolution, which for thirty years had been making Paris the leading manufacturing city in France, attracting a whole new population of workmen, not to mention the work on the fortifications, which had brought in a flood of labourers now out of work; the passion for material pleasures, which, spurred on by the government, was getting a firmer and firmer hold over the whole of this multitude, the democratic disease of envy silently at work; economic and political theories, which were beginning to attract notice and which tended to encourage the belief that human wretchedness was due to the laws and not to providence and that poverty could be abolished by changing the system of society; the contempt felt for the ruling class, especially its leaders — a contempt so deep and general that it paralyzed the resistance even of those who stood to lose most by the overthrow of authority; the centralization, thanks to which control of Paris and of the whole machinery of government was kept in working order, was all that was needed to complete a revolution; and lastly, the mobility of everything — institutions, ideas, mores and men — in a society on the move, which had lived through seven great revolutions within sixty years, not to mention numerous small secondary upheavals: such were the general causes without which the February Revolution would have been impossible. The main accidents that brought it on were the clumsy passions of the dynastic opposition, which prepared the ground for a riot when it wanted a reform; the attempts to suppress that riot, excessive at first, then abandoned; the sudden disappearance of the former ministers, which snapped the threads of power, threads that the new ministers, in their confusion, could neither pick up nor retie; the mistakes and mental disorientation of these ministers who were so inadequate in rebuilding what they had been strong enough to throw down; the vacillation of the generals; the absence of the only members of the royal family who had either popularity or energy, and above all the senile imbecility of King Louis-Philippe, a weakness nobody could have foreseen, and which even now after the event seems almost incredible.

I sometimes wonder what in the King's soul could have produced this unanticipated sudden collapse. Louis-Philippe's life had been passed amid revolutions, and he certainly lacked neither experience, nor courage, nor intelligence, although all those qualities deserted him on that day. I think his weakness was due to the intensity of his astonishment; he was knocked flat, unaware of what had hit him. The February Revolution was *unforeseen* by everybody, but by him most of all; no warning from the outside had prepared him for it, for his mind had retreated long ago into the sort of haughty loneliness inhabited by almost all kings whose long reigns have been prosperous, who mistake luck for genius, and who do not want to listen to anybody, because they think they have no more to learn. Besides, Louis-Philippe, like his ministers, had been misled, as mentioned before, by the will-o'-the-wisp light past history cast on the present. One could make a weird collection of all the utterly dissimilar mistakes that have been fathered one by the other. There is Charles I, being driven into arbitrary behaviour and violence by seeing how the spirit of opposition flourished under the kindly rule of his father; Louis XVI, determined to put up with everything because Charles I had perished unwilling to put up with anything; then Charles X provoking a revolution because he had witnessed Louis XVI's weakness; and finally Louis-Philippe, the most perspicacious of them all, who imagined that all he had to do to remain on the throne was, without violating the law, to pervert it, and that provided he himself observed the letter of the Charter, the nation would never go beyond it. To corrupt the people without defying them and to twist the spirit of the Constitution without changing the letter; to play off the country's vices one against the other; and gently to drown revolutionary passion in the love of material pleasures: this had been his idea throughout his life, and it gradually became, not just his main, but his only thought. He shut himself up in it; he lived inside it; and when he suddenly saw that it was wrong, he was like a man awakened at night by an earthquake, who, seeing his house falling down in the darkness and even the ground giving way under his feet, remains distracted and lost amid the universal unforeseen ruin.

I now sit back very comfortably to argue about the causes leading up to the 24th February, but on the afternoon of that day I had quite other thoughts in my head; the event itself filled my thoughts, and I was more concerned with what would follow than with what had produced it.

This was the second revolution within the space of seventeen years that I had seen accomplished before my eyes.

Both pained me; but how much more bitter were the impressions left by the second! Right up to the end I had felt some remnants of hereditary affection for Charles X, but that king fell because he had violated rights that were dear to me, and I was able to hope that my country's freedom would be revived rather than extinguished by his fall. Today that freedom seemed dead to me; the fugitive royal family meant nothing to me, but I felt that my own cause was lost.

I had spent the best year of my youth in a society that seemed to be regaining prosperity and grandeur as it regained freedom; I had conceived the idea of a regulated and orderly freedom, controlled by religious belief, mores and laws; I was touched by the joys of such freedom, and it had become my whole life's passion; I had felt that I could never be consoled for its loss, and now I clearly saw that I must give it up forever.

I had had too much experience of men to accept payment in idle words this time; I knew that, while one great revolution may be able to found a nation's liberty, several revolutions on top of each other make the enjoyment of an orderly liberty impossible there for a long time.

I still did not know what would come out of this one, but I was already certain that it would not be any result satisfactory to me; and I foresaw that, whatever might be the fate of our posterity, it was our lot to spend a wretched life between alternate swings to licence and oppression.

Mentally I reviewed the history of our last sixty years and smiled bitterly to myself as I thought of the illusions cherished at the end of each phase of this long revolution; the theories feeding these illusions; our historians' learned daydreams, and all the ingenious false systems by which men sought to explain a present still unclearly seen and to foresee the unseen future.

The Constitutional Monarchy had succeeded the Ancien Régime; the Republic followed the Monarchy; the Empire the Republic; after the Empire the Restoration; then there had come the July Monarchy. After each of these successive changes it was said that the French Revolution, having achieved what was presumptuously called its work, was finished: men had said that, and they had believed it. Under the Restoration, I, too, unfortunately hoped for that, and I continued to hope after the Restoration government had fallen; and here was the French Revolution Starting again, for it was always the same one. As we go on, its end seems ever farther off and hazier. Shall we reach, as other prophets as vain perhaps as their predecessors assure us, a more complete and profound social transformation than our fathers ever foresaw or desired, and which we ourselves cannot yet conceive; or may we not simply end up in that intermittent anarchy which is well known to be the chronic incurable disease of old peoples? I cannot tell, and do not know when this long voyage will end; I am tired of mistaking deceptive mists for the bank. And I often wonder whether that solid land we have sought for so long actually exists, and whether it is not our fate to rove the seas forever!

I passed the rest of that day with Ampère, my colleague at the Institute and one of my best friends. He came to find out what had become of me in the scuffle and to ask me to dinner. At first I wanted to console myself by getting him to share my grief. But almost at once I found that his impressions were not the same as mine, that he looked with other eyes on the revolution that was taking place. Ampère was an intelligent man, and what counts for more, a warm-hearted man, gentle and reliable in behaviour. He was loved for his good nature, and his versatile, intelligent, amusing, satirical conversation was a pleasure; he would throw out a whole lot of remarks [none of which, it is true, rose very high, but] which passed the time very agreeably. Unluckily, he was too much inclined to carry the spirit of a salon over into literature, and that of literature into politics. What I call the literary spirit in politics consists in looking for what is ingenious and new rather than for what is true, being fonder of what makes an interesting picture than what serves a purpose, being very appreciative of good acting and fine speaking without reference to the play's results, and, finally, judging by impressions rather than reasons. I need not say that this peculiarity is not confined to Academicians. To tell the truth, the whole nation shares it a little, and the French public as a whole often takes a literary man's view of politics. Ampère, who was kindness itself and had not adopted the life of the coterie to which he belonged except to become too indulgent to his friends, absolutely despised the government that had fallen, and its last acts on behalf of the Swiss ultramontanes had irritated him very much. His hatred for the latter, and especially their French friends, was his only feeling of that sort of which I am aware. He was mortally frightened of bores, but the only people he detested from the depths of his soul were the devout. That latter had, it is true wounded him very cruelly and clumsily, for he was not naturally their adversary, and nothing is better proof of their blind intolerance than that they should have roused such flaming hatred in so Christian a man as Ampère. I am not saying that he was a Christian by belief, but through goodwill, taste and, if I dare to put it so, temperament. Thus Ampère needed little consolation for the fall of a government that had served them so well. Moreover he had just witnessed instances of unselfishness, even generosity and courage among the insurgents; and he was carried away by the general emotion.

I saw that he not only failed to share my feeling but was inclined to take the opposite view. Such an attitude made all the indignation, grief and anger that had been piling up in my heart since the morning suddenly erupt against Ampère; and I addressed him with a violence of language that makes me a little ashamed whenever I think of it, and which only such a true friend as he would have excused. Among other things, I remember saying:

"You don't understand anything of what is happening; you judge it like some Parisian idler, or a poet. You call this the triumph of freedom when it is its final defeat. I tell you that this people whom you so naïvely admire has just proved that it is incapable and unworthy of living in freedom. Show me what it has learned form experience? What new virtues has it discovered, and what old vices has it discarded? No, I tell you, it is always the same; just as impatient, careless and contemptuous of the law as ever; just as easily led and as rash in the face of danger as its fathers before it. Time has wrought no change in it, but has left it as frivolous in serious matters as it used to be in trifles."

After a lot of shouting, we both agreed to leave the verdict to the future, that enlightened and just judge who, unfortunately, always arrives too late.

Pairs the day after the 24th February, and the days that followed—Socialist character of the new revolution

Started again at Sorrento in November 1850

The night passed without mishap for, although gunshots could be heard until morning, they were sounds of triumph, not of war. As soon as it was light I went out to see how the town looked and to find out what had happened to my two nephews. At the little seminary where they were being educated, they were being given no training to prepare them to live in a time of revolution such as ours, and it was not safe there with revolution abroad. The seminary was in the rue de Madame behind the Luxembourg, and so I had to go through a large part of Paris to get there.

I found the streets quiet and even half-deserted, as they usually are in Paris on a Sunday morning when the rich are still asleep and the poor resting. One did, of course, meet some of yesterday's victors from time to time along the walls, but most of them were on their way home and took no notice of passers-by. In the few shops that were open one saw frightened and, still more, astonished shopkeepers, looking like an audience at a theatre who, after the play is finished, still wonder what it was about. Soldiers were the commonest sight in these empty streets, some alone, others in small groups, all unarmed and homeward bound. Their recent defeat had left an acute sense of shame and anger in their souls, as became obvious later, but at the time it did not show; these lads' joy at finding themselves free seemed to swamp every other feeling; they went gaily along without a care in the world, like schoolboys home for the holidays.

No attack, or even insult, had disturbed the little seminary, and my nephews were not even there, having been sent the day before to their maternal grandmother's house. So I turned homewards, passing by the rue du Bac to find out if Lamoricière, who was then living there, had in fact been killed the day before, as his A.D.C. had said after seeing him fall. It was only after they had recognized me that his servants admitted he was at home and allowed me in to see him.

I found this uncommon man, of whom I shall have occasion to speak more than once later, stretched immobile on his bed, an unnatural and distasteful state for such as he. His head was half-broken open, his arms riddled with bayonet thrusts, and all his limbs bruised and crippled; but for the rest he was always the same, with his brilliant mind and indomitable heart. He told me all that had happened to him the day before, when only a miracle had saved him from a thousand dangers. I strongly urged him to stay quiet until he was recovered, and for a long time after that, so as not to risk his person and reputation uselessly in the ensuing chaos. Good advice, no doubt, to give to a man so much in love with action and so accustomed to act that, having accomplished things necessary and useful, he is always ready to undertake harmful and dangerous ones rather than do nothing at all, but as futile as advice that goes against the grain always is.

I spent the whole afternoon wandering about Paris and was particularly struck by two points: first, I will not say the mainly, but the uniquely and exclusively popular character of the recent revolution, and the omnipotence it had given the so-called people, that is to say, the classes who work with their hands, over all other classes. Secondly, how little hatred, or indeed any other acute feeling, was shown in this first moment of victory by the humble people who had suddenly become the sole masters of power.

Although the working classes had often played the principal part in the events of the first Republic, they had never been the leaders and sole masters of the State, in fact or in law; there was probably not a single man of the people in the Convention; it was full of the middle class and men of letters. The fight between the Mountain and the Gironde was between bourgeois on both sides, and the triumph of the former never brought power down into the hands of the people alone. The July Revolution was effected by the people, but they had been stirred up and led by the middle class who reaped the major advantages from it. But the February Revolution seemed to be entirely outside and against the bourgeoisie.

In the shock of conflict the two main parties composing the French body social had somehow separated, and the people, standing alone, remained in full possession of power. This was something completely new in our history. It is true that similar revolutions had taken place in other countries at other times; however new and unexpected contemporaries may find the particular events of any age, including our own, they are always part of the age-old history of humanity. In particular, Florence at the close of the Middle Ages presents many analogies with our conditions now; first the middle class had succeeded the nobility, and then one day the latter were driven out of government in their turn, and a barefoot *gonfalonier* marched at the head of the people and thus led the republic. But this popular revolution in Florence was the result of transitory and peculiar circumstances, whereas ours was due to very permanent and general causes, which, having thrown France into agitation, might be expected to stir up all the rest of Europe. For it was not just a party that triumphed this time; men aimed at establishing a social science, a philosophy, and I might almost say a common religion to be taught to all men and followed by them. Therein lay the really new element in the old picture.

Throughout this day in Paris I never saw one of the former agents of authority: not a soldier, or a gendarme, or a policeman; even the National Guard had vanished. The people alone bore arms, guarded public buildings, watched, commanded and punished; it was an extraordinary and a terrible thing to see the whole of this huge city, full of so many riches, or rather the whole of this great nation, in the sole hands of those who owned nothing; for thanks to centralization, whoever reigns in Paris controls France. Consequently the terror felt by all the other classes was extreme; I do not think that it had ever been so intense at any other moment of the revolution, and the only comparison would be with the feelings of the civilized cities of the Roman world when they suddenly found themselves in the power of Vandals or Goths.

Since nothing of the sort had happened before, many people anticipated unheard-of acts of violence. For my part, I never shared these fears. I noticed things that made me foresee strange perturbations and peculiar crises in the immediate future, but I never expected the rich to be looted. I knew the common people of Paris well enough to realize that their first impulses in times of revolution are usually generous, and that they like to pass the days immediately following their triumph in boasting about it, parading their authority and playing at being great men; during this interval some sort of authority is usually established, the policeman returns to his beat, and the judge to his bench. And when those great men of ours finally choose to come down again to the familiar, common ground of petty, evil human passions, they are no longer free to do so and are forced to live as simple honest people. Moreover we have passed through such long years of insurrections that a particular kind of morality of disorder and a special code for days of riot have evolved. These exceptional laws tolerate murder and allow devastation, but theft is strictly forbidden, which, whatever anybody says, does not prevent a lot of robbery on such days, for a society of rioters cannot be different from all others, and there are always rascals everywhere who jeer at the morality of the main body and are very contemptuous of its conception of honour when nobody is looking. I was further reassured by the feeling that the victors had been as surprised by their success as the losers by their defeat; there had been no time for passions to be enflamed and embittered in the fight; the government had fallen undefended by itself or others. Even those who in the depths of their hearts most regretted its fall had for a long time either fought against it or at least criticized it severely.

For the past year the dynastic opposition and the republican opposition had been living in deceptive harmony, performing the same acts for opposite reasons. This misunderstanding, which had facilitated the revolution, now made it more gentle. The Monarchy vanished, and the battlefield seemed empty; the people no longer saw clearly what enemies remained to be hunted down and defeated; the former objects of their anger were not there; the clergy had never been completely reconciled to the new dynasty and saw it fall without regret; the old nobility cheered, whatever the consequences might be. For the clergy had suffered form the intolerance of the middle classes, and the nobility from their pride. And both despised and feared their rule.

This was the first time in sixty years that priests, nobility and people had shared a common feeling — a longing for revenge, it is true, and not one of mutual affection. But in politics that is already much, for shared hatreds are almost always the basis of friendships. The real and only party defeated was the bourgeoisie, but even they had little to fear. Their rule had been exclusive rather than oppressive, and being corrupt rather than violent, it aroused more contempt than hatred. Moreover the middle class is never a compact body within the nation, nor does it form any very distinctive party within the whole. There is always something it shares with all the others, and in some places it becomes merged with them. This lack of homogeneity and of precise boundaries makes the rule of the middle class weak and vacillating. But it also makes it impossible to come to grips with that class, or even to see it, when it no longer rules, and others seek to strike it.

It was all these causes combined that resulted in the languor that, combined with omnipotence, struck me as so odd. And this languor stood out the more clearly in contrast with the over-blown language used, language that brought back terrible memories. M. Thiers' *History of the Revolution*, M. de Lamartine's *Girondins*, and other less famous but nonetheless well-known works, and especially some theatrical productions rehabilitated the Terror, and in a sense made it fashionable. So the tepid passions of our day were expressed in the burning language of '93, and the names and deeds of illustrious villains were continually on the lips of men who had neither the energy nor even the sincere desire to imitate them.

It was those socialist theories, which I have previously called the philosophy of the February Revolution, that later kindled real passions, embittered jealousies, and finally stirred up war between the classes. While at the beginning passions were less disorderly than one might have feared, on the morrow of the revolution there was certainly an extraordinary ferment and unheard-of disorder in the people's ideas.

After the 25th February a thousand strange systems poured from the impetuous imaginations of innovators and spread through the troubled minds of the crowd. Everything except Throne and Parliament was still standing; and yet it seemed that the shock of revolution had reduced society itself to dust, and that there was an open competition for the plan of the new edifice to be put in its place; each man had his own scheme; one might publish his in the papers; another might use the posters that soon covered the walls; a third might proclaim his to the listening winds. One was going to abolish inequality of fortunes; another that of education; while a third attacked the oldest inequality of all, that between men and women. There were remedies against poverty, and against that disease called work which has afflicted man since the beginning of his existence.

There was great variety in these theories; sometimes they were contradictory and sometimes hostile to one another. But all of them, aiming lower than the government and attempting to reach society itself, on which government stands, adopted the common name of socialism. Socialism will always remain the most essential feature of the February Revolution, and the one that left the most frightening memory. Seen from afar, the Republic will appear as a means, not an end.

It is no part of the plan of these *Recollections* to inquire into what gave the February Revolution this socialist character. I shall only say that it should not have surprised the world as much as it did. Had no one noticed that for a long time the people had been continually gaining ground and improving their condition, and that their importance, education, desires and power were all constantly growing? Their prosperity had also increased, but not so fast, and it was getting close to that limit which, in old societies, cannot be passed, when there are many candidates but few places. How could it have failed to occur to the poor classes, who were inferior but nonetheless powerful, that they might use their power to escape from their poverty and inferiority? For sixty years they had been working towards this end. At first the people hoped to help themselves by changing the political institutions, but after each change they found that their lot was not bettered, or that it had not improved fast enough to keep pace with their headlong desires. Inevitably they were bound to discover sooner or later that what held them back in their place was not the constitution of the government, but the unalterable laws that constitute society itself; and it was natural for them to ask whether they did not have the power and the right to change these too, as they had changed the others. And to speak specifically about property, which is, so to speak, the foundation of our social order, when all the privileges that cover and conceal the privilege of property, which is, so to speak, the foundation of our social order, when all the privileges that cover and conceal the privilege of property had been abolished and property remained as the main obstacle to equality among men and seemed to be the only sign thereof, was it not inevitable, I do not say that it should be abolished in its turns, but that at least the idea of abolishing it should strike minds that had no part in its enjoyment?

This natural restlessness in the minds of the people, with the inevitable ferment in the desires, thoughts, needs and instincts of the crowd, formed the fabric on which the innovators drew such monstrous and grotesque patterns. One may find their efforts ludicrous, but nothing merits the serious study of philosophers and statesmen more than the background on which they are working.

Will socialism remain buried in the contempt that so justly covers the socialists of 1848? I ask the question without answering it. I am sure that in the long run the constituent laws of our modern society will be drastically modified, many of the main parts of them have already been substantially modified. But will they ever be abolished and replaced by others? That seems impracticable to me. I say no more, for the more I study the former state of the world, and indeed even when I see the modern world in greater detail, when I consider the prodigious diversity found there, not just in the laws but in the principles of the laws and the different forms that the right of property has taken and, whatever anybody says, still takes on this earth, I am tempted to the belief that what are called necessary institutions are only institutions to which one is accustomed, and that in matters of social constitution the field of possibilities is much wider than people living within each society imagine.

Class Struggles in France

Karl Marx

With the exception of a few short chapters, every important part of the annals of the revolution from 1848 to 1849 carries the heading: Defeat of the revolution!

But what succumbed in these defeats was not the revolution. It was the pre-revolutionary traditional appendages, results of social relationships, which had not yet come to the point of sharp class antagonisms — persons, illusions, conceptions, projects, from which the revolutionary party before the February Revolution was not free, from which it could be freed, not by the victory of February, but only by a series of defeats.

In a word: revolutionary advance made headway not by its immediate tragi-comic achievements, but on the contrary by the creation of a powerful, united counter-revolution, by the creation of an opponent, by fighting whom the party of revolt first ripened into a real revolutionary party.

To prove this is the task of the following pages.

The Defeat of June 1848

After the July Revolution, when the Liberal banker, Laffitte, led his godfather, the Duke of Orleans, in triumph to the Hôtel de Ville, he let fall the words: "From now on the bankers will rule." Laffitte had betrayed the secret of the revolution.

It was not the French bourgeoisie that ruled under Louis Philippe, but a fraction of it, bankers, stock exchange kings, railway kings, owners of coal and ironworks and forests, a section of landed proprietors that rallied round them — the so-called finance aristocracy. It sat on the throne, it dictated laws in the Chambers, it conferred political posts from cabinet portfolios to the tobacco bureau.

The real industrial bourgeoisie formed part of the official opposition, *i.e.*, it was represented only as a minority in the Chambers. Its opposition was expressed all the more decisively, the more unalloyed the autocracy of the finance aristocracy became, and the more it itself imagined that its domination over the working-class was ensured after the mutinies of 1832, 1834 and 1839, which had been drowned in blood. *Grandin*, the Rouen manufacturer, the most fanatical instrument of bourgeois reaction, in the Constituent Assembly, as well as in the legislative National Assembly, was the most violent opponent of Guizot in the Chamber of Deputies. *Leon Faucher*, later renowned for his impotent endeavors to push himself forward as the Guizot of the French counter-revolution, in the last days of Louis Philippe, waged a war of the pen for industry against speculation and its train bearer, the government. *Bastiat* agitated against the ruling system in the name of Bordeaux and the whole of wine-producing France.

The petty bourgeoisie of all degrees, and the peasantry also, were completely excluded from political power. Finally, in the official opposition or entirely outside the *pays légal*, there were the ideological representatives and spokesmen of the above classes, their savants, lawyers, doctors, etc., in a word: their so-called talents.

From *The Class Struggles in France (1848–1850)* by Karl Marx.

The July monarchy, owing to its financial need, was dependent from the beginning on the big bourgeoisie, and its dependence on the big bourgeoisie was the inexhaustible source of a growing financial need. It was impossible to subordinate state administration to the interests of national production, without balancing the budget, establishing a balance between state expenses and income. And how was this balance to be established, without limiting state expenditure, *i.e.*, without encroaching on interests which were so many supports of the ruling system, and without redistributing taxes, *i.e.*, without putting a considerable share of the burden of taxes on the shoulders of the big bourgeoisie itself?

Rather the fraction of the bourgeoisie that ruled and legislated through the Chambers had a direct interest in state indebtedness. The state deficit was even the main object of its speculation and played the chief role in its enrichment. At the end of each year a new deficit. After expiry of four or five years a new loan. And every new loan offered new opportunities to the finance aristocracy for defrauding the state which was kept artificially on the verge of bankruptcy — it had to contract with the bankers under the most unfavorable conditions. Each new loan gave a further opportunity for plundering the public that had invested its capital in state bonds, by stock exchange manipulations into the secrets of which the government and the majority in the Chambers were admitted. In general, the fluctuation of state credits and the possession of state secrets gave the bankers and their associates in the Chambers and on the throne the possibility of evoking sudden, extraodinary fluctuations in the quotations of state bonds, the result of which was always bound to be the ruin of a mass of smaller capitalists and the fabulously rapid enrichment of the big gamblers. If the state deficit was in the direct interest of the ruling fraction of the bourgeoisie, then it is clear why extraordinary state expenditure in the last years of Louis Philippe's government was far more than double the extraordinary state expenditure under Napoleon, indeed reached a yearly sum of nearly 400,000,000 francs, whereas the whole annual export of France seldom attained a volume amounting to 750,000,000 francs. The enormous sums which, in this way, flowed through the hands of the state, facilitated, moreover, swindling contracts for deliveries, bribery, defalcations and all kinds of roguery. The defrauding of the state, just as it occurred on a large scale in connection with loans, was repeated in detail, in the state works. The relationship between Chamber and government multiplied itself as the relationship between individual departments and individual *entrepreneurs*.

In the same way as the ruling class exploited state expenditure in general and state loans, they exploited the building of railways. The Chambers piled the main burdens on the state, and secured the golden fruits to the speculating finance aristocracy. One recalls the scandals in the Chamber of Deputies, when by chance it came out that all the members of the majority, including a number of ministers, had taken part as shareholders in the very railway construction which as legislators they caused to be carried out afterwards at the cost of the state.

On the other hand, the smallest financial reform was wrecked by the influence of the bankers. For example, the postal reform. Rothschild protested. Was it permissible for the state to curtail sources of income out of which interest was to be paid on its ever increasing debt?

The July monarchy was nothing other than a joint stock company for the exploitation of French national wealth, the dividends of which were divided amongst ministers, Chambers, 240,000 voters and their adherents. Louis Philippe was the director of this company — Robert Macaire on the throne. Trade, industry, agriculture, shipping, the interests of the industrial bourgeoisie, were bound to be continually prejudiced and endangered under this system. The bourgeoisie in the July days had inscribed on its banner: *government à bon marché*, cheap government.

While the finance aristocracy made the laws, was at the head of the administration of the State, had command of all the organized public powers, dominated public opinion through facts and through the press, the same prostitution, the same shameless cheating, the same mania to get rich was repeated in every sphere, from the Court to the Café Borgne, to get rich not by production, but by pocketing the already available wealth of others. In particular there broke out, at the top of bourgeois society, an unbridled display of unhealthy and dissolute appetites, which clashed every moment with the bourgeois laws themselves, wherein the wealth having its source in gambling naturally seeks its satisfaction, where pleasure becomes *crapuleux*, where gold, dirt and blood flow together. The finance aristocracy, in its mode of acquisition as well as in its pleasures, is nothing but the resurrection of the lumpenproletariat at the top of bourgeois society.

And the non-ruling sections of the French bourgeoisie cried: corruption! The people cried: *à bas les grands voleurs! à bas les assassins!* when in 1847, on the most prominent stages of bourgeois society, the same scenes were publicly enacted which regularly lead the lumpenproletariat to brothels, to workhouses and lunatic asylums, before the Bench, to bagnos and to the scaffold. The industrial bourgeoisie saw its interests endangered, the petty bourgeoisie was filled with moral indignation, the imagination of the people was offended, Paris was flooded with pamphlets — "*la dynastie Rothschild*," "*les juifs rois de l'epoque*" etc. — in which the rule of the finance aristocracy was denounced and stigmatized with greater or less wit.

Rien pour la gloire! Glory brings no profit! *La paix partout et toujours!* War depresses the quotations of the Three and Four per Cents! the France of the Bourse Jews had inscribed on her banner. Her foreign policy was therefore lost in a series of mortifications to French national feeling, which reacted all the more vigorously when the robbery of Poland was brought to an end with the annexation of Cracow by Austria, and when Guizot came out actively on the side of the Holy Alliance in the Swiss separatist war. The victory of the Swiss liberals in this mimic war raised the self-respect of the bourgeois opposition in France; the bloody uprising of the people in Palermo worked like an electric shock on the paralyzed masses of the people and awoke their great revolutionary memories and passions.

The eruption of the general discontent was finally accelerated and the sentiment for revolt ripened by two economic world-events.

The potato blight and the bad harvests of 1845 and 1846 increased the general ferment among the people. The high cost of living of 1847 called forth bloody conflicts in France as well as on the rest of the Continent. As against the shameless orgies of the finance aristocracy, the struggle of the people for the first necessities of life! At Buzançais the hunger rioters executed; in Paris the over-satiated *escrocs* snatched from the courts by the Royal family.

The second great economic event which hastened the outbreak of the revolution, was a general commercial and industrial crisis in England. Already heralded in the autumn of 1845 by the wholesale reverses of the speculators in railway shares, delayed during 1846 by a number of incidents such as the impending abolition of the corn duties, in the autumn of 1847 the crisis finally burst forth with the bankruptcy of the London grocers, on the heels of which followed the insolvencies of the land banks and the closing of the factories in the English industrial districts. The after-effect of this crisis on the Continent had not yet spent itself when the February Revolution broke out.

The devastation of trade and industry caused by the economic epidemic made the autocracy of the finance aristocracy still more unbearable. Throughout the whole of France the bourgeois opposition evoked the banquet agitation for an electoral reform which should win for them the majority of the Chambers and overthrow the Ministry of the Bourse. In Paris the industrial crisis had, in particular, the result of throwing a number of manufacturers and big traders, who under the existing circumstances could no longer do any business in the foreign market, onto the home market. They set up large establishments, the competition of which ruined the *épiciers* and *boutiquiers en masse*. Hence the innumerable bankruptcies among this section of the Paris bourgeoisie, and hence their revolutionary action in February. It is known how Guizot and the Chambers answered the reform proposals with a plain challenge, how Louis Philippe too late resolved on a Ministry led by Barrot, how hand-to-hand fighting took place between the people and the army, how the army was disarmed by the passive conduct of the National Guard, how the July monarchy had to give way to a Provisional Government.

The Provisional Government which emerged from the February barricades, necessarily mirrored in its composition the different parties which shared in the victory. It could not be anything but a compromise between the different classes which together had overturned the July throne, but whose interests were mutually antagonistic. A large majority of its members consisted of representatives of the bourgeoisie. The republican petty bourgeoisie were represented by Ledru-Rollin and Flocon, the republican bourgeoisie by the people from the *National*, the dynastic opposition by Cremieux, Dupont de l'Eure, etc. The working class had only two representatives, Louis Blanc and Albert. Finally, Lamartine as a member of the Provisional Government; that was actually no real interest, no definite class that was the February Revolution itself, the common uprising with its illusions, its poetry, its imagined content and its phrases. For the rest, the spokesman of the February Revolution, by his position and his views, belonged to the bourgeoisie.

If Paris, as a result of political centralization, rules France, the workers, in moments of revolutionary earthquakes, rule Paris. The first act in the life of the Provisional Government was an attempt to escape from this overpowering influence, by an appeal from intoxicated Paris to sober France. Lamartine disputed the right of the barricade fighters to proclaim the republic, on the ground that only the majority of Frenchmen had that right; they must await their votes, the Parisian proletariat must not besmirch its victory by a usurpation. The bourgeoisie allowed the proletariat only one usurpation — that of fighting.

Up to noon on February 25, the republic had not yet been proclaimed; on the other hand, the whole of the Ministries had already been divided among the bourgeois elements of the Provisional Government and among the generals, bankers and lawyers of the *National*. But the workers were this time determined not to put up with any swindling like that of July 1830.

They were ready to take up the fight anew and to enforce the republic by force of arms. With this message, Raspail betook himself to the Hôtel de Ville. In the name of the Parisian proletariat he commanded the Provisional Government to proclaim the republic; if this order of the people were not fulfilled within two hours, he would return at the head of 200,000 men. The bodies of the fallen were scarcely cold, the barricades were not yet cleared away, the workers not yet disarmed, and the only force which could be opposed to them was the National Guard. Under these circumstances the prudent state doubts and juristic scruples of conscience of the Provisional Government suddenly vanished. The interval of two hours had not expired before all the walls of Paris were resplendent with the tremendous historical words:

République française! Liberté, Egalité, Fraternité!

Even the memory of the limited aims and motives which drove the bourgeoisie into the February Revolution was extinguished by the proclamation of the republic on the basis of universal suffrage. Instead of a few small fractions of the bourgeoisie, whole classes of French society were suddenly hurled into the circle of political power, forced to leave the boxes, the stalls and the gallery and to act in person upon the revolutionary stage! With the constitutional monarchy the semblance of a state power independently confronting bourgeois society also vanished, as well as the whole series of subordinate struggles which this semblance of power called forth!

The proletariat, by dictating the republic to the Provisional Government and through the Provisional Government to the whole of France, stepped into the foreground forthwith as an independent party, but at the same time challenged the whole of bourgeois France to enter the lists against it. What it won was the terrain for the fight for its revolutionary emancipation, but in no way this emancipation itself!

The first thing that the February republic had to do was rather to complete the rule of the bourgeoise by allowing, besides the finance aristocracy, all the propertied classes to enter the circle of political power. The majority of the great land-owners, the Legitimists, were emancipated from the political nullity to which they had been condemned by the July Monarchy. Not for nothing had the *Gazette de France* agitated in common with the opposition papers, not for nothing had Laroche-jaquelin taken the side of the revolution in the session of the Chamber of Deputies on February 24th. The nominal proprietors, who form the great majority of the French people, the peasants, were put by universal suffrage in the position of arbiters of the fate of France. The February republic finally brought the rule of the bourgeoisie clearly into prominence, since it struck off the crown behind which Capital kept itself concealed.

Just as the workers in the July days had fought and won the bourgeois monarchy, so in the February days they fought and won the bourgeois republic. Just as the July monarchy had to proclaim itself as a monarchy surrounded by republican institutions, so the February republic was forced to proclaim itself a republic surrounded by social institutions. The Parisian proletariat compelled this concession, too.

Marche, a worker, dictated the decree by which the newly formed Provisional Government pledged itself to secure the existence of the workers by work, to provide work for all citizens, etc. And when, a few days later, it forgot its promises and seemed to have lost sight of the proletariat, a mass of 20,000 workers marched on the Hôtel de Ville with the cry: Organization of labor! Formation of a special Ministry of Labor! The Provisional Government, with reluctance and after long debates, nominated a permanent, special commission, charged with finding means of improving the lot of the working classes! This commission consisted of delegates from the corporations of Parisian artisans and was presided over by Louis Blanc and Albert. The Luxembourg was assigned to it as a meeting place. In this way the representatives of the working class were exiled from the seat of the Provisional Government, the bourgeois section of which held the real state power and the reins of administration exclusively in its hands, and side by side with the Ministries of Finance, Trade and Public Works, side by side with the banks and the bourse, there arose a socialist synagogue whose high priests, Louis Blanc and Albert, had the task of discovering the promised land, of preaching the new gospel and of occupying the attention of the Parisian proletariat. Unlike any profane state power, they had no budget, no executive authority at their disposal. With their heads they had to break the pillars of bourgeois society. While Luxembourg sought the philosopher's stone, in the Hôtel de Ville they minted the current coinage.

And yet the claims of the Parisian proletariat, so far as they went beyond the bourgeois republic, could win no other existence than the nebulous one of the Luxembourg.

In common with the bourgeoisie the workers had made the February Revolution, and alongside the bourgeoisie they sought to put through their interests, just as they had installed a worker in the Provisional Government itself alongside the bourgeois majority. Organization of labor! But wage labor is the existing, bourgeois organization of labor. Without it there is no capital, no bourgeoisie, no bourgeois society. Their own Ministry of Labor! But the Ministries of Finance, of Trade, of Public Works — are not these the bourgeois Ministries of

Labor? And alongside these a proletarian Ministry of Labor must be a Ministry of impotence, a Ministry of pious wishes, a commission of the Luxembourg. Just as the workers thought to emancipate themselves side by side with the bourgeoisie, so they opined they would be able to consummate a proletarian revolution within the national walls of France, side by side with the remaining bourgeois nations. But French production relations are conditioned by the foreign trade of France, by her position on the world market and the laws thereof; how should France break them without a European revolutionary war, which would strike back at the despot of the world market, England?

A class in which the revolutionary interests of society are concentrated, so soon as it has risen up, finds directly in its own situation the content and the material of its revolutionary activity: foes to be laid low, measures, dictated by the needs of the struggle, to be taken; the consequences of its own deeds drive it on. It makes no theoretical inquiries into its own task. The French working class had not attained this standpoint; it was still incapable of accomplishing its own revolution.

The development of the industrial proletariat, is, in general, conditioned by the development of the industrial bourgeoisie. Only under its rule the proletariat wins the extensive national existence, which can raise its revolution to a national one and itself creates the modern means of production, which become just so many means of its revolutionary emancipation. Only bourgeois rule tears up the roots of feudal society and levels the ground on which a proletarian revolution is alone possible. In France industry is more developed and the bourgeoisie more revolutionary than elsewhere on the Continent. But was not the February Revolution directed immediately against the finance aristocracy? This fact proved that the industrial bourgeoisie did not rule France. The industrial bourgeoisie can only rule where modern industry shapes all property relations in conformity with itself, and industry can only win this power when it has conquered the world market, for national bounds are not wide enough for its development. But French industry, to a great extent, maintains its command even of the national market only through a more or less modified system of prohibitive duties. If, therefore, the French proletariat, at the moment of a revolution, possesses in Paris actual power and influence which spur it on to a drive beyond its means, in the rest of France it is crowded into single, scattered industrial centers, being almost lost in the superior numbers of peasants and petty bourgeois. The struggle against capital in its developed, modern form, in its culminating phase the struggle of the industrial wage worker against the industrial bourgeois, is in France partially a fact, which after the February days could supply the national content of the revolution so much the less, since the struggle against capital's secondary modes of exploitation, that of the peasants against the usury in mortgages, of the petty bourgeois against the wholesale dealer, banker and manufacturer, in a word, against bankruptcy, was still hidden in the general uprising against the general finance aristocracy. Nothing is more understandable, then, than that the Paris proletariat sought to put through its own interests along with those of the bourgeoisie, instead of enforcing them as the revolutionary interests of society itself, and that it let the red flag be lowered to the tricolor. The French workers could not take a step forward, could not touch a hair of the bourgeois order before the course of the revolution had forced the mass of the nation, peasants and petty bourgeois, standing between the proletariat and the bourgeoisie and in revolt not against this order, against the rule of capital, to attach itself to the proletariat as its vanguard. The workers could only buy this victory through the huge defeat of June.

To the Luxembourg commission, this creation of the Paris workers, remains the merit of having disclosed from the European tribune the secret of the revolution of the nineteenth century: the emancipation of the proletariat. The *Moniteur* raged when it had to propagate officially the "wild ravings" which up to that time lay buried in the apocryphal writings of the Socialists and only reached the ears of the bourgeoisie from time to time as remote, half terrifying, half ludicrous legends. Europe awoke astonished from its bourgeois doze. In the ideas of the proletarians, therefore, who confused the finance aristocracy with the bourgeoisie in general; in the imagination of good old republicans who denied the very existence of classes or, at most, admitted them as a result of the constitutional monarchy; in the hypocritical phrases of the sections of the bourgeoisie up till now excluded from power, the rule of the bourgeoisie was abolished with the introduction of the republic. All the royalists were transformed into republicans and all the millionaires of Paris into workers. The phrase which corresponded to this imagined liquidation of class relations was *fraternité*, universal fraternization and brotherhood. This pleasant abstraction from class antagonisms, this sentimental equalization of contradictory class interests, this fantastic elevation above the class struggle, *fraternité*, this was the special catch-cry of the February Revolution. The classes were divided by a mere misunderstanding and Lamartine baptized the Provisional Government on February 24 as "*un gouvernment qui suspende ce malentendu terrible qui existe entre les différentes classes.*" The Parisian proletariat reveled in this generous intoxication of fraternity.

The Provisional Government, on its side, once it was compelled to proclaim the republic, did everything to make it acceptable to the bourgeoisie and to the provinces. The bloody terror of the first French republic was disavowed by the abolition of the death penalty for political offenses; the press was opened to all opinions; the army, the courts, the administration remained with a few exceptions in the hands of their old dignitaries; none of the July monarchy's great offenders was brought to book. The bourgeois republicans of the *National* amused themselves by exchanging monarchist names and costumes for old republican ones. For them the republic was only a new ball dress for the old bourgeois society. The young republic sought its chief merit, not in being alarming, but rather in constantly taking fright itself, and through the soft compliance and non-resistance of its existence, sought to win existence and to disarm resistance. At home to the privileged classes, abroad to the despotic powers, it was loudly announced that the republic was of a peaceful nature. Live and let live was its motto. In addition thereto, shortly after the February Revolution the Germans, Poles, Austrians, Hungarians and Italians revolted, each people in accordance with its immediate situation. Russia and England — the latter itself agitated, the former cowed — were not prepared. The republic, therefore, had no national enemy. Consequently, there were no great foreign complications which could fire the energies, hasten the revolutionary process, drive the Provisional Government forward or throw it overboard. The Parisian proletariat, which recognized its own creation in the republic, naturally acclaimed each act of the Provisional Government which allowed it to take its place more easily in bourgeois society. It willingly allowed itself to be employed on police service by Caussidière, in order to protect property in Paris, just as it allowed Louis Blanc to arbitrate wage disputes between workers and masters. It was its *point d'honneur* to preserve unblemished the bourgeois honor of the republic in the eyes of Europe.

The republic encountered no resistance either abroad or at home. It was thereby disarmed. Its task was no longer the revolutionary transformation of the world, it was only to adapt itself to the relations of bourgeois society. Concerning the fanaticism with which the Provisional Government undertook this task, there is no more eloquent testimony than its financial measures.

Public and private credit were naturally shattered. Public credit rests on confidence that the state will allow itself to be exploited by the Jews of finance. But the old state had vanished and the revolution was directed above all against the finance aristocracy. The vibrations of the last European commercial crisis had not yet ceased. Bankruptcy still followed bankruptcy.

Private credit was therefore paralyzed, circulation restricted, production at a standstill before the February Revolution broke out. The revolutionary crisis increased the commercial crisis. And if private credit rests on confidence that bourgeoise production to the full extent of its relations, that the bourgeois order, is untouched and inviolate, what effect must a revolution have had, which questioned the basis of bourgeois production, the economic slavery of the proletariat, and set up against the Bourse the sphinx of the Luxembourg? The uprising of the proletariat is the abolition of bourgeois credit; for it is the abolition of bourgeois production and its order. Public and private credit are the economic thermometer, by which the intensity of a revolution can be measured. To the same degree as they fall, the glow and generative force of the revolution rises.

The Provisional Government wanted to strip the republic of its anti-bourgeois appearance. And so it had, above all, to try to ensure the exchange value of this new form of state, its quotation on the Bourse. With the current quotation of the republic on the Bourse, private credit necessarily rose again.

In order to turn aside the very suspicion that it would not or could not comply with the obligations assumed by the monarchy, in order to build up confidence in bourgeois morality and capacity to pay, the Provisional Government took refuge in a boast as undignified as it was childish. In advance of the legal date of payment they paid out 5 per cent, 4½ per cent and 4 per cent interest to the state creditors. The bourgeois aplomb, the self-respect of the capitalists suddenly awoke when they saw the anxious haste with which it was sought to buy their confidence.

The financial embarrassment of the Provisional Government was naturally not lessened by a theatrical stroke which robbed it of its stock of ready cash. The financial pinch could no longer be concealed and petty bourgeois, domestic servants and workers had to pay for the pleasant surprise which had been prepared for the state creditors.

The savings bank books with an amount of more than one hundred francs were declared no longer changeable into gold. The sums deposited in the savings banks were confiscated and by decree transformed into unredeemable state debt. This embittered the already hard pressed petty bourgeois against the republic. Since he received, in place of his savings bank books, state debt certificates, he was forced to go to the Bourse in order to sell them and in this way delivered himself directly into the hands of the Bourse Jews, against whom he had made the February Revolution.

The finance aristocracy which ruled under the July monarchy had its high church in the Bank. Just as the Bourse governs state credit, the Bank governs commercial credit.

The Bank, directly threatened not only in its rule, but in its very existence, by the February Revolution, tried from the beginning to discredit the republic by making the lack of credit general. It suddenly withdrew the credits of the bankers, the manufacturers and the merchants. This maneuver, as it did not immediately call forth a counter-revolution, necessarily reacted on the Bank itself. The capitalists drew out the money which they had deposited in the vaults of the Bank. The possessors of bank notes rushed the pay office in order to change them for gold and silver.

The Provisional Government could, without forcible interference, force the Bank into bankruptcy in a legal manner; it had only to remain passive and leave the Bank to its fate. The bankruptcy of the Bank — that was the deluge which in a trice would sweep away from French soil the finance aristocracy, the most powerful and dangerous enemy of the republic, the golden pedestal of the July monarchy. And once the Bank was bankrupt, the bourgeoisie itself would have to regard it as a last, desperate attempt at rescue if the government formed a national bank and subjected national credit to the control of the nation.

The Provisional Government, on the contrary, fixed a compulsory quotation for the notes of the Bank. It did more. It transformed all provincial banks into branches of the *Banque de France* and allowed it to cast its net over the whole of France. Later it pledged the state forests to the Bank as a guarantee for a loan that it contracted from it. In this way the February Revolution directly strengthened and enlarged the bankocracy which it was to have overthrown.

Meanwhile the Provisional Government was bowed beneath the burden of a growing deficit. In vain it begged for patriotic sacrifices. Only the workers threw in their alms. Recourse had to be had to an heroic measure, to imposition of a new tax. But whom to tax? The Bourse wolves, the bank kings, the state creditors, the *rentiers*, the manufacturers? That was not the way to ingratiate the republic with the bourgeoisie. That meant, on the one hand, to endanger state credit and commercial credit, which, on the other hand, it was sought to purchase with such great sacrifices and humiliations. But someone had to fork out the cash. Who was sacrificed to bourgeois credit? *Jacques le bonhomme*, the peasant.

The Provisional Government imposed an additional tax of 45 centimes in the franc on the four direct taxes. The government press humbugged the Paris proletariat into thinking that this tax would fall for preference on the big landed property, on the possessors of the milliard granted by the Restoration. But in truth it hit the peasant class above all, *i.e.*, the large majority of the French people. They had to pay the costs of the February Revolution; in them the counter-revolution gained its main material. The 45 centimes tax was a life question for the French peasant; he made it a life question for the republic. From that moment the republic meant the 45 centimes tax for the French peasant, and he saw in the Paris proletariat the spendthrift who did himself well at his expense.

Whereas the Revolution of 1789 began by shaking the feudal burdens off the peasants, the revolution of 1848 announced itself with a new tax on the rural population, in order not to endanger capital and keep its state machine going.

There was only one means by which the Provisional Government could set aside all these inconveniences and jerk the state out of its old rut — the declaration of state bankruptcy. We recall how Ledru-Rollin in the National Assembly subsequently recited the virtuous indignation with which he repudiated this demand of the Bourse Jew, Fould, now French Finance Minister. Fould had handed him the apple from the tree of knowledge.

The Provisional Government, having honored the bill drawn on the state by the old bourgeois society, succumbed to the latter. It had become the hard-pressed debtor of bourgeois society instead of confronting it as the pressing creditor that had to collect the revolutionary debts of many years. It had to consolidate the shaky bourgeois relationship, in order to fulfill obligations which are only to be fulfilled within these relationships. Credit becomes a condition of life for it and the concessions to the proletariat, the promises made to it, become so many fetters which had to be struck off. The emancipation of the workers — even as a phrase — became an unbearable danger to the new republic, for it was a standing protest against the restoration of credit, which rests on undisturbed and untroubled recognition of the existing economic class relations. Therefore, it was necessary to have done with the workers.

The February Revolution had cast the army out of Paris. The National Guard, *i.e.*, the bourgeoisie in its different grades, formed the sole power. Alone, however, it did not feel itself a match for the proletariat. Moreover, it was forced slowly and bit by bit to open its ranks and allow armed proletarians to enter the National Guard, albeit after the most tenacious resistance and after setting up a hundred different obstacles. There consequently remained but one way out: to set one part of the proletariat against the other.

For this purpose the Provisional Government formed 24 battalions of Mobile Guards, each of a thousand men, out of young men from 15 to 20 years. They belonged for the most part to the *lumpenproletariat*, which, in all big towns form a mass strictly differentiated from the industrial proletariat, a recruiting ground for thieves and criminals of all kinds, living on the crumbs of society, people without a definite trade, vagabonds, *gens sans feu et sans aveu*, with differences according to the degree of civilization of the nation to which they belong, but never renouncing their *lazzaroni* character; at the youthful age at which the Provisional Government recruited them, thoroughly malleable, capable of the most heroic deeds and the most exalted sacrifices, as of the basest banditry and the dirtiest corruption. The Provisional Government paid them 1 franc 50 centimes a day, *i.e.*, it bought them. It gave them their own uniform, *i.e.*, it made them outwardly distinct from the blouse of the workers. They had assigned to them as leaders, partly officers from the standing army; partly they themselves elected young sons of the bourgeoisie whose rhodomontades about death for the fatherland and devotion to the republic captivated them.

And so the Paris proletariat was confronted with an army, drawn from its own midst, of 24,000 young, strong and foolhardy men. It gave cheers for the Mobile Guard on its marches through Paris. It recognized in it its champions of the barricades. It regarded it as the proletarian guard in opposition to the bourgeois National Guard. Its error was pardonable.

Besides the Mobile Guard, the Government decided to gather round itself an industrial army of workers. A hundred thousand workers thrown on the streets through the crisis and the revolution were enrolled by the Minister Marie in so-called National *Ateliers*. Under this grand name was hidden nothing but the employment of the workers on tedious, monotonous, unproductive earthworks at a wage of 23 sous. English *workhouses* in the open — that is what these National *Ateliers* were. The Provisional Government believed that it had formed in them a second proletarian army against the workers themselves. This time the bourgeoisie was mistaken in the National *Ateliers*, just as the workers were mistaken in the Mobile Guard. It had created an army for mutiny.

But one purpose was achieved.

National *Ateliers* — that was the name of the people's workshops, which Louis Blanc preached in the Luxembourg. The *Ateliers* of Marie, devised in direct antagonism to the Luxembourg, thanks to the common name, offered occasion for a plot of errors worthy of the Spanish comedy of servants. The Provisional Government itself secretly spread the report that these National *Ateliers* were the discovery of Louis Blanc, and this seemed the more plausible because Louis Blanc, the prophet of the National *Ateliers*, was a member of the Provisional Government. And in the half naïve, half intentional confusion of the Paris bourgeoisie, in the artificially maintained opinion of France and of Europe, these workhouses were the first realization of socialism, which was put in the pillory with them.

In their title, though not in their content, the National *Ateliers* were the embodied protest of the proletariat against bourgeois industry, bourgeois credit and the bourgeois republic. The whole hate of the bourgeoisie was therefore turned upon them. At the same time, it had found in them the point against which it could direct the attack, as soon as it was strong enough to break openly with the February illusions. All the discontent, all the ill humor of the petty bourgeois was simultaneously directed against these National *Ateliers*, the common target. With real fury they reckoned up the sums that the proletarian loafers swallowed, while their own situation became daily more unbearable. A state pension for sham labor, that is socialism! they growled to themselves. They sought the basis of their misery in the National *Ateliers*, the declarations of the Luxembourg, the marches of the workers through Paris. And no one was more fantastic about the alleged machinations of the Communists than the petty bourgeoisie who hovered hopelessly on the brink of bankruptcy.

Thus in the approaching *mêlée* between bourgeoisie and proletariat, all the advantages, all the decisive posts, all the middle sections of society were in the hands of the bourgeoisie, at the same time as the waves of the February Revolution rose high over the whole Continent, and each new post brought a new bulletin of revolution, now from Italy, now from Germany, now from the remotest parts of South-Eastern Europe, and maintained the general exuberance of the people, giving it constant testimony of a victory that it had already lost.

March 17 and April 16 were the days on which occurred the first skirmishes in the big class struggle which the bourgeois republic hid under its wings.

March 17 revealed the ambiguous situation of the proletariat, which permitted no decisive act. Its demonstration originally had the purpose of pushing the Provisional Government back onto the path of the revolution, of effecting the exclusion of its bourgeois members according to circumstances, and of compelling the postponement of the election days for the National Assembly and the National Guard. But on March 16 the bourgeoisie represented in the National Guard made a hostile demonstration against the Provisional Government. With the cry: *à bas Ledru-Rollin!* it surged to the Hôtel de Ville. And the people was forced, on March 17, to shout: Long live Ledru-Rollin! Long live the Provisional Government! It was forced to take sides against the bourgeoisie with the party of the bourgeois republic, which seemed to it to be in danger. It strengthened the Provisional Government, instead of subordinating it to itself. March 17 went off in a melodramatic scene, and if the Paris proletariat on this day once more displayed its giant body, the bourgeoisie both inside and outside and the Provisional Government were all the more determined to break it.

April 16 was a misunderstanding organized by the Provisional Government and the bourgeoisie. The workers had gathered in great numbers in the Field of Mars and in the Hippodrome, in order to prepare their selections for the general staff of the National Guard. Suddenly throughout Paris, from one end to the other, a rumor spread as quick as lightning, to the effect that the workers had met, armed, in the Field of Mars, under the leadership of Louis Blanc, Blanqui, Cabet and Raspail, in order to march thence on the Hôtel de Ville, overthrow the Provisional Government and proclaim a Communist government. The general alarm is sounded — Ledru-Rollin, Marrast and Lamartine later contended for the honor of having initiated this — in an hour 100,000 men are under arms; the Hôtel de Ville is occupied at all points by the National Guard; the cry: Down with the Communists! Down with Louis Blanc, with Blanqui, with Raspail, with Cabet! thunders throughout Paris, and innumerable deputations pay homage to the Provisional Government, all ready to save the fatherland and society. When the workers finally appeared before the Hôtel de Ville, in order to hand over to the Provisional Government a patriotic collection which they had made in the Field of Mars, they learn to their amazement that bourgeois Paris had defeated their shadow in a very carefully calculated sham fight. The terrible attempt of April 16 furnished the excuse for recalling the army to Paris — the actual purpose of the clumsily constructed comedy — and for the reactionary federalist demonstrations in the provinces.

On May 4 the National Assembly met, the result of the direct general elections. Universal suffrage did not possess the magic power which republicans of the old school had ascribed to it. They saw in the whole of France, at least in the majority of Frenchmen, *citoyens* with the same interests, the same understanding, etc. This was their cult of the people. Instead of their imaginary people, the elections brought the real people to the light of day, *i.e.*, representatives of the different classes into which it falls. We have seen why peasants and petty bourgeois had to vote under the leadership of a bourgeoisie spoiling for fight and big landowners frantic for restoration. But if universal suffrage was not the miraculous magic wand for which the republican duffers had taken it, it possessed the incomparably higher merit of unchaining the class struggle, of letting the various middle sections of petty-bourgeois society rapidly live through their illusions and disappointments, of tossing all the fractions of the exploiting class at one throw to the head of the state, and thus tearing from them their treacherous mask, whereas the monarchy with its property qualification only let definite fractions of the bourgeoisie compromise themselves, and let the others lie hidden behind the scenes and surrounded them with the halo of a common opposition.

In the Constituent National Assembly, which met on May 4, the Bourgeois republicans, the republicans of the *National* had the upper hand. Legitimists and even Orleanists at first only dared to show themselves under the mask of bourgeois republicanism. Only in the name of the republic could the fight against the proletariat be undertaken.

The republic dates from May 4, not from February 25, *i.e.*, the republic recognized by the French people; it is not the republic which the Paris proletariat thrust upon the Provisional Government, not the republic with social institutions, not the dream picture which hovered before the fighters on the barricades. The republic proclaimed by the National Assembly, the sole legitimate republic, is the republic which is no revolutionary weapon against the bourgeois order, but rather its political reconstitution, the political reconsolidation of bourgeois society, in a word, the bourgeois republic. From the tribune of the National Assembly this contention resounded and in the entire republican and anti-republican bourgeois press it found its echo.

And we have seen how the February republic in reality was not and could not be other than a bourgeois republic; how the Provisional Government, nevertheless, was forced by the immediate pressure of the proletariat to announce it as a republic with social institutions, how the Paris proletariat was still incapable of going beyond the bourgeois republic otherwise than in ideas, in imagination; how it everywhere acted in its service when it really came to action; how the promises made to it became an unbearable danger for the new republic; how the whole life process of the Provisional Government was comprised in a continuous fight against the demands of the proletariat.

In the National Assembly all France sat in judgment on the Paris proletariat. It broke immediately with the social illusions of the February Revolution; it roundly proclaimed the bourgeois republic, nothing but the bourgeois republic. It at once excluded the representatives of the proletariat, Louis Blanc and Albert, from the Executive Commission appointed by it; it threw out the proposal of a special Labor Ministry, and received with stormy applause the statement of the Minister Trélat: "The question is merely one of bringing labor back to its old conditions."

But all this was not enough. The February republic was won by the workers with the passive support of the bourgeoisie. The proletarians regarded themselves, and rightly, as the victors of February, and they made the proud claims of victors. They had to be vanquished on the streets, they had to be shown that they were worsted as soon as they fought, not with the bourgeoisie, but against the bourgeoisie. Just as the February republic, with its socialist concessions, required a battle of the proletariat, united with the bourgeoisie, against monarchy, so a second battle was necessary in order to sever the republic from the socialist concessions, in order to officially work out the bourgeois republic as dominant. The bourgeoisie had to refute the demands of the proletariat with arms in its hands. And the real birthplace of the bourgeois republic is not the February victory; it is the June defeat.

The proletariat hastened the decision when, on the 15th of May, it pushed into the National Assembly, sought in vain to recapture its revolutionary influence and only delivered its energetic leaders to the jailers of the bourgeoisie. *Il faut en finir!* This situation must end! With this cry the National assembly gave vent to its determination to force the proletariat into a decisive struggle. The Executive Commission issued a series of provocative decrees, such as that prohibiting congregation of the people, etc. From the tribune of the Constituent National Assembly, the workers were directly provoked, insulted and derided. But the real point of the attack was, as we have seen, the National *Ateliers*. The Constituent National Assembly imperiously pointed these out to the Executive Commission, which only waited to hear its own plan put forward as the command of the National Assembly.

The Executive Commission began by making entry into the National *Ateliers* more difficult, by turning the day wage into a piece wage, by banishing workers not born in Paris to Sologne, ostensibly for the construction of earthworks. These earthworks were only a rhetorical formula with which to gloss over their expulsion, as the workers, returning disillusioned, announced to their comrades. Finally, on June 21, a decree appeared in the *Moniteur*, which ordered the forcible expulsion of all unmarried workers from the National *Ateliers*, or their enrollment in the army.

The workers were left no choice: they had to starve or start to fight. They answered on June 22 with the tremendous insurrection in which the first great battle was joined between the two classes that split modern society. It was a fight for the preservation or annihilation of the bourgeois order. The veil that shrouded the republic was torn to pieces.

It is well known how the workers, with unexampled bravery and talent, without chiefs, without a common plan, without means and, for the most part, lacking weapons, held in check for five days the army, the Mobile Guard, the Parisian National Guard, and the National Guard that streamed in from the provinces. It is well known how the bourgeoisie compensated itself for the mortal anguish it underwent by unheard of brutality and massacred over 3,000 prisoners.

The official representatives of French democracy were steeped in republican ideology to such an extent that it was only some weeks later that they began to have an inkling of the meaning of the June fight. They were stupefied by the gunpowder smoke in which their fantastic republic dissolved.

The immediate impression which the news of the June defeat made on us, the reader will allow us to describe in the words of the *N. Rh. Z.*:

> The last official remnant of the February Revolution, the Executive Commission, has melted away, like an apparition, before the seriousness of events. The fireworks of Lamartine have turned into the war rockets of Cavaignac. Fraternité, the fraternity of antagonistic classes of which one exploits the other, this fraternité, proclaimed in February, written in capital letters on the brow of Paris, on every prison, on every barracks—its true, unadulterated, its prosaic expression is civil war, civil war in its most fearful form, the war of labor and capital. This fraternity flamed in front of all the windows of Paris on the evening of June 25, when the Paris of the bourgeoisie was illuminated, whilst the Paris of the proletariat burnt, bled, moaned. Fraternity endured just as long as the interests of the bourgeoisie were in fraternity with the interests of the proletariat.—Pedants of the old revolutionary traditions of 1793; socialist doctrinaires who begged at the doors of the bourgeoisie on behalf of the people and were allowed to preach long sermons and to compromise

themselves as long as the proletarian lion had to be lulled to sleep; republicans who demanded the old bourgeois order in its entirety, with the exception of the crowned head; adherents of the dynasty among the opposition upon whom fortune foisted the overthrow of the dynasty instead of a change of Ministers; Legitimists who wanted, not to throw away the livery, but to change its cut, these were the allies with whom the people made its February.—The February Revolution was the beautiful revolution, the revolution of universal sympathy, because the antagonisms, which had flared up in it against the monarchy, slumbered peacefully side by side, still undeveloped, because the social struggle which formed its background had won only a joyous existence, an existence of phrases, of words. The June revolution is the ugly revolution, the repulsive revolution, because things have taken the place of phrases, because the republic uncovered the head of the monster itself, by striking off the crown that shielded and concealed it.—Order! was the battle cry of Guizot. Order! cried Sebastiani, the follower of Guizot, when Warsaw became Russian. Order! shouts Cavaignac, the brutal echo of the French National Assembly and of the republican bourgeoisie. Order! thundered his grape-shot, as it ripped up the body of the proletariat. None of the numeruous revolutions of the French bourgeoisie since 1789 was an attack on order; for they allowed the rule of the class, they allowed the slavery of the workers, they allowed the bourgeois order to endure, however often the political form of this rule and of this slavery changed. June has attacked this order. Woe to June! (N. Rh. Z., June 29, 1848.)

Woe to June! re-echoes Europe.

The Paris proletariat was forced into the June insurrection by the bourgeoisie. In this lay its doom. Neither its immediate, admitted needs drove it to want to win the forcible overthrow of the bourgeoisie, nor was it equal to this task. The *Moniteur* had to inform it officially that the time was past when the republic saw any occasion to do honor to its illusions, and its defeat first convinced it of the truth that the slightest improvement in its position remains an utopia within the bourgeois republic, an utopia that becomes a crime as soon as it wants to realize it. In place of its demands, exuberant in form, but petty and even still bourgeois in content, the concession of which it wanted to wring from the February republic, there appeared the bold slogan of revolutionary struggle: Overthrow of the bourgeoisie! Dictatorship of the working class!

By making its burial place the birthplace of the bourgeois republic the proletariat compelled the latter to come out forth-with in its pure form as the state whose admitted object is to perpetuate the rule of capital, the slavery of labor. With constant regard to the scarred, irreconcilable, unconquerable enemy — unconquerable because its existence is the condition of its own life — bourgeois rule, freed from all fetters, was bound to turn immediately into bourgeois terrorism. With the proletariat removed for the time being from the stage and bourgeois dictatorship recognized officially, the middle sections, in the mass, had more and more to side with the proletariat as their position became more unbearable and their antagonism to the bourgeoisie became more acute. Just as earlier in its upsurge, so now they had to find in its defeat the cause of their misery.

If the June insurrection raised the self-reliance of the bourgeoisie all over the Continent, and caused it to league itself openly with the feudal monarchy against the people, what was the first sacrifice to this alliance? The Continental bourgeoisie itself. The June defeat prevented it from consolidating its rule and from bringing the people, half satisfied and half out of humor, to a standstill at the lowest stage of the bourgeois revolution.

Finally, the defeat of June divulged to the despotic powers of Europe the secret that France under all conditions must maintain peace abroad in order to be able to wage civil war at home. Thus the peoples who had begun the fight for their national independence were abandoned to the superior power of Russia, Austria and Prussia, but, at the same time, the fate of these national revolutions was subordinated to the fate of the proletarian revolution, robbed of its apparent independence, its independence of the great social revolution. The Hungarian shall not be free, nor the Pole, nor the Italian, as long as the worker remains a slave!

Finally, with the victory of the Holy Alliance, Europe took on a form that makes every fresh proletarian upheaval in France directly coincide with a world war. The new French revolution is forced to leave its national soil forthwith and conquer the European terrain, on which alone the revolution of the nineteenth century can be carried through.

Only through the defeat of June, therefore, were all the conditions created under which France can seize the initiative of the European revolution. Only after baptism in the blood of the June insurgents did the tricolor become the flag of the European revolution — the red flag.

And we cry: *The revolution is dead! — Long live the revolution!*

My Indian Mutiny Diary

William Howard Russell

Edited by Michael Edwardes

February 12th

The scenes where great crimes have been perpetrated ever possess an interest, which I would not undertake to stigmatize as morbid; and surely among the sites rendered infamous for ever in the eyes of British posterity, Cawnpore will be pre-eminent as the magnitude of the atrocities with which it is connected. But, though pre-eminent among crimes, the massacre of Cawnpore is by no means alone in any of the circumstances which mark turpitude and profundity of guilt. We who suffered from it think that there never was such wickedness in the world, and the incessant efforts of a gang of forgers and utterers of base stories have surrounded it with horrors that have been vainly invented in the hope of adding to the indignation and burning desire for vengeance which the naked facts arouse. Helpless garrisons, surrendering under capitulation, have been massacred ere now; men, women, and children have been ruthlessly butchered by the enemies of their race ere now; risings, such as that of the people of Pontus under Mithridates, of the Irish Roman Catholics against the Protestant settlers in 1641, of the actors in the Sicilian vespers, of the assassins who smote and spared none on the eve of St. Bartholomew, have been over and over again attended by inhuman cruelty, violation, and torture.

In fact, the peculiar aggravation of the Cawnpore massacres was this, that the deed was done by a subject race — by black men who dared to shed the blood of their masters, and that of poor helpless ladies and children. Here we had not only a servile war and a sort of Jacquerie combined, but we had a war of religion, a war of race, and a war of revenge, of hope, of some national promptings to shake off the yoke of a stranger, and to re-establish the full power of native chiefs, and the full sway of native religions. There is a kind of God's revenge against murder in the unsuccessful issue of all enterprises commenced in massacre, and founded on cruelty and bloodshed. Whatever the causes of the mutiny and the revolt, it is clear enough that one of the modes by which the leaders, as if by common instinct, determined to effect their end was, the destruction of every white man, woman or child who fell into their hands — a design which the kindliness of the people, or motives of policy, frustrated on many remarkable occasions. It must be remembered that the punishments of the Hindu are cruel, and whether he be mild or not, he certainly is not, any more than the Mussulman, distinguished for clemency towards his enemies. But philosophize and theorize as we may, Cawnpore will be a name ever heard by English ears with horror long after the present generation has passed away.

After breakfast, Stewart, who is charged to put the end of a telegraph wire into Sir Colin's hand wherever he goes, sets off to the camp, which is at some distance from the hotel, on a sandy elevated plain near the *tête-de-pont* which defends the bridge across the Ganges. The camp consists of the tents of the Head-Quarters' Staff only, and is drawn in stiff precise lines, such as Indian quartermaster-generals delight in. Outside each tent hangs a little black board with the rank and title of the occupier described in white letters, thus: 'Military Secretary,' 'Deputy Adjutant-General, Queen's Troops,' 'Deputy Adjutant-General of the Army,' 'Commissariat Office Head-Quarters,' 'Chief of the Staff,' &c. The Commander-in-Chief's tent, undistinguished by aught

From *My Indian Mutiny Diary: A Diary of the Sepoy Rebellion (1857)* by William Howard Russell.

else except its position, is marked by a Union Jack pitched close to the adjacent mess-tent; and at the end of the street, a little in the rear, is the large tent of the Head-Quarters' Staff mess.

Whilst Stewart went off on his business, and to see his old friends, I made out Sir David Baird, senior aide-de-camp to the Commander-in-Chief, and sent in my card. The flap of the little tent was raised immediately, and I made my bow to Sir Colin. He was 'frank' and cordial. After a few remarks about the Crimea, his Excellency said, 'Now, Mr. Russell, I'll be candid with you. We shall make a compact. You shall know everything that is going on. You shall see all my reports, and get every information that I have myself, on the condition that you do not mention it in camp, or let it be known in any way, except in your letters to England.'

'I accept the condition, sir; and I promise you it shall be faithfully observed.'

'You see,' Sir Colin continued, 'you will be among a set of young fellows here, surrounded, as all of us are, by natives who understand all that is going on better than we think. They talk about what is happening, or what is going to take place; and all that gets to the ears of the enemy. So that our best plans may be frustrated. It is most essential for us to preserve secrecy in war, expecially in a country like this.' I could only assent to Sir Colin's remarks. As we were speaking, in came an officer with a number of despatches. 'See,' said Sir Colin, handing one to me, 'we will begin our compact at once.' (The despatch related to certain movements in the rebel force at Lucknow, and was of no great importance.) My interview was long and interesting — to me at least. Sir Colin seemed better, stronger, and more vigorous, than the last time I saw him, which was on his return to the Crimea.

Ere I left to-day, he gave me some information with regard to his plans, and showed me the necessity imposed on one in his position to act with such caution that success must be the certain concomitant of every step. The delay, at which some people were affecting ill-bestowed wonder, resulted, he said, from two causes: the one was the necessity of completing his arrangements and securing every gun and man that could be had ere he marched against Lucknow; the other, his desire to be assured of the safety of the women and children who were travelling down the main trunk-road from Agra, where they had been in a state of *quasi* siege, and of constant alarm in the fort. They were strongly escorted, but the relief of Lucknow would have met with a heavy counterpoise if any accident had happened to these ladies; and it must be remembered that, as they travel down the road, they have an enemy on their left flank, across the Ganges, that Kalpi is occupied by another enemy on their right, and that numerous bands of rebels, strong enough in numbers to be considered as separate corps, are scouring the country not yet held by our troops. Ere I left, Sir Colin was good enough to invite me to his table; but as he gave me the option of joining the Head-Quarters' Staff-mess, I preferred availing myself of the opportunity thus afforded me of subscribing to the expense of maintenance, at the same time that I felt very sensibly the kindness of his Excellency.

Those who have experienced the difficulty of living on one's private resources at this time in India, well know how great was the accommodation afforded to me in joining the Staff-mess, all the furniture being in the streets instead of in the houses, for it had been all tossed out of windows.

. . . .

Outside Lucknow proper, on the west and near the right bank of the Gumti, is a large palace, with gardens and enclosures, standing in the midst of an open country filled with trees, called the Musabagh. The approach to it lies through a dense suburb on one side, but a road and raised causeway, comparatively free, passes from the Hosseinabad to very spacious walled gardens, and the handsome summer residence of Ali Nucky Khan, late Prime Minister of

Oudh, now prisoner at Calcutta — beyond which is another way to the Musabagh. In the latter place the rebels were stationed to the number of 7,000 or 8,000, with guns, treasure, and ammunition, camels, elephants, and baggage. They were held together by Begum Huzrat Mahul and her son, Birjeis Kuddr, the *soi-distant* King of Lucknow, by Mummoo Khan, and by all the desperate rebels of the country. A considerable proportion of this force was cavalry. Nothing can show the odd nature of these people better than their attitude here; they can have no hope of taking the city, and yet they hang on in untenable positions in the presence of their enemy, as if they were quite satisfied they had nothing to fear from us.

It was resolved to attack, and, if possible, punish severely, those rebels. Sir Colin possibly fancied he might be fortunate enough to catch the Begum, the Moulvie, or some other great leader. Willie Campbell, of the Bays, brigadier of Cavalry, was sent round with one body of horse and some guns to cut off their retreat on the south of the Musabagh. Hope Grant, with a strong force of horse and artillery, moved along the left bank of the Gumti, so as to dispose of any rebels who might cross it and try to get away at the north side; the Gurkhas advancing into the city from the Charbagh line of road, toward the rear of the Hosseinabad. Thus there seemed fair grounds for believing that when Outram's corps attacked the rebels directly on the front, they would be certain to tumble, in their retreat, across some of the troops on their flanks. *Dis aliter visum est.*

March 19th

This morning Captain Oliver Jones — an enthusiastic naval officer, who has been fighting against the rebels for the last three or four months, wherever and whenever he had a chance, and who was foremost in the attack at Meeangunj — Stewart, and myself, set out for the Musabagh, which was to be attacked by the Chief and Outram with the dispositions I have mentioned above; but the advance had been rapid, and when we got up to the house of Ali Nucky Khan, the late Prime Minister, which stands outside the town, on the banks of the Gumti, before one comes to the Musabagh, we heard the latter had been evacuated and that the fighting was over: rode on, however, and found Napier in some distress, as the heavy guns were stuck in a narrow lane where there was not a soul to support them, and the sepoys, it appeared, had got in between us and the troops in possession of the Musabagh, some two miles away, so that it was not safe to go along the road. As we were speaking, a rascal started up in the narrow lane close at hand, and fired at us; but his bullet went far wide of the mark, though we were obliged to submit to the indignity of being potted at. It is not too much to say, that fifty determined sepoys, and a few horsemen, could have, at this moment, taken the heavy battery. Soon afterwards a young officer galloped up in some excitement. He had been sent to take prize charge of the Musabagh; but as he rode along, sepoys started up from the fields of corn and took steady shots at him in the coolest way, so that his escort turned tail, and he eventually very properly followed their example. After a time, a battalion of infantry came up to guard the guns, and as the day was so hot as to put any further excursion amid the list of tortures, I returned with my companions to camp after a canter up to the park of the Musabagh. Late this evening I heard the cavalry had made a complete blunder, and that the enemy had got away almost untouched, although we lost one or two good officers in an abortive charge. Pat. Stewart, who is really scarce able to sit on his horse, and is only kept in his saddle by sheer pluck and determination, is going to leave us at last, and now that the place has fairly fallen, he starts for England.

March 20th

The Commander-in-Chief tells me we shall have to wait here till he has placed Lucknow in a proper state of defence. There are copies of a Proclamation by Lord Canning to the people of Oudh which has caused much real alarm in the camp. Major Bouverie, aide to the Governor-General, has arrived on a mission, which is, I presume, connected with the restoration of the civil power in Lucknow; but if this Proclamation goes forth *pur et simple*, the duties of the Commissioner will become all but impossible of execution. Lord Canning confiscates the land of Oudh with the exception of the states of some seven or eight small chiefs. In cases of instant surrender he offers favourable consideration, life and honour to the rebel zemindars. This is what Turks and Englishman call 'bosh.' These words have no meaning in the ears of natives, and convey no idea to their minds; but at best they are *telum imbelle*, for we cannot really enforce them. Time must elapse ere Oudh be ours. It turns out unhappily that the fall of Lucknow has by no means secured the submission of Oudh as Lord Canning must have supposed it would when he hurled his bull from Allahabad. Stewart left for England this evening — *quod felix faustumque sit*.

Sunday, March 21st

Napier is engaged in drawing up a report on the alterations and defences of Lucknow, of a *grandiose* and very elevated character. It is imperial in conception; but where is the money to come from? We had, for a wonder, divine service in the Mess-tent to-day, at which there was a limited attendance. Sir Colin Campbell is of the Scotch Church; but he might have listened without harm to an eloquent but illogical sermon from the Rev. Mr. McKay, wherein that excellent divine sought to prove that England would not share the fate common to all the great empires of the world hitherto, because she was Christian and carried the ark of the covenant, whereas they had been heathen — *non constat domine*! Our tent was surrounded with Hindus and Mohammedans. They were our subjects, and part of our State. The Christianity of a Roman Emperor could not save his empire; and as 'Sarmatia fell unwept without a crime,' so might we fall unwept with many crimes, of which our people know nothing, in spite of our being Christian, with a Protestant constitution and an Empire of all religions in the world. I believe that we permit things to be done in India which we would not permit to be done in Europe, or could not hope to effect without public reprobation; and that our Christian character in Europe, our Christian zeal in Exeter Hall, will not atone for usurpation and annexation in Hindustan, or for violence and fraud in the Upper Provinces of India.

Monday, March 22nd

To-day I procured a copy of Lord Canning's Proclamation, which I sent to London, where no doubt it will excite as much disapprobation as it does here. I have not heard one voice raised in its defence; and even those who are habitually silent, now open their mouths to condemn the policy which must perpetuate the rebellion in Oudh. In fact, unless there be some modification of the general terms of the Proclamation, it will be but *irritamenta malorum* to issue it.

Having written till I was in a state of liquefaction, I rode over with Major Bruce to see the begums and their attendants, who are prisoners, or at least are guarded in the Martinière. Sir Colin gave me leave to do so; but he has been chary of granting permission to visit those ladies. We found them all in one large, low, dark and dirty room, without windows, on the ground floor, and Bruce's entrance was the signal for a shrill uplifting of voices, and passionate exclamations from the ladies, who were crouched down all round the walls. The begum, a shrivelled, wicked-looking old woman, led the chorus, complained of food, of loss of raiment, and of liberty, demanded money and life-allowances, and attendants, and many other things, receiving, at each request, the support of her followers in a sharp antistrophe. One of our difficulties was this — a fair, bright-eyed maid, who sat in the corner playing with the bangles around a very pretty instep, desired to go away into the town. We professed to detain the begums merely for their own safety, and of course we could not recognize the institution of slavery. The young lady, whom we declared we did not want to keep, was a slave, and it was our business to set her free; but, on the other hand, we knew she would not improve her condition by her liberty, and the begum to whom she belonged argued that we had no right to deprive her or let her be deprived of her property.

Thus we learn how very shallow is the influence of our government in India. It does not penetrate the institutions of the people. A domestic slavery is common which is not affected by our laws. At every step some little incident like this comes to light, which convinces me that in many parts of India our government is purely political, and that it is not social or deep searching.

I left the begums without reluctance, and as the heat was too great to permit me to write, I rode over to Banks' bungalow, where General Outram was busy sending out the Proclamation of the Governor-General with a rider of his own, which seemed to mean 'don't mind the Governor-General; his bark is worse than his bite; come in at once to me, and I'll make it all right for you and your lands.'

March 26th

Writing for the English Post. General Outram is going to Calcutta at his own request as soon as possible, inasmuch as he does not feel himself able to carry out the Governor-General's policy. Although the General will be well placed at the council-table, I regret that he does not remain in Oudh, where his name is well-known, and where he has many personal acquaintances among the great chiefs; but if he has not the support and confidence of the Governor-General in the discharge of his high duties, it is out of the question to expect a man like General Outram to retain a post in which he is called upon to carry out a policy of which he disapproves. It is strange that in the course of a few years the man who, as resident at Lucknow, recommended the annexation of the kingdom, should now, as commissioner of the revolted British province, feel himself obliged to force on the consideration of the supreme Government the claims of the rebels to more liberal treatment than Lord Canning is disposed to offer them. His Excellency has, indeed, made some concessions, but his general policy, as regards Oudh, is looked upon by all men here, political and military, as too harsh and despotic. In the abstract, and as a question of principle, I think Lord Canning may be right, with this single exception — he assumes that the fall of Lucknow has been followed by the submission of Oudh, and that he is in a position to confiscate all the lands of the province; but the fact is, that we are very far from such a consummation. So far the threat is mere *brutum fulmen*. Though it may be the bolt will fall some time or other, we cannot hurl it now. Mr. Montgomery is on his way to relieve General Outram.

March 27th

Rode out before breakfast, and visited Sir William Peel, whom I found in the same room with Gloster of the 38th Regt., who was shot right through the abdomen, and is nevertheless progressing fast towards convalescence. Peel looked thin and feverish, but he says he is much better, and is only waiting till he is strong enough to get down to Cawnpore on his way home. He is as much opposed to the Proclamation as any one I have spoken to. Dined at General Outram's mess. In the evening Mr. George Campbell, financial commissioner for Oudh, arrived, preceding Mr. Montgomery, who is expected in a few days. General Outram and he did not at all agree in the policy which should be adopted towards the rebellious native chiefs and others. The former is for a large and generous and general amnesty, except in the cases of actual murderers; the latter is for the most vigorous prosecution and punishment.

March 28th — Palm Sunday

The heat quite overpowering. Hope Grant is going out with a force to sweep away sundry collections of sepoys in the east of Oudh, notably one headed by the Begum at a fort on the Gogra called Bitowlee.

March 29th

Rode over to Banks' bungalow, and saw part of the column which is going under Lugard to clear the Azimghur district of the band under Koer Sing, on their way out. They have fifteen marches to make ere they reach the scene of their operations. Sir James Outram has received permission from Lord Canning to offer more liberal terms than are contained in the Proclamation to any of the great zemindars who show a disposition to surrender. From the bungalow rode with Morland through part of the city, and visited Duff, 23rd, and others in their quarters, near the Hosseinabad. The worst portion of the inhabitants have evidently returned to the city.

March 30th

Remained in my tent all day writing, with the perspiration streaming from every pore; had a ride of half an hour; to dinner and to bed.

The Mutinies and the People

A Hindu (Samhu Chandra Mookerjee)

&c.,   &c.,   &c.,

May It Please Your Lordship,

I the undersigned Rajah of Wunurputty, beg most respectfully to approach your Lordship with this humble address, earnestly hoping that it may meet with your favorable consideration.

With the deepest anxiety and horror have I heard and read of the barbarous and atrocious deeds of the mutineers of the Bengal Presidency; and their cold blooded and deliberate proceedings are of such a nature as to stamp them with infamy and brutality unknown in the histories of the most savage and uncivilized nations. Hence my sympathies towards the British have been roused, and my wrath against the rebels has been kindled; so that if the offer herein made is accepted, I am resolved to revenge the atrocities committed on the subjects of the Crown of England with an unsparing hand.

I beg to assure your Lordship in Council of my loyalty, affection and attachment to the British Government, to whose kind and paternal protection I owe my life, my liberty, my safety and my all, and it would be disloyal in me not to tender my services at this painful crisis to aid in quelling the disturbances and in destroying and dispelling the mutineers. On a former occasion I proposed to go to the Crimea with a force to join the allied armies against the Russians, but the proposal was declined by Lord Dalhousie, on the score that the force was ample, and that my services were then not required. Permit me to refer your Lordship in Council to the Governor General's letter No. 122, dated Ootacamund, 21st April, 1856.

With all due submission I take the liberty to intimate to your Lordship in Council, that I am resolved and prepared to start and join the English Army before Delhi, where the mutiny is concentrated, and to bring with me two complete Regiments of Infantry, one of Cavalry, and one Company of Artillery, which shall form a brigade under my command. I am well aware that my presence will unquestionably inspire the men with valour and confidence not easily to be shaken or intimidated. The body I intend raising, shall consist chiefly of Hindoos of my country, Seiks, Beloochees, &c. If your Lordship in Council should be pleased to acquiesce in the proposal now offered, I beg that the necessary instructions may be forthwith issued to the British Authorities, to afford me all the facilities I need towards the achievement of my design, and that preparations be made for the embarkation of my troops with the least practicable delay.

It may not be irrelevant here to inform your Lordship, that the country of Wunurputty and its dependencies in the Hyderabad, Deccan, were held by ancestral and hereditary right and succession for nearly six centuries and that since the treaty between His Highness the Nizam's Government and that of the British, the country has been more firmly established and greater security has been extended to life, property and freedom throughout my country. It is source of unbounded joy and gratification to learn that the friendship, alliance and

From *The Mutinies and the People or Statements of Native Fidelity*, 1859 by A Hindu (Samhu Chandra Mookerjee).

good feeling existing between the English and H. H. the Nizam have been unshaken and undisturbed, and the series of years that has revolved, tends incontestably to prove that the object of the treaty has been realized, matured and confirmed. H. H. the present Nizam, H. E. Salar Jung Bahadur, the Dewan than whom the State has never had a more equitable and able Minister, and all the leading noblemen of Hyderabad Deccan, are well affected towards the British Rule in India, and are deeply interested in their welfare, success and prosperity. They view with disgust and abhorrence the conduct and proceedings of the rebels, and can in no manner justify them from whatever cause they may have originated. I can speak from experience, that when required, the Hyderabad Deccan, is ready to put forth its colossal power in action against the insurgents and to crush the very name of mutiny.

In concluding this address I beg to assure your Lordship in Council, that we Hindoos and all the British Subjects in the Hyderabad Deccan, are deeply indebted to Colonel Davidson, British Resident, for the security of our lives, property and persons, owing solely and chiefly to his unwearied exertions and to the timely and suitable preparations he has made to meet any outbreak or rising, and we repose the utmost confidence in his judgment and prudence, and in all the plans and measures he has been pleased to adopt at this dreadful and critical juncture.

With sentiments of respectful submission, &c., &c.

Englishman, 20th November, 1857.

No. 4282

From

G. F. EDMONSTONE, Esquire,
Secretary to the Government of India,

To

His Highness W. RAMASWAR BULVENT BHYREE
BAHADUR,

Rajah of Wunurputty,
Dated Fort William, 21st October, 1857.

Sir,

I have received and laid before the Right Honorable the Governor General in Council, your letter to the address of His Lordship, dated the 12th ultimo, praying to be allowed to render the British Government some Military aid in quelling the present insurrection in its dominions.

2. In reply I am directed to acquaint you that, His Lordship in Council feels assured that your Highness's troops would, if called into the field, do excellent service. But the retaking of Delhi, and the arrangements that have been made for punishing the mutineers in all directions, renders it unnecessary for the Government to accept the aid of your troops. The Governor General in Council desires me, however, to express to you the thanks of the Government for your offers, and its approbation of your feelings of loyalty, and attachment to it.

I have the honor to be,

Sir,

Your most obedient Servant,

(Sd.)   G. F. EDMONSTONE,

Secretary to the Government of India.

Englishman, 15th Dec., 1857.

In reading the above correspondence we feel a thrill of pleasure matched only by the importance of the subject. Here is a Native Prince, with an ancestry of six centuries antiquity, and master of a principality in the heart of Central India Proper, volunteering his services with an earnestness, the very expression of which was a source of comfort, not to say strength, to the British Government when many other Native Potentates were in a doubtful neutrality. We scarcely remember having read an Oriental composition breathing such enlightened feelings and sentiments as the volunteering letter of the Rajah Wunurputty. Government must have had good reasons for declining the offer. One of the reasons which Mr. Secretary Edmonstone assigns, is the circumstance of the recapture of Delhi, but the important reason which influenced the mind of the Governor General was perhaps the rumour of an uneasy feeling about the tranquility of Hydrabad. Be it what it may, the good and earnest feeling of the Rajah was decidedly a great thing. We believe that similar letters have also been addressed to Government by other princes with the same object. We may say that imperial Rome was not more lamented and sympathized with by her dependant princes at the hour of her decline and fall than has Great Britain been during the sepoy revolution. If the termination of this struggle had been different from what it is, we think the British nation would have had this pride that their fate like that of the glorious Romans was universally lamented by Asiatic princes and people alike.

The following is a brief account of the services rendered by the Rajah of Benares:—

"And it seems as unnecessary for me to give proofs of the Rajah's undoubted loyalty, for which he received a letter of thanks from the Governor General. What few troops and armed men he has, have all along from the beginning of the disturbances, been at the service of the authorities; numbers of whom have been, and I believe still are employed at the Kotwallee, the thannahs and other places. He has done his best to prevent the mutineers from passing through his districts. His elephants, camels, horses, boats &c., have been at the entire disposal of Government, he has given supplies, — his two large houses, called the New Mint, have been occupied since May by British troops and others, for which he neither has received nor intends to receive any remuneration. And he has lately lent another large house, rent-free for Government purposes, formerly occupied by the late Major Stewart, Agent to the Governor General.

Mafeking Diary: A Black Man's View of a White Man's War

Sol T. Plaatje

Edited by John Comaroff with Brian Willan and Andrew Reed

October—November 1899

Sunday, 29th

Divine Services. No thunder. Haikonna terror; and I have therefore got ample opportunity to sit down and think before I jot down anything about my experiences of the past week. I have discovered nearly everything about war and find that artillery in war is of no use. The Boers seem to have started hostilities, the whole of their reliance leaning on the strength and number of their cannons — and they are now surely discovering their mistake. I do not think that they will have more pluck to do anything better than what they did on Wednesday and we can therefore expect that they will either go away or settle round us until the troops arrive.

To give a short account of what I found war to be, I can say: no music is as thrilling and as immensely captivating as to listen to the firing of the guns on your own side. It is like enjoying supernatural melodies in a paradise to hear one or two shots fired off the armoured train; but no words can suitably depict the fascination of the music produced by the action of a Maxim, which to Boer ears, I am sure, is an exasperation which not only disturbs the ear but also disorganizes the free circulation of the listener's blood. At the city of Kanya they have been entertained (I learn from one just arrived) with the melodious tones of big guns, sounding the 'Grand Jeu' of war, like a gentle subterranean instrument, some thirty fathoms beneath their feet and not as remote as Mafeking; they have listened to it, I am told, with cheerful hearts, for they just mistook it for what it is not. Undoubtedly the enrapturing charm of this delectable music will give place to a most irritating discord when they have discovered that, so far from it being the action of the modern Britisher's workmanship going for the Dutch, it is the 'boom' of the state artillerist giving us thunder and lightning with his guns.

I was roaming along the river at 12 o'clock with David yesterday when we were disgusted by the incessant sounds and clappering of Mausers to the north of the town: and all of a sudden four or five 'booms' from the armoured train quenched their metal. It was like a member of the Payne family silencing a boisterous crowd with the prelude of a selection she is going to give on the violin. When their beastly fire 'shut up' the Maxim began to play: it was like listening to the Kimberley R.C. choir with their organ, rendering one of their mellifluous carols on Christmas Eve; and its charm could justly be compared with that of the Jubilee Singers performing one of their many quaint and classical oratories. But like everything desirable it ceased almost immediately. The Maxim is everybody's favourite here. Whenever there is an almost sickening rattle of Mausers you can hear them enquiring amongst themselves when 'makasono' is going to 'kgalema'. Boers are fond of shooting. They do not wait until they see anything but let go at the rate of 100 rounds per minute at the least provocation. I am afraid if they could somehow or other lay their hands on a Maxim they would simply shake it until there is not a single round left to mourn the loss of the others. One can almost fancy that prior to their leaving the State their weapons were imprecated by empyrean authority — and the following are my reasons for believing that the State ammunition has been cursed: when I passed the gaol yesterday afternoon Phil told me that while some prisoners were working in front of the gaol one of them was hit by a Mauser bullet (from the Boer lines) on the ribs. They expected the man to drop down dead, but the bullet dropped down (dead) instead. Immediately after, another hit a European's thigh. It penetrated the clothes but failed to pierce his skin; and just as if to verify this statement, another came round and struck the shoulder of a white man, who was shocked but stood as firm as though nothing had happened, when the bullet dropped down in front of him.

I have already mentioned that on Wednesday (the day of the all-round attack) I was surprised to find that on getting to town not one person was killed — while the Dutch ambulances were busy all the afternoon.

On Friday morning Teacher Samson and 15 others crept along the river until they were very close to a party of Boers, who were busy sniping the location from an ambush. They killed eight of them and wounded several; they were all going to return without a hitch — but they advanced to disarm the dead men, and Samson received a slight wound on the shoulder.

· · · ·

Friday, 8th

We rose in high spirits preparing for a heavy day's shelling. We wonder whether yesterday's rapid outburst was because they received a fresh supply of ammunition or that Phil-june told them that they had just begun to do damage; but they only hit harder. During the day only an occasional Mauser and about six bangs from their thinner artillery kept us cognizant of the fact that we are beleaguered. What a contrast to unfortunate yesterday.

As a rule the 'Native Question' has, I believe, since the abolition of slavery, always been the gravest question of its day. The present siege has not been an exception to this rule for Natives have always figured pre-eminently in its chief correspondence. The following letter is public property and I have decided on reproducing it *in extenso*:

Mafeking, 8th Dec., 1899.

To General Snyman,
near Mafeking.

Sir,—I beg to thank you for having handed over Lady Sarah Wilson in exchange for the convict P. Viljoen.

At the same time, I beg to point out that I have only consented to the exchange under protest, as being contrary to the custom of civilized warfare.

In treating this lady as a prisoner-of-war, as well as in various other acts, you have in the present campaign, altered the usual conditions of war. This is a very serious matter; and I do not know whether it has the sanction of General Joubert or not, but I warn you of the consequences.

The war was at first, and would remain, as far as Her Majesty's troops are concerned, a war between one Government and another; but you are making it one of people against people in which women are considered as belligerents. I warn you that the consequence of this may shortly be very serious to your own people, and you yourself will be to blame for anything that may happen.

Regarding your complaint as to your being attacked by Natives I beg to refer you to my letter dated 14th November, addressed to your predecessor, General Cronje. In this letter I went out of my way, as one white man to another, to warn you that the Natives are becoming extremely incensed at your stealing their cattle, and the wanton burning of their kraals; they argued that the war lay only between our two nations, and that the quarrel had nothing to do with themselves, and they had remained neutral in consequence, excepting in the case of the Mafeking Baralongs, who had to defend their homes in consequence of your unjustifiable invasion. Nevertheless, you thought fit to carry on cattle thefts and raids against them, and, you are now beginning to feel the consequences; and, as I told you, I could not be responsible. And I fear from what I have just heard by wireless telegraph that the Natives are contemplating further operations should your forces continue to remain within or on the borders of their territories. Before the commencement of the war the High Commissioner issued stringent orders to all Natives that they were to remain quiet and not to take up arms unless their territory were invaded (in which case, of course, they had a perfect right to defend themselves).

Linchwe—of whom you complain—remained neutral until you brought a force into his principal town and looted his traders' stores, and were making preparations for shelling his stadt on the 26th ultimo. *Having obtained accurate information of these intentions of yours and, warned by what had happened to the Natives near Mafeking, he attacked your laager on the 24th in order to save his town from being shelled and consequent loss of life amongst his women and children. In this I consider he was quite justified, and you have no one but yourself to blame in the matter.*

While on the subject of Natives please do not suppose that I am ignorant of what you have been doing with regard to seeking the assistance of armed natives, nor of the use of the Natives by you in the destruction of the railway line south of Mafeking. However, having done my duty in briefly giving you warning on these points, I do not propose to further discuss them by letter.

I have the honour to be,

Sir,

Your obedient servant,

R. S. S. BADEN-POWELL,Col.

'Au Sanna' seems to have been blessed now. The only shot she discharged today did considerable damage. It came at 1.25, just when I was returning from town. It cut across my track and went for the B.S.A. camp in a most sickening whizz. It entered the stable and found several men of the Protectorate Regiment attending their horses; killed one and wounded two. The dead man was singing at the time it went for him.

It is marvellous that while we had 'Sanna's' shells at the rate of 50 per diem, besides hundreds from the thinner artillery, we lost no one; but now nearly every one of her shots kills a man and injures several. I am more keen about my impression of yesterday. People have started football, cricket and polo matches in defiance of shells. The Sunday is a day of gymkhana meetings and merriments which serve as strong counter-attractions to Divine Services. These surely must be one of the causes of the deadliness of the Dutch weapons now. I had entered my pony for a run in next Sunday's races — everybody who knows him was very sanguine that he would take the prize, but I had decided to withdraw him today lest I be guilty of blatant sacrilege and thereby further imperil my dangerous condition. Fancy, only one shot being fired during a very quiet day and carrying off three persons by a single stroke.

Saturday, 9th

Too little, if anything, has been said in praise of the part played by that gallant Britisher — the Barolong herdboy. Cattle are now grazing on what may be termed 'disputed' territory, just where the Dutch and English volleys cross each other; and it is touching to see how piccaninnies watch their flocks, and how in the bright sunshine along the wide plain south and west of the stadt — especially when after filling his belly with a lunch of black coffee and beef — the Dutch artillerist would turn his attention to them, and sate his iniquitous whims by sending a shell right in the midst of a group of them. God would guide it flying over their little heads and it would kindle a mortal fire near them: it is an imposing sight to see them each running after a fragment and calmly picking it up. They would quietly mind their stock or drive them home under a severe shell fire with the tenacity of the African in all matters where cattle are concerned. The chappie killed by that shell that struck the hospital last month was turning goats on the rushes at the back of the hospital. The Boers made a small retort within easy range of a Martini south of the stadt. They had intended to snipe the stadt from there, but the stadt folks made it hot for them. Last week a few herds went straight up to it and brought home some tinned beef biltong and two spades.

Two other herds went out last night. They went out as far as Jackal Tree, where they lay down on the grass near the Boer camp, when the enemy were busy outspanning. It was raining at the time and the oxen were tied up to the yokes. They waited until the owners sheltered themselves from the rain, then advanced and successfully loosened four of the oxen without detection. One of the smart thieves led them away by their riems, while his confederate drove their loot behind.

There is a regiment composed of a mixture of Zulu, Shangaan, Tembu and other Transkeian breeds under one McKenzie, styled the Black Watch. These are camped just where the railway passes Bokone. Some of these fellows on sentry duty saw their Barolong brethren advancing with their highly prized but 'nqabile' possession. The party was mad and an eruption, such as nearly started a revolution in the whole place, ensued. Their row was such as could have attracted considerable attention if 'Au Sanna' was not the lawful claimant for our attention. The case was 'sticking up' and the Colonel judged against the Transkeians, as the Barolong could substantiate their claims by the riems they carried in their hands. The Zulu swore that they brought the cattle from the Boer laager. The Colonel gave the Barolong the third ox and as they were abnormally fat animals he bought the others off them.

This cattle theft has put the Boers on the alert. On Thursday I sent out a man to Kimberley for Vere Stent; he and his companion tried to cross along the railway line but they found the country so excellently guarded by the Boers that to get through was an impossibility. They tried to north-west with the same result and they are now planning a scheme for a fresh try tomorrow. The Barolongs had a brush in miniature with the enemy this morning.

About 90 Boers were observed a half-mile to the south of the stadt waiting for our cattle. When the cattle were cleared away from the stadt range the Boers stormed the herds who, finding it impossible to drive the cattle, ran home for arms. Uncle Cornelius happened to be about and he alone managed to keep the Boers until his bandolier was empty. Just then about 40 men came up and drove the Boers off. One of our men got a slight wound and the Boers wounded three cows and a donkey. We only hope we have given them something in return.

Sunday, 10th

The usual holy holiday. No Mausering. We have not received any despatch since last week, when we heard of the relief of Kimberley. The story by our despatch-carrier that the Boer lines are impassable must be correct and this accounts for our not receiving any despatches. Some three of our men have been to the Transvaal to loot cattle. They went out on Friday and slept at a farmhouse occupied only by poultry. They killed half-a-dozen fowls and supped on them. They stayed in a hole all day Saturday and in the evening advanced towards a Boer homestead which they had been espying during the day. One of them went to guard the door of the homestead, with his Martini well cocked, and ready to 'Quma' — directly a Dutchman (or woman) put out his head — while the others went to empty a kraal of 14 heads of cattle that were in it. They took every one of them. They brought us some interesting news. While at the poultry-house they heard some voices in the dark, which they recognized as those of some of our Kalaharis in Rietfontein (now Boer territory). These Kalaharis were from delivering some Dutch letters, at the eastern laager, and expressed regret at not having met our men prior to delivering them as they would have handed them over for our information and let the Boers 'sweat'. These Bakgalagalis reported having heard at the laager that there was heavy fight between Kimberley and some river or other — probably the Vaal — towards the end of last moon (end of November) in which both sides lost heavily. The English lost 'vyf honderd' and the Dutch lost 'tien honderd'. Our friend Mnr Cronje was also there and his commando was scattered in every direction.

The usual gaiety and merriments took place in the afternoon.

There being no danger I took the pony and went out for a ride around 'disputed territory' and saw the Boers so close that I nearly felt inclined to go over and have a chat with them as they were seated on the ridges of their trenches looking at games played so merrily round our camp with longing eyes; this, however, is a serious crime and I cannot bring trouble upon myself in that manner. They undoubtedly wonder of what stuff we are made, to look so little the worse for this long siege. I wonder whether they have forgotten that while Cape Town and many important colonial towns have been seats of Dutch governments and still wear Dutch names, Mafikeng has since its creation never been cursed by being a Boer laager, despite strenuous endeavours to make it such. It still bears the name given it by Tau's band of Barolong, who came from Lake Ngami in about 1750. They were a peaceful lot of men, yet they plundered everybody who dared interfere with their migration, and earned for themselves the title of 'Baga Rungoana le Bogale'.

To return to our subject: these West Transvaalians ought to remember that Mafeking has always held her own against becoming Dutch and the only Boer who has owned Mafeking was the one who swore by the honour of the king. It is a pleasant day; fair and cloudy, with an occasional shower every now and then.

. . . .

Friday, 16th

The stadt has [for] once changed from its usual appearance and assumed a sullen aspect. We have not experienced it yet, but if the long look for the greatest day is unequalled, today was undoubtedly a second study of judgement day. People were almost disinclined to talk to one another, and there was dead silence in the green shrubbery which almost gave one the impression that on other days they were talkative. I spent my day in old Watermann's garden, without food of any sort: it was only [when] she, grand lady, brought me several sweet cones [that I could] break my fast. I felt very stimulated after being invigorated by them and tired of novel reading and shorthand exercises. I still retained a fresh enough memory to picture to myself the figure of a very young mother and a fat little piccaninny disturbing her peace (assisted by the absence of someone) somewhere about the Eastern Province.

Shelling was going on very lively, and fully justified the people's looks in the morning. The big gun only put in a few, but the show was generally kept up by the incendiary 9-pounders which put in about 30 during the day. It fired from Jackal Tree where it was on the morning that it killed poor Mamokoloi. It, however, went for our defence works like it ought to do. It went almost invariably for the forts of McKenzie's Black and the Barolong Watches — within two miles of the stadt. The former is on the railway line and the later one mile west of it.

Only the big gun went promiscuously for the stadt, and one woman at my friend Moathloli's house was only saved [from being decapitated] by a hair's breadth. The shell smashed the wall of the hut, burst inside it then found means of exit through another wall behind which the woman was sitting. One piece burst right opposite her head, but unlike the others it rebounded and fell inside. When the woman bowed her head a lot of earth fell from it and there was a hole in the wall.

The 'bad-night' shot was fired at 8.45. Emang had brought us tea early in the evening. At 8.00 I went home with her. I found Mafikeng sitting near the north-eastern corner of her house against the rising moon. We had not yet chatted to our heart's content when there was heavy rifle firing to the west. We had hardly passed remarks over it when 'tingalingal-ingaling' chimed the tocsins and we dodged like a couple of meercats. There was a heavy suspense when we were waiting for the blow — I think 20 seconds — when bang went a terrible smash. Then the usual row, terminating in a loud explosion that echoed through all the neighbourhood. Nothing would induce Mafie to remain to the open air and I believe she wanted to be dismissed for directly I suggested she should take to the shelter she leapt and bounded towards it with no less alacrity than Malibali or Emang could have mastered. I went round to see what [it] was like inside. The whole family was arraigned in it. There was old Masiako, the two girls and two old dames, and goodness knows too what more. This refuge was luminated with a candle that the old dame had sent Mamoathloli for just one hour previously. I strolled back to our quarters and jotted down these notes, while the evening was kept up by the usual rifle chatter which is forever the case in bright moonlight.

Saturday, 17th

Our troops kept up fire all night. The Maxim was going nobly all the time. By midnight it had become one of the grandest nights, watching our rifle flashes like a lot of fireworks to the south. Our volleys going for the Boers all night were worth listening to. We were press-ing away all night: the bright moonlit night being kept alive by the bombs of the 7-pounders and Nordenfeld, the cracks of rifles, and the tat-tat-tat of the firing. The Boers had worried the souls out of us during the day; and it is particularly consoling to see that they did it at the expense of their rest the next night. Not a single Dutch weapon was to be heard above the occasional Mauser or rifle.

We had a very quiet day. One often wondered if they exhausted themselves yesterday. 'Au Sanna' sent in a few shells to the women's laager.

Sunday, 18th

The usual thing. Runners came in from up north-east and south. They brought no news. It is difficult to describe one's feeling hearing that even now after four months Kimberley has not yet been relieved. The Imperial Government may be as good as we are told it is, but one thing certain is that it does not care a hang over the lives of its distant subjects. It is distressing to hear that troops are still having a holiday at Modder River, even now after we had been besieged over four months. In Kimberley, which is only a stone's-throw from Cape Town, they were still eating horseflesh with 10 000 troops at Modder River, and we may safely conclude that we, as far away as Mafeking, will have no more horseflesh to eat by the time they reach here.

The cattle and green mielie stocks have also been called in. No one is allowed to pick any green mielies for his or her village. They are going to be kept till they are ripe and then rationed out to people.

I am wondering if the heavens, like the Imperial Government, have also shut their ears to our prayers. Surely: 'Eare bo bisa go bitsa motho, go bitse molimo.' But was this so in our case?

I have a very strong appetite just now when food is very scarce. If I do not take a cup of cocoa at 10 p.m. (after suppering in the evening at 7) you may depend upon it I will never be able to sleep. This is an undesirable bad habit, and I almost feel inclined to consult the medico about it.

Monday, 19th

As quiet as last Saturday. 'Sanna' only sent in two shells (7 a.m.) which fell short of the town. The day was uneventful.

Tuesday, 20th

When the pass law was introduced for the time being I expected we would have about 20 convictions every week. We have up to date not had any infringers before the court. In fact when one is found minus the pass the policemen simply tell him to clear out of town.

'Au Sanna' sent in three miserable shots this morning. I believe there is something wrong with her. Only one of them burst and some people mistook the explosion for a Krupp 9-pounder's. One of them went into Moathloli's again but did no damage.

One medico of Mafeking (Dr Smythe) was, at the commencement of the row, appointed to doctor over the inmates of the women's laager. He had the funks and declined the appointment, fearing to leave his bomb-proof any day except Sundays. He has since been living at his house, which was also struck by a 94-pounder last week. I wonder where he intends going.

Wednesday, 21st

A calm and unusually lovely day! Eventually I got up early and went to town, returning at 12, and spent the day in the gardens. Joshua caught a thief in these gardens. He was a heathen, and in a farmer's employ. They nearly beat him to death. I returned to town again at 4.00, and found Weil's crowded with Fingoes and Zambezians, with no consciousness of the fact that the town store had closed its doors last night, and that they could get no more food.

They are only too anxious to avail themselves of the opportunity of going over to Kanya, as offered by the authorities. They were worrying me, and waiting for me to give them passes, when one of them fell in the courtyard of starvation — the poor fellow was taken to the hospital, where he died afterwards.

· · · ·

Wednesday, 14th

'Au Sanna' is still as hot as ever. We have heard this morning about 'relief of Ladysmith' in duplicated despatches from the north. The originals have been caught by the Boers evidently, for bearers state that the runners who preceded them have been caught.

A lot of women are always going out to their fields at Moleloane to gather melons and fresh kaffircorn. They go right across the Boer lines. There are so few Boers in the trenches that they cannot control the multitude of women. If they tell 16 to drop their stuff 'about 60' will bring in theirs from somewhere else. This shows that the Boer trenches are quite empty and 're tshosiwa ka merora fela'. They have all gone north to oppose Plumer. That is why Natives are guarding now.

Thursday, 15th

It rained during last night. We have rain nearly every day. Teacher Kolobe came back. His following of five supported him right through. They attacked a Boer homestead on Tuesday but failed to bag the cattle as the farmers were too numerous for them. They came back via Madibe and saw the dead and wounded horses shot by the balance of his party on Monday.

They killed one Boer in the attempt to capture cattle.

I had a very narrow escape at 4 o'clock this afternoon. My first warning was but the screeching of the shell when it came straight up to me. I was riding 'Pony' round from Lookoane and turning round the curve at Letsi's place. I hardly knew what to do as for six seconds (or thereabouts) I felt that it was coming straight to me. I have never felt so nasty as during that little period of my life, until it burst and the pieces flew overhead. The pony had already turned round and was going backwards with me.

The result was a bloodstirring whine amongst the womenfolk in the house next to me. I myself was so shaken that I scarcely felt anything when I heard that it had smashed old Letsi's head and killed the poor old fellow instantly.

These narrow escapades are not only undesirable because one barely escapes death, but surely because they give one the impression that many of them are in store for one in the little future left for one; and every one of them will be narrower than its predecessor — until he loses a leg, arm, some limb, or even life.

Many people are leaving Mafeking at night now. They experience no difficulty in crossing the outpost and the Boer lines. We are all convinced that the Boers have considerably diminished during the past week or two.

We are very restless about the safety of the two parties of cattle raiders still at large.

I heard something very extraordinary today. The administrators of martial law have authorized the municipality to levy a dog tax as they want to get rid of as many dogs as possible. Some unlicensed dogs were found, destroyed and buried by the town ranger.

Our local Zambesi friends unearthed them, immediately the ranger's assistants left the scene, and promptly cooked them for dinner, which gave the Barolong sections of the community the impression that there is more in a dog than they were ever told there was.

Friday, 16th

It was not so hot as we have had it from 'Sanna' since the beginning of the week.

McKenzie has taken Jackal Tree with his 'Black Watch' of which Titshalakazi's 'Gun' was a member when he got shot. They went to Jackal Tree at the beginning of the week and found no Boers there. He occupied the place but vacated it on account of it being so far away from here, and far away from any water. Last night, however, they went up there and took shelter in the Boer trench. They saw them coming: one Boer and three Natives.

Saturday, 17th

We are feeling the strain a little, not because we are defeated but simply because we have received no despatches this week.

There are some Shangaans and Zambesis — very few of them, as the majority have left this place and gone up country. They are going to be fed on soup, the 'stuff' we hear was used for white ladies in Kimberley. Here it is used by destitute people who cannot provide for themselves. It was not really a case of starvation but planned strategy on the part of the officers.

Two Treaties: from the *Hague Convention* and the *Treaty of Vereeniging*

[Great Britain was a signatory to the Hague Conventions on international rules of war in 1899.]

Section II. On Hostilities

Chapter I. On means of injuring the Enemy, Sieges, and Bombardments

Article 22

The right of belligerents to adopt means of injuring the enemy is not unlimited.

Article 23

Besides the prohibitions provided by special Conventions, it is especially prohibited:

a. To employ poison or poisoned arms;

b. To kill or wound treacherously individuals belonging to the hostile nation or army;

c. To kill or wound an enemy who, having laid down arms, or having no longer means of defence, has surrendered at discretion;

d. To declare that no quarter will be given;

e. To employ arms, projectiles, or material of a nature to cause superfluous injury;

f. To make improper use of a flag of truce, the national flag, or military ensigns and the enemy's uniform, as well as the distinctive badges of the Geneva Convention;

g. To destroy or seize the enemy's property, unless such destruction or seizure be imperatively demanded by the necessities of war.

Article 24

Ruses of war and the employment of methods necessary to obtain information about the enemy and the country, are considered allowable.

Article 25

The attack or bombardment of towns, villages, habitations or buildings which are not defended, is prohibited.

From *The Best of the Worst of Empires: Which?* (London: Review of Reviews Office, 1906) by William T. Stead.

Article 26

The Commander of an attacking force, before commencing a bombardment, except in the case of an assault, should do all he can to warn the authorities.

Article 27

In sieges and bombardments all necessary steps should be taken to spare as far as possible edifices devoted to religion, art, science, and charity, hospitals, and places where the sick and wounded are collected, provided they are not used at the same time for military purposes.

The besieged should indicate these buildings or places by some particular and visible signs, which should previously be notified to the assailants.

Article 28

The pillage of a town or place, even when taken by assault, is prohibited.

Source: University of Minnesota Human Rights Library: http://wwwi.umn.edu/humanarts/instree/1899b.htm.

Treaty of Vereeniging, 31 May 1902

[Peace was finally concluded in May 1902 in the peace treaty signed in Vereeniging, with severe conditions imposed on the Boer antagonists, but anticipating—in other clauses on reparations and culture—the union that would come in 1910.]

His Excellency General Lord Kitchener and his Excellency Lord Milner, on behalf of the British Government, and Messrs. M. T. Steyn, J. Brebner, General C. R. De Wet, General C. Olivier, and Judge J. B. M. Hertzog, acting as the Government of the Orange Free State, and Messrs. S. W. Burger, F. W. Reitz, Generals Louis Botha, J. H. Delarey, Lucas Meyer, and Krogh, acting as the Government of the South African Republic, on behalf of their respective burghers desirous to terminate the present hostilities, agree on the following Articles:—

1. The burgher forces in the field will forthwith lay down their arms, handing over all guns, rifles, and munitions of war in their possession or under their control, and desist from any further resistance to the authority of his Majesty King Edward VII., whom they recognise as their lawful Sovereign. The manner and details of this surrender will be arranged between Lord Kitchener and Commandant-General Botha, Assistant Commandant-General Delarey, and Chief Commandant De Wet.

2. All burghers in the field outside the limits of the Transvaal or Orange River Colony and all prisoners of war at present outside South Africa who are burghers will, on duly declaring their acceptance of the position of subjects of his Majesty King Edward VII., be gradually brought back to their homes as soon as transport can be provided and their means of subsistence ensured.

3. The burghers so surrendering or so returning will not be deprived of their personal liberty or their property.

4. No proceedings, civil or criminal, will be taken against any of the burghers surrendering or so returning for any acts in connection with the prosecution of the war. The benefit of this clause will not extend to certain acts, contrary to usages of war, which have been notified by Commander-in-chief to the Boer Generals, and which shall be tried by court-martial immediately after the close of hostilities.

5. The Dutch language will be taught in public schools in the Transvaal and Orange River Colony where the parents of the children desire it, and will be allowed in courts of law when necessary for the better and more effectual administration of justice.

6. The possession of rifles will be allowed in the Transvaal and Orange River Colony to persons requiring them for their protection on taking out a licence according to the law.

7. Military administration in the Transvaal and Orange River Colony will, at the earliest possible date, be succeeded by Civil Government, and, as soon as circumstances permit, by representative institutions, leading up to self-government, be introduced.

8. The question of granting the franchise to natives will not be decided until after the introduction of self-government.

9. No special tax will be imposed on landed property in the Transvaal and Orange River Colony to defray the expenses of the war.

10. As soon as conditions permit, a Commission, on which the local inhabitants will be represented, will be appointed in each district of the Transvaal and Orange River Colony, under the presidency of a Magistrate or other official, for the purpose of assisting the restoration of the people to their homes and supplying those who, owing to war losses, are unable to provide themselves with food, shelter, and the necessary amount of seed, stock, implements, etc., indispensable to the resumption of their normal occupations.

His Majesty's Government will place at the disposal of these Commissions a sum of £3,000,000 for the above purposes, and will allow all notes issued under Law 1 of 1900 of the South African Republic and all receipts given by officers in the field of the late Republics, or under their orders, to be presented to a Judicial Commission, which will be appointed by the Government, and if such notes and receipts are found by this Commission to have been duly issued in return for valuable considerations, they will be received by the first-named Commissions as evidence of war losses suffered by the persons to whom they were originally given.

In addition to the above-named free grant of £3,000,000, his Majesty's Government will be prepared to make advances on loan for the same purposes free of interest for two years, and afterwards repayable over a period of years with 3 per cent. interest. No foreigner or rebel will be entitled to the benefit of this clause.

Hymn of Hate

Ernst Lissauer

Translated by Barbara Henderson

French and Russian, they matter not,
A blow for a blow and a shot for a shot!
We love them not, we hate them not,
We hold the Weichsel and Vosges gate.
We have but one and only hate,
We love as one, we hate as one,
We have one foe and one alone.
He is known to you all, he is known to you all,
He crouches behind the dark gray flood,
Full of envy, of rage, of craft, of gall,
Cut off by waves that are thicker than blood.
Come, let us stand at the Judgment Place,
An oath to swear to, face to face,
An oath of bronze no wind can shake,
An oath for our sons and their sons to take.
Come, hear the word, repeat the word,
Throughout the Fatherland make it heard.
We will never forego our hate,
We have all but a single hate,
We love as one, we hate as one,
We have one foe and one alone —
            ENGLAND!

In the Captain's Mess, in the banquet hall,
Sat feasting the officers, one and all,
Like a sabre blow, like the swing of a sail,
One seized his glass and held high to hail;
Sharp-snapped like the stroke of a rudder's play,
Spoke three words only: "To the Day!"
Whose glass this fate?
They had all but a single hate.
Who was thus known?
They had one foe and one alone —
            ENGLAND!

Take you the folk of the Earth in pay,
With bars of gold your ramparts lay,

From *New York Times*, October 15, 1914 by Ernst Lissauer, Translated by Barbara Henderson.

Bedeck the ocean with bow on bow,
Ye reckon well, but not well enough now.
French and Russian, they matter not,
A blow for a blow, a shot for a shot,
We fight the battle with bronze and steel,
And the time that is coming Peace will seal.
You we will hate with a lasting hate,
We will never forego our hate,
Hate by water and hate by land,
Hate of the head and hate of the hand,
Hate of the hammer And hate of the crown,
Hate of seventy millions choking down.
We love as one, we hate as one,
We have one foe and one alone —
              ENGLAND!

The Return of the Soldier

Rebecca West

"Ah, don't begin to fuss!" wailed Kitty; "if a woman began to worry in these days because her husband hadn't written to her for a fortnight——! Besides, if he'd been anywhere interesting, anywhere where the fighting was really hot, he'd have found some way of telling me instead of just leaving it as 'Somewhere in France.' He'll be all right."

We were sitting in the nursery. I had not meant to enter it again after the child's death, but I had come suddenly on Kitty as she slipped the key into the lock and had lingered to look in at the high room, so full of whiteness and clear colours, so unendurably gay and familiar, which is kept in all respects as though there were still a child in the house. It was the first lavish day of spring, and the sunlight was pouring through the tall arched windows and the flowered curtains so brightly that in the old days a fat fist would certainly have been raised to point out the new translucent glories of the rose-buds; it was lying in great pools on the blue cork floor and the soft rugs, patterned with strange beasts; and it threw dancing beams, that should have been gravely watched for hours, on the white paint and the blue distempered walls. It fell on the rocking-horse which had been Chris's idea of an appropriate present for his year-old son and showed what a fine fellow he was and how tremendously dappled; it picked out Mary and her little lamb on the chintz ottoman. And along the mantelpiece, under the loved print of the snarling tiger, in attitudes that were at once angular and relaxed — as though they were ready for play at their master's pleasure but found it hard to keep from drowsing in this warm weather — sat the Teddy Bear and the chimpanzee and the woolly white dog and the black cat with the eyes that roll. Everything was there, except Oliver. I turned away so that I might not spy on Kitty revisiting her dead.

But she called after me:

"Come here, Jenny. I'm going to dry my hair."

And when I looked again I saw that her golden hair was all about her shoulders and that she wore over her frock a little silken jacket trimmed with rosebuds. She looked so like a girl on a magazine cover that one expected to find a large "7d." somewhere attached to her person. She had taken Nanny's big basket-chair from its place by the high chair and was pushing it over to the middle window.

"I always come in here when Emery has washed my hair; it's the sunniest room in the house. I wish Chris wouldn't have it kept as a nursery when there's no chance——"

She sat down, swept her hair over the back of the chair into the sunlight, and held out to me her tortoise-shell hairbrush.

"Give it a brush now and then like a good soul. But be careful. Tortoise snaps so."

I took the brush and turned to the window, leaning my forehead against the glass and staring unobservantly at the view. You probably know the beauty of that view; for when Chris rebuilt Baldry Court after his marriage, he handed it over to architects who had not so much the wild eye of the artist as the knowing wink of the manicurist, and between them they massaged the dear old place into matter for innumerable photographs in the illustrated papers.

The house lies on the crest of Harrow-weald, and from its windows the eye drops to miles of emerald pastureland lying wet and brilliant under a westward line of sleek hills blue with distance and distant woods, while nearer it ranges the suave decorum of the lawn and the Lebanon cedar whose branches are like darkness made palpable, and the minatory gauntnesses of the topmost pines in the wood that breaks downward, its bare boughs a close texture of browns and purples, from the pond on the hill's edge.

That day its beauty was an affront to me, because like most English women of my time I was wishing for the return of a soldier. Disregarding the national interest and every-thing except the keen prehensile gesture of our hearts towards him, I wanted to snatch my cousin Christopher from the wars and seal him in this green pleasantness his wife and I now looked upon. Of late I had had bad dreams about him. By night I saw Chris running across the brown rottenness of No Man's Land, starting back here because he trod upon a hand, not even looking there because of the awfulness of an unburied head, and not till my dream was packed full of horror did I see him pitch forward on his knees as he reached safety — if it was that. For on the war-films I have seen men slip down as softly from the trench parapet, and none but the grimmer philosophers would say that they had reached safety by their fall. And when I escaped into wakefulness it was only to lie stiff and think of stories I had heard in the boyish voice, that rings indomitable yet has most of its gay notes flattened, of the modern subaltern.

"We were all of us in a barn one night, and a shell came along. My pal sang out, '*Help me, old man, I've got no legs!*' and I had to answer, '*I can't, old man, I've got no hands!*'"

Well, such are the dreams of Englishwomen to-day; I could not complain. But I wished for the return of our soldier.

So I said: "I wish we could hear from Chris. It is a fortnight since he wrote."

And then it was that Kitty wailed, "Ah, don't begin to fuss," and bent over her image in her hand-mirror as one might bend for refreshment over scented flowers.

I tried to build about me such a little globe of ease as always ensphered her, and thought of all that remained good in our lives though Chris had gone. My eye followed the mellow brick of the garden wall through the trees, and I reflected that by the contriving of these gardens that lay, well-kept as a woman's hand, on the south side of the hill, Kitty and I had proved ourselves worthy of the past generation that had set the old house on this sunny ledge, overhanging and overhung by beauty. And we had done much for the new house.

I could send my mind creeping from room to room like a purring cat, rubbing itself against all the brittle beautiful things that we had either recovered from antiquity or dug from the obscure pits of modern craftsmanship, basking in the colour that glowed from all our solemnly chosen fabrics with such pure intensity that it seemed to shed warmth like sunshine. Even now, when spending seemed a little disgraceful, I could think of that beauty with nothing but pride. I was sure that we were preserved from the reproach of luxury because we had made a fine place for Chris, one little part of the world that was, so far as surfaces could make it so, good enough for his amazing goodness.

Here we had nourished that surpassing amiability which was so habitual that one took it as one of his physical characteristics, and regarded any lapse into bad temper as a calamity startling as the breaking of a leg. Here we had made happiness inevitable for him. I could shut my eyes and think of innumerable proofs of how well we had succeeded, for there never was so visibly contented a man: the way he lingered with us in the mornings while the car throbbed at the door, delighting just in whatever way the weather looked in the famil-iar frame of things, how our rooms burned with many coloured brightness on the darkest winter day, how not the fieriest summertime could consume the cool wet leafy places of our garden; the way that in the midst of entertaining a great company he would smile secretly to us, as though he knew we would not cease in our task of refreshing him; and all that he did on the morning just a year ago, when he went to the front. ...

First he had sat in the morning-room and talked and stared out on the lawn that already had the desolation of an empty stage although he had not yet gone; then broke off suddenly and went about the house, looking into many rooms. He went to the stables and looked at the horses and had the dogs brought out; he refrained from touching them or speaking to them, as though he felt himself already infected with the squalor of war and did not want to contaminate their bright physical well-being. Then he went to the edge of the wood and stood staring down into the clumps of dark-leaved rhododendra and the yellow tangle of last year's bracken and the cold winter black of the trees. (From this very window I had spied on him.) Then he moved broodingly back to the house to be with his wife until the moment of his going, when I stood with her on the steps to see him motor off to Waterloo.

He kissed us both; as he bent over me I noticed once again how his hair was of two colours, brown and gold. Then he got into the car, put on his Tommy air, and said, "So long! I'll write you from Berlin!" and as he spoke his head dropped back and he set a hard stare on the overarching house. That meant, I knew, that he loved the life he had lived with us and desired to carry with him to the dreary place of death and dirt the completest picture of everything about his home, on which his mind could brush when things were at their worst, as a man might finger an amulet through his shirt. This house, this life with us, was the core of his heart.

"If he could come back!" I said. "He was so happy here."

And Kitty answered: "He could not have been happier."

It was important that he should have been happy, for, you see, he was not like other city men. When we had played together as children in that wood he had always shown great faith in the imminence of the improbable. He thought that the birch tree would really stir and shrink and quicken into an enchanted princess, that he really was a Red Indian and that his disguise would suddenly fall from him at the right sundown, that at any moment a tiger might lift red fangs through the bracken; and he expected these things with a stronger motion of the imagination than the ordinary child's make-believe. And from a thousand intimations, from his occasional clear fixity of gaze on good things as though they were about to dissolve into better, from the passionate anticipation with which he went to new countries or met new people, I was aware that this faith had persisted into his adult life.

He had exchanged his expectation of becoming a Red Indian for the equally wistful aspiration of becoming completely reconciled to life. It was his hopeless hope that some time he would have an experience that would act on his life like alchemy, turning to gold all the dark metals of events, and from that revelation he would go on his way rich with an inextinguishable joy.

There had been, of course, no chance of his ever getting it. Literally there wasn't room to swing a revelation in his crowded life. First of all, at his father's death, he had been obliged to take over a business that was weighted by the needs of a mob of female relatives who were all useless either in the old way with antimacassars or in the new way with golf clubs.

Then Kitty had come along and picked up his conception of normal expenditure and carelessly stretched it as a woman stretches a new glove on her hand. Then there had been the difficult task of learning to live after the death of his little son. It had lain on us, as the responsibility that gave us dignity, to compensate him for his lack of free adventure by arranging him a gracious life. But now, just because our performance had been so brilliantly adequate, how dreary was the empty stage. ...

We were not, perhaps, specially contemptible women, because nothing could ever really become a part of our life until it had been referred to Chris's attention. I remember thinking, as the parlourmaid came in with a card on the tray, how little it mattered who had called and what flag of prettiness she flew, since there was no chance that Chris would come in and stand over her, his fairness red in the firelight, and show her that detached attention, such as an unmusical man pays to good music, which men of anchored affections give to attractive women.

Kitty read from the card, "'Mrs. William Grey, Mariposa, Ladysmith Road, Weald-stone.' I don't know anybody in Wealdstone." That is the name of the red suburban stain which fouls the fields three miles nearer London than Harrow-weald. One cannot now pro-tect one's environment as one could in the old days. "Do I know her, Ward? Has she been here before?"

"Oh, no, ma'am." The parlourmaid smiled superciliously. "She said she had news for you." From her tone one could deduce an over-confidential explanation made by a shabby visitor while using the door mat almost too zealously.

Kitty pondered and said, "I'll come down." As the girl went she took up the amber hairpins from her lap and began swathing her hair about her head. "Last year's fashion," she commented; "but I fancy it'll do for a person with that sort of address." She stood up and threw her little silk dressing-jacket over the rocking-horse. "I'm seeing her because she may need something, and I specially want to be kind to people while Chris is away. One wants to deserve well of Heaven."

For a minute she was aloof in radiance, but as we linked arms and went out into the corridor she became more mortal with a pout.

"The people that come breaking into one's nice quiet day," she moaned reproachfully, and as we came to the head of the broad staircase she leaned over the white balustrade to peer down on the hall, and squeezed my arm. "Look!" she whispered.

Just beneath us, on one of Kitty's prettiest chintz arm-chairs, sat a middle-aged woman. She wore a yellowish raincoat and a black hat with plumes whose sticky straw had but lately been renovated by something out of a little bottle bought at the chemist's. She had rolled her black thread gloves into a ball on her lap, so that she could turn her grey alpaca skirt well above her muddy boots and adjust its brushbraid with a seamed red hand which looked even more horrible when she presently raised it to touch the glistening flowers of the pink azalea that stood on a table beside her.

Kitty shivered and muttered, "Let's get this over," and ran down the stairs. On the last step she paused and said with a conscientious sweetness, "Mrs. Grey?"

"Yes," answered the visitor.

She lifted to Kitty a sallow and relaxed face whose expression gave me a sharp, pity-ing pang of prepossession in her favour; it was beautiful that so plain a woman should so ardently rejoice in another's loveliness.

"Are you Mrs. Baldry?" she asked, almost as if she were glad about it, and stood up.

The bones of her cheap stays clicked as she moved. Well, she was not so bad. Her body was long and round and shapely and with a noble squareness of the shoulders; her fair hair curled diffidently about a good brow; her grey eyes, though they were remote, as if anything worth looking at in her life had kept a long way off, were full of tenderness; and though she was slender there was something about her of the wholesome endearing heaviness of the draught-ox or the big trusted dog. Yet she was bad enough. She was repulsively furred with neglect and poverty, as even a good glove that has dropped down behind a bed in a hotel and has lain undisturbed for a day or two is repulsive when the chambermaid retrieves it from the dust and fluff.

She flung at us as we sat down:

"My general is sister to your second housemaid."

It left us at a loss. "You've come about a reference?"

"Oh, no. I've had Gladys two years now, and I've always found her a very good girl. I want no reference." With her finger-nail she followed the burst seam of the dark pigskin purse that slid about on her shiny alpaca lap. "But girls talk, you know. You mustn't blame them. ..."

She seemed to be caught in a thicket of embarrassment, and sat staring up at the azalea.

Kitty said, with the hardness of a woman who sees before her the curse of women's lives, a domestic row, that she took no interest in servants' gossip.

"Oh, it isn't" — her eyes brimmed as though we had been unkind — "servants' gossip that I wanted to talk about. I only mentioned Gladys" — she continued to trace the burst seam of her purse — "because that's how I heard you didn't know."

"What don't I know?"

Her head dropped a little.

"About Mr. Baldry. Forgive me, I don't know his rank."

"Captain Baldry," supplied Kitty wonderingly. "What is it that I don't know about him?"

She looked far away from us, to the open door and its view of dark pines and pale March sunshine, and appeared to swallow something.

"Why, that he's hurt," she gently said.

"Wounded, you mean?" asked Kitty.

Her rusty plumes oscillated as she moved her mild face about with an air of perplexity.

"Yes," she said, "he's wounded."

Kitty's bright eyes met mine and we obeyed that mysterious human impulse to smile triumphantly at the spectacle of a fellow-creature occupied in baseness. For this news was not true. It could not possibly be true. The War Office would have wired to us immediately if Chris had been wounded. This was such a fraud as one sees recorded in the papers that meticulously record squalor, in paragraphs headed "Heartless Fraud on Soldier's Wife."

Presently she would say that she had gone to some expense to come here with her news, and that she was poor, and at the first generous look on our faces there would come some tale of trouble that would disgust the imagination by pictures of yellow wood furniture that a landlord oddly desired to seize and a pallid child with bandages round its throat.

I turned away my eyes and tried to be inattentive Yet there was something about the physical quality of the woman, unlovely though she was, which preserved the occasion from utter baseness. I felt sure that had it not been for the tyrannous emptiness of that evil, shiny, pigskin purse that jerked about on her trembling knees, the poor driven creature would have chosen ways of candour and gentleness. It was, strangely enough, only when I looked at Kitty and marked how her brightly coloured prettiness arched over this plain criminal, as though she were a splendid bird of prey and this her sluggish insect food, that I felt the moment degrading.

She was, I felt, being a little too clever over it.

"How is he wounded?" she asked.

The caller traced a pattern on the carpet with her blunt toe.

"I don't know how to put it. ...

He's not exactly wounded. ... A shell burst. ..."

"Concussion?" suggested Kitty.

She answered with an odd glibness and humility, as though tendering us a term she had long brooded over without arriving at comprehension, and hoping that our superior intelligences would make something of it. "Shell-shock." Our faces did not illumine so she dragged on lamely. "Anyway, he's not well." Again she played with her purse. Her face was visibly damp.

"Not well? Is he dangerously ill?"

"Oh, no!" She was too kind to harrow us. "Not dangerously ill."

Kitty brutally permitted a silence to fall. Our caller could not bear it, and broke it in a voice that nervousness had turned to a funny diffident croak.

"He's in the Queen Mary Hospital at Boulogne." We did not speak, and she began to flush and wriggle on her seat, and stooped forward to fumble under the legs of her chair for her umbrella. The sight of its green seams and unveracious tortoise-shell handle disgusted Kitty into speech.

"How do you know all this?"

Our visitor met her eyes. This was evidently a moment for which she had steeled herself, and she rose to it with a catch of her breath.

"A man who used to be a clerk along with my husband is in Mr. Baldry's regiment." Her voice croaked even more piteously and her eyes begged, "Leave it at that! Leave it at that! If you only knew——"

"And what regiment is that?" pursued Kitty.

The poor sallow face shone with sweat.

"I never thought to ask!" she said.

"Well, your friend's name. ..."

Mrs. Grey moved on her seat so suddenly and violently that the pigskin purse fell from her lap and lay at my feet. I supposed that she cast it from her purposely because its emptiness had brought her to this humiliation, and that the scene would close presently in a few quiet tears.

I hoped that Kitty would let her go without searing her too much with words and would not mind if I gave her a little money. There was no doubt in my mind but that this queer ugly episode, in which this woman butted like a clumsy animal at a gate she was not intelligent enough to open, would dissolve and be replaced by some more pleasing composition in which we would take our proper parts; in which, that is, she should turn from our rightness ashamed.

Yet she cried, "But Chris is ill!"

It look a second for the compact insolence of the moment to penetrate: the amazing impertinence of the use of his name, the accusation of callousness she brought against us, whose passion for Chris was our point of honour, because we would not shriek at her false news, the impudently bright indignant gaze she flung at us, the lift of her voice that pretended she could not understand our coolness and irrelevance.

I pushed the purse away from me with my loe and hated her as the rich hate the poor, as insect things that will struggle out of the crannies which are their decent home, and introduce ugliness to the light of day. And Kitty said, in a voice shaken with pitilessness:

"You are impertinent. I know exactly what you are doing. You have read in the *Harrow Observer* or somewhere that my husband is at the front, and you come to tell this story because you think that you will get some money. I've read of such cases in the papers. You forget that if anything has happened to my husband the War Office would have told me. You should think yourself very lucky that I don't hand you over to the police." She shrilled a little before she came to the end. "Please go!"

"Kitty!" I breathed.

I was so ashamed that such a scene should spring from Chris's peril at the front that I wanted to go out into the garden and sit by the pond until the poor thing had removed her deplorable umbrella, her unpardonable raincoat, her poor frustrated fraud. But Mrs. Grey, who had begun, childishly and deliberately, "It's *you* who are being ..." and had desisted, simply because she realized that there were no harsh notes on her lyre and that she could not strike these chords that others found so easy, had fixed me with a certain wet, clear, patient gaze. It is the gift of animals and those of peasant stock. From the least regarded, from an old horse nosing over a gate or a drab in a workhouse ward, it wrings the heart. From this woman ... I said checkingly, "Kitty!" and reconciled her in an undertone ("There's some mistake. Got the name wrong, perhaps). Please tell us all about it, Mrs. Grey."

Mrs. Grey began a forward movement like a curtsey She was grovelling after that purse. When she rose her face was pink from stooping and her dignity swam uncertainly in a sea of half-shed tears. She said:

"I'm sorry I've upset you. But when you know a thing like that it isn't in flesh and blood to keep it from his wife. I am a married woman myself and I know. I knew Mr. Baldry fifteen years ago." Her voice freely confessed that she had taken a liberty. "Quite a friend of the family he was." She had added that touch to soften the crude surprisingness of her announcement. It hardly did. "We lost sight of each other. It's fifteen years since we last met. I had never seen or heard of him, nor thought to do again till I got this a week ago."

She undid the purse and took out a telegram. I knew suddenly that all she said was true; for that was why her hands had clasped that purse.

"He isn't well! He isn't well!" she said pleadingly. "He's lost his memory, and thinks — thinks he still knows me."

She passed the telegram to Kitty, who read it and laid it on her knee.

"See," said Mrs. Grey, "it's addressed to Margaret Allington, my maiden name, and I've been married these ten years. And it was sent to my old home, Monkey Island at Bray. Father kept the inn there. It's fifteen years since we left it. I never should have got this telegram if me and my husband hadn't been down there a little while back and told the folks who keep it now who I was."

Kitty folded up the telegram and said in a little voice:

"This is a likely story."

Again her grey eyes brimmed. People are rude to one, she visibly said, but surely not nice people like this. She simply continued to sit.

Kitty cried out, as though arguing:

"There's nothing about shell-shock in this wire."

She melted into a trembling shyness.

"There was a letter too."

Kitty held out her hand.

She gasped. "Oh, no! I couldn't do that."

"I must have it," said Kitty.

The caller's eyes grew great, she rose and dived clumsily for her umbrella, which had again slipped under the chair. "I can't," she cried, and scurried to the open door like a pelted dog. She would have run down the steps at once had not some tender thought arrested her.

She turned to me trustfully and stammered, "He is at that hospital I said," as if, since I had dealt her no direct blow, I might be able to salve the news she brought from the general wreck of manners. And then Kitty's stiff pallor struck to her heart, and she cried comfortingly across the distance, "But I tell you I haven't seen him for fifteen years." She faced about, pushed down her hat on her head, and ran down the steps on to the gravel. "They won't understand," we heard her sob.

For a long time we watched her as she went along the drive, her yellowish raincoat looking sick and bright in the sharp sunshine, her black plumes nodding like the pines above, her cheap boots making her walk on her heels; a spreading stain on the fabric of our life. When she was quite hidden by the dark clump of rhododendra at the corner Kitty turned and went to the fire-place. She laid her arms against the oak mantelpiece and cooled her face against her arms.

When at last I followed her she said, "Do you believe her?"

I started. I had forgotten that we had ever disbelieved her.

"Yes."

"What can it mean?" She dropped her arms and stared at me imploringly. "Think, think of something it can mean which isn't detestable!"

"It's all a mystery," I said; and added mildly, because nobody has ever been cross with Kitty, "You didn't help to clear it up."

"Oh, I know you think I was rude," she petulantly moaned, "but you're so slow, you don't see what it means. Either it means that he's mad, our Chris, our splendid sane Chris, all broken and queer, not knowing us. ... I can't bear to think of that. It can't be true. But if he isn't ... Jenny, there was nothing in that telegram to show he'd lost his memory. It was just affection — a name that might have been a pet name — things that it was a little common to put in a telegram. It's queer he should have written such a message, queer that he shouldn't have told me about knowing her, queer that he ever should have known such a woman. It shows there are bits of him we don't know. Things may be awfully wrong. It's all such a breach of trust. I resent it."

I was appalled by this stiff dignified gesture that seemed to be plucking Chris's soul from his body. She was hurt, of course. But there are ways pain should not show itself. ...

"But Chris is ill," I said.

She started at me. "You're saying what she said."

Indeed there seemed no better words than those Mrs. Grey had used. I repeated. "But he is ill."

She laid her face against her arms again. "What does that matter?" she said. "If he could send that telegram, he. ..." She paused, breathed deeply, and went on with the sick delight the unhappy sometimes find in ungraciousness. "If he could send that telegram he isn't ours any longer."

Civilization and Its Discontents

Sigmund Freud

Translated by James Strachey

Having reached the end of his journey, the author must ask his readers' forgiveness for not having been a more skilful guide and for not having spared them empty stretches of road and troublesome *détours*. There is no doubt that it could have been done better. I will attempt, late in the day, to make some amends.

In the first place, I suspect that the reader has the impression that our discussions on the sense of guilt disrupt the framework of this essay: that they take up too much space, so that the rest of its subject-matter, with which they are not always closely connected, is pushed to one side. This may have spoilt the structure of my paper; but it corresponds faithfully to my intention to represent the sense of guilt as the most important problem in the development of civilization and to show that the price we pay for our advance in civilization is a loss of happiness through the heightening of the sense of guilt. Anything that still sounds strange about this statement, which is the final conclusion of our investigation, can probably be traced to the quite peculiar relationship — as yet completely unexplained — which the sense of guilt has to our consciousness. In the common case of remorse, which we regard as normal, this feeling makes itself clearly enough perceptible to consciousness. Indeed, we are accustomed to speak of a 'consciousness of guilt' instead of a 'sense of guilt'. Our study of the neuroses, to which, after all, we owe the most valuable pointers to an understanding of normal conditions, brings us up against some contradictions. In one of those affections, obsessional neurosis, the sense of guilt makes itself noisily heard in consciousness; it dominates the clinical picture and the patient's life as well, and it hardly allows anything else to appear alongside of it. But in most other cases and forms of neurosis it remains completely unconscious, without on that account producing any less important effects. Our patients do not believe us when we attribute an 'unconscious sense of guilt' to them. In order to make ourselves at all intelligible to them, we tell them of an unconscious need for punishment, in which the sense of guilt finds expression. But its connection with a particular form of neurosis must not be over-estimated. Even in obsessional neurosis there are types of patients who are not aware of their sense of guilt, or who only feel it as a tormenting uneasiness, a kind of anxiety, if they are prevented from carrying out certain actions. It ought to be possible eventually to understand these things; but as yet we cannot. Here perhaps we may be glad to have it pointed out that the sense of guilt is at bottom nothing else but a topographical variety of anxiety; in its later phases it coincides completely with *fear of the super-ego*. And the relations of anxiety to consciousness exhibit the same extraordinary variations. Anxiety is always present somewhere or other behind every symptom; but at one time it takes noisy possession of the whole of consciousness, while at another it conceals itself so completely that we are obliged to speak of unconscious anxiety or, if we want to have a clearer psychological conscience, since anxiety is in the first instance simply a feeling, of possibilities of anxiety. Consequently it is very conceivable that the sense of guilt produced by civilization is not perceived as such either, and remains to a large extent unconscious, or appears as a sort of *malaise*, a dissatisfaction, for which people seek other motivations. Religions, at any rate, have never overlooked the part played in civilization by a sense of guilt. Furthermore — a point which I failed to appreciate elsewhere — they claim to redeem mankind from this sense of guilt, which they call sin. From the manner in which, in Christianity, this redemption is achieved — by the sacrificial death of a single person, who in this manner takes upon himself a guilt that is common to everyone — we have been able to infer what the first occasion may have been on which this primal guilt, which was also the beginning of civilization, was acquired.

Though it cannot be of great importance, it may not be superfluous to elucidate the meaning of a few words such as 'super-ego', 'conscience', 'sense of guilt', 'need for punishment' and 'remorse', which we have often, perhaps, used too loosely and interchangeably. They all relate to the same state of affairs, but denote different aspects of it. The super-ego is an agency which has been inferred by us, and conscience is a function which we ascribe, among other functions, to that agency. This function consists in keeping a watch over the actions and intentions of the ego and judging them, in exercising a censorship. The sense of guilt, the harshness of the super-ego, is thus the same thing as the severity of the conscience. It is the perception which the ego has of being watched over in this way, the assessment of the tension between its own strivings and the demands of the super-ego. The fear of this critical agency (a fear which is at the bottom of the whole relationship), the need for punishment, is an instinctual manifestation on the part of the ego, which has become masochistic under the influence of a sadistic super-ego; it is a portion, that is to say, of the instinct towards internal destruction present in the ego, employed for forming an erotic attachment to the super-ego. We ought not to speak of a conscience until a super-ego is demonstrably present. As to a sense of guilt, we must admit that it is in existence before the super-ego, and therefore before conscience, too. At that time it is the immediate expression of fear of the external authority, a recognition of the tension between the ego and that authority. It is the direct derivative of the conflict between the need for the authority's love and the urge towards instinctual satisfaction, whose inhibition produces the inclination to aggression. The superimposition of these two strata of the sense of guilt — one coming from fear of the *external* authority, the other from fear of the *internal* authority — has hampered our insight into the position of conscience in a number of ways. Remorse is a general term for the ego's reaction in a case of sense of guilt. It contains, in little altered form, the sensory material of the anxiety which is operating behind the sense of guilt; it is itself a punishment and can include the need for punishment. Thus remorse, too, can be older than conscience.

Nor will it do any harm if we once more review the contradictions which have for a while perplexed us during our enquiry. Thus, at one point the sense of guilt was the consequence of acts of aggression that had been abstained from; but at another point — and precisely at its historical beginning, the killing of the father — it was the consequence of an act of aggression that had been carried out [p. 94f.]. But a way out of this difficulty was found. For the institution of the internal authority, the super-ego, altered the situation radically. Before this, the sense of guilt coincided with remorse. (We may remark, incidentally, that the term 'remorse' should be reserved for the reaction after an act of aggression has actually been carried out.) After this, owing to the omniscience of the super-ego, the difference between an aggression intended and an aggression carried out lost its force. Henceforward a sense of guilt could be produced not only by an act of violence that is actually carried out (as all the world knows), but also by one that is merely intended (as psycho-analysis has discovered). Irrespectively of this alteration in the psychological situation, the conflict arising from ambivalence — the conflict between the two primal instincts — leaves the same result behind [p. 95f.]. We are tempted to look here for the solution of the problem of the varying relation in which the sense of guilt stands to consciousness. It might be thought that a sense of guilt arising from remorse for an evil *deed* must always be conscious, whereas a sense of guilt arising from the perception of an evil *impulse* may remain unconscious. But the answer is not so simple as that. Obsessional neurosis speaks energetically against it.

The second contradiction concerned the aggressive energy with which we suppose the super-ego to be endowed. According to one view, that energy merely carries on the punitive energy of the external authority and keeps it alive in the mind [p. 83]; while, according to another view, it consists, on the contrary, of one's own aggressive energy which has not been used and which one now directs against that inhibiting authority [p. 90]. The first view seemed to fit in better with the *history*, and the second with the *theory*, of the sense of guilt. Closer reflection has resolved this apparently irreconcilable contradiction almost too completely; what remained as the essential and common factor was that in each case we were dealing with an aggressiveness which had been displaced inwards. Clinical observation, moreover, allows us in fact to distinguish two sources for the aggressiveness which we attribute to the super-ego; one or the other of them exercises the stronger effect in any given case, but as a general rule they operate in unison.

This is, I think, the place at which to put forward for serious consideration a view which I have earlier recommended for provisional acceptance. In the most recent analytic literature a predilection is shown for the idea that any kind of frustration, any thwarted instinctual satisfaction, results, or may result, in a heightening of the sense of guilt. A great theoretical simplification will, I think, be achieved if we regard this as applying only to the *aggressive* instincts, and little will be found to contradict this assumption. For how are we to account, on dynamic and economic grounds, for an increase in the sense of guilt appearing in place of an unfulfilled *erotic* demand? This only seems possible in a round-about way — if we suppose, that is, that the prevention of an erotic satisfaction calls up a piece of aggressiveness against the person who has interfered with the satisfaction, and that this aggressiveness has itself to be suppressed in turn. But if this is so, it is after all only the aggressiveness which is transformed into a sense of guilt, by being suppressed and made over to the super-ego. I am convinced that many processes will admit of a simpler and clearer exposition if the findings of psycho-analysis with regard to the derivation of the sense of guilt are restricted to the aggressive instincts. Examination of the clinical material gives us no unequivocal answer here, because, as our hypothesis tells us, the two classes of instinct hardly ever appear in a pure form, isolated from each other; but an investigation of extreme cases would probably point in the direction I anticipate.

I am tempted to extract a first advantage from this more restricted view of the case by applying it to the process of repression. As we have learned, neurotic symptoms are, in their essence, substitutive satisfactions for unfulfilled sexual wishes. In the course of our analytic work we have discovered to our surprise that perhaps every neurosis conceals a quota of unconscious sense of guilt, which in its turn fortifies the symptoms by making use of them as a punishment. It now seems plausible to formulate the following proposition. When an instinctual trend undergoes repression, its libidinal elements are turned into symptoms, and its aggressive components into a sense of guilt. Even if this proposition is only an average approximation to the truth, it is worthy of our interest.

Some readers of this work may further have an impression that they have heard the formula of the struggle between Eros and the death instinct too often. It was alleged to characterize the process of civilization which mankind undergoes [p. 81] but it was also brought into connection with the development of the individual [p. 76], and, in addition, it was said to have revealed the secret of organic life in general [p. 77f.]. We cannot, I think, avoid going into the relations of these three processes to one another. The repetition of the same formula is justified by the consideration that both the process of human civilization and of the development of the individual are also vital processes — which is to say that they must share in the most general characteristic of life. On the other hand, evidence of the presence of this general characteristic fails, for the very reason of its general nature, to help us to arrive at any differentiation [between the processes], so long as it is not narrowed down by special qualifications. We can only be satisfied, therefore, if we assert that the process of civilization is a modification which the vital process experiences under the influence of a task that is set it by Eros and instigated by Ananke — by the exigencies of reality; and that this task is one of uniting separate individuals into a community bound together by libidinal ties. When, however, we look at the relation between the process of human civilization and the developmental or educative process of individual human beings, we shall conclude without much hesitation that the two are very similar in nature, if not the very same process applied to different kinds of object. The process of the civilization of the human species is, of course, an abstraction of a higher order than is the development of the individual and it is therefore harder to apprehend in concrete terms, nor should we pursue analogies to an obsessional extreme; but in view of the similarity between the aims of the two processes — in the one case the integration of a separate individual into a human group, and in the other case the creation of a unified group out of many individuals — we cannot be surprised at the similarity between the means employed and the resultant phenomena.

In view of its exceptional importance, we must not long postpone the mention of one feature which distinguishes between the two processes. In the developmental process of the individual, the programme of the pleasure principle, which consists in finding the satisfaction of happiness, is retained as the main aim. Integration in, or adaptation to, a human community appears as a scarcely avoidable condition which must be fulfilled before this aim of happiness can be achieved. If it could be done without that condition, it would perhaps be preferable. To put it in other words, the development of the individual seems to us to be a product of the interaction between two urges, the urge towards happiness, which we usually call 'egoistic', and the urge towards union with others in the community, which we call 'altruistic'. Neither of these descriptions goes much below the surface. In the process of individual development, as we have said, the main accent falls mostly on the egoistic urge (or the urge towards happiness); while the other urge, which may be described as a 'cultural' one, is usually content with the role of imposing restrictions. But in the process of civilization things are different. Here by far the most important thing is the aim of creating a unity out of the individual human beings. It is true that the aim of happiness is still there, but it is pushed into the background. It almost seems as if the creation of a great human community would be most successful if no attention had to be paid to the happiness of the individual. The developmental process of the individual can thus be expected to have special features of its own which are not reproduced in the process of human civilization. It is only in so far as the first of these processes has union with the community as its aim that it need coincide with the second process.

Just as a planet revolves around a central body as well as rotating on its own axis, so the human individual takes part in the course of development of mankind at the same time as he pursues his own path in life. But to our dull eyes the play of forces in the heavens seems fixed in a never-changing order; in the field of organic life we can still see how the forces contend with one another, and how the effects of the conflict are continually changing. So, also, the two urges, the one towards personal happiness and the other towards union with other human beings must struggle with each other in every individual; and so, also, the two processes of individual and of cultural development must stand in hostile opposition to each other and mutually dispute the ground. But this struggle between the individual and society is not a derivative of the contradiction — probably an irreconcilable one — between the primal instincts of Eros and death. It is a dispute within the economics of the libido, comparable to the contest concerning the distribution of libido between ego and objects; and it does admit of an eventual accommodation in the individual, as, it may be hoped, it will also do in the future of civilization, however much that civilization may oppress the life of the individual to-day.

The analogy between the process of civilization and the path of individual development may be extended in an important respect. It can be asserted that the community, too, evolves a super-ego under whose influence cultural development proceeds. It would be a tempting task for anyone who has a knowledge of human civilizations to follow out this analogy in detail. I will confine myself to bringing forward a few striking points. The super-ego of an epoch of civilization has an origin similar to that of an individual. It is based on the impression left behind by the personalities of great leaders — men of overwhelming force of mind or men in whom one of the human impulses has found its strongest and purest, and therefore often its most one-sided, expression. In many instances the analogy goes still further, in that during their lifetime these figures were — often enough, even if not always — mocked and maltreated by others and even despatched in a cruel fashion. In the same way, indeed, the primal father did not attain divinity until long after he had met his death by violence. The most arresting example of this fateful conjunction is to be seen in the figure of Jesus Christ — if, indeed, that figure is not a part of mythology, which called it into being from an obscure memory of that primal event. Another point of agreement between the cultural and the individual super-ego is that the former, just like the latter, sets up strict ideal demands, disobedience to which is visited with 'fear of conscience' [p. 90]. Here, indeed, we come across the remarkable circumstance that the mental processes concerned are actually more familiar to us and more accessible to consciousness as they are seen in the group than they can be in the individual man. In him, when tension arises, it is only the aggressiveness of the super-ego which, in the form of reproaches, makes itself noisily heard; its actual demands often remain unconscious in the background. If we bring them to conscious knowledge, we find that they coincide with the precepts of the prevailing cultural super-ego. At this point the two processes, that of the cultural development of the group and that of the cultural development of the individual, are, as it were, always interlocked. For that reason some of the manifestations and properties of the super-ego can be more easily detected in its behaviour in the cultural community than in the separate individual.

The cultural super-ego has developed its ideals and set up its demands. Among the latter, those which deal with the relations of human beings to one another are comprised under the heading of ethics. People have at all times set the greatest value on ethics, as though they expected that it in particular would produce especially important results. And it does in fact deal with a subject which can easily be recognized as the sorest spot in every civilization. Ethics is thus to be regarded as a therapeutic attempt — as an endeavour to achieve, by means of a command of the super-ego, something which has so far not been achieved by means of any other cultural activites. As we already know, the problem before us is how to get rid of the greatest hindrance to civilization — namely, the constitutional inclination of human beings to be aggressive towards one another; and for that very reason we are especially interested in what is probably the most recent of the cultural commands of the super-ego, the commandment to love one's neighbour as oneself, [Cf. p. 65ff. above.] In our research into, and therapy of, a neurosis, we are led to make two reproaches against the super-ego of the individual. In the severity of its commands and prohibitions it troubles itself too little about the happiness of the ego, in that it takes insufficient account of the resistances against obeying them — of the instinctual strength of the id [in the first place], and of the difficulties presented by the real external environment [in the second]. Consequently we are very often obliged, for therapeutic purposes, to oppose the super-ego, and we endeavour to lower its demands. Exactly the same objections can be made against the ethical demands of the cultural super-ego. It, too, does not trouble itself enough about the facts of the mental constitution of human beings. It issues a command and does not ask whether it is possible for people to obey it. On the contrary, it assumes that a man's ego is psychologically capable of anything that is required of it, that his ego has unlimited mastery over his id. This is a mistake and even in what are known as normal people the id cannot be controlled beyond certain limits. If more is demanded of a man, a revolt will be produced in him or a neurosis, or he will be made unhappy. The commandment, 'Love thy neighbour as thyself', is the strongest defence against human aggressiveness and an excellent example of the unpsychological proceedings of the cultural super-ego. The commandment is impossible to fulfil; such an enormous inflation of love can only lower its value, not get rid of the difficulty. Civilization pays no attention to all this; it merely admonishes us that the harder it is to obey the precept the more meritorious it is to do so. But anyone who follows such a precept in present-day civilization only puts himself at a disadvantage *vis-à-vis* the person who disregards it. What a potent obstacle to civilization aggressiveness must be, if the defence against it can cause as much unhappiness as aggressiveness itself!'Natural' ethics, as it is called, has nothing to offer here except the narcissistic satisfaction of being able to think oneself better than others. At this point the ethics based on religion introduces its promises of a better after-life. But so long as virtue is not rewarded here on earth, ethics will, I fancy, preach in vain. I too think it quite certain that a real change in the relations of human beings to possessions would be of more help in this direction than may ethical commands; but the recognition of this fact among socialists has been obscured and made useless for practical purposes by a fresh idealistic misconception of human nature. [Cf. p. 71 above.]

I believe the line of thought which seeks to trace in the phenomena of cultural development the part played by a super-ego promises still further discoveries. I hasten to come to a close. But there is one question which I can hardly evade. If the development of civilization has such a far-reaching similarity to the development of the individual and if it employs the same methods, may we not be justified in reaching the diagnosis that, under the influence of cultural urges, some civilizations, or some epochs of civilization — possibly the whole of mankind — have become 'neurotic'? An analytic dissection of such neuroses might lead to therapeutic recommendations which could lay claim to great practical interest. I would not say that an attempt of this kind to carry psycho-analysis over to the cultural community was absurd or doomed to be fruitless. But we should have to be very cautions and not forget that, after all, we are only dealing with analogies and that it is dangerous, not only with men but also with concepts, to tear them from the sphere in which they have originated and been evolved. Moreover, the diagnosis of communal neuroses is faced with a special difficulty. In an individual neurosis we take as our starting-point the contrast that distinguishes the patient from his environment, which is assumed to be 'normal'. For a group all of whose members are affected by one and the same disorder no such background could exist; it would have to be found elsewhere. And as regards the therapeutic application of our knowledge, what would be the use of the most correct analysis of social neuroses, since no one possesses authority to impose such a therapy upon the group? But in spite of all these difficulties, we may expect that one day someone will venture to embark upon a pathology of cultural communities.

For a wide variety of reasons, it is very far from my intention to express an opinion upon the value of human civilization. I have endeavoured to guard myself against the enthusiastic prejudice which holds that our civilization is the most precious thing that we possess or could acquire and that its path will necessarily lead to heights of unimagined perfection. I can at least listen without indignation to the critic who is of the opinion that when one surveys the aims of cultural endeavour and the means it employs, one is bound to come to the conclusion that the whole effort is not worth the trouble, and that the outcome of it can only be a state of affairs which the individual will be unable to tolerate. My impartiality is made all the easier to me by my knowing very little about all these things. One thing only do I know for certain and that is that man's judgements of value follow directly his wishes for happiness — that, accordingly, they are an attempt to support his illusions with arguments. I should find it very understandable if someone were to point out the obligatory nature of the course of human civilization and were to say, for instance, that the tendencies to a restriction of sexual life or to the institution of a humanitarian ideal at the expense of natural selection were developmental trends which cannot be averted or turned aside and to which it is best for us to yield as though they were necessities of nature. I know, too, the objection that can be made against this, to the effect that in the history of mankind, trends such as these, which were considered unsurmountable, have often been thrown aside and replaced by other trends. Thus I have not the courage to rise up before my fellow-men as a prophet, and I bow to their reproach that I can offer them no consolation: for at bottom that is what they are all demanding — the wildest revolutionaries no less passionately than the most virtuous believers.

The fateful question for the human species seems to me to be whether and to what extent their cultural development will succeed in mastering the disturbance of their communal life by the human instinct of aggression and self-destruction. It may be that in this respect precisely the present time deserves a special interest. Men have gained control over the forces of nature to such an extent that with their help they would have no difficulty in exterminating one another to the last man. They know this, and hence comes a large part of their current unrest, their unhappiness and their mood of anxiety. And now it is to be expected that the other of the two 'Heavenly Powers' [p. 96f.], eternal Eros, will make an effort to assert himself in the struggle with his equally immortal adversary. But who can foresee with what success and with what result?

A Writer at War

Vasily Grossman

The city of Stalingrad, some forty kilometres long, follows the western bank of the great Volga. After the sudden rush of XIV Panzer Corps to the northern tip of the city on 23 August, the Sixth Army's advance on the city slowed. The *Stavka*, under tremendous pressure from a very nervous Stalin, ordered attacks from the open steppe to the north against the left flank of XIV Panzer Corps. These were hurried and ill-prepared, leading to terrible losses of men and equipment, but they made Paulus cautious, diverted the Luftwaffe from the city, and provided more time for the *Stavka* to rush reinforcements forward.

To the south-west, part of General Hoth's Fourth Panzer Army advanced on Stalingrad relentlessly, even though Yeremenko had concentrated the bulk of his forces in that direction. Yeremenko's 'member of the Military Council', which meant chief political officer, was Nikita Khrushchev, who had been in charge of the evacuation of Soviet industry from the Ukraine. Grossman later crossed the Volga to visit Yeremenko and Khrushchev in the new headquarters of the Stalingrad Front.

The exhausted and demoralised remnants of the 62nd and 64th Armies had retreated across the last of the Don steppe in towards the city itself. By 12 September, the 62nd Army was reduced to a perimeter which was three kilometres deep at the southernmost point of the city and up to fifteen kilometres deep at the point of the northern suburbs. By the end of the month, the defensive perimeter was reduced to a strip of the northern part of the city, some twenty kilometres long and between one and five kilometres deep.

Without any sort of diary, it is hard to follow Grossman's movements precisely. One can, however, deduce from his notebooks that initially he seems to have been billeted in Dubovka, on the west bank of the Volga less than forty kilometres upstream from the northern part of Stalingrad. The west bank of the river, with a steep bank and sometimes with small cliffs, was much higher than the flat eastern side. The very idea of the German invaders reaching the Volga, the 'heart of Russia', did much to create a defeatist mood, as Grossman encountered in many conversations.

> Now, there is nowhere further to retreat. Every step back is now a big, and probably fatal, mistake. The civilians in the villages beside the Volga feel it, as well as the armies that are defending the Volga and Stalingrad.

> It is a joy and a pain at the same time to look at this most beautiful of rivers. Steamers painted grey green, covered with wilted branches, were standing by piers, with barely a light smoke rising from their smokestacks. . . Everywhere, also on the bank, there are trenches, bunkers, anti-tank ditches. The war has reached the Volga.

> We are staying in the house of a dispossessed kulak. Only we suddenly see that the old owner of the house has returned, God knows from where. She watches us day and night and says nothing. She is waiting. And there we are, living under her stare.

An old woman sits all night in the slit trench. The whole of Dubovka sits in slit trenches. A kerosinka is flying overhead. It rattles, lights candles and drops little bombs.

'Where's the babushka?'

'She's in the trench,' laughs the old man. 'She sometimes looks out like a suslik and then rushes back.'

'It's the end for us. That trickster [Hitler] has reached the heart of our land.'

A soldier with an anti-tank rifle is driving a huge flock of sheep through the steppe.

In the following description, Grossman appears to be close to the northern edge of the city near Rynok, where the parks and allotments full of ripening fruit appeared like a minor Garden of Eden to the men of the 16th Panzer Division who had spent the last two months crossing the sun-baked steppe.

Aircraft roar all night over our heads. The sky is humming day and night, as if we were sitting under the span of a huge bridge. This bridge is light blue during the day, dark blue at night, arched, covered with stars—and columns of five-ton trucks are thundering over this bridge.

Fire positions on the other side of the Volga, in a former sanatorium. A steep cliff. The river is blue and pink, like the sea. Vineyards, poplars. Batteries are camouflaged with vine leaves. Benches for the holidaymakers. A lieutenant is sitting on a bench, with a little table in front of him. He shouts: 'Battery fire!'

Beyond is the steppe. The air coming from the Volga is cool, and the steppe smells of warmth. Messers are up there. A sentry shouts: 'Air!' and the air is clear and smells of sagebrush.

Wounded men in their bloodstained bandages are walking along the Volga, right by the water. Naked people are sitting over the pink-evening Volga crushing lice in their underwear. Towing vehicles are roaring and skidding on the gravel by the bank. And then the stars at night. All one can see is a white church beyond the Volga.

A clear, cold morning in Dubovka. There is a bang, clinking of broken glass, plaster, dust in the air, haze. Screams and weeping over the Volga. Germans have dropped a bomb killing seven women and children. A girl in a bright yellow dress is screaming: 'Mama, Mama!'

A man is wailing like a woman. His wife's arm has been torn off. She is speaking calmly, in a sleepy voice. A woman sick with typhoid fever has been hit in the stomach by a shell fragment. She hasn't died yet. Carts are moving, and blood is dripping from them. And the screaming, the crying over the Volga.

Grossman managed to get permission to cross the Volga from the east, or left, bank over to the burned-out city on the west bank. The crossing points were strictly controlled by troops from the 10th NKVD Rifle Division to catch deserters and even prevent civilians from fleeing the city. Stalin felt that their presence would oblige the Soviet troops to fight harder to save the city. Grossman was accompanied by Kapustyansky, another correspondent from *Krasnaya Zvezda*. Just crossing the Volga was dangerous as the Luftwaffe continually targeted the crossing points.

A terrifying crossing. Fear. The ferry is full of vehicles, carts, hundreds of people crowded together, and it gets stuck. A Ju-88 drops a bomb from high above. A huge spout of water, upright, bluish-white in colour. The feeling of fear. There isn't a single machine gun at the crossing, not a single little anti-aircraft gun. The quiet, clear Volga is terrifying like a scaffold.

The city of Stalingrad, the last days of August, beginning of September, after the fire. Crossing the river to Stalingrad. At the start, for courage, we drink a huge amount of apple wine at a collective farm on the left bank.

Messers are howling over the Volga, there is haze and smoke over it, smoke canisters are burned constantly to camouflage the crossing.

The burned, dead city, the square of Fallen Warriors. Dedications on memorials: 'From the Proletariat of Red Tsaritsyn to the Fighters for Freedom who died at the hands of Wrangel's henchmen in 1919.'

Inhabitants of a burned building are eating shchi *in a gateway, seated upon a heap of belongings. A book entitled* The Insulted and the Injured *is lying on the ground nearby. Kapustyansky says to these people: 'You, too, are insulted and injured.'*

'We are injured, but not insulted,' a girl replies.

The two correspondents made their way beyond the western edge of Stalingrad where the right-hand corps of Paulus's Sixth Army was joining up with Hoth's Fourth Panzer Army advancing from the south-west. On this side, the Germans, with nine divisions, heavily outnumbered the 40,000 exhausted Soviet troops of the 64th and 62nd Armies, retreating back into the city.

Varapanovo, where there are old trenches overgrown with grass. The most severe battles of the civil war had taken place here, and now, once again, the heaviest enemy attacks are directed at this place.

Grossman and Kapustyansky appear, however, to have spent most of this visit in the city. They heard about the first worker battalions to be raised from various factories in the city. They were under the command of Colonel Sarayev of the 10th NKVD Rifle Division. The shock of battle proved too much for many in their ranks, so NKVD and Komsomol blocking detachments were used to prevent them running away. Political officers gave the correspondents stories of the determination of their troops.

A soldier shot his comrade who had been carrying a wounded man back from the battlefield and had raised his hands in surrender. After this the soldier brought the wounded man back himself. His father, when saying goodbye to him, had given him a towel his mother had embroidered as a girl and his four crosses from [the First World War].

Night in Stalingrad. Vehicles are waiting at the crossing point. Darkness. Fires are burning in the distance. A batch of reinforcements that has just crossed the Volga is moving slowly up [the steep river bank]. Two soldiers walk past us. I hear one of them say: 'They like an easy life, they hurry to live.'

Grossman used some of these notes as well as material from the previous visit in his article for *Krasnaya Zvezda* which was published on 6 September.

We arrived in Stalingrad soon after an air raid. Fires were still smoking here and there. Our comrade from Stalingrad who came there with us showed us his burned house. 'Here was the children's room,' he says. 'And here stood my bookcases, and I worked in that corner, where the distorted pipes now are. My desk stood there.' One could see the bent skeletons of children's beds under a pile of bricks. The walls of the house were still warm, like a dead man's body which hadn't had time to go cold.

Walls and the colonnade of the Physical Culture Palace are covered with soot after a fire, and two sculptures of naked young men are blindingly white on this velvet-black background. Sleek Siberian cats are sleeping on the windows of empty buildings. Near the statue of Kholzunov, boys are picking up fragments of bombs and antiaircraft shells. On this quiet evening, the pink beautiful sunset looks so melancholy through hundreds of empty eye sockets of windows.

Some people have instantly accustomed themselves to the war. The ferry which transports troops to the city is frequently attacked by enemy fighters and bombers. The crew are eating juicy watermelon slices, looking into the sky now and then. A boy is looking attentively at the float of his fishing angle, dangling his feet outside. An elderly woman is sitting on a little bench knitting a stocking during bursts of machine-gun fire and anti-aircraft guns firing away.

We entered a destroyed house. The inhabitants of the building were having dinner, sitting at tables made from planks of wood and boxes, children were blowing at hot shchi in their bowls.

For the Soviet military authorities, it seemed that the only way to save Stalingrad was to launch attack after attack against the northern flank of XIV Panzer Corps. But the three infantry armies involved, the 1st Guards, the 24th and the 66th, stood little chance, even though they vastly outnumbered their opponents. They were short of ammunition, had hardly any artillery and their ranks consisted mainly of reservists.

Stalin's furious orders urging speed led to total chaos. Divisions became confused as they marched forward from the railhead at Frolovo, north of the Don bend, with no idea of which army they were supposed to join or where they were going. The Luftwaffe strafed and bombed them on the open steppe, while the superiority of German tank-crew training made it an unequal struggle. Grossman, at Dubovka, was close to the forming-up areas for these ill-fated attacks.

Divisions on the move. People's faces. Engineers, artillery, tanks. They are moving day and night. Faces, faces, their seriousness, they are the faces of doomed people.

Before the advance began, Donbass proletarian Lyakhov, soldier from the motorised infantry battalion of a tank brigade, wrote this note to his commanders: 'Let Comrade Stalin know that I will sacrifice my life for the sake of the Motherland, and for him. And I won't regret it even for a second. If I had five lives, I would sacrifice them all for his sake, without hesitating, so dear is this man to me.'

Grossman was interested in the daily grumbles of soldiers. In the following case, a soldier talked about the open steppe, where Luftwaffe pilots could spot field kitchens easily, and then moved on to that other soldierly preoccupation: boots.

'Most men got killed because of kitchens. Corporals "get tanned" by the kitchens, waiting for food. It's usually gone off by the time we get it. I've suffered so much

because of my boots. I've been walking with blood blisters. I took the boots off a dead man because they didn't have any holes, but they were too small for me.'

'We, young soldiers, don't even think of home, it's mostly older soldiers who do. . . A corporal from the 4th Company called Romanov has let us down on the battlefield. We, the young soldiers who are properly brought up and conscientious, we endure all this with patience, but the moods of older soldiers are worse than ever.'

Grossman was particularly taken with Red Army soldier Gromov, an anti-tank rifleman, who at thirty-eight must have appeared ancient to the young conscripts. According to Ortenberg, Grossman spent a week with the anti-tank unit. 'He was not a stranger any more in their family,' he wrote. Ortenberg claimed the credit for the idea of writing about him, perhaps because Grossman's portrait of Gromov was later hailed as a masterpiece, particularly by Ilya Ehrenburg. These were Grossman's notes on what he called Gromov's story:

'When you've hit it, you see a bright flash on the amount. The shot deafens one terribly, one has to open one's mouth. I was lying there, I heard shouts: "They're coming!" My second shot hit the tank. The Germans started screaming terribly. We could hear them clearly. I wasn't scared even a little. My spirits soared. At first, there was some smoke, then crackling and flames. Evtikhov had hit one vehicle. He hit the hull, and how the Fritzes screamed!' (Gromov has light green eyes in a suffering, angry face.) 'The number one carries the anti-tank rifle. The number two carries thirty cartridges for it, a hundred cartridges for [an ordinary] rifle, two anti-tank grenades, and a rifle. What a noise the [anti-tank rifle] makes. The earth trembles from it.'

Our main losses occur because we have to go and get breakfast and dinner ourselves. We can only go and get them at night. There are problems with dishes, we should get hold of buckets.'

We used to lie down during the night and advance during the day. 'The ground's as flat as a tabletop.'

These notes, including Gromov's words, were then refashioned into the piece for *Krasnaya Zvezda*, which so impressed Ehrenburg and others.

When on the march, one's shoulder bone aches like hell from the anti-tank rifle, and the arm becomes numb. It's difficult to jump with the anti-tank rifle and difficult to walk on slippery ground. Its weight slows you down and upsets your balance.

Anti-tank riflemen walk heavily, in broad steps, and seem slightly lame—on the side where the rifle's weight is. [Gromov] was filled with the anger of a difficult man, a man whom the war has taken away from his field, from his izba, and from his wife who had given birth to his children. This was the anger of a doubting Thomas who saw with his own eyes the huge troubles of his people. . . Walls of white and black smoke and grey-yellow dust rose in front of the anti-tank riflemen and behind them. This was what one usually calls 'hell'. . . He was lying on the bottom of the slit trench. The hell was howling with a thousand voices, and Gromov was dozing, stretching his tired legs: a soldier's rest, poor and austere.

> *'I fired at [the tank] again,' [said Gromov]. 'And I saw at once that I'd hit it. It took my breath away. A blue flame ran over the armour, quick like a spark. And I understood at once that my anti-tank shell had got inside and gave off this blue flame. And a little smoke rose. The Germans inside began to scream. I'd never heard people scream this way before, and then immediately there was a crackling inside. It crackled and crackled. The shells had started to explode. And then flames shot out, right into the sky. The tank was done for.'*
>
> *Regimental commander Savinov, a wonderful Russian face. Blue eyes, red tan. There's a dimple from a bullet on his helmet. 'When the bullet hit me,' Savinov said, 'I became drunk and lay for fifteen minutes unconscious. A German had got me drunk.'*

Civilians too were caught up in what was seen by both sides as the key battle of the war.

> *Spies. A twelve-year-old boy who could report on where [German] headquarters had been situated by its signal cables, kitchens and dispatch riders. A woman, to whom the Germans had said: 'If you don't go and don't come back, we are going to shoot your two daughters.'*

Soviet pitilessness more than matched that of the Germans, when it came to forcing their own men into the attack, Stalin's Order No. 227

'Not One Step Back' — included the instruction to each army command to organise 'three to five well-armed [blocking] detachments (up to two hundred men each)' to form a second line to 'combat cowardice' by shooting down any soldier who tried to run away. In the factory district of northern Stalingrad, Grossman came across Colonel S.F. Gorokhov, then commanding the 124th Brigade.

> *After the seventh attack, Gorokhov said to the commander of the blocking detachment: 'Come on, that's enough shooting at their backs. Come on and join the attack.' The commander and his blocking detachment joined the attack, and the Germans were thrown back.*

The defence of Stalingrad was stiffened by the most terrifying discipline. Some 13,500 soldiers were executed during the five-month battle. Most of these were during the earlier days when many men broke. Grossman heard about an 'extraordinary event', which was the official Soviet term for 'betrayal of the Motherland', a very broadly defined crime.

> *An extraordinary event. Sentence. Execution. They undressed him and buried him. At night, he came back to his unit, in his blood stained underwear. They shot him again.*

This may possibly refer to another case, but it is almost exactly what happened in the 45th Rifle Division, when the execution squad from the NKVD Special Department attached to the division failed to kill the condemned man, perhaps because their aim was affected by alcohol. This soldier, like so many others, had been condemned to death for a self-inflicted wound. After shooting him, the execution squad buried him in a nearby shell-hole, but the condemned man dug himself out and returned to his company, only to be executed a second time. Usually, however, the prisoner was forced to undress before being shot so that his uniform could be issued to somebody else without too many discouraging bullet-holes.

A number of Soviet generals did not shrink from hitting even quite senior subordinates, although the striking of soldiers by officers and NCOs had been one of the most hated characteristics of the Tsarist Army.

Conversation of Colonels Shuba and Tarasov with the army commander:

"'What?'"

"'May I say again. . . ?'"

"'What?'"

"'May I say again. . . ?'"

'He hit Shuba in the mouth. I [presumably Tarasov] stood still, drew my tongue in and clenched my teeth, because I was afraid to bite my tongue off or be left with no teeth.'

At this critical moment of the war, Grossman recorded in his notebooks a number of stories about Soviet and military bureaucracy.

Aircraft had been bombing our tanks for three days, and all this time telegrams about it were travelling through different chains of command.

Provisions for an encircled division were to be dropped by parachute, but the quartermaster didn't want to issue the foodstuffs, because there was no one to sign the invoice.

A chief of reconnaissance could not get permission for half a litre of vodka, nor could he get a badly needed piece of silk which cost eighty roubles fifty kopecks.

Information on take-off. Applications for bombing missions.

A plane caught fire. The pilot wanted to save it and didn't bail out by parachute. He brought the burning plane back to the airfield. He was on fire himself. His trousers were burning. The quartermaster, however, refused to issue him with new trousers because the minimum period hadn't elapsed before a replacement could be provided for the old ones. The red tape lasted for several days.

A Yu-53 with a full load of fuel was burning in the clear evening sky. The crew bailed out with their parachutes.

Stalin was beside himself with rage when he heard on 3 September that Stalingrad was encircled on the western bank. For General Yeremenko, the commander-in-chief of the Stalingrad Front, and Nikita Khrushchev, the member of his Military Council and thus chief commissar, the key question was who should be given the responsibility of defending the city itself. The candidate would have to take over the thoroughly demoralised and battered 62nd Army, which was cut off from its neighbour to the south, the 64th Army, on 10 September.

On the following day, 11 September, Yeremenko's headquarters in a complex of tunnels in the Tsaritsa gorge came under direct fire. Grossman's editor, Ortenberg, accompanied by the writer Konstantin Simonov, reached the headquarters that day. They spoke to a 'gloomy' Khrushchev, who found it hard to light a cigarette due to the lack of oxygen in the tunnel. When Ortenberg and Simonov woke the next morning, they found that the headquarters had departed while they slept. Stalin, still in a foul temper, had been forced to agree that Yeremenko must withdraw Stalingrad Front headquarters across the Volga. General Vasily

Chuikov, a tough and thoroughly ruthless commander, was summoned to take command of the 62nd Army left on the west bank. Grossman later interviewed all those involved.

Khrushchev—Tired, white-haired, bloated. Looks perhaps like Kutuzov. Yeremenko—He has been wounded seven times in this war.

Yeremenko claimed the credit for selecting Chuikov.

'*It was I who promoted Chuikov. I knew him, he was never prone to panic. . . I knew Chuikov from peacetime. I used to drub him during manoeuvres. "I know how brave you are," [I told him], "but I don't need that sort of courage. Don't make hasty decisions, as you tend to."*'

According to Chuikov, the interview with Yeremenko and Khrushchev went as follows:

'*Yeremenko and Khrushchev said to me:*

"'You have to save Stalingrad. How do you feel about it?"

"'Yes, sir."

"'No, it isn't enough to obey, what do you think about it?"

"'It means to die. So we will die."'

In his memoirs written during the Khrushchev era, Chuikov recounted the conversation in a slightly different way:

'*Comrade Chuikov,' said Khrushchev, 'how do you interpret your task?*'

'*We will defend the city or die in the attempt,' came Chuikov's reply.*

Yeremenko and Khrushchev looked at him and said that he had understood his mission correctly.

As will be seen later, Grossman became disillusioned by the vanities and jealousies of the Stalingrad commanders after the battle, all of whom felt that their role had been insufficiently appreciated. Yeremenko was quite open in his boasting and his attempts to undermine Khrushchev.

'*I was a corporal during the last war and killed twenty-two Germans. . . Who wants to die? No one is particularly eager. . . I had to take terribly cruel decisions here: "Execute on the spot."*'

'*Khrushchev proposed that we should mine the city. I telephoned Stalin [about it]. "What for?" [Stalin] asked.*

"I am not going to surrender Stalingrad," I said. "I don't want to mine the city."

"'Tell him to fuck off, then," [Stalin replied].'

'*We have held on thanks to our [artillery] fire and thanks to the soldiers. The fortifications were fucking bad.*'

The inadequacy of Stalingrad's defences was just about the only matter on which all the senior officers agreed. Chuikov observed that the barricades could have been pushed over with a truck. Gurov, the chief commissar of the 62nd Army, said that no fortifications had existed, and Krylov, the chief of staff, said they were laughable. 'In the defence of

Stalingrad,' Chuikov said later to Grossman, 'divisional commanders counted on blood more than on barbed wire.'

Chuikov, whom Grossman came to know very well during the course of the war, also liked to expound on his past experience and his role at Stalingrad. 'I commanded a regiment at the age of fifteen,' he said to Grossman of his time in the Russian civil war. 'I was the chief adviser to Chiang Kai-shek,' Chuikov added when talking of 1941. He did not mention that it was a great advantage to have been absent in China during that first disastrous summer of the war.

Chuikov's army was not only exhausted and demoralised. Reduced to fewer than 20,000 men, it was heavily outnumbered and outgunned on the key sector of central Stalingrad, where four German infantry divisions, two panzer divisions and a motorised division attacked from the west towards the Volga. The two key objectives for them were the Mamaev Kurgan, a Tartar mound 102 metres high (and known as Point 102), and the Volga crossing point just beyond Red Square. Chuikov reached this landing stage on the night of 12 September immediately after his appointment as commander of the 62nd Army had been confirmed by Yeremenko and Khrushchev.

By the light from blazing buildings, he made his way to the Mamaev Kurgan where 62nd Army headquarters was temporarily established. The situation was even more desperate than he had feared. 'I see Mamaev Kurgan in my dreams.' Chuikov told Grossman later.

The only unmauled formation under his command was Colonel Sarayev's 10th NKVD Rifle Division, but its units were dispersed and Sarayev, who reported to the NKVD chain of command, was more than reluctant to put his men under Red Army control. Chuikov's commissar, Gurov, was scathing about the NKVD division.

> *The Sarayev division was scattered all over the front, and therefore there was practically no control over it. The Sarayev division did not fulfil its function. It hadn't held its defensive positions, and didn't maintain order in the city.'*

The previous year, no military commander had had the courage to face up to one of Beria's officers. But Chuikov, facing disaster, had no qualms. Evidently, his threat to Sarayev about Stalin's anger if the city fell had the required effect. Sarayev followed orders and placed one of his regiments in front of the vital landing stage, as instructed.

Grossman only discovered later that Chuikov was another commander who used to punch his subordinates when in a foul mood. Chuikov was indeed ruthless, as ready to execute a brigade commander who failed, in his duty as a simple soldier who turned tail in battle, but his own physical bravery was beyond question.

> *'A commander must feel that it is better for him to lose his head than to bow to a German shell. Soldiers notice these things.'*

> *'The first task was to instil in your [subordinate] commanders the idea that the Devil is not so terrible as he is painted.'*

> *'Once you are here, there is no way out. Either you will lose your head or your legs. . . Everyone knew that those who turn and run would be shot on the spot. This was more terrifying than the Germans. . . Well, there is also Russian zeal. We adopted a tactic of counter-attack. We attacked when they became tired of attacking.'*

In his memoirs, Chuikov openly acknowledged that when defending Stalingrad, he had followed the precept that 'Time is Blood'. He had to hold the Germans at all costs and that meant throwing fresh regiments and divisions into the hell of the city as soon as they reached the eastern bank and were ready to be ferried across.

The Sixth Army's major offensive into the city was launched just before dawn on 13 September. Chuikov had not even had time to meet his formation commanders when the German 295th Infantry Division came straight for the Mamaev Kurgan. Two other infantry divisions headed for the main station and the landing stage. Chuikov could only watch events from a slit trench through periscopic binoculars.

That evening, Führer headquarters celebrated the success of the 71st Infantry Division reaching the centre of the city. Stalin heard the same news in the Kremlin when Yeremenko telephoned him and warned that another major attack could be expected the next day. Stalin turned to General Vasilevsky. 'Issue orders immediately for Rodimtsev's 13th Guards Division to cross the Volga and see what else you can send over.' Zhukov, who was also with them, poring over a map of the area, was told to fly down again immediately. Nobody was in any doubt that the moment of crisis had arrived.

Chuikov's army headquarters now found itself in the front line, following the attack on the Mamaev Kurgan the day before. In the early hours they moved south to the tunnels of the Tsaritsa gorge, which Yeremenko and Khrushchev had so recently abandoned. Gurov told Grossman: 'When we were leaving Height 102, we felt that the worst thing of all was uncertainty. We didn't know how all this was going to end.'

The battle on 14 September went badly for the defenders. The German 295th Infantry Division captured the Mamaev Kurgan as Chuikov had feared, but the biggest threat came in the centre of the city, where one of Sarayev's NKVD regiments was thrown into a counter-attack on the main station. It changed hands several times during the day.

The key event, according to the Stalingrad legend, was the crossing of the Volga under fire by General Aleksandr Rodimtsev's 13th Guards Rifle Division. This formation had been hurried down by forced marches. Grossman recreated the march and the arrival on the bank of the Volga from participants.

> The road turned south-west, and soon we began to see maples and willows. Orchards with low apple trees in them stretched around us. And as the division was approaching the Volga, we saw a tall, dark cloud. One couldn't possible mistake it for dust. It was sinister, quick, light, and black as death: that was the smoke from burning oil-storage tanks rising over the northern part of the city. Big arrows nailed to the trunks of trees said 'Crossing'. They pointed towards the Volga … The division couldn't wait until night to cross the river. Men were hastily unloading crates of weapons and ammunition, and sugar and sausage.

> Barges were rocking on the waves, and men from the rifle division felt frightened because the enemy was everywhere, in the sky, on the opposite bank, but they had to encounter him without the comfort of solid earth under their feet. The air was unbearably transparent, the blue sky was unbearably clear, the sun seemed relentlessly bright and the flowing flat water seemed so tricky and unreliable. And no one felt happy about the clarity of the air, about the coolness of the river in the nostrils, about the tender and moist breath of the Volga touching their inflamed eyes. Men on the barges, ferries and motor boats were silent. Oh, why isn't there that suffocating and thick dust over the river? Why is the bluish smoke of the smoke-screen canisters so transparent and fine? Every head was turning from side to side in anxiety. Everyone was glancing at the sky.

> 'He's diving, the louse!' someone shouted.

Suddenly, a tall and thin bluish-white column of water sprang up about fifty metres from the barge. Immediately after it another column grew and collapsed even closer, and then a third one. Bombs were exploding on the surface of the water, and the Volga was covered with lacerated foamy wounds; shells began to hit the sides of the barge. Injured men would cry out softly, as if trying to conceal the fact of being wounded. By then, rifle bullets had already started whistling over the water.

There was one terrible moment when a large calibre shell hit the side of a small ferry. There was a flash of flame, dark smoke enveloped the ferry, an explosion was heard, and immediately afterwards, a drawling scream as if born from this thunder. Thousands of people saw immediately the green helmets of the men swimming among the wreckage of wood rocking on the surface of water.

Chuikov told Rodimtsev, who crossed to the west bank during the afternoon of 14 September to receive his orders, that the situation was so desperate that his men should leave behind all their heavy equipment, bringing just grenades and personal weapons. Rodimtsev described it to Grossman at a later stage in the battle.

'We began the crossing at 1700 hours on 14 September, preparing weapons as we went along. One barge was destroyed [by bombing] during the crossing; forty-one men were killed and twenty survived.'

Much has been written of the 13th Guards Rifle Division charging up the steep bank of the Volga and straight at the Germans, who had advanced to within two hundred metres of the river's edge. But Grossman heard about a special mission assigned to a small group of six men from the division.

Sapper Lieutenant Chermakov, Sergeants Dubovy and Bugaev, and Red Army soldiers Klimenko, Zhukov and Messereshvili carried out the task of blowing up a sealed building of the State Bank. Each carried 25kg of explosives. They made it to the bank and blew it up.

Inevitably, there was a less heroic aspect to the crossing of the river, which Soviet official accounts always suppressed.

Seven Uzbeks were guilty of self-inflicted wounds. They were all shot.

The exploits of the 13th Guards Rifle Division attracted a great deal of attention in the Soviet and international press. Rodimtsev, to Chuikov's furious jealousy, became a world-famous hero. Grossman, however, was more interested in the bravery of the soldiers and junior officers than in the squabbles of the commanders. He persuaded Rodimtsev's headquarters to let him have the report below, and he carried it with him in his fields bag all through the war. He mentioned it in his essay 'Tsaritsyn-Stalingrad' and included it in the novel *For a Just Cause*.

[Report]

Time: 11.30 hours, 20.9.42

To: Guards Senior Lieutenant Fedoseev (Commander of the Ist Battalion)

May I report to you, the situation is as follows: the enemy is trying to encircle my company, to send sub-machine-gunners round to our rear. But all their efforts have so far failed in spite of their superior strength. Our soldiers and officers are displaying courage and heroism in the face of the fascist jackals. The Fritzes won't succeed until they've stepped over my corpse. Guards soldiers do not retreat. Soldiers and officers may die like heroes, but the enemy mustn't be allowed to break our defence. Let the whole country learn about the 3rd Rifle Company of the 13th Guards Division. While the company commander is alive, not a single whore will break through. They might break though if the company commander is killed or heavily wounded. The commander of the 3rd Company is under stress and unwell physically himself, deafened and weak. He gets vertigo, is falling off his feet, his nose bleeds. In spite of all the hardships, the Guards, namely the 3rd and 2nd Companies, will not retreat. We will die like heroes for Stalin's city. Let the Soviet land be the [enemy's] grave. Commander of the 3rd Company Kolaganov has himself killed two Fritz machine-gunners and took from them a machine gun and documents which he has presented to the HQ of the battalion. [Signed] Kolaganov

The 62nd Army, continually outnumbered, held on as best it could within an ever diminishing perimeter along the west bank. Rodimtsev told Grossman: 'We operated with no reserves. A thin defence line, that was all we had.'

Yeremenko told him: 'I was sweating, [The Germans] were pressing hard, and we had positioned our troops stupidly. I felt hot all the time, [even though] I am a very healthy man. We were just feeding soldiers [into the battle]. That was it.'

Gurov, the chief commissar of the 62nd Army, pointed out: 'There were days when we evacuated 2,000–3,000 injured men.'

Krylov, the chief of staff of the 62nd Army, remarked on the German conduct of the battle.

'They rely on the massive use of fire-power, to stunning effect. Their powerful materiel is in inverse proportion to the potential of German infantry. German middle-rank commanders completely lack initiative.

'The first days of September were particularly hard, the beginning of chaos. In the evenings I could pull myself together in order to give instructions to the troops. During the day, we just counted down minutes till the evening.'

The Germans knew only too well that they needed to break the 62nd Army's life lines across the Volga, using artillery as well as the Luftwaffe. That was why there were so many struggles back and forth to secure the Mamaev Kurgan, the one hill from which direct fire could be concentrated on the landing stages. The river-transport troops, many of them Volga boatmen and fishermen, faced dangers as great as those of the *frontoviki* on the west bank.

The officer in charge of the crossing, Lieutenant Colonel Puzyrevsky, has been here about two weeks. His predecessor, Captain Eziev, a Chechen, was killed by a bomb on a barge. Perminov, the military commander, has been here for fifty-seven days. Deputy Battalion Commander Ilin has been taken away by air, heavily wounded. Smerechinsky—killed—was the chief of the crossing before Eziev. The battalion commander, who set up the Volga crossing, was killed by a bomb splinter. Sholom Akselrod, commander of the technical platoon, was killed on a barge by a mine. Politruk Samotorkin was wounded by a mine. Politruk Ishkin's leg was torn off by a shell.

For the reinforcements assembling on the west bank opposite, the 1,300 metres of open water was enough to break anyone's nerve. But Chuikov, with his characteristically brutal humour, observed that the crossing was just the start.

'Approaching this place, soldiers used to say: "We are entering hell." And after spending one or two days here, they said: "No, this isn't hell, this is ten times worse than hell." [It produced] a wild anger, an inhuman anger, towards Germans. [Some Red Army soldiers] were escorting a prisoner, but he never reached his destination. The poor chap died from fear. "Would you like to drink some water from the Volga?" [they asked], and they rammed his face into the water ten or twelve times.'

Suffering seemed to have become a universal fate. Towards the end of the month, Grossman received a letter from his wife, Olga Mikhailovna, in which she recounted the death of her son, Misha, who had been killed by a bomb. He wrote back in a clumsy attempt to mitigate her despair.

My own one, my good one. Today I received your letter which someone had brought from Moscow. It grieved me deeply. Don't let your spirits sink, Lyusenka. Don't give way to despair. There is so much sorrow around us. I see so much of it. I've seen mothers who have lost three sons and a husband in this war, I've seen wives who've lost husbands and children, I've seen women whose little children have been killed in a bombing raid, and all these people don't give way to despair. They work, they look forward to victory, they don't lose their spirits. And in what hard conditions they have to survive! Be strong, too, my darling, hold on. . . You've got me and Fedya, you have love and your life has a meaning.

'I've been recommended for the Order of the Red Star for the second time, but to no effect so far, just as before. I've got this letter taken from a dead soldier; it's written in a child's scribble. There are the following words at the end: 'I miss you very much. Please come and visit, I so want to see you, if only for one hour. I am writing this, and tears are pouring. Daddy, please come and visit.'

He also wrote to their old German-speaking nanny, Zhenni Genrikhovna. Henrichson, whom many years later he put into his novel *Life and Fate*.

You already know about our terrible grief: the death of Misha. Sorrow has come to our family too, Zhenni Genrikhovna. Please write to me at my new address: 28 Field Post, 1st Unit, V.S. Grossman (don't mention my position in the address). Have you heard from Papa? Where is he now? I don't know at what address to write to him.

Grossman at this point had no idea that his nephew, Yura Benash, a young lieutenant in Stalingrad who had been trying to contact him having read his articles, had been killed in the fighting.

Survival at Auschwitz

Primo Levi

Iwas captured by the Fascist Militia on 13 December 1943. I was twenty-four, with little wisdom, no experience and a decided tendency — encouraged by the life of segregation forced on me for the previous four years by the racial laws — to live in an unrealistic world of my own, a world inhabited by civilized Cartesian phantoms, by sincere male and bloodless female friendships. I cultivated a moderate and abstract sense of rebellion.

It had been by no means easy to flee into the mountains and to help set up what, both in my opinion and in that of friends little more experienced than myself, should have become a partisan band affiliated with the Resistance movement *Justice and Liberty*. Contacts, arms, money and the experience needed to acquire them were all missing. We lacked capable men, and instead we were swamped by a deluge of outcasts, in good or bad faith, who came from the plain in search of a non-existent military or political organization, of arms, or merely of protection, a hiding place, a fire, a pair of shoes.

At that time I had not yet been taught the doctrine I was later to learn so hurriedly in the Lager: that man is bound to pursue his own ends by all possible means, while he who errs but once pays dearly. So that I can only consider the following sequence of events justified. Three Fascist Militia companies, which had set out in the night to surprise a much more powerful and dangerous band than ours, broke into our refuge one spectral snowy dawn and took me down to the valley as a suspect person.

During the interrogations that followed, I preferred to admit my status of 'Italian citizen of Jewish race.' I felt that otherwise I would be unable to justify my presence in places too secluded even for an evacuee; while I believed (wrongly as was subsequently seen) that the admission of my political activity would have meant torture and certain death. As a Jew, I was sent to Fossoli, near Modena, where a vast detention camp, originally meant for English and American prisoners-of-war, collected all the numerous categories of people not approved of by the new-born Fascist Republic.

At the moment of my arrival, that is, at the end of January 1944, there were about one hundred and fifty Italian Jews in the camp, but within a few weeks their number rose to over six hundred. For the most part they consisted of entire families captured by the Fascists or Nazis through their imprudence or following secret accusations. A few had given themselves up spontaneously, reduced to desperation by the vagabond life, or because they lacked the means to survive, or to avoid separation from a captured relation, or even — absurdly — 'to be in conformity with the law.' There were also about a hundred Jugoslavian military interness and a few other foreigners who were politically suspect.

The arrival of a squad of German SS men should have made even the optimists doubtful; but we still managed to interpret the novelty in various ways without drawing the most obvious conclusions. Thus, despite everything, the announcement of the deportation caught us all unawares.

On 20 February, the Germans had inspected the camp with care and had publicly and loudly upbraided the Italian commissar for the defective organization of the kitchen service and for the scarce amount of wood distribution for heating; they even said that an infirmary would soon be opened. But on the morning of the 21st we learned that on the following day the Jews would be leaving. All the Jews, without exception. Even the children, even the old, even the ill. Our destination? Nobody knew. We should be prepared for a fortnight of travel. For every person missing at the roll-call, ten would be shot.

Only a minority of ingenuous and deluded souls continued to hope; we others had often spoken with the Polish and Croat refugees and we knew what departure meant.

For people condemned to death, tradition prescribes an austere ceremony, calculated to emphasize that all passions and anger have died down, and that the act of justice represents only a sad duty towards society which moves even the executioner to pity for the victim. Thus the condemned man is shielded from all external cares, he is granted solitude and, should he want it, spiritual comfort; in short, care is taken that he should feel around him neither hatred nor arbitrariness, only necessity and justice, and by means of punishment, pardon.

But to us this was not granted, for we were many and time was short. And in any case, what had we to repent, for what crime did we need pardon? The Italian commissar accordingly decreed that all services should continue to function until the final notice: the kitchens remained open, the corvées for cleaning worked as usual, and even the teachers of the little school gave lessons until the evening, as on other days. But that evening the children were given no homework.

And night came, and it was such a night that one knew that human eyes would not witness it and survive. Everyone felt this: not one of the guards, neither Italian nor German, had the courage to come and see what men do when they know they have to die.

All took leave from life in the manner which most suited them. Some praying, some deliberately drunk, others lustfully intoxicated for the last time. But the mothers stayed up to prepare the food for the journey with tender care, and washed their children and packed the luggage; and at dawn the barbed wire was full of children's washing hung out in the wind to dry. Nor did they forget the diapers, the toys, the cushions and the hundred other small things which mothers remember and which children always need. Would you not do the same? If you and your child were going to be killed tomorrow, would you not give him to eat today?

. . . .

Next to me, crushed against me for the whole journey, there had been a woman. We had known each other for many years, and the misfortune had struck us together, but we knew little of each other. Now, in the hour of decision, we said to each other things that are never said among the living. We said farewell and it was short; everybody said farewell to life through his neighbour. We had no more fear.

The climax came suddenly. The door opened with a crash, and the dark echoed with outlandish orders in that curt, barbaric barking of Germans in command which seems to give vent to a millennial anger. A vast platform appeared before us, lit up by reflectors. A little beyond it, a row of lorries. Then everything was silent again. Someone translated: we had to climb down with our luggage and deposit it alongside the train. In a moment the platform was swarming with shadows. But we were afraid to break that silence: everyone busied himself with his luggage, searched for someone else, called to somebody, but timidly, in a whisper.

A dozen SS men stood around, legs akimbo, with an indifferent air. At a certain moment they moved among us, and in a subdued tone of voice, with faces of stone, began to interrogate us rapidly, one by one, in bad Italian. They did not interrogate everybody, only a few: 'How old? Healthy or ill?' And on the basis of the reply they pointed in two different directions.

Everything was as silent as an aquarium, or as in certain dream sequences. We had expected something more apocalyptic: they seemed simple police agents. It was disconcerting and disarming. Someone dared to ask for his luggage: they replied, 'luggage afterwards'. Someone else did not want to leave his wife: they said, 'together again afterwards'. Many mothers did not want to be separated from their children: they said 'good, good, stay with child'. They behaved with the calm assurance of people doing their normal duty of every day. But Renzo stayed an instant too long to say good-bye to Francesca, his fiancée, and with a single blow they knocked him to the ground. It was their everyday duty.

In less than ten minutes all the fit men had been collected together in a group. What happened to the others, to the women, to the children, to the old men, we could establish neither then nor later: the night swallowed them up, purely and simply. Today, however, we know that in that rapid and summary choice each one of us had been judged capable or not of working usefully for the Reich; we know that of our convoy no more than ninety-six men and twenty-nine women entered the respective camps of Monowitz-Buna and Birkenau, and that of all the others, more than five hundred in number, not one was living two days later. We also know that not even this tenuous priciple of discrimination between fit and unfit was always followed, and that later the simpler method was often adopted of merely opening both the doors of the wagon without warning or instructions to the new arrivals. Those who by chance climbed down on one side of the convoy entered the camp; the others went to the gas chamber.

This is the reason why three-year-old Emilia died: the historical necessity of killing the children of Jews was self-demonstrative to the Germans. Emilia, daughter of Aldo Levi of Milan, was a curious, ambitious, cheerful, intelligent child; her parents had succeeded in washing her during the journey in the packed car in a tub with tepid water which the degenerate German engineer had allowed them to draw from the engine that was dragging us all to death.

Thus, in an instant, our women, our parents, our children disappeared. We saw them for a short while as an obscure mass at the other end of the platform; then we saw nothing more.

Instead, two groups of strange individuals emerged into the light of the lamps. They walked in squads, in rows of three, with an odd, embarrassed step, head dangling in front, arms rigid. On their heads they wore comic berets and were all dressed in long striped overcoats, which even by night and from a distance looked filthy and in rags. They walked in a large circle around us, never drawing near, and in silence began to busy themselves with our luggage and to climb in and out of the empty wagons.

We looked at each other without a word. It was all incomprehensible and mad, but one thing we had understood. This was the metamorphosis that awaited us. Tomorrow we would be like them.

Without knowing how I found myself loaded on to a lorry with thirty others; the lorry sped into the night at full speed. It was covered and we could not see outside, but by the shaking we could tell that the road had many curves and bumps. Are we unguarded? Throw ourselves down? It is too late, too late, we are all 'down'. In any case we are soon aware that we are not without guard. He is a strange guard, a German soldier bristling with arms. We do not see him because of the thick darkness, but we feel the hard contact every time that a lurch of the lorry throws us all in a heap. At a certain point he switches on a pocket torch and instead of shouting threats of damnation at us, he asks us courteously, one by one, in German and in pidgin language, if we have any money or watches to give him, seeing that they will not be useful to us any more. This is no order, no regulation: it is obvious that it is a small private initiative of our Charon. The matter stirs us to anger and laughter and brings relief.

. . . .

Ka-Be is the abbreviation of Krankenbau, the infirmary. There are eight huts, exactly like the others in the camp, but separated by a wire fence. They permanently hold a tenth of the population of the camp, but there are few who stay there longer than two weeks and none more than two months: with-in these limits they are held to die or be cured. Those who show signs of improvement are cured in Ka-Be, those who seem to get worse are sent from Ka-Be to the gas chambers. All this because we, fortunately, belong to the category of 'economically useful Jews'.

. . . .

Some more hours pass before all the inmates are seen, are given a shirt and their details taken. I, as usual, am the last. Someone in a brand-new striped suit asks me where I was born, what profession I practised 'as a civilian', if I had children, what diseases I had had, a whole series of questions. What use could they be? Is this a complicated rehearsal to make fools of us? Could this be the hospital? They make us stand naked and ask us questions.

Finally the door is opened, even for me, and I can enter the dormitory.

Here as everywhere there are bunks on three levels, in three rows throughout the hut, separated by two narrow corridors. The bunks are 150, the patients 250; so there are two in almost all the bunks. The patients in the upper bunks, squashed against the ceiling, can hardly sit up; they lean out, curious to see the new arrivals of today. It is the most interesting moment of the day, for one always finds some acquaintances. I am assigned bunk number 10 — a miracle! It is empty! I stretch myself out with delight, it is the first time since I entered the camp that I have a bunk all to myself. Despite my hunger, within ten minutes I am asleep.

The life of Ka-Be is a life of limbo. The material discomforts are relatively few, apart from hunger and the inherent pains of illness. It is not cold, there is no work to do, and unless you commit some grave fault, you are not beaten.

The reveille is at 4 a.m., even for the patients. One has to make one's bed and wash, but there is not much hurry and little severity. The bread is distributed at half past five, and one can cut it comfortably into thin slices and eat it lying down in complete peace; then one can fall asleep again until the soup is distributed at midday. Until about 4 p.m. it is *Mittagsruhe*, afternoon rest-time; then there is often the medical visit and dispensing of medicines, and one has to climb down from the bunks, take off one's shirt and file past the doctor. The evening ration is also served in bed, after which, at 9 p.m., all the lights are turned off except for the shaded lamp of the nightguard, and there is silence.

... And for the first time since I entered the camp the reveille catches me in a deep sleep and its ringing is a return from nothingness. As the bread is distributed one can hear, far from the windows, in the dark air, the band beginning to play: the healthy comrades are leaving in squads for work.

One cannot hear the music well from Ka-Be. The beating of the big drums and the cymbals reach us continuously and monotonously, but on this weft the musical phrases weave a pattern only intermittently, according to the caprices of the wind. We all look at each other from our beds, because we all feel that this music is infernal.

The tunes are few, a dozen, the same ones every day, morning and evening: marches and popular songs dear to every German. They lie engraven on our minds and will be the last thing in Lager that we shall forget: they are the voice of the Lager, the perceptible expression of its geometrical madness, of the resolution of others to annihilate us first as men in order to kill us more slowly afterwards.

When this music plays we know that our comrades, out in the fog, are marching like automatons; their souls are dead and the music drives them, like the wind drives dead leaves, and takes the place of their wills. There is no longer any will: every beat of the drum becomes a step, a reflected contraction of exhausted muscles. The Germans have succeeded in this. They are ten thousand and they are a single grey machine; they are exactly determined; they do not think and they do not desire, they walk.

At the departure and the return march the SS are never lacking. Who could deny them their right to watch this choreography of their creation, the dance of dead men, squad after squad, leaving the fog to enter the fog? What more concrete proof of their victory?

Even those in Ka-Be recognize this departure and return from work, the hypnosis of the interminable rhythm, which kills thought and deadens pain; they have experienced it themselves and they will experience it again. But one had to escape from the enchantment, to hear the music from outside, as happened in Ka-Be, and as we think back now after the liberation and the rebirth, without obeying it, without enduring it, to understand what it was, for what meditated reason the Germans created this monstrous rite, and why even today, when we happen to remember some of those innocent songs, our blood freezes in our veins and we become aware that to escape from Auschwitz was no small fortune.

I have two neighbours in the adjoining bunk. They lie down all day and all night, side by side, skin against skin, crossed like the Pisces of the zodiac, so that each has the feet of the other beside his head.

One is Walter Bonn, a Dutchman, civilized and quite well mannered. He sees that I have nothing with which to cut my bread and loans me his knife, and then offers to sell it to me for half a ration of bread. I discuss the price and then turn it down, as I think that I will always find someone to lend me one here in Ka-Be, while outside it only costs a third of a ration. Walter is by no means less courteous because of this, and at midday, after eating his soup, he cleans his spoon with his mouth (which is a good rule before loaning it, so as to clean it and not to leave waste any traces of soup which may still be there) and spontaneously offers me it.

'What are you suffering from, Walter?'

'*Körperschwäche*', organic decay. The worst disease: it cannot be cured, and it is very dangerous to enter Ka-Be with such a diagnosis. If it had not been for the oedema of his ankles (and he shows me it) which binders him from marching to work, he would have been very cautious about reporting ill.

I still have quite confused ideas about this kind of danger. Everybody speaks about it indirectly, by allusions, and when I ask some question they look at me and fall silent.

Is it true what one hears of selections, of gas, of crematoriums?

Crematoriums. The other one, Walter's neighbour, wakes up startled and sits up: who is talking about the crematorium? what is happening? cannot a sleeping person be left in peace? He is a Polish Jew, albino, with an emaciated and good-natured face, no longer young. His name is Schmulek, he is a smith. Walter tells him briefly.

So, '*der Italeyner*' does not believe in selections. Schmulek wants to speak German but speaks Yiddish; I understand him with difficulty, only because he wants to be understood. He silences Walter with a sign, he will see about persuading me:

'Show me your number: you are 174517. This numbering began eighteen months ago and applies to Auschwitz and the dependent camps. There are now ten thousand of us here at Buna-Monowitz; perhaps thirty thousand between Auschwitz and Birkenau. *Wo sind die Andere?* Where are the others?'

'Perhaps transferred to other camps?' I suggest.

Schmulek shakes his head, he turns to Walter.

'*Er will nix verstayen,*' he does not want to understand.

But destiny ordained that I was soon to understand, and at the expense of Schmulek himself. That evening the door of the hut opened, a voice shouted '*Achtung!*' and every sound died out to give way to a leaden silence.

Two SS men enter (one of them has many chevrons, perhaps he is an officer?). One can hear their steps in the hut as if it was empty; they speak to the chief doctor, and he shows them a register, pointing here and there. The officer notes down in a book. Schmulek touches my knee:

'*Pass' auf, pass' auf,*' keep your eyes open.

The officer, followed by the doctor, walks around in silence, nonchalantly, between the bunks; he has a switch in his hand, and flicks at the edge of a blanket hanging down from a top bunk, the patient hurries to adjust it.

One has a yellow face; the officer pulls away his blankets, he starts back, the officer touches his belly, says, '*Gut, gut,*' and moves on.

Now he is looking at Schmulek; he brings out the book, checks the number of the bed and the number of the tattoo. I see it all clearly from above: he has drawn a cross beside Schmulek's number. Then he moves on.

I now look at Schmulek and behind him I see Walter's eyes, so I ask no questions.

The day after, in place of the usual group of patients who have recovered, two distinct groups are led out. The first have been shaved and sheared and have had a shower. The second left as they are, with long hair and without being treated, without a shower. Nobody said good-bye to the latter, nobody gave them messages for healthy comrades.

Schmulek formed part of this group.

In this discreet and composed manner, without display or anger, massacre moves through the huts of Ka-Be every day, touching here and there. When Schmulek left, he gave me his spoon and knife; Walter and I avoided looking at each other and remained silent for a long time. Then Walter asked me how I manage to keep my ration of bread so long, and explained to me that he usually cuts his bread lengthwise to have longer slices in order to smear on the margarine more easily.

Walter explains many things to me: *Schonungsblock* means the rest hut, where there are only the less serious patients or convalescents, or those not requiring attention. Among them, at least fifty more or less serious dysentery patients.

These are checked every third day. They are placed in a line along the corridor. At the end there are two tin-plate pots, and the nurse with a register, watch and pencil. Two at a time, the patients present themselves and have to show, on the spot and at once, that they still have diarrhoea; to prove it, they are given exactly one minute. After which, they show the result to the nurse who looks at it and judges. They wash the pots quickly in a wash-tub near by and the next two take over.

Of those waiting, some are contorted in the pain of keeping in their precious evidence another ten, another twenty minutes; others, without resources at the moment, strain veins and muscles in a contrary effort. The nurse watches, impassive, chewing his pencil, one eye on the watch, one eye on the specimens gradually presented him. In doubtful cases, he leaves with the pot to show it to the doctor.

I receive an unexpected visit: it is Piero Sonnino, my friend from Rome. 'Have you seen how I have fixed it?' Piero has mild enteritis, has been here for twenty days, and is quite happy, rested and growing fatter; he could not care less about the selections and has decided to stay in Ka-Be until the end of the winter, at all costs. His method consists of placing himself in line behind some authentic dysentery patient who offers a guarantee of success; when it is his turn he asks for his collaboration (to be rewarded with soup or bread), and if the latter agrees, and the nurse has a moment of inattention, he switches over the pots in the middle of the crowd, and the deed is done. Piero knows what he is risking, but it has gone well so far.

But life in Ka-Be is not this. It is not the crucial moments of the selections, it is not the grotesque episodes of the diarrhoea and lice controls, it is not even the illnesses.

Ka-Be is the Lager without its physical discomforts. So that, whoever still has some seeds of conscience, feels his conscience re-awaken; and in the long empty days, one speaks of other things than hunger and work and one begins to consider what they have made us become, how much they have taken away from us, what this life is. In this Ka-Be, an enclosure of relative peace, we have learnt that our personality is fragile, that it is much more in danger than our life; and the old wise ones, instead of warning us 'remember that you must die', would have done much better to remind us of this great danger that threatens us. If from inside the Lager, a message could have seeped out to free men, it would have been this: take care not to suffer in your own homes what is inflicted on us here.

When one works, one suffers and there is no time to think: our homes are less than a memory. But here the time is ours: from bunk to bunk, despite the prohibition, we exchange visits and we talk and we talk. The wooden hut, crammed with suffering humanity, is full of words, memories and of another pain. 'Heimweh' the Germans call this pain; it is a beautiful word, it means 'longing for one's home'.

We know where we come from; the memories of the world outside crowd our sleeping and our waking hours, we become aware, with amazement, that we have forgotten nothing, every memory evoked rises in front of us painfully clear.

But where we are going we do not know. Will we perhaps be able to survive the illnesses and escape the selections, perhaps even resist the work and hunger which wear us out — but then, afterwards? Here, momentarily far away from the curses and the blows, we can re-enter into ourselves and meditate, and then it becomes clear that we will not return. We travelled here in the sealed wagons; we saw our women and our children leave towards nothingness; we, transformed into slaves, have marched a hundred times backwards and forwards to our silent labours, killed in our spirit long before our anonymous death. No one must leave here and so carry to the world, together with the sign impressed on his skin, the evil tidings of what man's presumption made of man in Auschwitz.

· · · ·

The Story of Ten Days

Already for some months now the distant booming of the Russian guns had been heard at intervals when, on 11 January 1945, I fell ill of scarlet fever and was once more sent into Ka-Be. 'Infektionsabteilung': it meant a small room, really quite clean, with ten bunks on two levels, a wardrobe, three stools and a closet seat with the pail for corporal needs. All in a space of three yards by five.

It was difficult to climb to the upper bunks as there was no ladder; so, when a patient got worse he was transferred to the lower bunks.

When I was admitted I was the thirteenth in the room. Four of the others — two French political prisoners and two young Hungarian Jews — had scarlet fever; there were three with diphtheria, two with typhus, while one suffered from a repellent facial erysipelas. The other two had more than one illness and were incredibly wasted away.

I had a high fever. I was lucky enough to have a bunk entirely to myself: I lay down with relief knowing that I had the right to forty days' isolation and therefore of rest, while I felt myself still sufficiently strong to fear neither the consequences of scarlet fever nor the selections.

Thanks to my by-now long experience of camp life I managed to bring with me all my personal belongings: a belt of interlaced electric wire, the knife-spoon, a needle with three needlefuls, five buttons and last of all eighteen flints which I had stolen from the Laboratory. From each of these, shaping them patiently with a knife, it was possible to make three smaller flints, just the right gauge for a normal cigarette lighter. They were valued at six or seven rations of bread.

I enjoyed four peaceful days. Outside it was snowing and very cold, but the room was heated. I was given strong doses of sulpha drugs, I suffered from an intense feeling of sickness and was hardly able to eat; I did not want to talk.

The two Frenchmen with scarlet fever were quite pleasant. They were provincials from the Vosges who had entered the camp only a few days before with a large convoy of civilians swept up by the Germans in their retreat from Lorraine. The elder one was named Arthur, a peasant, small and thin. The other, his bed-companion, was Charles, a school teacher, thirty-two years old; instead of a shirt he had been given a summer vest, ridiculously short.

On the fifth day the barber came. He was a Greek from Salonica: he spoke only the beautiful Spanish of his people, but understood some words of all the languages spoken in the camp. He was called Askenazi and had been in the camp for almost three years. I do not know how he managed to get the post of *Frisör* of Ka-Be: he spoke neither German nor Polish, nor was he in fact excessively brutal. Before he entered, I heard him speaking excitedly for a long time in the corridor with one of the doctors, a compatriot of his. He seemed to have an unusual look on his face, but as the expressions of the Levantines are different from ours, I could not tell whether he was afraid or happy or merely upset. He knew me, or at least knew that I was Italian.

When it was my turn I climbed down laboriously from the bunk. I asked him in Italian if there was anything new: he stopped shaving me, winked in a serious and allusive manner, pointed to the window with his chin, and then made a sweeping gesture with his hand towards the west.

'*Morgen, alle Kamarad weg.*'

He looked at me for a moment with his eyes wide-open, as if waiting for a reaction, and then he added: '*todos, todos*' and returned to his work. He knew about my flints and shaved me with a certain gentleness.

The news excited no direct emotion in me. Already for many months I had no longer felt any pain, joy or fear, except in that detached and distant manner characteristic of the Lager, which might be described as conditional: if I still had my former sensitivity, I thought, this would be an extremely moving moment.

My ideas were perfectly clear; for a long time now Alberto and I had foreseen the dangers which would accompany the evacuation of the camp and the liberation. As for the rest, Askenazi's news was merely a confirmation of rumours which had been circulating for some days: that the Russians were at Censtochowa, sixty miles to the north; that they were at Zakopane, sixty miles to the south; that at Buna the Germans were already preparing the sabotage mines.

I looked at the faces of my comrades one by one: it was clearly useless to discuss it with any of them. They would have replied: 'Well?' and it would all have finished there. The French were different, they were still fresh.

'Did you hear?' I said to them. 'Tomorrow they are going to evacuate the camp.'

They overwhelmed me with questions. 'Where to? On foot? ... The ill ones as well? Those who cannot walk?' They knew that I was an old prisoner and that I understood German, and deduced that I knew much more about the matter than I wanted to admit.

I did not know anything more: I told them so but they continued to ask questions. How stupid of them! But of course, they had only been in the Lager for a week and had not yet learnt that one did not ask questions.

In the afternoon the Greek doctor came. He said that all patients able to walk would be given shoes and clothes and would leave the following day with the healthy ones on a twelve mile march. The others would remain in Ka-Be with assistants to be chosen from the patients least ill.

The doctor was unusually cheerful, he seemed drunk. I knew him: he was a cultured, intelligent man, egoistic and calculating. He added that everyone, without distinction, would receive a triple ration of bread, at which the patients visibly cheered up. We asked him what would happen to us. He replied that probably the Germans would leave us to our fate: no, he did not think that they would kill us. He made no effort to hide the fact that he thought otherwise. His very cheerfulness boded ill.

He was already equipped for the march. He had hardly gone out when the two Hungarian boys began to speak excitedly to each other. They were in an advanced state of convalescence but extremely wasted away. It was obvious that they were afraid to stay with the patients and were deciding to go with the healthy ones. It was not a question of reasoning: I would probably also have followed the instinct of the flock if I had not felt so weak; fear is supremely contagious, and its immediate reaction is to make one try to run away.

Outside the hut the camp sounded unusually excited. One of the two Hungarians got up, went out and returned half an hour later laden with filthy rags. He must have taken them from the store-house of clothes still to be disinfected. He and his comrade dressed feverishly, putting on rag after rag. One could see that they were in a hurry to have the matter over with before the fear itself made them hesitate. It was crazy of them to think of walking even for one hour, weak as they were, especially in the snow with those broken-down shoes found at the last moment. I tried to explain, but they looked at me without replying. Their eyes were like those of terrified cattle.

Just for a moment it flashed through my mind that they might even be right. They climbed awkwardly out of the window; I saw them, shapeless bundles, lurching into the night. They did not return; I learnt much later that, unable to continue, they had been killed by the SS a few hours after the beginning of the march.

It was obvious that I, too, needed a pair of shoes. But it took me an hour to overcome the feeling of sickness, fever and inertia. I found a pair in the corridor. (The healthy prisoners had ransacked the deposit of patients' shoes and had taken the best ones; those remaining, with split soles and unpaired, lay all over the place.) Just then I met Kosman, the Alsatian. As a civilian he had been a Reuter correspondent at Clermont Ferrand; he also was excited and euphoric. He said: 'If you return before me, write to the mayor of Metz that I am about to come back.'

Kosman was notorious for his acquaintances among the Prominents, so his optimism seemed a good sign and I used it to justify my inertia to myself; I hid the shoes and returned to bed.

Late that night the Greek doctor returned with a rucksack on his shoulders and a woollen hood. He threw a French novel on my bed. 'Keep it, read it, Italian. You can give it back to me when we meet again.' Even today I hate him for those words. He knew that we were doomed.

And then finally Alberto came, defying the prohibition, to say good-bye to me from the window. We were inseparable: we were 'the two Italians' and foreigners even mistook our names. For six months we had shared a bunk and every scrap of food 'organized' in excess of the ration; but he had had scarlet fever as child and I was unable to infect him. So he left and I remained. We said good-bye, not many words were needed, we had already discussed our affairs countless times. We did not think we would be separated for very long. He had found a sturdy pair of leather shoes in a reasonable condition: he was one of those fellows who immediately find everything they need.

He also was cheerful and confident, as were all those who were leaving. It was understandable: something great and new was about to happen; we could finally feel a force around us which was not of Germany; we could concretely feel the impending collapse of that hated world of ours. At any rate, the healthy ones who, despite all their tiredness and hunger, were still able to move, could feel this. But it is obvious that whoever is too weak, or naked or barefoot, thinks and feels in a different way, and what dominated our thoughts was the paralysing sensation of being totally helpless in the hands of fate.

All the healthy prisoners (except a few prudent ones who at the last moment undressed and hid themselves in the hospital beds) left during the night of 18 January 1945. They must have been about twenty thousand, coming from different camps. Almost in their entirety they vanished during the evacuation march: Alberto was among them. Perhaps someone will write their story one day.

So we remained in our bunks, alone with our illnesses, and with our inertia stronger than fear.

In the whole Ka-Be we numbered perhaps eight hundred. In our room there were eleven of us, each in his own bunk, except for Charles and Arthur who slept together. The rhythm of the great machine of the Lager was extinguished. For us began the ten days outside both world and time.

. . . .

26 January

We lay in a world of death and phantoms. The last trace of civilization had vanished around and inside us. The work of bestial degradation, begun by the victorious Germans, had been carried to its conclusion by the Germans in defeat.

It is man who kills, man who creates or suffers injustice; it is no longer man who, having lost all restraint, shares his bed with a corpse. Whoever waits for his neighbour to die in order to take his piece of bread is, albeit guiltless, further from the model of thinking man than the most primitive pigmy or the most vicious sadist.

Part of our existence lies in the feelings of those near to us. This is why the experience of someone who has lived for days during which man was merely a thing in the eyes of man is non-human. We three were for the most part immune from it, and we owe each other mutual gratitude. This is why my friendship with Charles will prove lasting.

But thousands of feet above us, in the gaps in the grey clouds, the complicated miracles of aerial duels began. Above us, bare, helpless and unarmed, men of our time sought reciprocal death with the most refined of instruments. A movement of a finger could cause the destruction of the entire camp, could annihilate thousands of men; while the sum total of all our efforts and exertions would not be sufficient to prolong by one minute the life of even one of us.

The saraband stopped at night and the room was once again filled with Sómogyi's monologue.

In full darkness I found myself suddenly awake. 'L' pauv' — vieux' was silent; he had finished. With the last gasp of life, he had thrown himself to the ground: I heard the thud of his knees, of his hips, of his shoulders, of his head.

'La mort l'a chassé de son lit,' Arthur defined it.

We certainly could not carry him out during the night. There was nothing for it but to go back to sleep again.

27 January

Dawn. On the floor, the shameful wreck of skin and bones, the Sómogyi thing.

There are more urgent tasks: we cannot wash ourselves, so that we dare not touch him until we have cooked and eaten. And besides: '... rien de si dégoutant que les débordements,' said Charles justly; the latrine had to be emptied. The living are more demanding; the dead can wait. We began to work as on every day.

The Russians arrived while Charles and I were carrying Sómogyi a little distance outside. He was very light. We over-turned the stretcher on the grey snow.

Charles took off his beret. I regretted not having a beret.

Of the eleven of the *Infektionsabteilung* Sómogyi was the only one to die in the ten days. Sertelet, Cagnolati, Towarowski, Lakmaker and Dorget (I have not spoken of him so far; he was a French industrialist who, after an operation for peritonitis, fell ill of nasal diphtheria) died some weeks later in the temporary Russian hospital of Auschwitz. In April, at Katowice, I met Schenck and Alcalai in good health. Arthur has reached his family happily and Charles has taken up his teacher's profession again; we have exchanged long letters and I hope to see him again one day.

The People Who Walked On (This Way to the Gas, Ladies and Gentlemen)

Tadeusz Borowski

It was early spring when we began building a soccer field on the broad clearing behind the hospital barracks. The location was excellent: the gypsies to the left, with their roaming children, their lovely, trim nurses, and their women sitting by the hour in the latrines; to the rear — a barbed-wire fence, and behind it the loading ramp with the wide railway tracks and the endless coming and going of trains; and beyond the ramp, the women's camp — *Frauen Konzentration Lager*. No one, of course, ever called it by its full name. We simply said F.K.L. — that was enough. To the right of the field were the crematoria, some of them at the back of the ramp, next to the F.K.L., others even closer, right by the fence. Sturdy buildings that sat solidly on the ground. And in front of the crematoria, a small wood which had to be crossed on the way to the gas.

We worked on the soccer field throughout the spring, and before it was finished we started planting flowers under the barracks windows and decorating the blocks with intricate zigzag designs made of crushed red brick. We planted spinach and lettuce, sunflowers and garlic. We laid little green lawns with grass transplanted from the edges of the soccer field, and sprinkled them daily with water brought in barrels from the lavatories.

Just when the flowers were about to bloom, we finished the soccer field.

From then on, the flowers were abandoned, the sick lay by themselves in the hospital beds, and we played soccer. Every day, as soon as the evening meal was over, anybody who felt like it came to the field and kicked the ball around. Others stood in clusters by the fence and talked across the entire length of the camp with the girls from the F.K.L.

One day I was goalkeeper. As always on Sundays, a sizeable crowd of hospital orderlies and convalescent patients had gathered to watch the game. Keeping goal, I had my back to the ramp. The ball went out and rolled all the way to the fence. I ran after it, and as I reached to pick it up, I happened to glance at the ramp.

A train had just arrived. People were emerging from the cattle cars and walking in the direction of the little wood. All I could see from where I stood were bright splashes of colour. The women, it seemed, were already wearing summer dresses; it was the first time that season. The men had taken off their coats, and their white shirts stood out sharply against the green of the trees. The procession moved along slowly, growing in size as more and more people poured from the freight cars. And then it stopped. The people sat down on the grass and gazed in our direction. I returned with the ball and kicked it back inside the field. It traveled from one foot to another and, in a wide arc, returned to the goal. I kicked it towards a corner. Again it rolled out into the grass. Once more I ran to retrieve it. But as I reached down, I stopped in amazement — the ramp was empty. Out of the whole colourful summer procession, not one person remained. The train too was gone. Again the F.K.L. blocks were in unobstructed view, and again the orderlies and the patients stood along the barbed-wire fence calling to the girls, and the girls answered them across the ramp.

Between two throw-ins in a soccer game, right behind my back, three thousand people had been put to death.

In the following months, the processions to the little wood moved along two roads: one leading straight from the ramp, the other past the hospital wall. Both led to the crematoria, but some of the people had the good fortune to walk beyond them, all the way to the Zauna, and this meant more than just a bath and a delousing, a barber's shop and a new prison suit. It meant staying alive. In a concentration camp, true, but — alive.

Each day, as I got up in the morning to scrub the hospital floors, the people were walking — along both roads. Women, men, children. They carried their bundles.

When I sat down to dinner — and not a bad one, either — the people were walking. Our block was bathed in sunlight; we threw the doors and the windows wide open and sprinkled the floors with water to keep the dust down. In the afternoons I delivered packages which had been brought that morning from the Auschwitz post office. The clerk distributed mail. The doctors dressed wounds and gave injections. There was, as a matter of fact, only one hypodermic needle for the entire block. On warm evenings I sat at the barracks door reading *Mon frère Yves* by Pierre Loti — while the procession continued on and on, along both roads.

Often, in the middle of the night, I walked outside; the lamps glowed in the darkness above the barbed-wire fences. The roads were completely black, but I could distinctly hear the far-away hum of a thousand voices — the procession moved on and on. And then the entire sky would light up; there would be a burst of flame above the wood ... and terrible human screams.

I stared into the night, numb, speechless, frozen with horror. My entire body trembled and rebelled, somehow even without my participation. I no longer controlled my body, although I could feel its every tremor. My mind was completely calm, only the body seemed to revolt.

Soon afterwards, I left the hospital. The days were filled with important events. The Allied Armies had landed on the shores of France. The Russian front, we heard, had started to move west towards Warsaw.

But in Birkenau, day and night long lines of trains loaded with people waited at the station. The doors were unsealed, the people started walking — along both roads.

Located next to the camp's labour sector was the deserted, unfinished Sector C. Here, only the barracks and the high voltage fence around them had been completed. The roofs, however, were not yet covered with tar sheets, and some of the blocks still had no bunks. An average Birkenau block, furnished with three tiers of bunks, could hold up to five hundred people. But every block in Sector C was now being packed with a thousand or more young women picked from among the people on the ramp ... Twenty-eight blocks — over thirty thousand women. Their heads were shaved and they were issued little sleeveless summer dresses. But they were not given underwear. Nor spoons, nor bowls, nor even a rag to clean themselves with. Birkenau was situated on marshes, at the foot of a mountain range. During the day, the air was warm and so transparent that the mountains were in clear view, but in the morning they lay shrouded in a thick, icy mist. The mornings were cold and penetrating. For us, this meant merely a refreshing pause before a hot summer day, but the women, who only twenty yards to our right had been standing at roll-call since five in the morning, turned blue from the cold and huddled together like a flock of partridges.

We named the camp — Persian Market. On sunny, warm days the women would emerge from the barracks and mill around in the wide aisles between the blocks. Their bright summer dresses and the gay kerchiefs on their shaved heads created the atmosphere of a busy, colourful market — a Persian Market because of its exotic character.

From afar, the women were faceless and ageless. Nothing more that white blotches and pastel figures.

The Persian Market was not yet completed. The Wagner Kommando began building a road through the sector, packing it down with a heavy roller. Others fiddled around with the plumbing and worked on the washrooms that were to be installed throughout all the sectors of Birkenau. Still others were busy stocking up the Persian Market with the camp's basic equipment — supplies of blankets, metal cups and spoons — which they arranged carefully in the warehouses under the direction of the chief supervisor, the assigned S.S. officer. Naturally, much of the stuff evaporated immediately, expertly 'organized' by the men working on the job.

My comrades and I laid a roof over the shack of every Block Elder in the Persian Market. It was not done on official order, nor did we work out of charity. Neither did we do it out of a feeling of solidarity with the old serial numbers, the F.K.L. women who had been placed there in all the responsible posts. In fact, we used 'organized' tar-boards and melted 'organized' tar, and for every roll of tar-board, every bucket of tar, an Elder had to pay. She had to pay the Kapo, the Kommandoführer, the Kommando 'bigwigs'. She could pay in various ways: with gold, food, the women of her block, or with her own body. It depended.

On a similar basis, the electricians installed electricity, the carpenters built and furnished the shacks, using 'organized' lumber, the masons provided metal stoves and cemented them in place.

It was at that time that I came to know the anatomy of this strange camp. We would arrive there in the morning, pushing a cart loaded with tar-sheets and tar. At the gate stood the S.S. women-guards, hippy blondes in black leather boots. They searched us and let us in. Then they themselves went to inspect the blocks. Not infrequently they had lovers among the masons and carpenters. They slept with them in the unfinished washrooms or the Block Elders' shacks.

We would push our cart into the camp, between the barracks, and there, on some little square, would light a fire and melt the tar. A crowd of women would immediately surround us. They begged us to give them anything, a penknife, a handkerchief, a spoon, a pencil, a piece of paper, a shoe string, or bread.

'Listen, you can always manage somehow,' they would say. 'You've been in the camp a long time and you've survived. Surely you have all you need. Why won't you share it with us?'

At first we gave them everything we happened to have with us, and then turned our pockets inside out to show we had nothing more. We took off our shirts and handed them over. But gradually we began coming with empty pockets and gave them nothing.

These women were not so much alike as it had seemed when we looked at them from another sector, from a distance of twenty metres.

Among them were small girls, whose hair had not been shaved, stray little cherubs from a painting of the Last judgment. There were young girls who gazed with surprise at the women crowding around us, and who looked at us, coarse, brutal men, with contempt. Then there were married women, who desperately begged for news of their lost husbands, and mothers trying to find a trace of their children.

'We are so miserable, so cold, so hungry,' they cried. 'Tell us, are they at least a little bit better off?'

'They are, if God is just,' we would answer solemnly, without the usual mocking and teasing.

'Surely they're not dead?' the women asked, looking searchingly into our faces.

We would walk away without a word, eager to get back to work.

The majority of the Block Elders at the Persian Market were Slovak girls who managed to communicate in the language of the new inmates. Every one of these girls had behind her several years of concentration camp. Every one of them remembered the early days of the F.K.L., when female corpses piled up along the barracks walls and rotted, unremoved, in hospital beds — and when human excrement grew into monstrous heaps inside the blocks.

Despite their rough manner, they had retained their femininity and human kindness. Probably they too had their lovers, and probably they too stole margarine and tins of food in order to pay for blankets and dresses, but ...

... but I remember Mirka, a short, stocky 'pink' girl. Her shack was all done up in pink too, with pink ruffled curtains across the window that faced the block. The pink light inside the shack set a pink glow over the girl's face, making her look as if she were wrapped in a delicate misty veil. There was a Jew in our Kommando with very bad teeth who was in love with Mirka. He was always running around the camp trying to buy fresh eggs for her, and then throwing them, protected in soft wrapping, over the barbed-wire fence. He would spend many long hours with her, paying little attention to the S.S. women inspecting the barracks or to our chief who made his rounds with a tremendous revolver hanging from his white summer uniform.

One day Mirka came running over to where several of us were laying a roof. She signalled frantically to the Jew and called, turning to me:

'Please come down! Maybe you can help too!'

We slid off the roof and down the barracks door. Mirka grabbed us by the hands and pulled us in the direction of her shack. There she led us between the cots and pointing to a mass of colourful quilts and blankets on top of which lay a child, she said breathlessy:

'Look, it's dying! Tell me, what can I do? What could have made it so sick so suddenly?'

The child was asleep, but very restless. It looked like a rose in a golden frame — its burning cheeks were surrounded by a halo of blond hair.

'What a pretty child,' I whispered.

'Pretty!' cried Mirka. 'All you know is that it's pretty! But it can die any moment! I've had to hide it so they wouldn't take it to the gas! What if an S.S. woman finds it? Help me!'

The Jew put his arm around her shoulders. She pushed him away and suddenly burst into sobs. I shrugged, turned around, and left the barracks.

In the distance, I could see trains moving along the ramp. They were bringing new people who would walk in the direction of the little wood. One Canada group was just returning from the ramp, and along the wide camp road passed another Canada group going to take its place. Smoke was rising above the treetops. I seated myself next to the boiling bucket of tar and, stirring it slowly, sat thinking for a long time. At one point a wild thought suddenly shot across my mind: I too would like to have a child with rose-coloured cheeks and light blond hair I laughed aloud at such a ridiculous notion and climbed up on the roof to lay the hot tar.

And I remember another Block Elder, a big redhead with broad feet and chapped hands. She did not have a separate shack, only a few blankets spread over the bed and instead of walls a few other blankets thrown across a piece of rope.

'I mustn't make them feel,' she would say, pointing to the women packed tightly in the bunks, 'that I want to cut myself off from them. Maybe I can't give them anything, but I won't take anything away from them either.'

'Do you believe in life after death?' she asked me once in the middle of some lighthearted conversation.

'Sometimes,' I answered cautiously. 'Once I believed in it when I was in jail, and again once when I came close to dying here in the camp.'

'But if a man does evil, he'll be punished, won't he?'

'I suppose so, unless there are some criteria of justice other than the man-made criteria. You know ... the kind that explain causes and motivations, and erase guilt by making it appear insignificant in the light of the overall harmony of the universe. Can a crime committed on one level be punishable on a different one?'

'But I mean in a normal, human sense!' she exclaimed.

'It ought to be punished. No question about it.'

'And you, would you do good if you were able to?'

'I seek no rewards. I build roofs and want to survive the concentration camp.'

'But do you think that they', she pointed with her chin in an indefinite direction, 'can go unpunished?'

'I think that for those who have suffered unjustly, justice alone is not enough. They want the guilty to suffer unjustly too. Only this will they understand as justice.'

'You're a pretty smart fellow! But you wouldn't have the slightest idea how to divide bread justly, without giving more to your own mistress!' she said bitterly and walked into the block. The women were lying in the rows of bunks, head to head. Their faces were still, only the eyes seemed alive, large and shining. Hunger had already started in this part of the camp. The redheaded Elder moved from bunk to bunk, talking to the women to distract them from their thoughts. She pulled out the singers and told them to sing, the dancers — and told them to dance, the poets — and made them recite poetry.

'All the time, endlessly, they ask me about their mothers, their fathers. They beg me to write to them.'

'They've asked me too. It's just too bad.'

'Ah, you! You come and then you go, but me? I plead with them, I beg them — if anyone is pregnant, don't report to the doctor, if anyone is sick, stay in the barracks! But do you think they believe me? It's no good, no matter how hard you try to protect them. What can you do if they fall all over themselves to get to the gas?'

One of the girls was standing on top of a table singing a popular tune. When she finished, the women in the bunks began to applaud. The girl bowed, smiling. The redheaded Elder covered her face with her rough hands.

'I can't stand it any longer! It's too disgusting!' she whispered. And suddenly she jumped up and rushed over to the table. 'Get down!' she screamed at the singer.

The women fell silent. She raised her arm.

'Quiet!' she shouted, though nobody spoke a word. 'You've been asking me about your parents and your children. I haven't told you, I felt sorry for you. But now I'll tell you, so that you know, because they'll do the same with you if you get sick! Your children, your husbands and your parents are not in another camp at all. They've been stuffed into a room and gassed! Gassed, do you understand? Like millions of others, like my own mother and father. They're burning in deep pits and in ovens ... The smoke which you see above the rooftops doesn't come from the brick plant at all, as you're being told. It's smoke from your children! Now go on and sing.' She finished calmly, pointing her finger at the terrified singer. Then she turned around and walked out of the barracks.

It was undeniable that the conditions in both Auschwitz and Birkenau were steadily improving. At the beginning, beating and killing were the rule, but later this became only sporadic. At first, you had to sleep on the floor lying on your side because of the lack of space, and could turn over only on command; later you slept in bunks, or wherever you wished, sometimes even in bed. Originally, you had to stand at roll-call for as long as two days at a time, later — only until the second gong, until nine o'clock. In the early years, packages were forbidden, later you could receive 500 grams, and finally as much as you wanted. Pockets of any kind were at first strictly taboo, but eventually even civilian clothes could sometimes be seen around Birkenau. Life in the camp became 'better and better' all the time — after the first three or four years. We felt certain that the horrors could never again be repeated, and we were proud that we had survived. The worse the Germans fared at the battle front, the better off we were. And since they fared worse and worse …

At the Persian Market, time seemed to move in reverse. Again we saw the Auschwitz of 1940. The women greedily gulped down the soup which nobody in our blocks would even think of touching. They stank of sweat and female blood. They stood at roll-call from five in the morning. When they were at last counted, it was almost nine. Then they were given cold coffee. At three in the afternoon the evening roll-call began and they were given dinner: bread with some spread. Since they did not work, they did not rate the *Zulage*, the extra work ration.

Sometimes they were driven out of the barracks in the middle of the day for an additional roll-call. They would line up in tight rows and march along the road, one behind the other. The big, blonde S.S. women in leather boots plucked from among them all the skinny ones, the ugly ones, the big-bellied ones — and threw them inside the Eye. The so-called Eye was a closed circle formed by the joined hands of the barracks guards. Filled out with women, the circle moved like a macabre dance to the camp gate, there to become absorbed by the great, camp-wide Eye. Five hundred, six hundred, a thousand selected women. Then all of them started on their walk — along the two roads.

Sometimes an S.S. woman dropped in at one of the barracks. She cased the bunks, a woman looking at other women. She asked if anyone cared to see a doctor, if anyone was pregnant. At the hospital, she said, they would get milk and white bread.

They scrambled out of the bunks and, swept up into the Eye, walked to the gate — towards the little wood.

Just to pass the time of day — for there was little for us to do at the camp — we used to spend long hours at the Persian Market, either with the Block Elders, or sitting under the barracks walls, or in the latrines. At the Elders' shacks you drank tea or dozed off for an hour or two in their beds. Sitting under the barracks wall you chatted with the carpenters and the bricklayers. A few women were usually hanging around, dressed in pretty little pullovers and wearing sheer stockings. Any one of them could be had for a piece of bright silk or a shiny trinket. Since time began, never has there been such an easy market for female flesh!

The latrines were built for the men and the women jointly, and were separated only by wooden boards. On the women's side, it was crowded and noisy, on ours, quiet and pleasantly cool inside the concrete enclosure. You sat there by the hour conducting love dialogues with katia, the pretty little latrine girl. No one felt any embarrassment or thought the set-up uncomfortable. After all, one had already seen so much …

That was June. Day and night the people walked — along the two roads. From dawn until late at night the entire Persian Market stood at roll-call. The days were warm and sunny and the tar melted on the roofs. Then came the rains, and with them icy winds. The mornings would dawn cold and penetrating. Then the fair weather returned once again. Without interruption, the trains pulled up to the ramp and the people walked on … Often we had to stand and wait, unable to leave, for work, because they were blocking the roads. They walked slowly, in loose groups sometimes hand in hand. Women, old men, children. As they passed just outside the barbed-wire fence they would turn their silent faces in our direction. Their eyes would fill with tears of pity and they threw bread over the fence for us to eat.

The women took the watches off their wrists and flung them at out feet, gesturing to us to take them.

At the gate, a band was playing foxtrots and tangos. The camp gazed at the passing procession. A man has only a limited number of ways in which he can express strong emotions or violent passions. He uses the same gestures as when what he feels is only petty and unimportant. He utters the same ordinary words.

'How many have gone by so far? It's been almost two months since mid-May. Counting twenty thousand per day ... around one million!'

'Eh, they couldn't have gassed that many every day. Though ... who the hells knows, with four ovens and scores of deep pits ...'

'Then count it this way: from Koszyce and Munkacz, almost 600,000. They got 'em all, no doubt about it. And from Budapest? 300,000, easily.'

'What's the difference?'

'Ja, but anyway, it's got to be over soon. They'll have slaughtered every single one of them.'

'There's more, don't worry.'

You shrug your shoulders and look at the road. Slowly, behind the crowd of people, walk the S.S. men, urging them with kindly smiles to move along. They explain that it is not much farther and they pat on the back a little old man who runs over to a ditch, rapidly pulls down his trousers, and wobbling in a funny way squats down. An S.S. man calls to him and points to the people disappearing round the bend. The little old man nods quickly, pulls up his trousers and, wobbling in a funny way, runs at a trot to catch up.

You snicker, amused at the sight of a man in such a big hurry to get to the gas chamber.

Later, we started working at the warehouses, spreading tar over their dripping roofs. The warehouses contained mountains of clothing, junk, and not-yet-disembowelled bundles. The treasures taken from the gassed people were piled up at random, exposed to the sun and the rain.

Every day, after lighting a fire under the bucket of tar, we went to 'organize' a snack. One of us would bring a pail of water, another a sack of dry cherries or prunes, a third some sugar. We stewed the fruit and then carried it up on the roof for those who took care of the work itself. Others fried bacon and onions and ate it with corn bread. We stole anything we could get our hands on and took it to the camp.

From the warehouse roofs you could see very clearly the flaming pits and the crematoria operating at full speed. You could see the people walk inside, undress. Then the S.S. men would quickly shut the windows and firmly tighten the screws. After a few minutes, in which we did not even have time to tar a piece of roofing board properly, they opened the windows and the side doors and aired the place out. Then came the *Sonderkommando* to drag the corpses to the burning pits. And so it went on, from morning till night — every single day.

Sometimes, after a transport had already been grassed, some late-arriving cars drove around filled with the sick. It was wasteful to gas them. They were undressed and Oberscharführer Moll either shot them with his rifle or pushed them live into a flaming trench.

Once, a car brought a young woman who had refused to part from her mother. Both were forced to undress, the mother led the way. The man who was to guide the daughter stopped, struck by the perfect beauty of her body, and in his awe and admiration he scratched his head. The woman, noticing this coarse, human gesture, relaxed. Blushing, she clutched the man's arm.

'Tell me, what will they do to me?'

'Be brave,' said the man, not withdrawing his arm.

'I am brave! Can't you see, I'm not even ashamed of you! Tell me!'

'Remember, be brave, come. I shall lead you. Just don't look.'

He took her by the hand and led her on, his other hand covering her eyes. The sizzling and the stench of the burning fat and the heat gushing out of the pit terrified her. She jerked back. But he gently bent her head forward, uncovering her back. At that moment the Oberscharführer fired, almost without aiming. The man pushed the woman into the flaming pit, and as she fell he heard her terrible, broken scream.

When the Persian Market, the gypsy camp and the F.K.L. became completely filled with the women selected from among the people from the ramp, a new camp was opened up across from the Persian Market. We called it Mexico. It, too, was not yet completed, and there also they began to install shacks for the Block Elders, electricity, and windows.

Each day was just like another. People emerged from the freight cars and walked on — along both roads.

The camp inmates had problems of their own: they waited for packages and letters from home, they 'organized' for their friends and mistresses, they speculated, they schemed. Nights followed days, rains came after the dry spells.

Towards the end of the summer, the trains stopped coming. Fewer and fewer people went to the crematoria. At first, the camp seemed somehow empty and incomplete. Then everybody got used to it. Anyway, other important events were taking place: the Russian offensive, the uprising and burning of Warsaw, the transports leaving the camp every day, going West towards the unknown, towards new sickness and death; the revolt at the crematoria and the escape of a *Sonderkommando* that ended with the execution of all the escapees.

And afterwards, you were shoved from camp to camp, without a spoon, or a plate, or a piece of rag to clean yourself with.

Your memory retains only images. Today, as I think back on that last summer in Auschwitz, I can still see the endless, colourful procession of people solemnly walking — along both roads; the woman, her head bent forward, standing over the flaming pit; the big redheaded girl in the dark interior of the barracks, shouting impatiently:

'Will evil be punished? I mean in human, normal terms!'

And I can still see the Jew with bad teeth, standing beneath my high bunk every evening, lifting his face to me, asking insistently:

'Any packages today? Couldn't you sell me some eggs for Mirka? I'll pay in marks. She is so fond of eggs ...'